AMERICA IN 1492

AMERICA IN 1492

The World of the Indian Peoples
Before the Arrival of Columbus

EDITED AND WITH AN INTRODUCTION BY

Alvin M. Josephy, Jr.

DEVELOPED BY FREDERICK E. HOXIE

VINTAGE BOOKS
A DIVISION OF RANDOM HOUSE, INC.
NEW YORK

FIRST VINTAGE BOOKS EDITION, FEBRUARY 1993

Library of Congress Cataloging-in-Publication Data
America in 1492: the world of the Indian peoples before the arrival of Columbus / edited
with an introduction by Alvin M. Josephy; developed by Frederick E. Hoxie.
p. cm.
Originally published: New York: Knopf, 1992.
Includes index.
ISBN 0-679-74337-5 (pbk.)
1. Indians—History. 2. Indians—Antiquities. 3. America—Antiquities.
I. Josephy, Alvin M., 1915– . II. Hoxie, Frederick E., 1947–
[E58.A526 1993]
970.01'1—dc20 92-56363
CIP

Catalogue numbers for artifacts from the Field Museum:
Point Hope mask, p. 46, (#53479); Nootka salmon mask, p. 57, (#85844); Pai baskets,
p. 100, (#63118, 63117, #63091, #17621); polychrome bowl, p. 113, (#98069);
Aztec stone corn spirit, p. 168, (#164772); Cubeo mourning costume, p. 208, (#143840,
#243837, #243836); Chimu pottery cat jar, p. 218, (#100012); Tsimshian mask,
p. 276, (#18124); Arizona stone woman, p. 288, (#280951); Midewiwin scroll,
p. 295, (#84383); Eskimo shaft wrench, p. 370, (#13617); Pawnee star chart,
p. 378, (#718-9810); Mochica squash pot, p. 384, (#1156); Mochica popcorn popper,
p. 398, (#4801); Ohio bone panpipes, p. 414, (#56708); Papago flutes, p. 415, (#63477).

Manufactured in the United States of America
10 9 8 7 6 5 4 3 2 1

To the Indian peoples of the Americas
and to the memory of
D'Arcy McNickle, a member of the
Confederated Salish and Kutenai Tribes
of Montana who, in his career of
scholarship and public service, explored
America as it was and might be

CONTENTS

A NOTE ON THE ILLUSTRATIONS

Because so few Native American illustrations of life before 1492 have survived, and because Europeans so frequently misunderstood the peoples they encountered, it is difficult to illustrate a book on the American continents as they were at the end of the fifteenth century. Illustrations for this volume were selected largely from the Newberry Library's matchless holdings of early books, manuscripts, and art on the native peoples of the New World. From this collection we have chosen drawings and engravings that best represent native life in 1492. These visual representations have been supplemented by illustrations from: The Field Museum of Chicago; The National Museum of the American Indian, New York City; The Milwaukee Public Museum; Museum für Völkerkunde, Berlin; The Library of Congress; The Peabody Museum, Harvard University; The Regenstein Library Rare Book Room, University of Chicago; The University of Utah Press; The American Museum of Natural History, New York; Museum für Völkerkunde, Vienna; The University of Turin, Italy. There are also four original drawings designed to illustrate topics of special interest. Hugh Claycombe prepared the drawings under the direction of Jay Miller and Frederick Hoxie, who benefited from the assistance of Robert Hall, Anthony Mattina, Barry Carlson, Tony Incashola, and Barbara Tedlock. Unless otherwise indicated, all illustrations are reproduced through the courtesy of the Newberry Library.

ACKNOWLEDGMENTS

Even though seventeen names adorn this book's title page and table of contents, there are many other people and institutions that deserve special acknowledgment here.

The D'Arcy McNickle Center for the History of the American Indian was created by Chicago's Newberry Library in 1972 to improve the quality of teaching and research in Indian history through the use of the institution's outstanding collections of books, manuscripts, and art. In 1983, believing that the approaching quincentennial of the Columbus voyages offered an opportunity for the Center to contribute to a better understanding of the significance of those voyages, its director, Frederick E. Hoxie, proposed the idea of this book to the Center's national Advisory Council. The Council helped refine the scope of the proposal before endorsing it late in 1985. Particularly helpful at this stage were advisers Raymond J. DeMallie, Charlotte Wilson Heth, R. David Edmunds, and the group's chairman, Alfonso Ortiz. Three other advisers were so enthusiastic that they became more directly involved in the project. Raymond D. Fogelson helped select and contact authors, Francis Jennings agreed to write a chapter, and—most generous of all—Alvin Josephy agreed to edit the volume. The enthusiastic support of Julian Bach, Ann Close of Alfred A. Knopf, Inc., and the Newberry's academic vice president, Richard H. Brown, enabled the enterprise to begin formally in January 1986.

Throughout the preparation of *America in 1492,* a number of McNickle Center staff members and volunteers from other institutions have provided valuable editorial assistance. These include Colin G. Calloway, William R. Swagerty, Jonathan Haas, Jane Levin, Violet Brown, and Margaret Curtis. In addition, a number of other Newberry Library personnel have helped with a variety of research and production tasks. These include Ayer reference librarian John Aubrey, Robert Karrow and his outstanding Department of Special Collections, Ruth Hamilton, Ken Cain, and Claudette Aho. Jay Miller, in addition to his labors as an author, has undertaken a number of editorial tasks and contributed significantly to the production of captions. Harvey Markowitz spent several months searching the collections of the Newberry, the Field Museum of Natural History, and other institutions for illustrations. Hugh Claycombe prepared both the maps and the special drawings that appear in several chapters.

Finally, an acknowledgment of *future* contributions. The bulk of the anticipated royalties from this book will go to the McNickle Center to support its fellowship programs for Native Americans. Fellowships are awards to researchers that enable them to travel to Chicago to use the Newberry's collections. We wish to recognize in advance the contributions these new scholars will surely make to the public's understanding of the Indian past as we collectively embark on a new chapter in the Indian future.

Frederick E. Hoxie
D'Arcy McNickle Center for the
History of the American Indian,
The Newberry Library

Acknowledgments

AMERICA IN 1492

INTRODUCTION
The Center of the Universe

ALVIN M. JOSEPHY, JR.

IN THE LUSH northeastern hills of Dominica, one of the loveliest of the Windward Islands that help shelter the Caribbean Sea from the rough Atlantic, is a tiny, almost forgotten group of Carib Indians. Five hundred years ago, their ancestors were among the first inhabitants of the Western Hemisphere to gaze upon white men. Along with the members of other small Carib communities on St. Vincent and in Belize and northern South America, they are today among the most remarkable—and most maligned—humans on earth.

There is good reason to regard Caribs with awe and respect. During the course of half a millennium, commencing with Columbus's arrival among them, Spanish, French, and English invaders, colonizers, pirates, and imperial exploiters all but exterminated them, slaughtering Caribs wholesale with fire, steel, European tortures, and savage dogs, working thousands of them to death as slaves, and wiping out their settlements with the pox, measles, diphtheria, and other white men's diseases to which the Indians had no resistance. But the Caribs' determination to survive (their name means "valiant people") and the astonishing spiritual strength of their culture have carried some of them through the terrible five-century American Indian holocaust—the greatest and longest-lasting in history—and the tribe is still here.

At the same time, the Caribs bore—and still bear before the world—a horrendous stigma, false and undeserved, but fastened on them by a muddled, ambitiously scheming Columbus. "Cannibal," dictionaries relate, "comes from the name Cariba, or Caniba (Carib), who Columbus reported were man-eating Indians." Like various other peoples in different parts of the world—and with a spiritual purpose matching that of the symbolic partaking by Christians of the body and blood of Christ—the Caribs in 1492 may have engaged in ceremonies that included the ritual eating of parts of the body of an enemy. However, there is no credible evidence from anyone who claimed to have witnessed such a ceremony, and none at all that the Caribs ate or relished human flesh as food. All is lurid hearsay, embellishing original—and quite possibly mis-understood—reports conveyed to Columbus by Arawak Indians, the Caribs' enemies.

Columbus nevertheless clutched at the tale, announcing that the Caribs were the ferocious, man-eating savages described in his well-thumbed copy of *The Travels of Marco Polo* as inhabiting islands of the East Indies, which Co-lumbus thought he had reached. From that conclusion, it was a short step for him to propose and justify to the Spanish monarchs the profitable enslavement of such debased beings. For a while, the Crown hesitated. But Columbus's voyages produced disappointingly little gold or other material wealth, and at length the Court saw things his way: the Caribs, from whose name was taken the word "cannibal" and who were equated in the Europeans' mind with the works of the Devil and all that was dark and evil, would enrich Spain and the Admiral by the labor of their bodies. "Being as they are hardened in their bad habits of idolatry and cannibalism," proclaimed Queen Isabella in 1503, "I hereby give license and permission . . . to capture them . . . paying us the share that belongs to us, and to sell them and utilize their services. . . ." Thus offi-cially began the nefarious American slave trade. Adopted also by competing European powers, it played a paramount role in bringing about the near-annihilation of both the Caribs and the Arawaks, as well as the actual extinc-tion of other tribes on both American continents.

The unquestioned acceptance of the fierce and inhuman image of the Ca-ribs clearly served the self-interest of an expansive Spanish empire. In later years similar stories circulated in other European capitals, fueling the engines of imperialism in the New World. But the savage image of the Caribs and their kinsmen served more than political ends. Tales of inhuman Carib ferocity, of-ten enhanced by toothsome details stemming from dramatic but largely fic-tional accounts of the past, have continued to this day. From the chronicles of early exploration, one prominent example is the well-read *Admiral of the Ocean Sea* by the late distinguished American historian Samuel Eliot Morison. In the century after Columbus, Morison wrote, the Caribs of Dominica "made a practice of killing and eating anyone who ventured ashore. On one occasion the natives were made so violently sick by eating a friar that thereafter anyone in ecclesiastical garb was let strictly alone. When Spaniards were forced to call at Dominica for water, they either sent a friar ashore or rigged up the boat's crew with sacking and the like to fool the natives."

The point of this ludicrous picture is that on the one hand all that has seemed important for the rest of the world to know about the Carib peoples is the belief, substantiated or not, that they were cannibals and on the other that everything else about the Caribs or their culture has been treated as of little or no consequence. Such historical stereotyping, in the context of the last five hundred years, exemplifies the misshapen collection of largely false, distorted, or half-true images that has passed for scholarship and has shaped the public's understanding of Indians and their universes. From 1492 on, Spaniards and the Europeans who followed in their wake to the Americas, with rare exceptions, observed and judged Indian societies from their own self-centered European points of view. Interpreting Indian life and customs entirely in terms that were familiar to themselves, they failed habitually to comprehend the truth or the sophisticated complexities and richness of the Indian cultures and ignored or condemned as inferior, savage, and barbaric much of what they did not understand or what they deemed strange or different from their own customs and outlook.

In the long run, indeed, no adverse impact visited on the Indians by the 1492 voyage of "discovery" was more profound in its consequences in every nook and cranny of the Americas than Columbus's introduction of Western European ethnocentricity to the Indians' worlds. Asserting the superiority of the white aggrandizers' religious, political, and social universe over those of each of the many different indigenous peoples from the Arctic to Tierra del Fuego at the southern tip of South America, this ethnocentricity was an arrogant vice, backed by superior firepower and boundless gall, that never faltered or weakened. It continues unabashedly on both continents today, and its impact has been felt long after the conquest of the continents was complete. The failure to recognize the coherence and humanity of Indian traditions has allowed the hemisphere's governments to persist in subjecting Indian populations to unequal treatment, gross indignities, and worse, from Canada and the United States to Guatemala and Brazil, where genocide against Indians is still widely practiced.

The ethnocentricity of the Euroamericans had—and still has—many forms and faces. The following few examples from yesterday and today demonstrate the broad range of their malignance: the sixteenth-century Spanish bishop Landa destroying Mayan books in Yucatan, and nineteenth- and twentieth-century government officials stamping out Indian languages and culture in the United States; scientists asserting that American tribes could not have built the burial mounds of the eastern North American woodlands, and French scholar Jacques Soustelle pronouncing learnedly in the 1950s that the high civilizations of pre-Columbian Mesoamerica were too advanced to have been Indian; seventeenth-century Spanish monks, French priests, and English missionaries like John Eliot in New England trying to induce Indians to shed the spiritual beliefs and values of their fathers as sorcery, and crass modern-day developers bulldozing sacred Indian cemeteries and shrines while insisting that Indian religion is only "mumbo jumbo." At their most benign, white ethnocentricity and ignorance have insulted, demeaned, and crushed out the self-esteem of Indian peoples; at their worst, they have fostered violent hatred and racism, massacres, and the plundering and dispossession of the Indians.

The character of the American natural environment, and with it any possibility of a rewarding understanding of the Indians' unique and special relationship to it, were also victimized. History still teaches falsely that pre-Columbian America was a wilderness, a virgin land, virtually untenanted, unknown, and unused, waiting for the white explorers and pioneers, with their superior brains, brawn, and courage, to conquer and "develop" it. "For thousands of centuries," reads the 1987 edition of *American History: A Survey,* co-authored by three eminent American historians, Richard N. Current, T. Harry Williams, and Alan Brinkley, "centuries in which human races were evolving, forming communities, and building the beginnings of national civilizations in Africa, Asia, and Europe—the continents we know as the Americas stood empty of mankind and its works. . . . The story of this new world . . . is a story of the creation of a civilization where none existed."

That image, leaving out the almost 75 million Indians who demographers now estimate may have been living in the Americas in 1492 (almost 6 million of them, perhaps, in the area of the present-day contiguous United States), perpetuates the myth of Euroamerican superiority. It says nothing of the challenges met and overcome by the Indians as the *original* pioneers, the first occupiers of a truly uninhabited hemisphere, of the thousands of years of their tenancy, of the many marvelous innovations, inventions, and adaptations of their societies and civilizations that enabled the Indians to live and govern themselves in America's different environments, of the distinctiveness, diversity, and complexity of their numerous cultures, developed without benefit of Western European advice and assistance, and of such Indian attainments and institutions as intricate calendrical systems, land and sea trade networks extending for hundreds and even thousands of miles, cities larger at the time than any in Europe, and political and social systems that, long before the Age of Enlightenment in Europe, recognized the dignity, worth, and liberty of the individual.

One should not pull the pendulum all the way over and pretend that pre-Columbian America was a paradise with no ills or vices—which, as this book makes clear, it was not. But we should recognize that while Western European—and, later, American—ethnocentricity was wreaking havoc among Indians, it was also adversely affecting whites—denying them knowledge of, and access to, much that Indians could have taught them to benefit their own lives. Examples like that offered at Plymouth in New England, where Wampanoag Indians met the boat, so to speak, and taught its Pilgrim passengers how to survive in their new home, were quickly forgotten. Instances of interracial cooperation, often symbolized by the marriage of John Rolfe and Pocahontas in Virginia in 1614, were very few. In succeeding years—even as Indians guided white "pathfinders" across the prairies, mountains, and deserts of their homelands and Indian resources enriched the European colonies—few whites understood or respected indigenous American traditions and values, and fewer still saw them as an asset in their own lives and affairs.

Despite the horrors of the past five hundred years, there has been a continuing—if muted—minor theme of curiosity and openness in the European expansion into the New World. And despite the violence and dislocations experienced by native peoples during these centuries, there have been Indians willing to share their knowledge with those few newcomers who were seriously interested in them. As a consequence, we have accumulated an incomplete but sizable body of information about the indigenous cultures of the hemisphere. While much has been lost, it is possible for modern scholars to assemble and analyze what has been recorded and shared in order to re-create in words what so many Europeans have sought to destroy.

Today, the five-hundredth anniversary of Columbus's voyage has focused attention on questions only rarely confronted in the past. What was life truly like in the Americas of 1492? How did American cultures and civilizations resemble, and how did they differ from, those of fifteenth-century Europe, Asia, and Africa? If one sheds long-observed stereotypes and delusions—both, for instance, that there was nothing worthwhile in pre-Columbian America and that America was a Garden of Eden peopled by happy noble savages—what can be said of the reality? In a rootless and drifting modern-day era, the information gathered and presented by Indians and non-Indians alike has risen immeasurably in value. It is possible today that exploring the Americas of 1492 will provide pertinent and valuable information on such basic subjects as man's relation with fellow man, with nature, and with the supernatural. It is possible the Indians who lived five hundred years ago in what we now think of as "our continents" will be found to have much to teach present-day humanity as it struggles to fashion a world for tomorrow.

With this book, much of which may be as foreign to many readers as a history of another planet, we move from the center of the universe of the white man to the centers of those of the different Indian peoples of 1492. It will describe America and its traditions on the eve of the Columbus voyages. Its point of reference is America, not Europe. Such a perspective reveals not unexpectedly a long-overdue need to retell the history of America and the Western Hemisphere, restructuring it more wholly and accurately to include the participation of the Indians and the roles and contributions of their cultures and traditions that have been misunderstood, traduced, and ignored.

Several other points should be made about the book. Each of its chapters has been written by a respected authority, and the factual substance as closely as possible reflects what is currently known of the pre-holocaust Indian world of 1492. But the written records of the first years of Indian–white contact are scanty and for many parts of the hemisphere nonexistent until later time periods. Many tribes, moreover, were devastated and became extinct—some by the spread of European diseases—even before white men had met them, leaving behind little or no evidence of their existence. In addition, there have been continual changes and assaults on cultures—among them, migrations, acculturation, white destruction, and distorted documentation—that have clouded or concealed what existed in 1492. In a number of chapters, particularly those dealing with languages and social relationships as they were, or may have been, in 1492 and with areas and people about whom there is little or no documentation, the authors' task has been a difficult and hesitant one of extrapolation—projecting backward carefully to make inferences from relevant linguistic or ethnographic material of later times that in some instances can be supported by archaeological or other evidence. Although the result enfolds interpretations that future scholarship may alter or improve upon, the authors in each case have done their best to use known materials in an intelligent and careful way to look backward to 1492.

Additionally, the reader will note that the book demolishes many stereotypes. There are no descriptions, for instance, of the familiar war-bonneted Indians of the North American Plains fighting each other on horseback, because no Indians had horses until Columbus and his followers introduced them into the Americas after 1492. Plains Indians at the time bore no resemblance to today's stereotyped image of them, but essentially were farmers who planted gardens along the Plains rivers and hunted deer, buffalo, and other game animals on foot. Moreover, the Sioux and many other tribes that became famous as Plains warriors in the nineteenth century were not yet living on the Plains in 1492. On the whole, in fact, this book, eliminating another well-publicized stereotype, examines the full array of human activity, from religion to child-rearing to trade. There is relatively little here about warriors and warfare.

The chapters, it should also be emphasized, are about the American world of the period of 1492, and about no other time in the past. With the exception of occasional brief descriptions of earlier occurrences to provide necessary background information about a chapter's subject, the book tries not to tell the histories of Indian societies from their beginning—again, only what they were like in 1492. Nor do the chapters digress more than is necessary into post-1492 history. The book's purpose, in short, is to familiarize the reader with an accurate portrait and understanding of the Indian world on the eve of Columbus's first voyage. To facilitate that end, the volume is divided into two parts. The first takes the reader, chapter by chapter, geographically through the Western Hemisphere in 1492 from the Arctic of North America to the Southern Cone of South America, picturing each area and describing who lived there and what their lives and cultures were like. The second part examines topics—Indian languages, religion, social organization, intertribal trade and relations, science and technology, and arts—hemisphere-wide, dealing not with one tribe or group of tribes, but drawing specifically on the cultural traits and values of various indigenous peoples on both continents. These chapters will describe aspects of American culture that were distinctive, that set it apart from the traditions of Asia, Africa, and Europe.

Finally, the book is addressed primarily to the general reader. It is hoped, however, that even the scholar and specialist, Indian or non-Indian, will find in it much that is new and provocative, for by accurately portraying this moment in the American past, the pages to follow are intended to help chart a new course for the American future.

Part One

WE THE PEOPLE, 1492

The Becoming of the Native: Man in America before Columbus

N. SCOTT MOMADAY

THURSDAY, 11 OCTOBER 1492

The moon, in its third quarter, rose in the east shortly before midnight. I estimate that we were making about 9 knots and had gone some 67½ miles between the beginning of night and 2 o'clock in the morning. Then, at two hours after midnight, the *Pinta* fired a cannon, my prearranged signal for the sighting of land.

FRIDAY, 12 OCTOBER 1492

At dawn we saw naked people. . . .

—*The Log of Christopher Columbus*

IT WAS NOT UNTIL 1498, when he explored what is now Venezuela, that Columbus realized he had touched upon a continent. On his last voyage, in 1502, he reached Central America. It is almost certain that he never knew of the great landmass to the north, an expanse that reached almost to Asia and to the top of the world, or that he had found a great chain of land that linked two of the earth's seven continents. In the little time that remained to him (he died in 1506) the enormity of his discovery was virtually unknown and unimagined. Christopher Columbus, the Admiral of the Ocean Sea, went to his grave believing he had reached Asia. But his accomplishment was even greater than he dreamed. He had in fact sailed beyond the *orbis,* the circle believed to

Giuliano Dati executed this woodcut to accompany the Italian edition of Columbus's report of his first voyage to America. Published in 1493, the image depicts King Ferdinand declaring his dominion over a group of frightened Caribbean natives. While highlighting European ambition, the woodcut does contain a few accurate elements: open-sided dwellings, tropical foliage, and inhabitants with long hair.

describe the limits of the earth, and beyond medieval geography. His voyage to the New World was a navigation in time; it was a passage from the Middle Ages to the Renaissance.

There are moments in history to which one can point and say, "At this hour, on this day, the history of the world was changed forever." Such a moment occurred at two o'clock on the morning of October 12, 1492, when a cannon, fired from the Spanish caravel *Pinta,* announced the sighting of land. The land sighted was probably Samana Cay in the Bahamas. It was the New World.

It is this term, "New World," with which I should like to begin this discussion, not only because it is everywhere a common designation of the Americas but also because it represents one of the great anomalies of history. The British writer J. B. Priestley, after visiting the United States, commented that "New World" is a misnomer. The American Southwest seemed to him the oldest landscape he had ever seen. Indeed, the New World is ancient. Here is a quintessential irony.

For Americans in general, a real part of the irony consists of their Eurocentric understanding of history. Columbus and his Old World contemporaries knew a good deal about the past, the past that was peculiarly theirs, for it had been recorded in writing. It was informed by a continuity that could be traced back to the story of Creation in the Old Testament. Most Americans have inherited that same understanding of the past. American history, therefore, as distinct from other histories, begins in the popular mind with the European intercession in the "New World." Relatively little is known of the Americas and their peoples before Columbus, although we are learning more all the time. On the far side of 1492 in the Americas there is a prehistoric darkness in which are mysteries as profound and provocative as are those of Stonehenge and Lascaux and Afrasiab.

Who were the "naked people" Columbus and his men observed at dawn on that autumn day five hundred years ago? Columbus, the first ethnographer in the New World, tells us a few things about them. They were broad in the forehead, straight and well-proportioned. They were friendly and bore gifts to their visitors. They were skilled boat-builders and boatmen. They painted their faces and their bodies. They made clothes and hammocks out of cotton. They lived in sturdy houses. They had dogs. And they too lived their daily lives in the element of language; they traded in words and names. We do not know what name or names they conferred upon their seafaring guests, but on October 17, on the sixth day of his sojourn among them, Columbus referred to them in his log as "Indios."

In 1492 the "Indians" were widespread in North, Central, and South America. They were the only human occupants of a third of the earth's land surface. And by the year 1492 they had been in the New World for untold thousands of years.

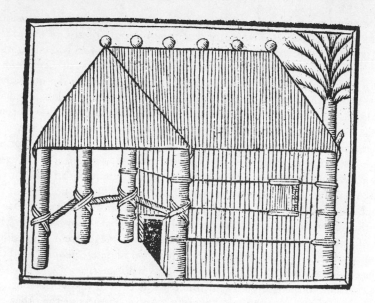

In contrast to Dati's fanciful image, Gonzalo Fernández de Oviedo y Valdés presented his European readers with this comprehensive picture of a Carib dwelling in 1547. Uniting several perspectives, the illustration shows a house made with solid corner poles, an open entryway, and a window cut in the thatch wall.

The "Paleo-Indians," as they are known, the ancestors of modern American Indians, came from Asia and entered upon the continent of North America by means of the Bering land bridge, a wide corridor of land, now submerged, connecting Siberia and Alaska. During the last glaciation (20,000 to 14,000 years ago) the top of the world was dominated by ice. Even so, most of Asia and most of Beringia were unglaciated. From Alaska to the Great Plains of the present United States ran a kind of corridor between the Cordilleran and Laurentide ice sheets, a thoroughfare for the migration of hunters and the animals they hunted. It is known that human bands had reached the Lena River drainage in northeastern Siberia at least 18,000 years ago. Over the next 7,000 years these nomads crossed the Bering bridge and dispersed widely throughout the Americas.

This dispersal is one of the great chapters in the story of mankind. It was an explosion, a revolution on a scale scarcely to be imagined. By 1492 there were untold numbers of indigenous human societies in the New World, untold numbers of languages and dialects, architecture to rival any monument of the Old World, astronomical observatories and solar calendars, a profound knowledge of natural medicine and the healing arts, very highly developed oral

The Becoming of the Native   **15**

traditions, dramas, ceremonies, and—above all—a spiritual comprehension of the universe, a sense of the natural and supernatural, a sense of the sacred. Here was every evidence of man's long, inexorable ascendancy to civilization.

It is appropriate that I interject here my particular point of view. I am an American Indian, and I believe that I can therefore speak to the question of America before Columbus with a certain advantage of ancestral experience, a cultural continuity that reaches far back in time. My forebears have been in North America for many thousands of years. In my blood I have a real sense of that occupation. It is worth something to me, as indeed that long, unbroken tenure is worth something to every Native American.

I am Kiowa. The Kiowas are a Plains Indian people who reside now in Oklahoma. But they are newcomers to the Southern Plains, not having ventured below the Arkansas River until the eighteenth century. In 1492 they were near the headwaters of the Yellowstone River, in what is now western Montana. Their migration to the Southern Plains is the most recent migration of all those which have described the great dispersal of native peoples, and their Plains culture is the last culture to evolve in North America.

According to their origin myth, the Kiowas entered the world through a hollow log. Where was the log, I wonder. And what was at the other end? When I imagine my blood back through generations to the earliest man in America, I see in my mind's eye a procession of shamanistic figures, like those strange anthropomorphic forms painted on the cliffs of Barrier Canyon, Utah, emerging from the mists. They proceed, it seems, from the source of geology itself, from timelessness into time.

When man set foot on the continent of North America he was surely an endangered species. His resources were few, as we think of them from our vantage point in the twentieth century. He was almost wholly at the mercy of the elements, and the world he inhabited was hard and unforgiving. The simple accomplishment of survival must have demanded all of his strength. But he had certain indispensable resources. He knew how to hunt. He possessed tools and weapons, however crude. He could make fire. He probably had dogs and travois, perhaps sleds. He had some sense of society, of community, of cooperation. And, alone among the creatures of the earth, he could think and speak. He had a human sense of morality, an irresistible craving for order, beauty, appropriate behavior. He was intensely spiritual.

The Kiowas provide us with a fortunate example of migration and dispersal, I believe. Although their migration from the Yellowstone to the Wichita Mountains is recent (nonetheless prehistoric in the main), it was surely preceded by countless migrations of the same kind in the same landscape, generally speaking, over a period of some thousands of years. The experience of the Kiowas, then, from earliest evidence to the present, may serve to indicate in a general way the experience of other tribes and other cultures. It may allow

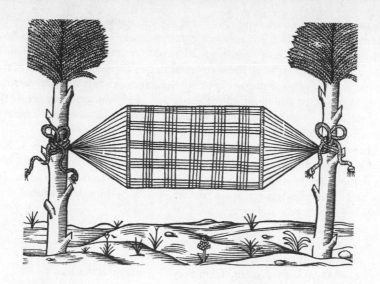

Oviedo introduced European readers to the hammock. This ubiquitous feature of tropical life caught the European fancy because it was light, cool, and comfortable. As with his other illustrations, Oviedo's drawing combines both a side and a top view.

us to understand something about the American Indian and about the condition of his presence in America in 1492.

The hollow log of the Kiowa origin myth is a not uncommon image in comparative mythology. The story of the tree of life is found throughout the world, and in most instances it is symbolic of passage, origination, evolution. It is tempting to associate the hollow log with the passage to America, the peopling of the Americas, to find in it a metaphorical reflection of the land bridge.

We tell stories in order to affirm our being and our place in the scheme of things. When the Kiowas entered upon the Great Plains they had to tell new stories of themselves, stories that would enable them to appropriate an unknown and intimidating landscape to their experience. They were peculiarly vulnerable in that landscape, and they told a story of dissension, finally of a schism in the tribe, brought about by a quarrel between two great chiefs. They encountered awesome forces and features in nature, and they explained them in story too. And so they told the story of Man-Ka-Ih, the storm spirit, which speaks the Kiowa language and does the Kiowas no harm, and they told of the tree that bore the seven sisters into the sky, where they became the stars of the Big Dipper. In so doing they not only accounted for the great monolith that is Devils Tower, Wyoming (in Kiowa, Tsoai, "rock tree"), but related themselves to the stars in the process. When they came upon the Plains they were befriended by the Crows, who gave them the sun-dance fetish Tai-Me, which was from that time on their most powerful medicine, and they told a story of the coming of Tai-Me in their hour of need. Language was their element. Words, spoken words, were the manifestations of their deepest belief, of their deepest feelings, of their deepest life. When Europeans first came to America, having had writing for hundreds of years and lately the printing press, they could not conceive of the spoken word as sacred, could not understand the American Indian's profound belief in the efficacy of language.

I have told the story of the arrowmaker many times. When I was a child I heard it told more times than I can say. It was at the center of my oral tradition long before I knew what that tradition was, and that is as it should be. The story had never been written down. It had existed, perhaps hundreds of years, at the level of the human voice.

> If an arrow is well made, it will have tooth marks upon it. That is how you know. The Kiowas made fine arrows and straightened them in their teeth. Then they drew them to the bow to see that they were straight. Once there was a man and his wife. They were alone at night in their tipi. By the light of a fire the man was making arrows. After a while he caught sight of something. There was a small opening in the tipi where two hides were sewn together. Someone was there on the outside, looking in. The man went on with his work, but he said to his wife, "Someone is standing outside. Do not be afraid. Let us talk easily, as of ordinary things." He took up an arrow and straightened it in his teeth; then, as it was right for him to do, he drew it to the bow and took aim, first in this direction and then in that. And all the while he was talking, as if to his wife. But this is how he spoke: "I know that you are there on the outside, for I can feel your eyes upon me. If you are a Kiowa, you will understand what I am saying, and you will speak your name." But there was no answer, and the man went on in the same way, pointing the arrow all around. At last his aim fell upon the place where his enemy stood, and he let go of the string. The arrow went straight to the enemy's heart.

Only after I had lived with the story for many years did I understand that it is about language. The storyteller is anonymous and illiterate, but he exists in his words, and he has survived for untold generations. The arrowmaker is a man made of words, and he too is a storyteller. He achieves victory over his enemy by exerting the force of language upon the unknown. What he does is far less important than what he says. His arrows are words. His enemy (and the presence outside *is* an enemy, for the storyteller tells us so) is vanquished by the word. The story is concise, beautiful, and alive. I know of nothing in literature that is more intensely alive.

Concurrent with the evolution of an oral tradition is the rise of ceremony. The sun dance was the preeminent expression of the spiritual life of the Plains culture. And it was a whole and intricate and profound expression.

And within the symmetry of this design of language and religion there came art. Universal in the world of the American Indian is a profound aesthetic sense. From ancient rock paintings to contemporary theater, through such forms as beadwork, featherwork, leathercraft, wood carving, ceramics, ledger-book drawing, music, and dance, American Indian art has rivaled other great art of the world. In museums and galleries around the globe are treasures of that art that are scarcely to be imagined.

These various expressions of the human spirit, emblematic of the American Indian today and five hundred years ago and long before that, are informed by an equation of man and the landscape that has had to be perceived, if neither appreciated nor acknowledged, by every society that has made contact with it. The naked people Columbus saw in 1492 were the members of a society altogether worthy and well made, a people of the everlasting earth, possessed of honor and dignity and a generosity of spirit unsurpassed.

ROBIN RIDINGTON

IT IS THE SPRING of 1492 on the treeless shores of the Arctic Ocean. The sea hunters have been waiting eagerly for migrating herds of bowhead whales to return to their summering waters at the edge of the polar pack ice. Throughout the long dark night of an Arctic winter, these northern sea-mammal hunters have lived in sod houses roofed over with whalebone. In renewing their equipment for the hunt, the people of this closely knit community have also been experiencing a sense of world renewal. Now, a lookout has given the call.

Their delicate skin boat is made of tough but translucent split walrus hide stretched tightly over a light driftwood frame held together by rawhide lashings. Ten men, dressed in water-repellent sealskin parkas, paddle it effortlessly through the sun-sparkled water at the speed of an easy jog. The boat, an umiak, is capable of carrying more than a ton, but it is light enough so that the crew can lift it from the water and place it on a specially made rack above the high-tide line. Now, in the rapidly increasing sunlight of a long Arctic day, they are confident of their knowledge of the sea and its rich resources. They know that the tools and skills their ancestors handed down to them will bring them once again into contact with the great whales that migrate past their coast. They know that the umialik, or hunt captain, has already made contact with the spirits of the whales. They look forward to the ceremonial greeting his wife

In 1736 Hans Egede published an account of Eskimo life based on his fifteen years as a missionary in western Greenland. His report was the first reliable European description of life along the Davis Strait. Here Egede illustrates a variety of seal-hunting methods: sitting in a chair near a tiny breathing hole (used in the winter), stalking a seal while it rests beside a hole, circling an opening in the ice to harpoon animals that gather there, and spying on a seal while a partner stands at the ready with a long harpoon.

Arctic and Subarctic

Miles 0   200   400   600   800   1000
Kms 0   400   800   1200

Language group **ALEUTIAN**
Modern tribe name *(INUPIAQ)*

Lena River

Siberia

Chukchi Peninsula

Bering
Sea

ALEUTIAN

Seward
Peninsula

Bering Strait

Norton Sound

Kotzebue Sound

(YUPIK)

ESKIMOAN

Point
Barrow

Yukon

NORTH
POLE

Arctic
Ocean

Beaufort
Sea

Pacific
Ocean

Copper

ATHAPASKAN

(TAGISH)

ATHAPASKAN

Mackenzie

Great Bear
Lake

ESKIMOAN

*(COPPER
ESKIMO)*

WAKASHAN

Peace

Great Slave Lake

ESKIMOAN

(INUPIAQ)

Greenland

Baffin
Bay

ESKIMOAN

(INUGSUK)

ESKIMO

SALISHAN

(BEAVER)

Lake
Athapaska

(SKAGIT)

SIOUAN

Reindeer
Lake

Hudson
Bay

Davis
Strait

NORTH
POLE

USSR

Alaska
(USA)

Canada

Greenland

United States

Lake
Winnipeg

ALGONQUIAN

ESKIMOAN

Labrador

(NASKAPI)

Lake
Superior

Lake
Huron

Newfoundland

Lake
Michigan

IROQUOIAN

Lake
Erie

Lake
Ontario

ALGONQUIAN

(BEOTHUK)

Mississippi

will give the whale as the successful hunters finally bring one of these great creatures ashore to feed the people.

A thousand miles away, another group of hunters has just returned to their forest camp with the neatly divided quarters, ribs, head, and hide of a moose that, hours before, was grazing on willows in country that the people had cleared by burning in years past. A hunter's wife takes charge of the meat. Her sharp stone blade finds the joints at which the animal's body falls apart naturally. She distributes the smaller pieces to women and children who arrive from every family of the band. The people of this band have camped together through the hot months of the northern forest's summer. They know the stories of one another's lives as they know the lives of the animals.

By evening, drying racks above each family's fire will be full of meat hanging in thin rippled sheets. Relatives who come to visit from another band will be able to identify each piece of the animal from which these women of knowledge have unrolled the thin ribbons of meat. People will talk quietly as they savor freshly spitted moose ribs and listen to the story of the hunt. As the outlines of constellations become visible in the dusk that passes for night at this time of year, people of all ages will dance in a circle around a common fire. Hunters will cast their voices into the taut heads of hand drums, upon which they sound pulses like the beating of a heart. The singing and drumming will last until the dusk transforms itself into an early dawn.

Soon daylight will begin to shorten throughout the north country as each day the sun moves "one grouse step" farther south in its points of rising and setting. Water will turn to crystal as night returns the stars to view. Water surfaces will be painted into those of the land, and both will become snow country. The story of this land and its life will be written in the tracks that animals and people leave in the snow. It will be written in the dream trails on which hunters and animals encounter one another. It will be lived in the snow houses and lodges in which these people make community with one another. The story will be passed on from season to season, generation to generation, just as it has been for thousands of years. The people will continue to live their lives like a story, adding whatever new experiences may come their way.

In 1492, hunting people occupied the entire northern third of North America. They lived well from the animals with whom they shared these lands. They lived well because they knew the land and its animals in the same way that they knew one another. By 1492, hunters had already known the north country for thousands of years. Sea mammal hunters had colonized the Arctic coasts of Canada and Greenland between four and five thousand years before. Land hunting people had lived throughout much of the northern interior for at least 12,000 years. No other lands in the New World had been known to human beings as long as these.

Northern North America is part of a larger circumpolar ecological domain

Hans Egede reported that when Greenland Eskimos went whaling "they put on their best gear," believing that whales hated "dirty habits." As many as fifty men and women occupied each skin boat, the men to stalk their prey and the women to mend tears in the hull. They attached inflated sealskins to lines tied to their harpoons to mark their prey and slow their flight. Once the whales were killed, the entire boat would join in butchering them.

that continues across the narrow Bering Strait into Siberia and Northern Europe. The overall circumpolar environment in 1492 was not very different from the present. This vast landmass had a continental climate, and was dominated by cold Arctic air throughout a long winter and spring season. Summer temperatures ranged from near freezing to the mid-70s, while winter temperatures were often as low as 40 degrees below zero. Air flowing in from warmer lands in the south was responsible for higher summer temperatures in southern parts of the region.

Geographers divide the overall circumpolar domain into two zones, the Arctic and, below it, the Subarctic. They refer to the landforms of these areas as tundra and taiga, respectively.

Temperatures in the northern lands were below freezing for eight or nine months of the year. Subsurface soil in the Arctic's tundra remained permanently frozen. Even when summer temperatures were above freezing and the top inches of earth became saturated with water, the soil below remained frozen into a permafrost, as hard as rock. When water flowed out upon the surface of permanently frozen tundra, it made overland travel extremely difficult. Summer travel in the boggy lands, or muskeg country, of the Subarctic's taiga was also slow and arduous. Tracking animals was more difficult under such conditions than it was during the winter, when the swampy ground was frozen solid and covered with snow. In both tundra and taiga, hordes of mosquitoes and biting flies bred in the standing pools of water. Clothing lost its thermal efficiency when it became damp. Northern people in 1492, like their descendants today, looked forward to the turn of the season to bring the easier traveling conditions associated with cold weather. In the Arctic, they could haul food and supplies by dogsled. In the Subarctic, people could travel quickly and efficiently by snowshoes and toboggan. Northern hunting people experienced the cold of their country as a valued resource.

Hunting and gathering are as ancient as our species. Until about 10,000 years ago, all human cultures were based on these ways of life. While agriculture and industry replaced hunting in many parts of the world, the native peoples of the Northern American Arctic and Subarctic continued hunting as the dominant way of life until recent times. Many of them still rely on hunting to supply an important part of their subsistence. Significantly, moreover, the ideas and institutions of all Native American cultures throughout the hemisphere evolved over the millennia from the culture of hunting ancestors.

More than a simple matter of subsistence, hunting was a way of thinking about humans in relation to all other beings and natural forces of a living and sentient environment. Animals were more than food to sustain people's bodies; they were parts of creation with whom humans had to establish a sense of trust and understanding. Hunters touched the spirits as well as the bodies of animals that gave them life. They felt responsible to the animals they hunted, in the same way that they felt responsible to one another. Respecting the autonomy of the game as they respected that of other humans, they did not take animals against their wills.

Metaphors about the relations of people to animals and natural forces were essential to the adaptive strategies of people who lived by hunting. The northern native people of 1492 had evolved both ways of thinking and institutions which balanced individual autonomy with the interdependence of community living. They valued knowledge as a source of personal power, but they also recognized that the stories a community holds in common are a fundamental source of all knowledge. They shared information with one another in the same way that they shared meat.

The hunting people also shared the experience of coming together in ceremony, to sing and to dance. They came together to affirm ties of kinship and their common bonds to relatives who had gone before them. They came together because they were people of a common country. The sound of drumming and singing was a keynote of that country. Dancing in a circle was a way of saying that people who lived together shared the trails of a common world. Dancing also affirmed their recognition of a common connection to the spirit world.

The hunting people of the north listened to spirit voices in the buzz of rawhide snares stretched tightly across the heads of their single-sided hand drums. Singers cast their voices into the resonating skin heads of their drums as a way of making contact with that spirit world. In times of celebration, or times of need, the northern peoples sang and danced together, singing the songs that connected them to the animals and to their ancestors. When the continuous light of a northern spring turned the night-world to day, people in Inuit (Eskimo) communities of the central Arctic would join several of their snow houses together to create a communal space for singing and dancing. In the Subarctic, Athapaskan- and Algonquian-speaking people made their dance lodges in the form of large conical structures covered with skins or bark.

When people of the northern forest came together from distant hunting camps to the circles of their dancing places, they would find the dance lodge crowded with relatives, many of whom they had not seen since the previous season. People danced in a circle together around the heat and light of their common fire. The dancing bodies touched one another closely. From time to time, the singers would stop to tune their drums. Holding their instruments before the heat of the fire, singers tapped lightly, listening to a rising tone, as heat waves stretched the skins tight against the birch frames. Drumheads became taut and bright with sound, and the tuning gently turned into a rhythm that emerged and established itself like the sound of one's own heart beating. Then someone took up the lead. The song may have been learned from one of the animals in a vision quest. It may have been dreamed by one of the hunters

Three skin boats filled with Eskimos meeting at the head of Kotzebue Sound in the summer of 1826, by William Smyth. Smyth accompanied the Arctic expedition of the British naval officer F. W. Beechey. Many of the boatmen use individualized paddles and are adorned with lip labrets; the women have chin tattoos.

or by a spiritual leader known as a Dreamer. The lead singer gathered his breath and started out fresh upon the song's trail. Its rhythm was steady, like the rise and fall of tracking feet. The melody was intricate in its turns, as the knowledge a hunter gains of the trail ahead was complex in its pattern of meaning. The songs took people into the mythic time, the time of animal powers, the time of natural and spiritual forces. The songs took people into the times of their ancestors.

In the Arctic, the people had to adapt not only to cold but to alternating periods of continuous night and continuous day, when the sun for long periods stayed either below or above the horizon. The people's deepest thoughts were molded by this fundamental alternation of darkness and light. The dark of a winter solstice night and its opposite, the midnight sun of the summer day, suggested moments of the soul's confrontation with fear and loneliness, and also with hope. An ancient spirit song documented by the Arctic explorer Knud Rasmussen in 1921 described feelings possessed by the Inuit of the central Arctic of northern Canada about their environment:

> There is fear
> In the longing for loneliness

When gathered with friends,
And longing to be alone.
Iyaiya-yaya!
There is joy
In feeling the summer
Come to the great world,
And watching the sun
Follow its ancient way.
Iyaiya-yaya!
There is fear
In feeling the winter
Come to the great world,
And watching the moon
Now half-moon, now full,
Follow its ancient way.
Iyaiya-yaya!
Where is all this tending?
I wish I were far to the eastward.
And yet I shall never again
Meet with my kinsman.
Iyaiya-yaya!

Much of the Arctic land in North America is coastal. A maritime climate and the physical effects of sea ice have always strongly influenced that part of the continent. In 1492, as now, ocean currents from the Pacific warmed northern Alaska and the lands adjacent to the Bering Strait, but waters surrounding the high Arctic islands of present-day Canada often remained locked in polar ice packs throughout the year. In winter, ice covered almost all water surfaces everywhere in the Arctic. With the coming of spring, ice on rivers and lakes began to break up, but the sea ice gave up its great jumbled packs of ice floes only later and with reluctance. In southern waters, summer melting and wind action eventually dislodged most of the sea ice, but in some years, drifting pack ice continued to obstruct certain bays and channels until winter closed in again.

In the summer, the Arctic lands were visibly distinct from their adjacent waters, but throughout the long winter, land and sea gave the appearance of a continuous frozen landmass. People could travel and even live offshore during the winter, gaining access to the high productivity of a marine ecology. Two species, the ringed seal and the bearded seal, were particularly important to hunters of the central Arctic coast. The continuing availability of marine resources during the winter was a primary factor in the adaptation of people to the coastal north. Winter seal hunting on the sea ice was a basic adaptive technique in the central Arctic.

The Arctic landmasses were largely treeless in 1492, as they are today, but during the summer they supported a luxuriant growth of lichen (reindeer moss) and flowering plants. These plants, in turn, provided food for herds of caribou that migrated seasonally between the taiga and the tundra, as well as for more localized populations of musk-oxen. Other animals of the tundra included grizzly bears, wolves, wolverines, Arctic hares, Arctic foxes, weasels, ground squirrels, lemmings, mice, and voles. The Arctic environments offered far less cover for small land mammal populations than did those of the Subarctic. Ravens, ptarmigan, and snowy owls were the only birds that stayed in the Arctic throughout the winter, but during the short summer, fifty or more species of migratory land and shore birds returned to the area from the south to nest and breed.

Without the protective canopy of a forest, snow that fell in the treeless tundra underwent many physical transformations. The wind moved and compacted it into a great variety of forms. Some types of snow had properties

Igloos under construction, as recorded by Captain William Parry's expedition to the Arctic in the early 1820s. Eskimo families would lay a circular foundation from eight to fifteen feet in diameter, adding spiraling tiers of snow slabs until a complete dome was formed. The lower left-hand corner shows a tunnel entrance, which was later added.

Northern Hunters   **29**

similar to those of geological deposits. Temperature variation was less extreme in the Arctic than in the Subarctic, but the absence of a forest cover made the wind force a powerful fact of life. In the mythology of central Arctic people the winds, called annorait, issued from two holes in the sky. Canadian anthropologist Diamond Jenness wrote that in stormy weather, according to Copper Eskimo traditions, "the shamans sometimes tie them all [the annorait] together with a cord of fur taken from the throat of a caribou and push them back into one of their holes. Then the Eskimos enjoy fine weather again until the malignant spirits of the dead, desiring destruction of people still living, untie them again and let them loose."

Although the winds of an Arctic winter could produce conditions under which travel was virtually impossible, they also created types of compacted snow that people could cut into blocks for building snow houses. These elegant and economical dwellings provided an ideal wind shelter and insulation from the bitter cold. The Arctic people of 1492 had a rich vocabulary for different kinds of snow and ice, and they also possessed an elaborate set of tools and techniques for the manipulation of snow. One of these was the snow probe, a composite tool described by anthropologist Asen Balikci as "a long thin rod of antler, three or four feet long, with an ovoid ferrule at one end and a small handle at the other." Using this implement, a person could probe beneath the softer surface snow to locate a layer suitable for cutting into blocks. A complementary tool was the snow shovel, used for digging down to the compacted snow that the builder had located with the probe. Once he had found suitable building material, the snow house builder then used his pana, or caribou-antler snow knife, to cut and trim blocks of snow.

South of the tundra, the Subarctic taiga was covered with boreal forests of spruce, tamarack, balsam, jack pine, aspen, and poplar. In the northern margins of the forest, permafrost was common. Then, as now, the permafrost covered about 50 percent of the land that is now Canada and 20 percent of the entire North American continent.

Wintry snow conditions in the taiga were very different from those of the Arctic's open tundra. Protected by the forest cover, the taiga snow was not easily modified by external factors such as wind or incoming solar radiation. During the long winter, the forest provided an insulating shelter for a variety of plants and animals. Tracks of the many animals that made their homes within the cover left signatures on the snow. Native peoples read the tracks as stories of the lives the animals led, knowing how to interpret them, also, as episodes in the stories of their own lives.

Temperature variation was more extreme in the boreal forest than in the high Arctic. Some of the lowest winter temperatures recorded for inhabited areas of the earth have come from the Subarctic regions of North America, while in summer the heat could rise well above 80 degrees. Yet the Subarctic

When Captain James Cook embarked on his final voyage of discovery in the eighteenth century, he was accompanied by John Webber, an accomplished draftsman and engraver. Here, Webber's drawing of the interior of a semi-subterranean Aleut house at Unalaska gives us a glimpse of domestic life. Each family is assigned a compartment (marked by a basketlike stone lamp) according to social rank. The families wear clothes made from the hides of many animals: seals, fish, and birds.

had a maximum of only 100 to 120 frost-free days each year, making it unsuitable for the cultivation of crops and the use of farming techniques that, by 1492, were available to native peoples farther south on the continent.

Instead, the crops harvested by the inhabitants of the Subarctic's boreal forest were the annual growths of berries, succulent wild plants such as cow parsnip, and the nourishing spring inner bark of trees like the poplar. But principally they were hunters and fishermen, subsisting on beaver, moose, caribou, deer, whitefish, pike, waterfowl, grouse, and fur-bearing animals. The hunters knew the local populations of the animals they took for food. They harvested the animals and all the resources with care and attention, understanding and respecting the carrying capacities of their lands and knowing how to manage the resources—setting fires, for example, to increase the growth of subclimax plants like willows that supported moose and other game animals.

Thus, in 1492, the hunting peoples of the northern part of North America lived in a variety of extreme environments, in each environment making their living through their intimate knowledge of the plants, animals, birds, and fishes

Northern Hunters

with whom they shared the country. The Inupiaq-speaking people of northern Alaska and the Bering Strait hunted walrus and whales from their umiaks. In the central Arctic, Inuktitut speakers migrated far out on the sea ice to hunt seals by waiting patiently at the breathing holes those mammals kept open through the winter. Algonquian-speaking peoples of the eastern Subarctic moved with the seasons, from summer fishing camps and fall berry patches to winter moose and caribou hunting grounds. In the western Subarctic, Athapaskan speakers caught fish and hunted caribou, moose, and mountain-dwelling animals like sheep, goats, and marmots. They used a variety of techniques, some relatively complex and high-yielding, which included trapping fish in weirs built across streams and driving caribou between lines of fences.

Throughout the vast lands of the north, groups of people moved seasonally within their own territories from one resource area to another. Each knew the importance of scheduling their activities according to the availability of the local resources. When Arctic char or caribou became available in large numbers during their annual migrations, people came together and formed cooperative work groups to harvest them. When animals like moose were the main source of food, people lived in smaller bands that could move easily from one hunting area to another. The hunting peoples were wise in the knowledge of the seasons, and they planned and carried out their movements and activities in accordance with the wisdom they bore with them from past generations.

To non-natives, the northern tundra and taiga lands seem empty, alien, and unproductive. They exist there only with the help of supplies brought in from elsewhere, and maintain themselves with artifacts that protect them from the environment. Non-natives do not truly live there, even though they believe the north belongs to them. The northern peoples of 1492 thought differently. They did not think of the land as a resource that could be sold or otherwise disposed of, but knew that they were the people who belonged to the land and were responsible to and for it. Men and women of the Arctic and Subarctic knew, named, and dreamed the intricate features of a vast and complex network of northern forests, lakes, rivers, tundra, and coastlines. Some knew and were bonded to the sea ice and the warm-blooded creatures that lived in the cold and dark waters beneath its surface. Others were linked to the forest animals. All knew the places where animal trails came together with those of humans.

In their universe of physical landscape and natural forces, the northern peoples also saw signs of events that took place in a mythic time of essential meanings. They knew the rocks and mountains, rivers and lakes, sun, moon, and stars—like the plants and animals—as sentient beings with whom they were constantly negotiating the unfolding of life-giving relationships. They lived in lands that were storied with knowledge about the interdependence of people, animals, and natural phenomena. They studied the lands and the animals, and they studied one another. Native people communicated the results of their studies through myths and oral traditions that tell of a people's understanding of human life and the land.

The Inuit people who lived in the western part of the central Arctic islands, for instance, thought of the places over which they could travel as "a flat unbroken expanse of land and sea—the earth—covered over during the greater part of the year with snow and ice; of undefined limits but stretching farther than any man knows." Above this surface that was accessible to the physical presence of humans was another unbroken expanse, the sky, held up at each corner with a pillar of wood. Above and beyond this sky realm, according to Diamond Jenness, was another land "abounding in caribou and other animals like our own earth." Wandering with these animals were beings who were part human and part spirit, the sun, the moon, and the stars. The moon was a man. The sun was a woman who walked across the sky and beneath the earth each day. She followed a mighty power, known as Sila, into the dark of the sea each winter. Sometimes people heard the hiss of her body as it passed from sky to sea.

The Arctic people of 1492 knew Sila as the spirit of nature that supported the world, the weather, and all life on earth. During the long night of winter when the sun remained in Sila's sea world, the Arctic people had ample opportunity to study the movements of these celestial persons who continued their journeys above the open, treeless snowscape. The mountains on the moon, they said, were the dogs of people who had been hoisted up to the sky realm through the power of an angakoq, the Inuit shaman who knew the secrets of spirit travel. Similarly, the stars were humans or animals who had fled, like shamans, from earth to the sky world. Unlike shamans, they were unable to return to earth in human form. Falling stars were feces of the larger ones. The three bright stars of Orion's belt were three sealers who had never returned to earth after following a polar bear that fled into the sky world. The undulating splendor of the Arctic aurora, the northern lights, was a sign of celestial spirits that brought good weather.

Northern hunting people also knew the birds and animals as people with special gifts and powers. The Inuit angakoq was able to converse with them and to observe them changing from animal to human form. Jenness recounted a Copper Eskimo story of such an encounter, describing the experience of two brothers, Annarvik and Angivranna. They sighted a brown bear on the opposite bank of a river. They began to cross over toward it, but they had hardly reached halfway when the bear's ears began to enlarge and gradually cover its whole body. Annarvik turned and fled to shore. When he looked around again a man had sprung out from beside the bear and entered the water. The creature disappeared below the surface, and presently the terrified Angivranna disappeared also, pulled under by his adversary. No sooner had he sunk than the brown bear vanished into the ground, but on the same spot appeared a mysterious man. Annarvik fled to his camp and told his companions of Angivranna's fate. The brown bear had killed him, the people said, because he was too good a hunter.

People of the Subarctic also viewed the animals and natural forces of their environment as persons. Subarctic hunters expected to encounter their game in dreams before the physical contact of the hunt itself. Dreaming was a way of visualizing and organizing the hunter's information about the complex pattern of potential relationships between humans and animals. Subarctic people often personified the spirits of animals as game masters, or keepers, with whom the hunters were required to negotiate a relationship in order to gain success in the hunt. Elders trained their young people to make such contact by sending them out into the bush alone on vision-quests. There, they would learn to understand the speech of an animal friend. They would experience a transformation from ordinary human life into the mythic time in order to learn the powers of these animal people.

Subarctic people also understood that hunting was an essentially mental and spiritual activity. They knew that a hunt could succeed only through the hunter's informed understanding of both the environment and the animal's state of mind. Thus, they viewed success in the hunt as evidence of the hunter's knowledge and power. They believed that animals had a reciprocal understanding of the hunter's state of mind. Animals gave themselves only to generous people with whom they had made spiritual contact. Knowledge, power, and individual intelligence were central to the adaptive competence of northern hunting people. The hunters expected each individual to be capable of understanding the complex and intelligent animals of the northern environment. Subarctic people were individualistic, but not selfish. They shared meat with one another in the understanding that animals would be generous to hunters who shared meat freely. Animals would visit these hunters in their dreams.

The Subarctic hunting people were individualistic and often egalitarian, as well as being responsible to one another and to the sentient beings of their environment. The metaphors of their discourse elaborated relations of power and negotiation, rather than those of authority and hierarchy. Northern hunting people typically negotiated social relations with both human and transhuman persons through a vocabulary of "supernatural power." Both men and women established personal and empowering relationships with the world of sentient beings. They often did this through a childhood vision-quest encounter with an animal friend, spirit helper, or game master. A person who had acquired supernatural power from a vision-quest demonstrated it by showing competence and social power. A person with power was well connected, both to the social world of humans and to the world of transhuman persons. A person with power was said to "know something." The Subarctic people recognized shamans as people with special powers to make contact with the spirit world on behalf of others. Shamans, in turn, used their powers to cure illness and identify the causes of misfortune.

Children returning from their vision-quest experiences were expected to keep their newly acquired knowledge and power secret. As they grew into adulthood, they would then find opportunities to demonstrate their powers and gradually reveal the stories of their vision-quests. A person could indicate "knowing something" by hanging a medicine bundle behind his or her sleeping place, by revealing personal food and behavior taboos, by using medicine songs in healing, and by making subtle references to vision-quest powers in story-telling. These stories, in turn, enacted events from stories about the mythic time. Subarctic people shared stories in the same way that they shared meat. Each person nourished, and was nourished by, the stories of other people's lives. Each person's life was a story known to every other person in his or her social world. As a Tagish Athapaskan woman from the Yukon, Angela Sidney, told Canadian anthropologist Julie Cruikshank, a person's life was "lived like a story." The story of each person's life contributed to the ongoing story of life in a closely knit kin-based community.

In 1492, most Subarctic people lived in small nomadic bands that were well adapted to taking advantage of seasonal and regional variations in the availability of resources. The people of related bands held in common a great deal of information about social and natural conditions. They communicated this information through oral tradition. Band composition was quite flexible. People speaking related dialects maintained mutually accepted access to larger areas. They often intermarried. Although people of the Subarctic did not have tribes as formal political units, members of a particular band generally knew how they were related to the people of other related bands. They usually thought of themselves as the People of an area.

Most of the several dozen Athapaskan-speaking language groups used some variation of the term Dene, "the People," to refer to the group's identity. Eskimo people of the Arctic identified particular areas by the name of a group of people who had the right to live upon its resources. They called these groups by a place-name followed by the suffix "miut," meaning "people of that place." People had rights to a variety of places but were not limited to particular territories. They moved cyclically with the seasons, and freely from one area to another as the availability of resources changed. It was not unusual for one individual to have lived in areas many hundreds of miles apart during the course of a lifetime.

Most individuals within a northern hunting band were able to trace their relationship to a primary relative within the band. Typically, groups of siblings and their spouses formed the core of a band. The core composition of a band would change gradually over time as people died, married, and were born. People would often travel with more than one band during the course

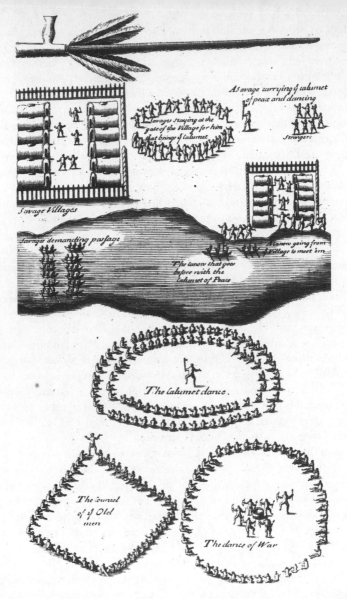

The various labels within the illustration read:

Savage Villages

Savages staying at the gate of the Village for him that brings y calumet

A savage carrying y calumet of peace and dancing

Strangers

Savages demanding passage

Canow going from ye Village to meet 'em

The canow that goes before with the calumet of Peace

The calumet dance.

The Council of ye Old men

The dance of War

This illustration from Baron Lahontan's account of his travels in French Canada reveals the many uses of the pipe, or calumet, among the Indians of the St. Lawrence. Lahontan, who first traveled to Canada in 1683, published his book in both England and France in 1703. The drawing shows the pipe as an instrument of diplomacy when two groups met along a river, or when visiting, and it demonstrates the use of the pipe in ceremonies and celebrations.

of a lifetime. A person had access to any band in which he or she had a sibling, a spouse, a parent, or a child. Northern hunters typically used systems of kinship that classified large numbers of people as relatives. Thus, one would have access to another band not only through full siblings but also through cousins, who would be regarded and referred to as being like one's own brothers and sisters.

In the north, individuals lived not only with human families but in the company of animal and spiritual kin. Thus, understanding individual experiences with these beings is a key to seeing how native people identified animals and natural phenomena as a part of their community. Because this tradition has endured, we can look to recent ethnographic accounts to increase our understanding of the people of 1492. In 1964, I was present as an old man named Japasa of the Athapaskan Beaver Indians (Dunne-Za) from the Peace River area of western Canada told the story of his vision-quest to his relatives a week before he died. His son, Johnny Chipesia, put it into English. The story described a vision-quest experience like those that must have been common to native people of the Subarctic in 1492.

> My dad said that when he was a boy, about nine years old,
> he went into the bush alone.
> He was lost from his people. In the night it rained.
> He was cold and wet from the rain,
> but in the morning he found himself warm and dry.
> A pair of silver foxes had come and protected him.
> After that, the foxes kept him and looked after him.
> He stayed with them and they protected him.
> Those foxes had three pups.
> The male and female foxes brought food for the pups.
> They brought food for my dad too.
> They looked after him as if they were all the same.
> Those foxes wore clothes like people.
> My dad said he could understand their language.
> He said they taught him a song.

As he told the story, the old man began to sing. The song seemed to be part of his story. It must have been a song the foxes gave him, one of the songs from his vision-quest. He sang the song because he knew that soon he would follow his dreams toward Yagatunne, the Trail to Heaven. Each song had the power to restore life, or to take it away. As he prepared for death, the old man was both revealing and letting go of power the foxes had given him in a time out of time, alone in the bush.

My dad said he stayed out in the bush for twenty days.
Ever since that time, foxes have been his friends.
Anytime he wanted to, he could set a trap and get foxes.
When he lived with the foxes that time, he saw rabbits too.
The rabbits were wearing clothes like people.
They were packing things on their backs.
The first night out in the bush
he was cold and wet from the rain.
In the morning he woke up warm and dry.
The wind came to him too.
The wind came to him in the form of a person.
That person said:
"See, you're dry now. I'm your friend."
The wind has been his friend ever since.
He can call the wind. He can call the rain.
He can also make them go away.
One time when I was twelve,
I was with my dad and some other people
when we got trapped by a forest fire.
My dad told all the people to look for clouds
even though it hadn't rained for a long time.
They found a little black cloud and my dad called it to help us.
In just about ten minutes, there was thunder and lightning,
and heavy rain that put out the fire.
We were really wet but we were glad to be saved from that fire.
My dad sang for rain to come a couple of days ago.
He sang for it to come and make him well.
That rain came right away.
This morning he called the wind and rain.
They came to him right away.
Then he told them to go away.
He told them he was too old and didn't need them.
He said it was time to die.
He told the wind and rain they could leave him now.
After he had been in the bush twenty days,
he almost forgot about his people.
Then he remembered them.
The old people must have been dreaming about him.
He heard a song.
He went toward the song.
Every time he got to where the song had been,
it moved farther away.

Every time he followed it, he moved a little farther.
Finally, by following that song,
he found his way back to his people.

The story of this vision-quest illustrates the importance Subarctic people placed on the knowledge gained through personal experience of animal powers. "Knowing something" empowered a person to make contact with the animals. Many Subarctic people sent both boys and girls on vision-quests. They were trained to be competent in the bush on their own.

The following story, also from the Dunne-Za Indians, illustrates the kind of self-reliance expected of children in the Subarctic. It shows that women as well as men made contact with animals and fed their people. The story was told to me by an old woman named Nacheen about her experience as a girl during a period of hard times when the hunters of her band had been unsuccessful in making contact with the game animals. Rather than staying in camp passively, the girl and her father's sister set out on their own into the bush to find food.

One time I was camping with my two grandfathers, my father's sister (aspe), and some other people. We were starving. We moved from place to place. We moved to another place and those two men didn't even go out hunting for moose. So my aspe and I decided to hunt for porcupines. We set out, and aspe went along the river. I went up along the crest of some mountains. It was late wintertime and there was deep snow. I looked down the slope but I didn't see any porcupines. The days were getting long but already it was getting dark, so I started straight down the mountainside. There was a river at the bottom, and I thought that if I followed it back to camp I might find something. The snow was deep down there and there was lots of brush. I was wearing snowshoes but the snow was too deep for them too. I was walking slowly when I saw some sticks broken under a medium-size spruce tree. It looked like something had broken them. I went over there. There were no tracks. I was on top of a bear's den but I didn't know it.

I took off my snowshoes and started to look around. There was a small hole where the snow was falling in. I took a stick and poked it. It went inside. I looked inside. There seemed to be something in there but I couldn't see. It was dark. I poked again with a long stick. It felt like there was something in there, but it didn't move. It didn't growl. I was wondering what it could be. I threw lots of sticks and stones in there but nothing moved. Then I noticed a stick by the entrance that had been chewed, so I put it in my pack and started back. It was late. I was tired.

It was after the middle of the night when I got back. My grandfather was angry. "I thought you got a porcupine or something. I thought you were carrying some kind of meat in your pack. That's why you were late, but you didn't bring anything." I showed my grandfather the chewed stick. "I found a bear's den, but I don't think he is in there now." My grandfather called to the other people. "Hey, my granddaughter found a bear's den."

That same night we all set out to find it in the moonlight. I drank tea and then I went on with them. We took a dog with us. After we had gone some way he could smell the bear, and he started barking. He wanted to chase it but we held him. When we came to the hole we took the bear and killed him. It was a big black bear, the kind that is almost like a grizzly, and it was very fat. They started to skin it while I made a fire. We were so hungry we ate the bear's liver and guts. That night we packed the bear meat back and we ate it. The next day we were feeling better and we moved camp again. A chinook wind came and it turned nice and warm. Then we got two moose. It was all right then.

Although the hunting peoples of both the Arctic and the Subarctic possessed in common a sense of being connected to the natural forces and animal persons of their lands, the different environments, resources, and ecologies of the two regions resulted in different adaptations. Tundra and taiga conditions respectively called for different tools, different techniques, and different strategies to enable people to take advantage of their local resources. Life in the Arctic would have been impossible without thermally efficient clothing and a source of light, while in the Subarctic it would have been impossible without snowshoes for traveling through the deep snow of winter. Similarly, the people of the tundra and those of the taiga used fundamentally different strategies to keep warm. In the treeless tundra, people depended almost entirely on internally generated body heat as their source of thermal energy, while the taiga people of the forest relied on the external heat of fires.

An essential feature of Eskimo adaptation—employing skills evolved by their ancestors to colonize the Arctic coasts of Canada and Greenland thousands of years earlier—was the use of efficiently tailored clothing. Clothes worn by the Arctic people consisted of double caribou-skin parkas with matching pants and boots. The hair faced outward on the outer parka and in toward the body on the inner one. Caribou hair was hollow and provided excellent insulation. The combination of the two parkas allowed for air circulation within the garment, while retaining a very high overall thermal efficiency. As a result,

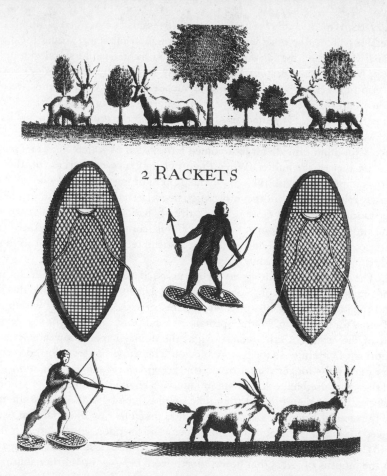

2 RACKETS

Here Baron Lahontan presents his European readers with their first accurate drawings of snowshoes. These native inventions were two and a half feet long and laced with rabbit or elk hide. They were essential for hunting elk in the deep Canadian winter snows. "The fatigue" of this hunt, the young soldier wrote, "equaled the pleasure of it."

an Eskimo hunter could stand motionless at a seal's breathing hole for hours at a time in severely cold weather. Eskimo clothing was designed to retain body heat, even at the low metabolic rate necessary for such an activity.

Breathing-hole sealing required a social, as well as a physical, technology. The winter sea-ice sealing communities of the central Arctic were integrated by formal and complex rules of reciprocity known as nigaiturasuaktut—a term that also referred to the sealskin bag in which seal-sharing partners carried

Northern Hunters   **41**

away their meat and blubber. Because the seals maintained a number of breathing holes, the odds were not terribly good that a seal would use a particular one during the few hours that an Inuit hunter could stand motionless by it, waiting in the extreme cold. The only way to improve the odds was to position hunters at more of the holes. Such a strategy could be effective only if the hunters were part of a cooperative, sharing network, assuring that each hunter would get a fair share of any seal taken in the jointly conducted hunt.

When the hunters brought a seal back to the sea-ice village, the wife of the successful hunter divided it into named parts, each of which went to a particular partner of the hunter. When the other hunters were successful, they, in turn, reciprocated with the same-named piece of meat. People who were not closely related to one another most often negotiated these partnerships, the understanding being that close relatives already had an obligation to share with one another in a more general fashion. Thus, communities of unrelated families could live interdependently, using a social technology relevant to the requirements of sea-ice sealing.

The Arctic peoples designed their houses, like their caribou-skin clothing, for a maximum degree of thermal efficiency. The most common land dwelling was the karmat, a hut of stone, whalebone, or sod, covered over with blocks of snow for insulation. For the specialized conditions of life on the sea ice, people of the central Arctic built igluviga, the dome-shaped snow houses made entirely of carefully shaped snow blocks. The snow houses allowed them to live during the longer winter on marine resources. The high insulation value of the snow used in both karmat and igluviga enabled people to live comfortably with only their body heat and the small flame of a seal-oil lamp. In much of the central Arctic, wood was a rare and precious raw material that people saved for making implements such as spear and harpoon shafts, kayak frames, and sledge runners. It was unavailable for shelter or as a source of heat, except at the mouths of rivers that flowed north from headwaters farther south.

Archaeologists call the first inhabitants of the central and eastern Arctic coasts the Dorset People. These northern hunters had migrated rapidly from Alaska to Greenland because their inventions had included such fundamental enabling features of Arctic life as the dome-shaped snow house, seal-oil lamps for light, and tailored caribou-skin clothing, as well as recurved bows, kayaks, and hand-drawn sledges. To prevent snow blindness, Dorset People had also created snow goggles, and had fitted their harpoons with detachable heads that toggled to form a secure anchor attached to a lanyard, or line. Their tools had been both elegant and intricate in design and function.

In addition to this ancient legacy from Dorset times, the Arctic hunters of 1492 also employed techniques developed by more immediate ancestors, the Thule People, who had spread across the Arctic about A.D. 1000, replacing the Dorset People. The Thule People were more mobile than their Dorset predecessors, and were probably specialized large-sea-mammal hunters able to take advantage of the relatively open waters that prevailed at the time. Their umiaks enabled them to carry heavy loads and dozens of people on the water, and on the snow and ice they used teams of dogs to draw their sledges.

By 1492, the Arctic coastal climate was colder than it had been during the time of the Thule migration. Whales were no longer able to pass freely through the narrow passages of the central Arctic islands. All along the Arctic coast, people were developing specialized adaptations to the local resources of their individual areas. Their Thule heritage of a rich and varied inventory of tools and implements enabled them to live in environments that ranged from the Bering Strait with its bounteous maritime ecology to the severe high Arctic of northern Greenland, where, at 79 degrees north latitude, polar Eskimos (known to archaeologists as those of the Inugsuk culture) were the most northerly-dwelling people on the planet.

In the western Arctic, from Point Barrow on the north coast of Alaska to the Mackenzie River delta, people continued to hunt whales, but by 1492 Eskimos of the central Arctic islands of northern Canada had become specialized sea-ice seal hunters. No people lived in the barren territory inland from the northwestern shore of Hudson's Bay. On Greenland's western coast, at that time, Inugsuk Eskimos may still have been in contact with remnants of European settlements that Norse colonizers had established about A.D. 1000 but that had probably lost contact with Europe by around 1350. Although the Inugsuk people had traded with the Norse, their culture and adaptation had remained essentially a variation on the Thule pattern. Using traditional native technology, they had continued to make a living as hunters while the herding and farming Europeans died out. By 1492, Norse influence was an insignificant factor in the lives of the Inugsuk Eskimos.

The seasonal rounds of the Arctic's economy consisted of a series of functionally interrelated activities, and the technology of the people flowed from the principle of constructing tool kits of objects that were also functionally interrelated. The technology of the Eskimo people in 1492 was remarkable for its proliferation of tools used in the making of other tools and artifacts. They had tool kits for working snow, tool kits for hide working, and tool kits for bone working or stone carving and chipping. They often constructed individual tools using multiple, interrelated parts made from a variety of materials. Eskimo tools were, in a sense, small machines. Among the more ingenious and sophisticated of them were the bow drill, which used the mechanical principle of converting linear motion into the rotation of a shaft; the complete multiple-part toggle harpoon, without which sea-ice sealing would have been impossible; fishing leisters; and a multiple-part, sinew-backed recurved bow.

The multiple-part tools were an elaboration of a 4,000-year-old complex known as the Arctic small tool tradition, which may have originated in Asia.

A ceremonial headpiece worn by an Athapaskan leader from the interior of modern British Columbia. It was constructed on a netted sinew cap to which were attached twists of human hair and rows of dentalium shells (acquired by trade from the Pacific coast), both topped with a band of either ermine or sea-lion whiskers. A train of decorated strands added to the dramatic impact. When used in rituals, the headpiece was covered with swan down that floated through the room as the wearer danced.

By 1492, most of the specialized tool kits and artifacts were variations of those developed and used by the Thule People. Each area had its variations of the general Thule assemblage, tailored to the limitations and opportunities of the local environment. In 1492 the Eskimos were still in the process of diversifying their adaptations to a variety of local environments, following the decline of the relatively warm conditions that had previously allowed the summer whale migrations through the central Arctic.

The Eskimo peoples of the coastal tundra had different histories, different languages, and even looked different from the native people of the Subarctic taiga. Physically, they resembled the peoples of eastern Siberia rather than their Subarctic Indian neighbors. The Eskimo peoples spoke closely related languages and dialects of the Eskimo-Aleut language family, while Subarctic people spoke a variety of distinct languages belonging to two separate language families, Athapaskan and Algonquian.

In 1492, Eskimo-Aleut-speaking people lived throughout the Arctic lands, from eastern Greenland to eastern Siberia and the Aleutian Islands, spanning almost halfway around the world at the latitude of the Arctic Circle. Languages of the Eskimo-Aleut family fell into two distinct branches. People of the Aleutian Islands spoke Aleut. The Eskimo branch consisted of two subgroups. One of these was Yupik, encompassing five languages spoken by people on the coasts of the Chukchi Peninsula in Siberia and in Alaska south of Norton Sound below the Seward Peninsula. The other branch, according to linguist Anthony Woodbury, was Inuit-Inupiaq, "a continuum of closely related dialects [that] extended north from Norton Sound and east across Arctic Alaska and Canada to the coasts of Labrador and Greenland." These closely related speech communities spanned an astonishing distance of 3,500 miles, or 140 degrees of longitude. Their close relationship to one another clearly reflected the relatively recent expansion of common Thule ancestors across the Arctic coast, about five hundred years before 1492.

Subarctic culture history was more complex than that of the Arctic. As a result of the greater complexity, the Subarctic people in 1492 spoke a variety of languages within the Athapaskan and Algonquian language families. The Beothuk people of Newfoundland, who became extinct early in the nineteenth century, may have spoken a language belonging to a different family. People speaking dozens of Athapaskan languages occupied the more varied, sometimes mountainous lands of the western Subarctic. People speaking a smaller number of languages belonging to the Algonquian family occupied the more homogeneous lake and river country of the eastern Subarctic. Despite their differences in language, the Subarctic people of 1492 shared a common set of ideas about individual knowledge and power in relation to the environment. Those ideas were an essential part of the adaptive strategy that enabled them to live successfully in the northern forest environment.

The Subarctic people kept warm in very different ways from those developed in the Arctic. They made clothing of supple, scraped hide from which the hair had been removed. Such clothing had freedom of movement and protection from abrasion, but did not provide the thermal efficiency required for keeping warm at low metabolic rates in cold weather. Instead, people kept warm by building fires and shelters whenever they were not actually generating heat by moving. Because wood was an abundant source of fuel, they made large open fires whenever they stopped on the trail. For overnight bivouacs they built windbreaks or lean-tos to enhance the efficiency of their fires. They made more permanent dwellings in the form of double lean-tos or conical, tipi-shaped frames covered with bark or hides. A central fire within these dwellings provided both heat and light.

Unlike modern non-natives, who are able to live in the north because they possess the artifacts of industrial technology—guns, knives, vehicles, and clothing—the northern forest hunting people of 1492 understood that their lives depended entirely upon their knowledge of the environment. Their technology was a system of information rather than an inventory of objects. They understood that the objects they made from stone, hide, wood, and bone were merely

Mask excavated at Point Hope, Alaska, on the north coast of Kotzebue Sound. The Ipiutak peoples who used this mask emerged at the beginning of the Christian era and are generally regarded as forerunners of modern Eskimos. Masks of this kind were frequently used in curing rituals. Courtesy of the Field Museum of Natural History.

the manifestations of empowering ideas they held in mind. Stories about a mythic time, for instance, explained the existence of every animal, place, and natural force in relation to mythic events. Similarly, a hunter's contact with his game on the trail of a "hunt dream" explained his physical contact with an animal on the actual trails of the world. Northern hunting people viewed the world itself as a realization of the images, thoughts, and events of mythic time. Creation, they believed, was an ongoing and inherent outcome of mental and spiritual processes. A common creation story explained that a diving animal such as Muskrat discovered the world in germinal form, as a speck of dirt beneath his claws following his dive beneath a primordial body of water in mythic times. He found the world there, the story related, because he dove down from the center of a cross, a place where the four directions and the three domains of a stratified cosmos, zenith, nadir, and center, came together.

The songs that Subarctic people sang in 1492 were like trails they could "grab hold of" with their minds. Their song trails led them into a world of myth and dream. They led them toward the mythic time of creation. The dancers of 1492 circled their fires, their movable centers of the cosmos. Their tracks came together on an earth brought up from a primordial body of water as their minds came together with those of the old people who went before them. Their songs were trails that took them to the world of myth and spirit. Hunters and Dreamers knew that their trails always returned to complete a circle. They knew that, like swans, they could fly through to heaven and return. Dreamers came back to the bodies they had left in the care of their people. They came back to the centers of their creation. Hunters came back from their hunt dreams with renewed spirits. They came back from their hunts with meat to feed the people. They came back to their centers with renewed life.

Dreamers said that the place they dreamed toward was beautiful, in the way that people coming together after a long winter of isolation was beautiful. The old people of past generations came close to the others when people came close to one another in the dance lodge. When people danced and listened to the Dreamers' songs, they knew what it was like to be with their relatives who had danced in the generations before them. The dancers would follow a common trail around the fire in the sun's direction, leaning into the heat, until smoke got in their eyes, and they would hold their breath, and hold it, like the diving animal who brought up the world, until they were once again upwind of the searing center. It seemed to take so long to move clear of the heat, because one old woman was dancing serenely in the song's tracks, taking tiny little "grouse steps," like the sun as it moved from one season to another. It seemed to take so long because the old woman was up there at the trail's beginning, and the others were dancing in the smoke and heat that rose toward the place from which the swans returned each spring. Because of the old woman, people would be dancing close together, getting close enough to feel how the others danced. They would feel the touch of bodies pass from person to person around the circle.

Someone would give the fire hotly rising breath with fresh wood, and then stand, stamping feet in the dust of the many tracks, the one trail, as spirits of all the living powers circled around the center conjured there. A person's mind would rise with the smoke while feet would circle like the hunter's trail. Dreams would incline toward the sun. Singing was the sound of people breathing together. The voices would float toward where the old people were dancing in the shimmering waves of the aurora, somewhere far above the dance lodge. People would share breath with one another as they danced around a fire in the northern country, where Swan and Muskrat made a world together. The people pressed together into the night that carried them through to dawn. In the still distance of the bush that encircled the camp, waves of song flowed over the animals until the sound diminished into a throbbing heartbeat that merged with silence, and then subsided.

RICHARD D. DAUGHERTY

SOME FIVE HUNDRED years ago, just about the time of Columbus's voyages to the New World, a massive springtime mud slide, set off possibly by a small earthquake, swept out of a canyon during the night, burying a large part of the village of Ozette in the territory of the Makah Indians on the northern Pacific coast of present-day Washington State's Olympic Peninsula. In a few frightful minutes, humans and their buildings, canoes, utensils, and other possessions were covered under many feet of silt and sand.

For centuries, they lay hidden in silence. Then, beginning in the 1960s and continuing for eleven years, archaeologists excavated this remarkable miniature New World Pompeii, revealing—in a completeness almost unparalleled in American archaeology—the details of Native American life as it existed in this part of the continent about 1492. Because of subsurface drainage, the silt and clay deposits above the village had remained moist throughout the years, preserving in excellent condition the lower walls of the structures and a stunning variety of the contents of the houses. Although animal tissue, hair, and feathers had not survived as well, objects made of wood and other vegetable fibers were found in almost the exact condition they were in at the time when the spirits turned against the people.

Ozette, at Cape Alava, the westernmost point in the contiguous United States, had been probably the largest of five main villages of the Makah, a maritime-oriented people, and had been occupied for at least 2,000 years. With

During the nineteenth century, James Swan lived in close proximity to the Makah Indians of the Washington coast and recorded many aspects of their cultural life. The Makah reservation encompasses the site of Ozette. In this drawing a Makah man stands wearing clothes and holding tools like those found by archaeologists at Ozette. The fish spear and paddle represent vital activities. His woven basketry hat and his fur cloak are emblems of rank.

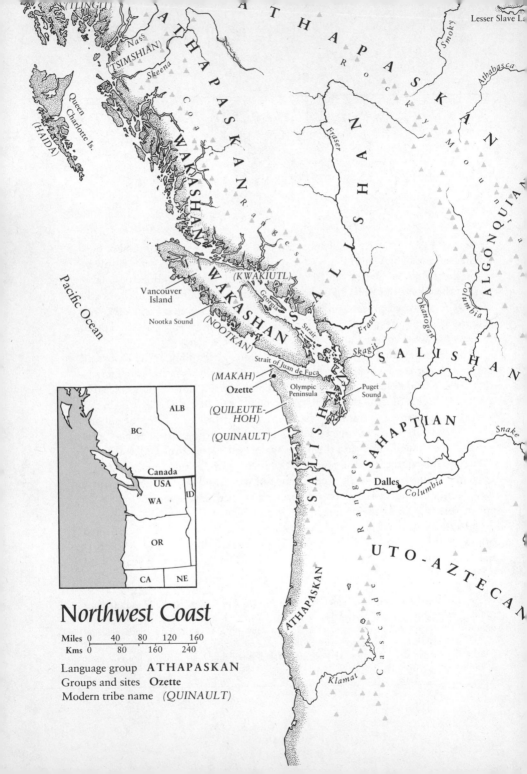

(TLINGIT)

ATHAPASKAN

Nass
(TSIMSHIAN)

Skeena

Queen
Charlotte Is.
(HAIDA)

ATHAPASKAN

Smoky

Lesser Slave La

Athabasca

R o c k y

Coast

Fraser

WAKASHAN

ATHAPASKAN

M o u n t a i n s

ALGONQUIAN

Ranges

SALISHAN

Columbia

(KWAKIUTL)

Vancouver
Island

Georgia

WAKASHAN

Fraser

Okanogan

Nootka Sound

(NOOTKAN)

Strait

SALISHAN

Skagit

Fraser

Pacific Ocean

Strait of Juan de Fuca

Puget
Sound

(MAKAH)
Ozette

Olympic
Peninsula

(QUILEUTE-
HOH)

(QUINAULT)

SALISHAN

SAHAPTIAN

Snake

Dalles

Columbia

R a n g e s

UTO-AZTECAN

ATHAPASKAN

Klamat

Cascade

C a s c a d e

ALB

BC

Canada

USA

WA   ID

OR

CA   NE

Northwest Coast

Miles 0   40   80   120   160
Kms   0   80   160   240

Language group **ATHAPASKAN**
Groups and sites **Ozette**
Modern tribe name *(QUINAULT)*

a permanent population of about 300 (which almost doubled, perhaps, during sea-mammal hunting season), it was the premier site for deep-water hunting on the entire Pacific coast of North America south of the Aleutian Islands. Here, in spring, the passing pods of whales and herds of fur seals came closest to land during their annual northward migration. In many ways, the particular, specialized traits and ways of life of the people of Ozette illustrated the sharp variants that existed among the numerous Native American groups inhabiting the Northwest Coast in 1492. But in broad outline their rich and dramatic culture exemplified that of all of them, and we will return shortly to a detailed look at life in the village before it was destroyed.

Actually, the vast northwestern section of North America—the coast and the interior south and west of the Subarctic taiga—was in 1492 the home of people of two thoroughly different overall cultures that had been developed within the two adjoining, but starkly contrasting, environments. The first were those who, like the Ozette, dwelled along the ocean on the relatively narrow strip of the Northwest Coast. The second lived inland to the east, in the arid plateau, or intermontane, region between the Coast and Cascade ranges and the Rocky Mountains. Although the primary economic orientation of most of the tribes in both areas was toward the seasonal runs of salmon, the adaptive responses of the peoples of each area to their own environment and its distinctive resources had produced by 1492 lifeways of quite different character. As "people of the salmon," the Indians in both areas, some of whom frequently met and influenced each other, will be the subject of this chapter, but attention will be given first to those who were living along the sea.

The Northwest Coast, a complex pattern of islands, coastal plains, foothills, and mountain ranges, extended from Yakutat Bay in Alaska to northern California, encompassing all of the territory west of the Coast Ranges of Alaska and British Columbia and west of the Cascades in Washington and Oregon. Its climate was one of even, moderate temperatures (except in the mountains) and relatively heavy rainfall. Warm, moisture-laden air masses generated by the warm offshore Japan Current moved inland and were forced up the slopes of the coastal mountains. Expanding and cooling as they rose, they lost much of their moisture as rain at the lower elevations, but in winter at the higher elevations heavy snowfalls nourished glaciers and snowfields, which in turn fed numerous coastal rivers. In the northern and central sections of the coastal strip, this combination of mild temperatures and abundant rainfall produced a lush, dense forest vegetation of conifers, deciduous trees, mosses, and ferns, but in the drier and warmer southern portion of the coast, open interior valleys with groves of oak trees were not uncommon.

To its inhabitants of 1492, the long, slender coastal region presented both a favorable and a forbidding environment. The sea and the rivers held many resources, but to exploit them had required the development of superb craft to navigate waters that were often stormy and rough. The forests were rich with game and many edible plant foods, but the vegetation of much of the area was so dense that land travel was extremely difficult, and large parts of the heavily forested foothills and rugged mountains were unsuitable for human settlement. Villages, instead, were located along the rivers, on the shores of bays and low-lying offshore islands, and occasionally even at sheltered locations fronting on the open ocean. The people had no agriculture, but over thousands of years had developed techniques and equipment to exploit their environment, basing their economy on fishing in streams and coastal waters that teemed with salmon, halibut, and other varieties of fish, gathering abalone, mussels, clams, and other shellfish from the rocky coastline, hunting land and sea mammals, and collecting wild plant foods. By 1492, they had reached a high cultural level usually found only among agricultural people, enjoying a stability that for some had allowed the development of a complex social and ceremonial life, an elaborate technology, and one of the world's great art styles.

On the basis of nineteenth-century census figures, corrected for earlier devastating losses from smallpox and other diseases introduced by white explorers and traders, it is estimated that the Northwest Coast had a population of about 130,000 in 1492. Thus, it was one of the most heavily populated areas of North America north of Mexico.

From the perspectives of habitat, economy, social and ceremonial life, languages, and arts and crafts, the full coastal strip could be divided into three subareas: northern, central, and southern.

Tlingit-speaking peoples were the northernmost inhabitants of the Northwest Coast, occupying the rugged coast and offshore islands of southeastern Alaska. South of them were Tsimshian Indians, whose territory included the Nass and Skeena rivers and the associated deep fjords and broken shoreline of the British Columbia coast. Offshore from the mainland, along the coast of the Queen Charlotte Islands and on part of Prince of Wales Island, were the villages of various groups of Haida speakers. The Tlingits, Tsimshians, and Haidas were set apart from their neighbors to the south, largely because of the richness of their social and ceremonial life and the elaboration of their technology, particularly the size and construction of their houses and canoes. They were also distinctive because of their art, especially the carving of large totem poles and house posts.

In the central section of the coastal region were groups of Kwakiutl, who lived on the southern British Columbia coast and the northern end of Vancouver Island; Nuuchanuth (Nootkan) people of the west coast of Vancouver Island; their close relatives, the Makahs of the northern Washington coast; and the Quileute-Hohs, the southern neighbors of the Makahs along the coast. The Nootkan, Makah, and Quileute-Hoh people were the great sea mammal hunters of the Northwest Coast, pursuing whales and fur seals in the open ocean,

A Tlingit warrior, wearing cedar-slat armor and helmet, stands at the ready. A wooden collar protects his throat, and a dagger (made from traded metal or hardwood) hangs at his side. Throughout the Northwest Coast, such coverings and designs have heraldic import indicating membership in a select group. By the Spanish explorer Alessandro Malaspina, eighteenth century. Courtesy Beinecke Library, Yale University.

harpooning them, and bringing them back to their villages to be butchered and have their blubber rendered into oil. All of the Indians of the central coastal area had a social structure and ceremonial life quite different from those of their northern neighbors, although the Kwakiutl had blended many northern traits into their culture.

The southern area included all of the tribes, principally Salishan speakers, from the Georgia Strait and Puget Sound southward along the southern Washington coast; Chinookan-speaking peoples along the lower Columbia River; and all the tribes along the coasts of Oregon and northern California. Because of cultural influences from central California and the interior plateau region east of the Cascades, the Indians of the southern Oregon and northern California coasts were a distinctive variant within this southern area. Not blessed with the abundance of economic resources enjoyed by the coastal tribes farther north, they nonetheless fished for salmon, hunted deer and elk, and gathered a wide variety of plant foods.

It is not known for certain how long people had been living along the Northwest Coast, or how early they developed the special technological and social adaptations that allowed them to exploit fully their coastal riverine and maritime environment. Archaeologists have discovered that people hunted mastodons on the Olympic Peninsula 12,000 years ago, and that groups were living along the panhandle coast of southeastern Alaska 10,000 years ago. In addition, numerous sites dating from 9,000 to 6,000 years ago have been found from southern Alaska to southern Oregon. But it is not clear just how early salmon became a significant part of their diet, although evidence from the lower Fraser River in British Columbia indicates that it was at least 9,000 years ago. Probably the use of shellfish, gathered from rocky reefs and shoals, began at least as early. At the same time, it is not established just how early watercraft was developed to the point where the coastal people could exploit the bottom fish and other resources of the offshore waters, although what was found at Ozette suggests that a fully developed sea mammal hunting culture existed by A.D. 800 (or 1,200 years ago).

Linguistic evidence, in time, may throw further light on such unanswered questions. The various tribes living along the Northwest Coast spoke many different languages and different dialects of the same language. But this great mix of languages and the widespread distribution of some of them do tell of longtime habitation of the coast and of major movements of people in the area over thousands of years.

By 1492, at any rate, fishing had become established as the economic foundation of the Northwest Coast tribes. Many edible species of fish filled the coastal waters and streams, and most were caught and eaten. Those taken in greatest numbers, and of prime economic significance, were salmon, halibut, rockfish, eulachon, and smelt. Five species of salmon were found in the area, but an individual locality might have had sizable runs of only two or three species. The salmon lived in salt water, but returned up the freshwater streams to spawn. The new, young salmon then moved down to salt water for two to four years, depending on the species, and at length returned to the stream of their birth to spawn and die.

The most productive way to catch salmon was to take them in the rivers on their way upstream to spawn. Different runs of salmon occurred in incredible numbers from spring until fall, and the Indians planned their economic life around being at their favored fishing stations when the runs appeared. Salmon were caught in weirs and traps, or were harpooned or dipnetted. The catching, butchering, drying, and storing of great quantities of salmon for winter use was a long and laborious process. The men caught the fish, and the women did the butchering; both sexes worked at drying the fish. Children helped whenever they were needed.

Halibut were caught off the coast at "banks," shallow areas with a sandy bottom where the fish came to feed. An ingenious device that employed multiple hooks was used to catch them. Several hooks were baited and tied to a spreader bar, which was simply a wooden pole about an inch and a half in diameter and four or five feet long. A stone anchor was attached by a short line to the center of the bar, and a long kelp line led from the bar to the surface of the water and was attached to a float. A number of these "sets" were left at the halibut bank for a day or so and then checked by the fishermen. Halibut, some weighing over 400 pounds, were caught, not only providing savory on-the-spot eating but drying well in the air for winter storage. Other fish, such as cod, perch, and rockfish, were caught with hook and line along the rocky shores throughout the year.

Some northern and central coastal groups lived in areas with particularly large runs of eulachon, a small fish rich in oil. The Nass River in Tsimshian territory was such a locale. The fish were taken in large funnel-shaped nets that were emptied into the canoes. When a canoe was full, it was paddled to shore, where the piles of fish were thrown into large pits to partially decompose, which aided the process of extracting their oil. When the eulachon were sufficiently "ripe," they were placed in large boxes of water in which heated stones were dropped. As the water boiled, the oil was skimmed from the surface and set aside to cool and thicken into grease. The grease was an important item in the people's diet and was consumed in great quantities. Tsimshian eulachon grease was highly valued by other tribes. Haida voyaged from the Queen Charlotte Islands to trade canoes, carved wooden boxes, and food for it. Tlingit from the north brought items made of native copper to trade, and tribes from the interior plateau region traded furs and tanned hides.

The hunting of land animals was not a major economic activity for the coastal people, but to those living in upriver villages who did not have access to the sea mammals of the coast, land mammals were a major resource. Group drives, snares, deadfalls, and the use of bows and arrows were some of the hunting techniques employed.

Sea mammal hunting was practiced by all coastal groups to a greater or lesser extent, depending on the local environmental situation. Whales, harbor seals, fur seals, sea otters, sea lions, and porpoises were found in the offshore waters. Although seals, sea lions, and sea otters were pursued by many coastal groups, only the Nootkan villages of Vancouver Island, the Makahs, the Quileute-Hohs, and, to a lesser extent, the Salish-speaking Quinaults were truly maritime peoples, hunting whales and fur seals in the spring in the open ocean.

Whales provided oil, baleen for fishhook leaders, bone for making tools, and food for the villagers. Even the barnacles on the whale's skin were relished. Fur seals contributed oil, meat, and skins. All of the sea mammals were a source for that very important dietary item, oil. Consumed in great quantities by the coastal people, seal oil and whale oil were also major trade items for the sea mammal hunting tribes.

Whaling was not only an important economic activity; it was integrated prominently in the hunting peoples' social and ceremonial life. Traveling back in time to 1492, let us now return to the Makah village of Ozette. The whales are passing by on their northern migration, a hunt is about to occur, and we have been invited to join it.

It is springtime, a season of unsettled weather conditions along the central part of the coast. Alders, willows, and salmonberry bushes are getting new leaves, and the bracken ferns are growing. Our trip to the village is in a dugout canoe, one that is used for whaling and is about forty-five feet long and nearly six feet wide in the center. The brother-in-law of the man who will be our host sits in the stern and steers with a long, tapered paddle, while other young men sweep the canoe along at a swift speed with their rhythmic strokes. From the sea, the coastline is rugged and forbidding. Small, rocky islands and sea stacks, sculptured by the incessant battering of the waves and used as rookeries by swarms of gulls, cormorants, and puffins, line the shore. It is a dull, misty day with low clouds and a snapping wind, and the water is a dark gray color with heaving swells and small whitecaps. We ask one of the paddlers what would happen if fog suddenly enveloped us; how would we know which way to go to reach land? He replies confidently that along this stretch of the coast the swells always move toward the land. If one knows the direction of the swells, one will know where the land is.

Soon we see three islands forming a protective arc around a point of land. Above the beach at the point, we make out more than a dozen flat-roofed, wooden houses, seemingly arranged in two rows with their long axes paralleling the beach. As we pass between the two northernmost islands, we cross a barely submerged, rocky shelf. It is half tide, and large boulders project above the water. At low tide, the entire flat will be exposed, leaving only scattered tidal pools. It is an ideal location for a coastal village, because the offshore islands and the rocky shelf protect it from the battering of winter storms and afford a safe and sheltered canoe landing throughout the year.

Dozens of large canoes, mostly for whaling and sealing, are pulled up on the Ozette beach, which is littered with whale and seal bones. A short distance away, the butchered carcass of a humpback whale lies rotting in the shallow surf. Crows, gulls, and village dogs have picked the skeleton nearly clean. As we step ashore, we are met by our host and members of his family, who, with

This carved Nootkan (Nuuchahnuth) mask, with movable eyes and mouth, represents the spirit who first brought salmon (represented by hanging wooden fish) to the west coast of Vancouver Island. A food staple throughout the region, salmon were a major concern of economic and religious life. The mask pictured here was carved by native artists in the nineteenth century for use in ceremonies. Courtesy of the Field Museum of Natural History.

hand-held skin drums and rattles of pecten shells, sing us a family song of welcome. Then our host leads us to his house, which is located in the first row, just above the beach. The buildings are on a bank, ten feet high, that is climbed by a series of shallow steps dug into its slope. The bank, we see, is really a great pile of clam and mussel shells, animal bones, charcoal, and fire-cracked rock, refuse from the economic activities of the village that has accumulated over the many centuries that the site has been occupied.

Our host's house is a large, multifamily structure entered through a door on the seaward side. The building, about 65 feet long and 35 feet wide, has a framework of logs covered with hand-split cedar planks. The flat roof slopes from front to back. The wall planks, which run horizontally, are tied to the upright logs with split cedar limbs or spruce roots. Each plank slightly overlaps the one below it; gaps between the planks are chinked with seaweed and moss. The roof has been fashioned from carefully adzed cedar planks about ten inches wide and from ten to twelve feet long. One face of each plank has been adzed to form a raised lip along each edge. These have been laid tile-fashion, with the raised edges overlapping to prevent rain from leaking into the house. Heavy stones and large whale vertebrae have been placed on the roof planks to keep them from blowing off in a storm. In the summer, many of the wall and roof planks will be removed and taken to Tatoosh Island, about twelve miles to the north, where our host's family goes at that time of the year to fish for halibut.

Inside the building, the walls are lined with low benches or sleeping platforms that rest on short wooden stakes driven in the house floor. The fronts of some of the benches have been inlaid in patterned designs with the opercula of the red turban shell. Several flat cedar planks, covered with woven cedar-bark mats, lie on the ground in front of the benches. Dividers made of planks and mats separate the interior into six family living compartments, each with its own fire hearth. The center of the house has been left open as the main traffic area. Several of the roof planks have been pushed aside with a long pole to permit light to enter and smoke to escape. Because the house has no eave troughs, drainage ditches, lined and covered with planks, have been dug across the hard-packed earth floor to maintain a dry interior.

Our quarters are in the southwest corner of the house, next to the compartment of our host. In addition to our host and his wife, the building is occupied by two married sons and their wives and small children, our host's mother, an elderly aunt, and a slave woman who was captured during a raid on a village of another tribe down the coast. Most of the possessions of the building's occupants are stored under the sleeping benches and in boxes and baskets that are stacked behind the benches; some are tied to the inside walls of the house. Our host is a whaler, a man of prominence, and two whale harpoons and a large, plaited cedar-bark basket containing harpoon heads and lanyards hang from the wall above his bed. At its foot, six tips of whale harpoon, broken and retrieved during the hunts, are driven a few inches into the ground.

Near his sleeping bench, also, rests a carved cedar effigy of a whale fin, inlaid with over 700 sea otter molar and canine teeth, some forming the design of a thunderbird grasping a double-headed serpent in its talons. Along one wall is a large carved and painted cedar plank, approximately twelve feet long and two feet wide, depicting two thunderbirds, each being followed by a wolf. Another wall has a similar carved and painted panel, showing a whale. Black and red pigments predominate in the artwork, all of which has personal meaning to our host.

In front of one of the compartments is a large loom. Two uprights set into the ground support two roller bars, around which the yarn is stretched. Spindles and spindle whorls, weaver's combs and swords, and baskets full of dyed yarn of dog hair rest on a mat near the loom. A partially finished blanket on the loom—or perhaps it is only yardage material—has a plaid design in gray and black.

Hanging from the roof beams are long, slender sticks on which dozens of smelt have been threaded through their gills. The fish were smoke-dried in this fashion and then brought into the house and hung from the ceiling so that smoke from the cooking fires can complete the curing process and help keep away flies.

Preparations for a special feast in our honor are underway. The main dishes will be steamed clams and mussels, boiled seal meat, dried smelt and salmon, seal oil, and salmonberries that have been preserved in a box of seal oil. A fire has been burning for some time in a large pit, the bottom of which is lined with rocks. Now that the rocks are sufficiently hot, the fire has been allowed to burn down. The pit is being lined with kelp, on which will be dumped basketfuls of mussels and clams. More kelp will be added and the pile allowed to steam until the food is cooked. Fresh meat is either roasted in a pit, cooked over an open fire, or boiled in wooden boxes into which heated stones are dropped. Our boiled seal meat is cut up into chunks in such a way that each piece is part lean and part fat. Fat and rendered seal and whale oil are important parts of the meal. Dried meat is dipped into the seal oil before it is eaten, berries are preserved in the oil, and seal blubber is eaten with the lean meat.

After the "welcoming feast," a number of invited guests, all important leaders in the village, stand and make welcoming speeches to us. Songs of welcome are then sung, and several individuals perform special dances. The party ends early, because tomorrow we will hunt whales.

To be a successful whale hunter, a man must possess the proper spiritual power. Our host inherited his power from his father, who had also been a whaler, but he has enhanced his spiritual help by acquiring a whaling power of his own. He spends this night before the hunt at a lonely spot on the coast, communicating with his spirit powers and asking for success the next day.

It is not yet light when the whaling crews assemble on the beach, checking their equipment and stowing it properly in the canoes. We will be riding in a canoe that will not be hunting, since the activities of a highly trained whaling crew will not permit the presence of a nonfunctioning observer in their midst. The head whaler's position is in the bow of the canoe, with his harpoon resting in a notch in the raised prow. His gear consists of a heavy, tapered shaft of yew wood made in three sections. The lower section is often damaged after the

Nootka people traveling by canoe, the essential mode of transportation throughout the Pacific coastal area. The knobbed hat of the man in the center indicates his high rank, as does the sloped forehead of the woman passenger. Often, slaves would paddle, but these paddlers are too well dressed to be slaves. This drawing was part of the log of the brigantine *Hope*, which traveled from Boston to the Northwest Coast in 1790. Courtesy of the Library of Congress.

whale is struck. Thus, the entire harpoon shaft does not have to be replaced. A large woven bag contains eight harpoon heads, each in a small cedar-bark pouch. The harpoon head has a large mussel-shell blade and two barbs made of elk bone or antler. To each harpoon head is tied a lanyard about twenty feet long made of whale sinew. This lanyard attaches to the whaling rope. Finally, a long, slender killing lance rests next to the harpoon.

As we head out to sea, the whaler stands at the bow of his canoe, scanning the ocean for sight of a whale and continuing to ask for help from his spirit power. Behind the whaler are six paddlers, who will also manage the whaling lines and floats. More than a hundred feet of cedar-bark and spruce-limb rope are coiled in baskets at the men's feet. Eight sealskin floats, to be inflated when the whaling grounds are reached, lie with the rope. In the stern is the man who steers the canoe. It is his job to bring the canoe up next to the whale as it surfaces, so that the whaler can plunge his harpoon into the huge animal's side.

We reach the area where the hunt is to begin, the open ocean beyond the outermost island, and follow our host's canoe closely. His crew is inflating the floats and attaching them to the line. The "guide" in our canoe explains that they seldom go more than five miles out to sea, because if they are successful in killing a whale, it must be towed back to shore, a lot of hard work.

At last, our host's canoe sights a whale. Soon we see it too, when it surfaces and blows. But it dives again and is gone for several minutes. Suddenly it comes up, blows, and dives again. The whaler's canoe marks its path and times its dives. The steersman must place the canoe right next to where the whale will surface again. A miscalculation could be disastrous.

Suddenly the whale surfaces alongside the canoe. The whaler instantly plunges his harpoon into the animal, and at the same moment the paddlers throw the floats and the baskets full of line into the water and attempt to back the canoe away from the rising flukes. The whale dives, and the baskets that contained the line are retrieved. A small, brightly colored telltale float at the end of the line marks the direction of the whale. The whaler prays that the whale will not swim out to sea. His spirit power is strong, and the frantic whale swims gradually closer to the coast. As it tires, it surfaces more and more frequently; the sealskin floats have done their work. Finally, exhausted and unable to dive, it lies blowing on the surface. The whaling canoe approaches cautiously. The whaler plunges the killing lance into the whale's heart. One of the paddlers leaps onto the head of the whale once it is dead with a short piece of line and a knife. Cutting holes in the upper and lower jaws, he lashes the mouth shut to make towing the animal easier. The floats are now tied on each side of the whale to make it ride higher in the water. The towing line is attached, and the exhilarated whalers begin the voyage home. The singing of rhythmical towing songs eases their work.

The whale was killed not too far from the village, allowing the carcass to be brought to the beach directly in front of the houses. Relatives of the successful whaling crew immediately begin the butchering process. Each knows the proper portion to remove because of the degree of their relationship to a member of the crew. Our host, the killer of the whale, does not participate in the butchering. He must appease the spirit of the dead whale. Ceremonies celebrating the successful hunt will take place in the village that evening, and the next day we will leave.

Unlike whale hunters, three-man crews, using smaller canoes and double-pointed harpoons attached to a line, hunted the fur seals. After a seal was harpooned, it was pulled to the canoe and clubbed to death. Harbor seals and sea lions were usually hunted on offshore rocky islets where they "hauled out" to rest. Most of the meat of the seals, like that of the whales, was eaten fresh, because its high fat content did not permit it to cure well for storage. The oil, on the other hand, could be stored for several years. Shellfish, abundant along most of the coast, were harvested throughout the year except during the summer. Clams, mussels, native oysters, limpets, and barnacles were among the shellfish that the people gathered. Dried clams and mussels and certain shells like dentalium were traded to inland groups.

The lush forests of the coastal region contained a wealth of edible plants, useful also for medicines, dyestuffs, and raw materials for making most of the villagers' goods. Studies indicate that some peoples may have utilized as many as 150 different plants. Although edible berries, greens, roots, and shoots were abundant, there were few starchy food plants that could be gathered in large quantities and stored for winter use. In the more southerly areas, however, camas bulbs and acorns were gathered and stored, and formed an important part of people's diets. In the northern and central areas, berries were one of the few plant foods that could be kept satisfactorily for winter use. For storage, some berries were placed in a wooden box and covered with seal or whale oil, while others were put in baskets and buried in the soft mud along a riverbank. On the whole, vegetable foods comprised a very small part of the Northwest Coast Indians' diet. It was important, nevertheless, that because of the seasonal nature of most of the food resources, a plentiful supply be stored for the winter. In addition, substantial quantities of stored food enabled large numbers of people from different villages to come together for winter ceremonials.

By 1492, the tribes of the Northwest Coast had well-developed technologies for making objects of stone, bone, antler, and shell. They also possessed excellent techniques for weaving a wide variety of baskets, soft bags, and mats, and some groups made superb blankets out of such materials as mountain goat wool, shredded cedar bark, and dog hair. But it was in their woodworking that they really excelled—a fact driven home by the five-hundred-year-old buildings and objects unearthed at Ozette.

A detailed study of the species of wood that the occupants of the village selected for different uses indicated that they had a comprehensive knowledge of the properties and characteristics of each wood available to them, and selected the wood most suitable for a given project. Because of its straight grain, ease of splitting, workability, and resistance to decay, western red cedar was used for house construction, canoe building, fashioning arrow shafts, shaping bentwood boxes, and making a myriad of other objects, large and small. Red alder was used for carving food bowls, dishes, and trays because it did not split readily and had no strong resinous smell or taste. Where great strength was required, such as in the making of canoe paddles, harpoon shafts, bows, and clubs for killing seals and fish, Pacific yew was the choice.

The principal tools employed in woodworking were stone mauls; wedges made of wood, bone, and antler; mussel-shell knives; stone adze blades set in handles of wood, antler, or bone; hafted beaver-tooth knives; and stone drills. Slabs of sandstone and dried pieces of sharkskin were used as sandpaper.

Uncovering Ozette also revealed that prior to the mud slide—at a time shortly before that of Columbus—the villagers were using steel tools. Small steel adze blades and large and small steel knives were found in the silt deposits; each was hafted in a handle of native manufacture. The most likely source

Set at the edge of an evergreen forest, this village was typical of settlements along the southern coast of modern-day British Columbia. The drawing by William Alexander, who accompanied Captain George Vancouver on his voyage around the world in the 1790s, contains many features that would have existed in 1492: cedar-plank houses, several types of canoes, and a fish weir, shown at the lower right.

of the metal was wrecked Asian junks that had crossed the Pacific on the Japan Current and been cast ashore on the rugged American coast. This probably meant that metal tools were in use all along the Northwest Coast by five hundred years ago; how much earlier is at present not known.

All of the Northwest Coast houses were similar in form to those at Ozette, but geographic variants did exist. In the northern section, among the Tlingits, Haidas, and Tsimshians, the houses were beautifully made and decorated. Nearly square in ground plan, they had a gabled roof whose ridgepoles were supported at each end by often elaborately carved and painted wooden posts. The vertical wall planks were held in place between slotted lower and upper timbers that had been carefully adzed to shape, and the ends tenoned to fit into mortises in vertical posts at the corners of the house. The door was at the center under the gable.

Often these houses were constructed over a central pit five or six feet deep

The interior of a Nootkan house by John Webber, the draftsman on Captain Cook's voyage to the Northwest Coast. Here, fish hang from the ceiling to dry, food is cooked in a wooden box, and sleeping cubicles line the walls. In the middle rear is a carved wooden effigy of a whale fin, emblematic of the high status accorded whalers. It is much like one found by archaeologists at Ozette.

and perhaps thirty feet square that had been lined with planks. The storage, lounging, and sleeping areas were between the walls of the house and the edge of the central pit. The cooking area was a sand-filled hearth in the central pit.

The shed-roof houses at Ozette were more or less characteristic of those of the Nootka on Vancouver Island and the Salishan-speaking tribes of Puget Sound and the Washington coast. Occasionally, very large houses were constructed in the Puget Sound area by the practice of simply building adjoining houses having common walls. One of them, known as "Old Man House," was 540 feet long and 60 feet wide.

From the mouth of the Columbia River southward along the Oregon coast, the houses were made of split cedar or redwood planks tied vertically to a frame. These buildings had gable roofs and were often constructed over a pit. Similar structures were built along the northern California coast, but in that area they often had double- or triple-pitched gabled roofs.

The skill of Northwest Coast Indians as woodworkers was expressed not only in their houses but also in their large and finely crafted canoes, which were their primary means of travel and were essential to their economic pursuits. The canoes were made in various sizes to suit the intended use. In the northern area, large freight or traveling canoes were as long as fifty feet, with a beam of over six feet.

Rarely was any wood other than red or yellow cedar or redwood used for canoe making. After a suitable tree was found, felled, and cut to the appropriate length, a long and laborious task, the log was split in half using large wooden wedges and heavy stone or wooden mauls. The canoe log was roughly hollowed out in the woods to decrease its weight, and then dragged to the nearest water and floated to the village, where the work could be completed in a more leisurely and convenient manner. Working carefully with adzes and chisels, the hull was shaped to near its final form. Elaborately carved bow and stern pieces were fitted, pegged, and sewn to the hull. After the final shaping and sanding, the craft was ready to be steamed and spread. The canoe was filled with water, into which heated stones were dropped, and fires were built at a safe distance along the outer sides of the hull. As the hull grew hot, water was splashed against it to hasten the steaming process. After the sides were sufficiently pliable, wooden thwarts cut to the correct lengths were forced into the canoe, spreading the sides. This was done with great care in order to maintain a uniform curve along the gunwales. The slight outward flare of the sides of the hull caused by this spreading would help deflect the waves and make the craft more seaworthy. Long, tapering paddles propelled the canoes in deep water, but the smaller river canoes were often poled.

On the northern part of the coast, the canoes had projecting bows and sterns, while those of the central region and the Washington and Oregon coasts had projecting bows but vertical sterns. The canoes of the northern California area were heavier, less finely made, and more suited for river travel than for use in open coastal waters.

The political and social organization of the Northwest Coast tribes in 1492 was based upon rigidly defined principles of kinship, class affiliation, and wealth. It was a class-structured society that recognized a nobility, commoners, and slaves, and determined a person's position primarily by birth. The highest goals in life were the accumulation and dispersal of wealth, and the acquisition of status, privilege, and prestige. High-ranking individuals achieved their position largely through inheriting material wealth, songs, dances, and certain social prerogatives. Most often, they had enhanced their status through astute potlatching (a ceremony marking a change of status where gifts were given) and success in such activities as whaling. Below them were the commoners, including some who were related to the high-ranking individuals and gained some measure of social standing through their relationship. At the bottom were slaves, usually women and children who had been captured in raids on other villages, purchased, or received as gifts, or who were the offspring of a man of high rank and a slave woman. Because of the stigma attached to being a slave, they had no status and virtually no hope of ever gaining any.

The high-ranking men were the village political leaders. However, the family was the primary social and political unit, and control of individuals within the community rested with the family. There were few decisions to be made that affected the entire village. There were no public works, no taxes, and scarcely even a community-organized defense effort in case of an attack by another tribe. The highest-ranking person in the community might be referred to as the village leader, but he had no absolute power or authority. It was largely an honorary title, and he received respect only because of his status and prestige.

There were three different systems of kinship reckoning along the coast. Among the Tlingits, Haidas, and Tsimshians in the north, descent was traced through the mother's side of the family, and a complex clan structure was developed. In the central area, among the Kwakiutls, Nootkas, Makahs, and Quileute-Hohs, descent was traced through both sides of the family, but definitely favored the father's side. Among the rest of the tribes, descent was patrilineal.

The Tsimshians in 1492 were an excellent example of the intricacy of the northern social system. The Tsimshians comprised fourteen tribes, eleven scattered in villages along the inland waters and three on the outer coast. These tribes, which were not of equal size, each possessed one or more villages made up of a number of households, or "houses."

All of the people of the fourteen tribes belonged to one or another of four clans based upon kinship. The clans determined the descent of their members, and who they could and could not marry. Descent within each clan was from the mother's side of the family, and marriage had to be with someone of another clan. To marry within one's own clan was considered incestuous. The names of the Tsimshian clans were Wolf, Eagle, Raven, and Blackfish or Killerwhale, and all four clans had members in each of the fourteen tribes. Within each clan were a number of family lineages with myths of a common origin.

Each house in a village was constructed cooperatively by members of a particular lineage and was owned by that lineage, but because polygamous marriages were permitted, and because of the restrictions against marrying within the clan, several families representing several lineages and more than one clan might occupy a single large house. Each household owned a fund of things which it considered its personal property, including names, crests, privileges, songs, dances, and myths, to which all the household members, regardless of lineage or clan, had a right. Households also owned rights to fish, hunt, gather shellfish, and collect berries at certain locations. The highest-ranking member of a lineage owning a house and residing in it was the household leader.

Within each village, one household and one lineage was recognized as most prominent because of its wealth and inherited privileges. The leader of such a house and lineage was the village chief, who was able to lead because of his prestige and personality. In the same manner, a village chief who outranked the other village chiefs within a tribe was recognized as the tribal chief. The village or tribal chief was the social and ceremonial figurehead of the group. Succession to his position was largely by inheritance and ideally fell to the chief's younger brother. It could not descend to a son, since a man's sons belonged to a different lineage and clan, that of their mother.

In addition to kinship ties and affiliation with local villages and households, the Tsimshians of 1492 were born into what amounted to a caste system. The highest-ranking individuals within the system were the chiefs and their lineage members, who tended to marry within their prestigious group in order to maintain their superior position. Below them, the commoners, or middle class, comprised the bulk of the population. By accumulating a great deal of wealth and by careful potlatching, it was possible—though rare—for a commoner to elevate himself into the highest status group. At the bottom were the slaves and their children. The basic political unit—the extended family or lineage with its own leader and ownership of economic resources—governed itself, settled disputes, and knew no higher authority. Only in time of war, for purposes of offense or defense, would local groups join together.

Among the tribes of the central and southern sections of the coast, who had either a bilateral or a patrilineal system of tracing descent, the functioning of the kinship structure was less complex. But for the central area groups, at least, the ideas about rank, wealth, and social privilege were as strong as among the Tsimshian in the north.

Basic to the social, economic, and political systems of the peoples all along the coast was the institution known as the potlatch, a ceremony involving feasting, singing, dancing, and the giving of gifts to invited guests for the purpose of announcing a change in status. The change might be a wedding, the birth or naming of a child, the giving or taking of a name important in the history of the lineage, or perhaps the assumption of an hereditary title and all of the rights and privileges inherent in it. Any such change had to be recognized by the community and even by members of other villages. Hence, the practice of giving gifts, for the acceptance of a gift by a guest was tacit recognition of the new status announced by the host or his spokesman. A potlatch was also an occasion for young people to socialize and an enjoyable opportunity for relatives and friends from different villages to see each other.

Let us return again to Ozette in 1492. We have been invited to a potlatch being given by a high-ranking man, the head of a large and important family that has been preparing for it for more than a year. This potlatch will probably last for several days. The host family has set aside enough food to feed nearly two hundred guests, some from villages several days' journey from Ozette. They have also accumulated a great store of objects to give away as gifts, including several canoes, carved and inlaid boxes, food dishes, blankets, and shell beads and other trinkets. Everyone will receive a gift, the most valuable going to the highest-ranking individuals.

Canoeloads of guests have been arriving all day. They are greeted with great ceremony and escorted to the houses where they will be staying. Fortunately for the occasion, the weather has cleared and the temperature is mild. At the appropriate time, the people are gathered, and an announcement is made concerning the event being celebrated. This involves a lengthy recitation of the legendary history of the family or lineage to demonstrate the right of the person giving the potlatch to assume the new status, with its name, title, and rights. There then follow songs, dances, feasts, and the distribution of the gifts to all of the invited guests in the order of their recognized personal importance. The event, continuing for several evenings, is notable for the huge quantities of food consumed and the resplendent garb and masks of the dancers. Eventually, the ceremony ends and, taking the gift we have received, we leave with the other guests.

Economically, the potlatch was a very serious undertaking. Material wealth was important in Northwest Coast society, but only insofar as it could purchase through potlatching the thing that was of even greater value: higher personal status. A person who received a gift at a potlatch was placed in the debt of the man who gave the gift and would in time hold his own potlatch and return a gift of equal or higher value. In this way, the potlatch actually served as a vehicle for passing around among the members the surplus wealth of a society; the only thing that changed was the status of the individuals.

In the intertribal relationships along the coast, life was often unfriendly and violent. Through native traditions and the modern distribution of different languages, there is abundant evidence of large-scale warfare in the northern and central sections of the coast. There is little question that some Tsimshian groups had originally pushed downriver to the coast from the interior, probably displacing Tlingit people who were already living there. Also, the Nootkan-speaking Makahs had crossed the Strait of Juan de Fuca from their homeland on the west coast of Vancouver Island and driven out the Quileute-Hohs, taking over a part of their territory. Prominent geographic features in Makah territory still retained their Quileute-Hoh names.

There was also another kind of conflict, carried on not for territorial gain but for the purpose of acquiring personal prestige. This was persistent small-scale raiding, usually conducted by canoe-borne war parties, to capture slaves and other booty. Slaves were wealth, and to own them enhanced an individual's status.

The religion of the coastal tribes in 1492 was an individualistic and highly personal part of daily life. Among all the groups, there was a general belief in supernatural beings who existed everywhere in nature. Human contact with the supernatural could be fortunate or disastrous. The supernatural beings appeared in various guises, some as animal spirits and others as monsters. The thunderbird, who lived on mountaintops and could carry a whale in its talons, was one of the most widely recognized monsters. Some of the beings of the spirit world functioned as guardian spirits to protect and bring good fortune to those who possessed their spiritual power.

Most guardian spirits were thought to be rather specialized in the type of assistance they could provide. For example, a person could receive a power for seal hunting, halibut fishing, gambling, or for being a shaman. Spirit powers were acquired through ritualized quests or inheritance, though sometimes they even came unsolicited. A song and a dance came with the power. A person might have more than one spiritual "helper," and some powers were considered to be stronger than others.

In addition to the belief in spirit powers, which they considered to reside outside of a person's body, they also believed in something that might be thought of as a "soul," which they regarded as the animating force within the body. If a soul wandered from the body or was stolen by a malevolent shaman, death was sure to follow unless the soul could be found and restored by another shaman.

The principal religious practitioner among the Northwest Coast people was the shaman, who interpreted the spiritual world to the layperson and employed his special spiritual powers and certain magical practices to cure individuals who were ill. Although the Indians cured most of their sicknesses with a vast lore of herbal remedies, in case of serious and prolonged illness a shaman was called in and paid to effect a cure. Concepts of illness included soul loss, spirit loss, or intrusion of a foreign spirit or object into the body, perhaps caused by a malevolent shaman. Through often very dramatic public performances, the shaman would attempt to heal the individual.

The art of the Northwest Coast Indians, as made manifest most prominently in the masks, garb, rattles, and other paraphernalia of religious ceremonies, was one of the most distinctive in the world, and generally depicted animals, birds, fish, and supernatural beings that figured prominently in these peoples' mythology and family crest designs. Much of the art was rendered in two- and three-dimensional carvings that were often also painted. Sometimes, the designs were inlaid with shell. The carving tools included knives, chisels, and adzes with blades of metal, stone, or shell, and handles of wood, bone, or antler. The chisels were struck with mauls made of artistically ground stone or carved from bone or wood.

Such art reached its highest and most dramatic development in the northern section of the coast, where the Tlingits, Tsimshians, and Haidas carved

While Northwest Coast peoples wore few clothes, rain gear was ubiquitous. Poorer people wore capes woven of cedar bark, but well-to-do people like this man wore fur robes and woven hats. Courtesy Beinecke Library, Yale University.

large, massive totem poles with the crests of their personal or clan lineage, built magnificent houses with highly carved, ornamented, and painted fronts, constructed huge, artistically rendered canoes, and made intricate, painted wooden masks and decorated headdresses, blankets, and ceremonial garments. While some of the art was realistic, much of it consisted of conventionalized designs that produced the distinctive Northwest Coastal style. In many cases, it appeared that a two-dimensional graphic design had been applied to a three-dimensional form. Many of the totem poles, for example, were really low-relief carvings of designs wrapped around a cylindrical form. The distortion of the anatomical features that of necessity had to take place was one of the characteristics of the style. In the same manner, when these motifs were depicted on a flat surface such as the side of a wooden box, the animal appeared to be split down the middle into two halves that were spread over the design field.

Another characteristic of this northern style was the feeling that all available space had to be filled. Eyelike designs, U-forms, and ovoids were employed in a strikingly patterned manner to cover every blank area on the design field. Much of the art was rendered by carving and painting on wood surfaces, whether it was a canoe prow, a house post, a feast dish, a halibut hook, or any of dozens of utilitarian objects. There also was some carving on bone, antler, stone, and shell.

The art of the tribes of the central part of the coast, although it contained some of the northern design elements, was of a rather different, more realistic style. Humans, as well as whales, seals, wolves, and birds, were common subjects, and were rendered in a representational, nondistorted manner. Many utilitarian objects were decorated with either realistic forms or geometric designs. It was primarily in the ceremonial art that a conventionalized rendering of real animals or mythic beings took place. The art of the Kwakiutl appeared to be a blend of the basic central area forms and those from farther north.

Among the Salish and Chinookan tribes, art was much more attenuated in amount and form. Much of the art of these more southerly people was applied to ritual paraphernalia, such as masks, rattles, drums, and spirit figures. It was not that they could not carve or paint, but simply that art was not as great a part of their everyday life. There are excellent examples of Salish art in masks and spindle whorls, for example. Among the tribes of the southern Oregon and northern California coasts, there was considerably less artistic carving and painting than among their northern neighbors. However, considerable effort went into weaving intricate geometric designs in beautifully made coiled baskets.

Along the whole coast, artistic expression also found outlet in personal decoration. Except in inclement weather, the Indians wore few clothes in their daily life, leaving large areas of the body exposed. Tattooing was common, and in some cases tattoo artwork covered the entire body. Whereas everyday utilitarian garb for wet, windy, or cold weather was mostly unadorned— usually a simple protective covering like a cloak of fur, hide, or shredded cedar bark—ceremonial garments were elaborately decorated. In the far northern area, cone-shaped basketry hats with wide rims often had designs woven into them, and headdresses and beautifully woven blankets, worn on important occasions, were accented with beads, strips of fur, and pendants of shell, bone, or stone.

EAST of the central and southern coastal tribes and the formidable mountain ranges that hemmed them to the fringe of the continent was a vast interior country of a totally different environment, inhabited in 1492 by peoples of a different culture from that of the coastal area, but who also depended on fish, particularly salmon, for much of their diet. This great inland region was bounded on the north by the great bend of the Fraser River in modern-day British Columbia and on the south by the country of the headwaters of rivers in today's Oregon and western Idaho that flowed northward into the Snake and Columbia. The region extended from the Cascades in the west to the Rockies in the east.

Physiographically, it was a very diverse region. In the north, parallel ranges of forested hills and mountains separated valleys containing rivers, lakes, and scattered grasslands. Farther south, in present-day eastern Washington and north-central Oregon, lay one of the largest basalt plateaus in the world, formed millions of years before by layers of molten lava that had spread across the land from fissures in the earth's surface. It gave a modern descriptive name, the Plateau, to the whole region. Later, along the eastern slopes of the Oregon Cascades, vulcanism that had deposited ash over a huge area had produced cinder cones and enormous flows of obsidian, which the Indians for thousands of years used for making many of their stone tools. On the region's western and eastern borders, much of the Cascade and Rocky Mountain foothill country was forested, but south of the basalt plateau was an extensive arid and largely treeless grassland.

Because air masses moving inland from the coast had much of their moisture wrung from them as they were forced up over the Cascade and Coast ranges, far less rain fell on the interior side, and most of the region's moisture came as snow in the winter. The driest areas, toward the southern end, received only 11 to 20 inches of moisture annually. Throughout the region, temperatures lower than 20 degrees below zero in the winter and above 100 degrees in the summer were not uncommon.

The population—concentrated in 1492 in the major river valleys, where winter villages and salmon-fishing stations were located—was probably not much more than 50,000. The areas away from the rivers and lakes were used only on a temporary basis for hunting and gathering wild plant foods. None of the Indians practiced agriculture, and the locations of their somewhat widely scattered groups were directly related to the ability of those areas to support nonagricultural peoples.

In the northern part of the region, in modern-day British Columbia, were groups of Salishan speakers, ancestors in 1492 of today's Okanagon, Shuswap, Thompson, and Lillooet tribes. Their territory covered a variety of terrain, including forested mountain ranges and grassy lowland river valleys dotted with large and small lakes. South of them, other Salishan speakers, ancestors of a host of modern-day tribes, including the Coeur d'Alene, Kalispel, Spokane, Sanpoil, and southern Okanagon, inhabited a somewhat similar country of open river valleys, scattered lakes, grassy flats, and pine-covered hills. However, one group, known today as the Columbia, for the river along which they

A Chinook woman decorated with tattoos holds a baby bound in a cradleboard. A sloping board is attached to the cradleboard to mold the infant's head to resemble his mother's. The effect was a mark of beauty, prestige, and rank.

lived, dwelled in the arid, open-steppe environment of present-day Washington State's Big Bend country on the central area's southern fringe.

The dry southern section of the region, a country of grasslands and sagebrush, with juniper stands in sandy areas and pine forests at higher elevations, was the territory of Sahaptin-speaking peoples, forebears of such modern-day tribes as the Nez Perce, Palouse, Cayuse, Walla Walla, Tenino, Molala, Klickitat, Yakima, and Kittitas. In addition, the upper Klamath, physically remote from the rest of the Plateau tribes, lived in the southern foothills of the Oregon Cascades, an environment that in many ways was more like that of the northern part of the region. Along the Plateau's eastern flank, finally, ancestors of the Kutenai and the Salish-speaking Flathead (who did not flatten their heads and were grossly misnamed by whites in the nineteenth century) occupied territories that lay wholly or in part east of the Rocky Mountains. They did not have access to salmon streams and developed a more generalized economy with greater emphasis on hunting.

Let us return once more to 1492 and visit a Plateau village of Salishan speakers. They live far inland in the arid southern portion of the region, and the best way to reach them from the coast, where we have been, is by canoe up the great river which one day will be called the Columbia.

It is a beautiful clear fall day as we leave the broad mouth of the river and a village of coastal Chinooks, who have suspended salmon fishing at their tidal fish traps and begun readying their large plank houses for the winter rains. We begin our journey in a coastal river canoe, about twenty-five feet long, but much narrower than those used in the open ocean.

As we head upstream, we pass high, snow-covered mountains bordered by ranges of forested foothills. The river becomes narrow and swift, and we encounter numerous rapids. For two days, we move steadily inland and, leaving the slow-moving tidal waters, enter a stretch of river where wooded shores plunge steeply to the river and numerous waterfalls cascade down awesome cliffs. We pass several Indian camps and villages, located at the mouths of tributary rivers and small streams where fresh water and firewood are always available. These small streams also have huge runs of spawning salmon.

As we pass a long, lightly timbered island, we see that it is used as an Indian cemetery. Many canoes, each containing the remains and possessions of a deceased person, have been dragged up and left on the island's rocky surface.

At one point, we have to portage our canoes and possessions around impassable rapids. Finally, we leave the heavily forested slopes behind us and enter a region of tall, brown, grass-covered hills and precipitous basalt cliffs. A long stretch of rapids here is one of the most famous salmon fisheries on the entire river, and is also a major trading center where members of tribes from the interior come to trade with those who bring goods upstream from the coast. There is also much gambling and socializing.

The method of taking salmon from the big river is different from anything we have seen before. At places where the water cascades through narrow, vertical-walled canyons, the fishermen construct small platforms, tied and wedged to the precipitous cliffs and projecting out over the rushing water. In such fast water, the salmon moving upstream hug the rock walls, where the current is less strong. Standing on the platforms, the Indian fishermen sweep their long-handled dip nets downstream to catch the migrating fish.

Above these rapids, the canoe we transfer into for the rest of our upstream journey differs from the coastal river canoe. Roughly twenty-two feet long, it was shaped from half a tree that had been hollowed out along much of its length to leave a flat, rounded, and projecting bow and stern. These canoes are propelled through the shallow waters close to the shore by a boatman using a long pole as he stands on the flat stern.

As we continue upstream, we pass a number of areas where designs have been painted and incised into the rocky cliffs bordering the river. Some designs are of deer, mountain sheep, and other animals, and others are purely geometric, consisting of parallel zigzag lines, concentric circles, or what appear to be sun figures with rays radiating from a circle. Still other designs are highly stylized anthropomorphic figures. No one can tell us the significance of these pictographs and petroglyphs. They were put there in the distant past, and no one in 1492 knows what they mean.

Gradually, the valley broadens, the tan hills become lower with more gentle slopes, and there are fewer basalt cliffs. On our right, where the river makes a bend to the north and a small river enters from the east, is a large village. A few miles farther upstream, we pass the mouth of a bigger river, also flowing from the east. Although we will not follow this stream, we are told that it would take us to many villages of Sahaptin-speaking people.

A long day's trip, still on the great river, brings us to the foot of another major series of rapids. We decide to spend the night here and explore our surroundings. A village of a dozen long, mat-covered lodges, the first of this style that we have seen, is situated on a sagebrush-covered flat overlooking the river. The structures vary in size, the largest being about 70 feet long and 20 feet wide, with a triangular cross section. A framework of poles covered by multiple layers of tule and cattail mats is constructed over a shallow depression. One of these structures houses several families, each with its own living compartment. Mats and skins cover the floor except for the fire hearths, which run along the center under the smoke vent.

The next morning, we observe numerous caves and rock-shelters in the cliffs bordering the river. We learn that hunting parties and small groups of travelers occasionally camp in one of these natural shelters, but no one lives in them permanently. Often, they are used to store food, which is buried in the floors in mat-lined pits to safeguard it from coyotes and other predators.

Late in the afternoon, we arrive at our destination, a village just within the canyon of a small stream near its junction with the big river. The location is a good one, for it protects the village from the strong, icy winds that sweep up the river valley in the winter. Many of the villagers, curious to see the strangers who are visiting them, gather on the sandy beach as we land. Eager hands seize our belongings and carry them to the house we will occupy. It is a structure like many we have seen along the river, the basic Plateau semi-subterranean winter dwelling. These structures, roughly circular in ground plan and varying in diameter from 15 to 30 feet, are formed by a framework of radiating poles and horizontal crosspieces, supported by one or more center posts, constructed over a pit three to six feet deep. Several layers of tule or cattail mats cover the entire structure except for a smoke hole at the center of the top. The aboveground doorway faces the stream. The floor inside is covered with layers of mats, except for the area of the fire hearth in the center beneath the smoke hole. Earth is piled up around the base of the lower roof mats to keep out drafts. When it rains, the mats swell and become watertight, and in the winter they become frozen and often snow-covered. These are very warm structures and admirably suited for winter use when the temperatures drop well below freezing.

There are other structures besides houses in the village. One small semi-subterranean shelter is used only for cooking; almost its entire interior is a fire hearth. Several small mat-covered huts are located close to the stream; these are sweat lodges.

Every village or camp has at least one sweat lodge. Sweat bathing is done by both sexes on an almost daily basis for personal cleanliness, for ceremonial purification, and, when necessary, for curing an illness. A permanent sweat lodge in a winter village is usually a mat-covered structure, but a temporary sweat lodge can be readily made of bent willow poles covered with mats or hides. To take a sweat bath it is first necessary to heat some stones, preferably vesicular basalt rocks that will not explode when water is splashed on them. When the rocks are white hot, several are placed in a small pit just inside the door of the sweat lodge, and a container of water is also placed within. The nude bathers then crawl into the sweat lodge and lower the door covering. The degree of heat is controlled by the number of heated rocks inside the lodge, and the steam by the amount of water that is splashed on the rocks. The sweat lodge is always constructed near a stream or a lake so that when the bathers emerge they can leap into the cold water.

Because the Plateau bands must move seasonally in search of food, their material possessions are kept to a highly efficient minimum. Unlike their coastal neighbors, they have no concept of accumulating material possessions as an indication of wealth and higher status. It is their belief that all persons are equal, although they recognize and accept individual differences in abilities.

Their environment provides a great variety of resources to use in manufacturing the material goods they need. An abundance of cryptocrystalline stone and obsidian has allowed them to develop a real artistry in the flaking of stone tools, and the stone projectile points found in this area are some of the finest made anywhere in the world. Game animals furnish bone and antler, from which they make a variety of implements, and the hides are worked into skin garments. Their baskets and mats are well made, but they ornament only certain styles. It is only in the area of woodworking that their efforts do not reach above the utilitarian level. The people of the village are technologically very competent in working all of the materials available to them, but even though some of their manufactured objects are ornamented, they stress utility above all else.

Clothing is rather simple and functional, particularly in the summertime. The men's usual garb is a breechcloth, a buckskin shirt, leggings, and moccasins. They add a fur robe and a fur cap for winter wear. Customarily, the women wear a short apron front and back, and a poncho-like garment which they weave of bast fiber or make from soft buckskin. They also wear leggings and moccasins, and often a basketry hat. Fur robes are worn in the winter.

For a time, the villagers busily engage in repairing their houses for winter and in bringing in loads of dried food to be stored for winter use. Throughout the year, in their hunting, fishing, and plant-food-gathering activities, they had dried and cached quantities of food, much of which is now collected and brought to the village. Dried salmon, meat, and roots are stored in large pits in talus slopes near the village.

As the weeks pass, we learn about the political and social life of the people. The village is its own political unit and owes no allegiance to any larger organization. In this area of the Plateau, the village, or at most a small cluster of villages that occupy a recognized territory, speak a common dialect, and accept a chosen leader, is the only political entity. This grouping is best referred to as a band. They choose their leaders on the basis of character, leadership ability, wisdom, and hunting and fishing skills. In general, a band leader directs the seasonal movements of the group, acts as judge and counselor, and looks after the welfare of the group, but he has no absolute authority. The band, in addition, has a council made up of older and more influential men and women who assist the leader.

The band's territory is rather vaguely defined except along the river where the fishing stations are located. Fishing sites are owned by the band, and are equally accessible to all members. Hunting and gathering territories—largely in the hills and mountain meadows to the west—are used in common with other bands.

Unlike the Northwest Coast villages, in which extended kinship ties form the basis for a tight village organization, the Plateau bands or villages are loose groupings of small family units; any of these are free to move at will to any other friendly village. In fact, except during the winter, when the people come together in their villages, the bands break up into smaller units of one or two families, who pursue their seasonal economic activities on their own.

Marriages are normally arranged by the couple's parents, although the couple are usually consulted. When marriages occur between members of different villages, as they often do, the couple will live in the village of the groom. For economic reasons, maintaining family kin relationships among other bands is particularly important because in times of food shortages individuals and families will have access to the food resources of their kindred. These same ties also permit a person or a family to change their band affiliation.

As winter settles in, the time of year arrives when all Plateau peoples participate in their most important religious ceremonies. Their religious practices center on a belief in guardian spirit powers, much the same as on the Northwest Coast. The principal difference is that in the Plateau region spiritual power must be obtained through a series of personal quests; guardian spirit powers are not inherited. These spirits are conceived of as being nonhuman in form, and may assume the guise of animals or be inanimate objects. An elder in the village, while refusing to speak specifically about any individual, explains to us that every young boy and most of the young girls are sent out on a series of one-night quests just before they reach the age of puberty. Prior to the quests, they are taught the ways of the spirit world by one of the elders. The seekers after the spirit power are dispatched alone and naked to some lonely spot and told to do certain physical tasks, such as piling rocks, and to stay awake and be vigilant. If successful, a guardian spirit will appear in human form, tell the supplicant how it will assist, and give him or her a song and perhaps a dance. As the spirit leaves, it will assume its real form, such as a blue jay, an elk, or some other creature or inanimate object. The young visionary is instructed by the elder never to reveal the nature of the vision-quest and to try to forget the experience for the present, for sometime later the spirit power will return and stay with the person for the rest of his or her life. For an adult, the guardian spirit exists apart, but is always around to be talked to and to be asked for assistance. Like their Northwest Coast neighbors, Plateau people also believe in the concept of an animating force within the body, the soul.

By late winter, the major religious ceremonies are fully under way. Participation in them is open only to those possessing spirit powers, but anyone can attend. They are held in the larger houses and involve the singing of personal spirit songs and the performing of dances. Often during a ceremony, a shaman will put on a performance demonstrating the strength of his spiritual power. Part of the reason for storing a large supply of food for winter is that the religious ceremonies also involve feasting, and the village must have enough food to feed the guests from other villages who come to participate in the events.

A drawing of the wooden column of painted figures (more crudely executed than the actual native designs) that would rise up magically from behind a blanket at a Kwakiutl winter ceremonial. Its mechanics and aesthetics were carefully guarded family secrets. Singing and drumming accompanied the erection of the column, a display of both family treasure and technical skill.

In this village, as on the coast, the religious leader is the shaman. To become one requires the support and preparation of another shaman. The aspiring shaman goes on quests of longer duration and receives special guardian spirit powers. Both men and women can become shamans. Among them, some are recognized as having special talents and abilities and possessing powers of different strengths.

Since most illnesses are diagnosed as somehow related to the supernatural world, the shaman is the medical practitioner. A malevolent shaman "shoot-

This nineteenth-century drawing from the report of the Charles Wilkes expedition in 1838, the first American scientific voyage around the world, shows a Kalapuya hunter from the Willamette Valley of present-day Oregon. He is wearing moccasins, an elkskin robe, and a foxskin cap, and carrying a sealskin quiver. The hat and robe were particularly effective in shedding the rain.

ing" a pebble, feather, or some other material object into a person's body can cause illness. Another person's spirit being intruded into one's body will also cause sickness. The loss of one's guardian spirit can produce lingering illness, and the loss of the soul, death. In all cases, a shaman is called to effect a cure.

As the winter season passes, the first signs of spring make the villagers restless to move out of their confining, smoky winter houses and begin their economic foraging activities that by midsummer will take them to the mountains.

Already, preparations are under way. Some of the families have rolled up the mats from the roofs of their winter dwellings and placed them on raised platforms of poles to protect them until they return in the fall. A few of the mats will be taken along to make temporary shelters whenever they camp.

Fishnets and spears that have been made or repaired during the winter are now being readied, for the entire village will move to the salmon-fishing sites along the river. One location is a salmon weir on a small tributary stream, but we will go to a place where more than a dozen fishing platforms are suspended from cliffs. These must be inspected and repaired before they can be used.

A temporary fishing camp is under construction. It consists of shelters of poles and mats that are little more than windbreaks, and fish-drying racks of poles that are tied together. We will camp here for a few weeks until the spring runoff makes the river too high and muddy to be fishable. As the salmon are scooped from the water, the women and children carry them to the area of the drying racks, where the fish are processed and hung to dry. The smoke from small fires built below the racks imparts a delicious smoky flavor to the fish.

Prolonged spring rains at length make the river high and muddy, so we will leave this fishing camp with one of the village families and move inland to a large marsh where duck eggs can be gathered. But, first, the dried salmon must be loaded into the canoes and taken back to the winter village and cached.

When traveling inland, only necessities are taken, because everything, including some dried food, must be carried. A man has his weapons, a kit for flaking new arrow points of stone, the clothing he is wearing, and little else. As the small group travels, the men do not take a direct route to the next camp, but hunt deer and small game in the country along the way. The women carry their digging sticks, gathering baskets, clothing, and some of the mats for the shelter. They frequently stop to gather roots and other plant foods, or to capture ground squirrels or other small animals.

When we reach the marsh, poles are cut for the mat shelters, and the fires are built. Food will be whatever has been gathered or caught during the day. We will spend several days here gathering duck eggs and collecting cattails. Since the eggs cannot be stored, they are eaten fresh and considered a great delicacy. Several of the old worn mats are discarded, and new ones made from the cattails that have been collected.

Again we are on the move, this time heading for a large meadow where roots can be gathered, cooked, and prepared for storage. The women dig up a number of different kinds of roots, but camas, bitterroot, and biscuitroot are the most important. Roots, along with salmon, are the staples of the diet. They are dug up with a slightly curved wooden digging stick that has a T-shaped handle made from the tine of an elk antler. After large quantities of roots have been gathered, they are roasted in an underground oven. A large hole is dug and the bottom lined with rocks. A fire is kept burning on the rocks until they are sufficiently hot. Then the fire is allowed to die down and the rocks are covered with grass and leaves. The roots are then piled on, and old mats are used to cover them; the entire pile is covered with earth. After the roasted roots are dug out, they are pulverized into a coarse flour in an open-ended basket hopper that is placed over a smooth flat rock. A stone pestle, elaborately shaped, is used to pound the roots. Much of this flour will later be mixed with dried and pounded salmon or deer or elk meat, plus some animal fat or fish oil, and perhaps some dried berries, to form a nourishing pemmican.

In addition to the roots, the women have collected the inner bark of certain trees, fern sprouts, seeds, and various leaves—all of them edible.

After several weeks at the camas meadows, where we have met members of a number of different bands who also came to dig roots, it is time to continue our slow journey into the mountains. The time spent at the root grounds was not only one of hard work but also a happy social occasion. Singing and dancing in the evenings, trading, young people courting, and the reunion with kin and old friends from other bands made the time of root gathering very special.

We are in no hurry to get to the mountains, because we are following the ripening of plants at higher and higher elevations. Also, we must wait until the mountain meadows are free of snow and until the deer and elk have moved up into the subalpine regions.

The meat of land mammals figures prominently in the villagers' diet. They hunt a considerable variety of animals, but deer, elk, black bears, rabbits, and beavers are of greatest importance. Deer are sometimes hunted in communal drives, but most often by individuals stalking them or lying in wait at salt licks or along game trails. Bears are usually hunted in the winter, when they are hibernating. The men's principal hunting weapon is a sinew-backed bow and arrows tipped with stone points.

Other animals hunted include mountain sheep, mountain goats, and raccoons. The animals furnish not only food but hides or skins for clothing, sinew used in the manufacture of many tools and the sewing of garments, and horn, bone, and antler for tools.

Finally, we reach a hunting camp, located in a beautiful subalpine valley with a clear, cold lake at its center. The shelters are erected and more poles gathered for the drying racks that, hopefully, will soon be loaded with elk meat. Huckleberry bushes are everywhere, and the women and children will soon be busy picking and drying berries, as well as helping to butcher the elk and dry the meat. Although there is much work to be done, this is a pleasant and relaxing time of the year. There is abundant food to be had, the weather is warm, and the scenery spectacular. It is little wonder that the people view this as the ideal season, for the return to the river means the heavy work of fall fishing and then getting the village ready again to be occupied for the winter.

Here in the mountains the women gather certain grasses for their baskets, and occasionally visitors from the west side of the mountains arrive for trading. They bring beautiful shells from the coastal waters, dentalium, olivella, and abalone, to trade for stone arrowheads.

The men are successful in hunting elk, and quantities of meat are dried. The hides of several animals are staked out, scraped, and soaked. Selected pieces, to be used for making moccasins, are rolled up to be carried back to the village.

The leaves of the birches and tamaracks are beginning now to turn yellow, and we have had one light snowfall. It is time to head back to the river and get ready for the major run of salmon. After the fall fishing, we will leave the Plateau people and start downstream again, back to the mouth of the great river and the people of the coast.

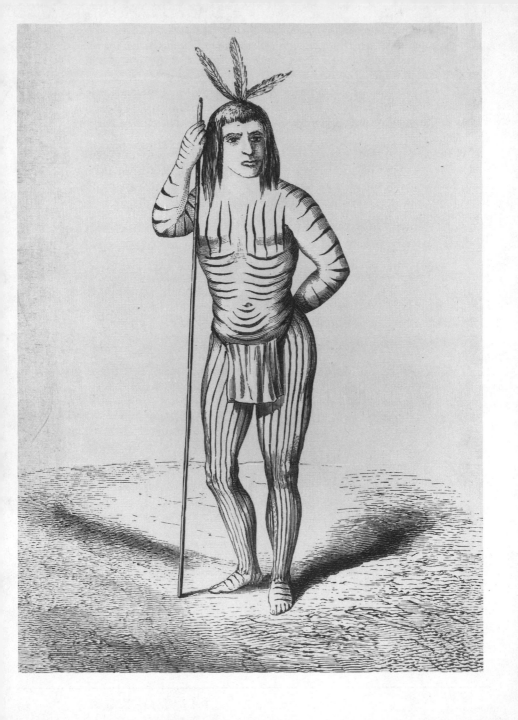

Taking Care of the Earth and Sky   4

PETER IVERSON

IN PERHAPS NO OTHER part of the New World was one so conscious of the earth and sky as in the extensive western half of the North American continent. The broad, sweeping country of 1492 was one of spirits and powers. Vast deserts and badlands spoke to its harshness. Deep canyons and long rivers testified to its immensity. The highest mountains, the farthest horizons, the most severe climates existed there. From carpets of bright wildflowers that emerged in spring to forests of towering saguaro cacti, the flora varied dramatically in size, composition, age, and use. The birds and animals were equally wondrous in their variety: magpies and eagles, coyotes and Gila monsters, grasshoppers, pronghorn antelopes, ravens, horned toads, and bison— it was home to all of them.

This arid and semi-arid landmass stretched roughly from the 98th meridian and the eastern plains, where the woodlands of the modern-day Midwest ended, to southern California, and from the prairies of Canada to central Mexico. Within this huge region, the sky and earth were different from the more humid lands to the east. Traveling west, one literally felt it as well as saw it. The vegetation became more sparse and the land more open. The cloud patterns changed, and the air became drier and clearer. As the 98th meridian and the woodlands were left behind, the sky and earth grew bigger, closer together, and seemingly all-encompassing. The Navajos spoke in their Blessingway ceremonial of the sky taking care of the earth and the earth taking care of the sky. Both required the kind of homage and understanding reflected in the rituals and daily lives of many different Native American groups who accepted the

A Mohave man in body paint. Living along the lower reaches of the Colorado River, the Mohaves were skilled farmers and hunters. While their desert homes seemed remote to early European travelers, the Mohaves played a pivotal role in trade between the Pacific coast and the Southwest.

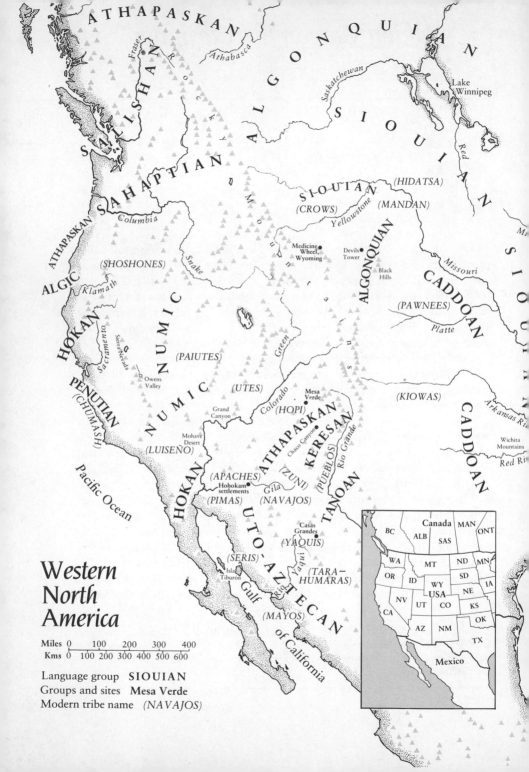

ATHAPASKAN

ALGONQUIAN

Fraser

Athabasca

Saskatchewan

Lake
Winnipeg

SALISHAN

SAHAPTIAN

SIOUIAN

Columbia

Red

SIOUIAN
(CROWS)

(HIDATSA)

(MANDAN)

Yellowstone

Snake

(SHOSHONES)

Medicine
Wheel,
Wyoming

Devils
Tower

Black
Hills

Missouri

Mi

ALGIC

Klamath

ALGONQUIAN

CADDOAN

HOKAN

Sacramento

Sierra Nevada

NUMIC

Green

(PAWNEES)

Platte

PENUTIAN
(CHUMASH)

(PAIUTES)

Owens
Valley

(UTES)

Grand
Canyon

Colorado

Mesa
Verde

(KIOWAS)

Arkansas Ri

CADDOAN

HOKAN

NUMIC

Mohave
Desert

(HOPI)

ATHAPASKAN

KERESAN

(ZUNI)

(PUEBLOS)

Rio Grande

Wichita
Mountains

Red Ri

(LUISEÑO)

Pacific Ocean

(APACHES)

Hohokam
settlements

(PIMAS)

Gila

(NAVAJOS)

TANOAN

Casas
Grandes

Canyon

UTO-AZTECAN

(YAQUIS)

(SERIS)

Isla
Tiburon

Yaqui

(TARA-
HUMARAS)

Gulf

Mayo

(MAYOS)

of California

Western
North
America

Miles 0   100   200   300   400
Kms 0 100 200 300 400 500 600

Language group **SIOUIAN**
Groups and sites **Mesa Verde**
Modern tribe name *(NAVAJOS)*

BC   Canada   MAN
ALB   SAS   ONT

WA
OR   ID   MT   ND   MN
SD   IA

NV   WY   USA   NE
CA   UT   CO   KS

AZ   NM   OK
TX

Mexico

challenge of carving out their future in this part of the hemisphere. One may properly see these native peoples as pioneers, unaided by written guidebooks or imperfect maps. As with pioneers of all eras, they shared motivations and aspirations, fears and anxieties. In 1492, their communities were carrying out diverse efforts at the least to survive and at best to prosper.

It is said of this western country that it has more rivers with less water, and that one can see farther yet see less, than anywhere in the world. Even its great rivers, including the Missouri, Rio Grande, and Colorado, have long stretches where their breadth is far from impressive. And where they widen, they compensate by shallowness: the Platte River can be a mile wide and an inch deep. There are also dry creeks, washes, arroyos, and other watercourses of different names that are empty of water for most of the year and then without warning are transformed by sudden storms into dangerous torrents.

When one moves beyond the Missouri or any point near the 98th meridian, the land—except for the breaks that flank the rivers—is generally unrelieved in its flatness. But if one persists westward, one is rewarded ultimately by increasing natural features that break the monotonous landscape: mesas, buttes, eroded formations, and range after range of great mountains. One can appreciate why such land formations have always been important to humans, for whom they acquired religious, economic, and social significance.

Still, the ultimate character of the region does not lie in its heights. Rather, one has to look beyond the peaks to the vast dry spaces of plains, basin, and desert. To the uninitiated, the desert especially seems without redemption. It seems empty. And it often is largely bare of plant life and other forms that are familiar to those who have lived where there is more moisture. There are few trees and fewer lakes. But the desert is hardly empty of flora and fauna and not without essential resources for the sustenance of knowledgeable human populations.

It is this environmental feature—aridity—often in the form of desert, that gives the entire region its underlying temperament and what unity it possesses. Not all of the huge region can be termed arid, for some of it attracts sufficient precipitation to allow it to bear the more generous label of semi-arid. Yet what is nearly universal in this part of North America is both the unpredictability of precipitation and the limits of it.

Geographically and in other ways, the region can be subdivided into three overlapping and sizable areas: the Plains, the Great Basin, and the Southwest. Such a division is somewhat artificial, for there are common elements and qualities in each of the areas, and there were native peoples who migrated from one of them to the next. Still, each possesses enough of a distinctive geographical and historical identity to make meaningful such a division and permit the giving of separate attention to the native peoples who inhabited each of them at the time of Columbus.

A group of Seris on the move near the Gulf of California. This seventeenth-century drawing by the Jesuit Adamo Gilg shows two men carrying bows and dressed in breechcloths made from animal skins. They are accompanied by a woman who is balancing a basket containing a baby in a cradleboard while carrying a rolled mat and leading a child.

To people in much of the world today, the tribes of one of those sections, the Plains, were the stereotypical American Indians. The feathered headdress, the warrior on horseback, the portable villages of hide tipis, all contributed to an image now well established through film and other media. Since the Spaniards brought the horse to the Americas, however, there were no horses on the Plains—or anywhere else in the New World—in 1492, and we have to pull back the layers of that image to a time when the Indians on the Plains made their living without the knowledge or use of that animal.

The people we think of today as Plains Indians, in fact, were not yet living on the Plains in 1492. Rather, they were still dwelling in the woodlands farther east. Only later did they move their way westward onto the Plains, which they then called home, giving sacred significance to the land formations of their new country. The most powerful peoples on the Plains at the time of Columbus's voyages were not mounted bison hunters but soil-working farmers who had successfully conquered the age-old scourge of hunger through their determined agrarian efforts. For centuries, these peoples, living mostly along the tree-lined streams and rivers of the Plains, had been masters of the world they occupied. They were village people, and were known by such names as Mandan, Hidatsa, and Pawnee.

The Mandans lived in the upper Missouri River country, primarily in present-day North Dakota. By 1492, they had large villages of houses built closely together. The tight arrangement enabled the Mandans to protect themselves more easily from the attacks of others who might seek to obtain some of the food these highly capable farmers stored from one year to the next.

Mandan housing at the time included two forms. The older type used center poles to hold up a hide covering, with other posts flaring out on the sloped roof. Probably influenced by peoples to the south, the Mandans had also developed a new kind of dwelling, rounder in its shape and covered with earth. Such houses, supported by frameworks made of native cottonwood and willow, afforded protection from four enemies: humans, the cold of winter, the heat of summer, and that ubiquitous companion of the plains, the wind.

Though the Mandans were hunters as well as farmers, hunting on foot was difficult for the sedentary villagers. Bison were plentiful in the region, but the effort to kill these enormous, cantankerous beasts required considerable ingenuity and cooperation. Mandan men worked together in large groups in order to drive bison over cliffs or trap them in corrals. The leader of the hunting party occupied a place of special honor. Recognized for his exploits in war or on the hunt, he was selected for the role by the head men of the village.

Hunting provided an excellent means to socialize younger men into the larger order of the people. A young man perceived the skill and knowledge of an older man in the hunt and began to appreciate the kind of roles he would play as he matured. Success of the hunt demonstrated the importance of cooperative endeavor, in placing the value of the group over that of the individual. Bison yielded not only food but clothing, shelter, implements, and other additions to the lives of the Mandans. The many purposes to which they put a bison exemplified the need of the people to make maximum use of the land's resources and the benefits that accrued from such thorough employment.

The women had primary responsibilities for the fields. The lands nearer the Missouri River could be cultivated more easily because of their moisture and their relatively sheltered position. The upper Missouri River country was lightly populated, and no major problem loomed with disputes over territory between tribes. In the Mandan community, extended families had responsibilities for the generous garden plots. These farmers had to exercise considerable skill to produce desired results, for their northern location meant fleeting growing seasons. Winter often lingered; autumn could be ushered in by severe frost. For good measure, during the spring and summer, drought, heat, hail, grasshoppers, and other frustrations might await the wary grower.

Under such conditions, Mandan women had to grow maize capable of weathering adversity. They began as early as it appeared feasible to do so in the spring, clearing the land, using fire to prepare the earth for planting. The women altered the specific places slightly from year to year for their maize seeds, planted in hills formed a few feet apart. From this point until the first green corn could be harvested in August, the crop required labor and vigilance. The young plants had to be thinned and protected during the summer from birds and animals and hungry human outsiders.

Harvesting proceeded in two stages. The Mandans picked a smaller amount of the crop before it had matured fully. This green corn was boiled, dried, and shelled, with some of the maize slated for immediate consumption and the rest stored in animal-skin bags. Later in the fall the people picked the rest of the corn. They saved the best of the harvest for seed or for trade, with the remainder eaten right away or stored for later use in underground reserves. With appropriate banking of the extra food, the Mandans protected themselves against the disaster of crop failure and accompanying hunger.

The Mandans grew other vegetables besides maize. The women planted another staple, squash, about the first of June and harvested it near the time of the green corn harvest. After they picked it, they sliced it, dried it, and strung the slices before they stored them. Once again, they saved the seed from the best of the year's crop. They also grew sunflowers and tobacco; the latter was the particular task of the old men.

In common with Indians across the continent, the Mandans performed religious ceremonies to aid them with their efforts in the fields. They prayed to the gods that the seeds they planted would reach fruition. Their rituals reflected a general understanding that, just as with farming, life itself was difficult, complicated, fragile. The well-being of the community could also be ensured through proper conduct and appropriate ritual. Just as economic activities promoted group cohesion, particular ceremonies encouraged solidarity.

The high point of the Mandan year came with the Okeepa, a midsummer ceremony that was as intense as any religious observance on the Plains in any era. The Okeepa gave symbolic expression to every aspect of tribal existence. All of the people participated, either as spectators or as actors in this literal act of passage. The Okeepa necessitated extended preparation, for its proper observance was essential for prosperity during the coming year.

The interior of an Omaha earth lodge near the Missouri River. Cottonwood posts support a covering of logs, which are in turn covered with layers of grass, branches, and earth. Sleeping benches circle a central hearth. Lodges of this kind were large enough to accommodate as many as forty people. (This nineteenth-century drawing also shows the Omahas' adoption of an iron hook to suspend pots over the hearth.)

The ceremony took place over a period of four days—traditionally an important number because of the four cardinal directions. Before sunrise, a religious leader alerted the people that a single person, Lone Man, would soon approach the village from the west at the time that the sun appeared. All eyes were directed to the west, and soon the people perceived the figure of Lone Man in the distance. Warriors in their regalia advanced to meet the stranger in order to ask his purpose. Lone Man responded the he had come to open the ceremonial lodge. He then encountered the newly arrived leaders, faces painted black, who brought him into the village itself. At the ceremonial lodge he began to retell the great stories of the people, from the creation of the world down to the present.

During the four days, remarkable characters presented themselves. At one point, eight men, painted identically in black, red, or brown, took the part of buffalo bulls. Wearing the skins of the bison, they mimicked the actions of the huge animals. Joining them were four other men, two representing the night

A Wichita village of thatched-grass houses near the Red River in what is now eastern Oklahoma. The artist, an Army captain who traveled through the region in the mid-nineteenth century, has enlarged the smoke holes of these conical dwellings, but his presentation of houses clustered at the center of radiating cornfields reflects long-standing practice. Actually, smoke seeped through the thatch, which entirely covered the top of the houses.

and painted all in black with white stars all over their bodies and two painted red with white stripes for the rays of the sun, symbolizing the day. The twelve danced in the ritual, while other men, attired as grizzly bears, bald eagles, antelopes, swans, rattlesnakes, beavers, vultures, or wolves, also participated.

In the course of the second, third, and fourth days, young men underwent torturous physical ordeals that were part of the requirements they had to fulfill in order to join the buffalo bull society. On the second day, knife cuts were made in the legs, chests, backs, and arms of the men, and wooden splints were inserted in the cuts. Thongs were attached to the splints in the men's chests and backs; the men were raised and suspended in the air and, with heavy bison skulls attached to their legs and arms, were dangled from the ceiling of the ceremonial lodge. The men twisted and turned and cried out in agony before fainting from the pain. Then they were lowered to the floor. They endured comparable trials on the remaining two days. For the rest of their lives the men wore the scars of the ceremony as badges of honor for their courage, stamina, and dedication to the ways of their people.

Such torture was part of an overall ritual that depicted graphically the struggle the people had sustained. The Okeepa Ceremony theatrically portrayed the association of the Mandans with the animals and plants of the earth and with the earth itself. It demonstrated the intertwining of their fates with other occupants of the earth, and it provided a link with the supernatural through the appearance of a heroic figure such as Lone Man, responsible for instruction in the right ways of ceremonial activities. The opening of sacred bundles during the ceremony ritually revealed the items of utmost religious importance that they contained. At the end of the four days, all the participants, regardless of their role in the annual rite, felt a sense of renewal, both individually and collectively.

The Mandans were related linguistically to another village community in this region. The Hidatsas were also horticulturalists and carried on sedentary lifestyles similar to those of the Mandans. They had migrated to the upper Missouri River country from the east, believing traditionally that they had emerged from Devils Lake in eastern North Dakota. At one time they had lived beneath the surface of that lake. Hunters came upon a root of a vine and climbed up it to the earth's surface. Half the people joined them and climbed up the vine to leave the lake, but the vine broke as a pregnant woman was

Bull boats on the upper Missouri River. A Swiss artist, Rudolf Friedrich Kurz, sketched these families in 1851 as they prepared to cross the river in boats made from buffalo hide stretched over a willow frame. When dry, the boats were light enough to be carried.

Taking Care of the Earth and Sky

attempting to ascend it, relegating the other half of the people to permanent existence beneath the lake.

When the Hidatsas migrated west they met the Mandans, who introduced them to corn. The first Hidatsas who sampled it liked its taste, and soon thereafter when a Mandan leader gave them half an ear of yellow corn, they took it back and planted the seed. Perhaps the Mandans introduced them to squash, sunflowers, and beans as well. In any event, their pattern of planting and tending their crops became similar to that of the Mandans, and the Hidatsas became excellent farmers in their own right.

The Hidatsas grew five different kinds of beans. They called them ama'ca ci'pica (black bean), ama'ca hi'ci (red bean), ama'ca pu'xi (spotted bean), ama'ca ita' wina'ki matu'hica (shield-figured bean), and ama'ca ata'ki (white bean). The Hidatsas planted each variety separately and threshed and stored them separately as well. They took particular care with the selection of seed beans, checking the seeds for ripeness, color, plumpness, and size. They planted the seed right after they planted the squash, using small hills about four feet apart, often between the corn rows. Using the same methods they employed with the raising of maize, the women hoed and cultivated the beans during the summer and harvested them in the fall. The beans were threshed quickly, winnowed, dried, and packed in sacks for storage.

As the young men did in hunting, young women learned through their responsibilities in the fields about being a woman in Hidatsa society. In the years when the corn grew quickly, the weeds grew just as promptly and one had to be out early in the morning each day with a hoe. Birds were a constant irritant, especially the crows, who were particularly fond of young corn. Hidatsa girls and women nurtured the growing crop and developed a fondness for it that they likened to that for growing children. They sang to the corn as they would to a young child.

Since the young women spent so much time in the fields, young men often sought their company there. Rules of proper behavior limited the nature of conversation, and mothers kept a hawklike watch on their daughters. Twelve-year-old girls teased boys of their age with songs such as:

> You bad boys, you are all alike!
> Your bow is like a bent basket hoop;
> You poor boys, you have to run on the prairie barefoot;
> Your arrows are fit for nothing but to shoot up into the sky!

As the girls matured, their songs changed, but teasing still might be a prominent element in a chorus designed for the ears of a young man.

The Hidatsa migration illustrated a larger point about the movement of the peoples on the Plains. Even if the ancestors of the Cheyennes, Sioux, and others—who much later would become quintessential Plains Indians—were still living farther east, there was already considerable resettlement and new settlement occurring on the Plains by the end of the fifteenth century. Much of this movement was voluntary. Communities sought new locations for economic or social reasons. Perhaps the bison could be hunted more effectively in this direction. Perhaps a certain crop could be grown more productively along a river. Perhaps a neighboring tribe had become so powerful that wisdom dictated a change of scenery where greater autonomy could be established. The move might be impelled by new opportunities or be a response to decline—the absence of game, the failure of crops, or some other downturn in community fortunes. Thus, a map of the peoples of the Plains five hundred years ago can do little to suggest its key ingredient: change.

The Plains did not always know peace. Despite trading networks and the benefits of reciprocity, hostilities did erupt. War provided the chance for glory, for distinction; individual men brought special attention to themselves through their bravery. Yet war was more than a great game, a kind of bloodless touch football where counting coups were recorded on an invisible scoreboard. The losers in battle might be killed or captured. Farmers might lose their lands or their treasured caches of food and seed.

When migration did take place, the people carried much with them. Not only did they take along material possessions but, as the Hidatsa story of Devils Lake illustrates, they packed various forms of cultural baggage. In the northern Plains country, the Kiowas began to make their way toward the southern plains of Oklahoma. Along the journey they added stories about Devils Tower in northeastern Wyoming and about the Black Hills of western South Dakota to the anthology of tales passed down from one generation to the next. Centuries later, in western Oklahoma, they told of seven sisters who escaped from a bear by remaining on top of a gigantic rock formation that rose miraculously into the sky, where the sisters became the stars of the Big Dipper. The strange gray thrust of rock (Devils Tower) remained, scarred by the claw marks of the bear that had tried to reach them.

So too the ancestors of the Absarokas, known later as the Crows, moved away from their association with the Hidatsas and traveled westward toward a new home in the Montana country. Among other things, they took with them the story of Old Woman's Grandchild, a tale told also by the Hidatsas. Old Woman's Grandchild was the son of the Sun and a Hidatsa woman. As was true of many such offspring in different tribal traditions, he was a hero figure who eventually embarked upon a great adventure. He destroyed the evil monsters on the earth, and after this successful mission he became the North Star, while his grandmother became the moon. In the same manner, the Absarokas may also have learned the cultivation of tobacco from the Hidatsas. The old men grew this crop, deemed necessary for human well-being. The Absarokas distinguished between tobacco raised for ceremonial purposes and that smoked recreationally. Tobacco was a crop mentioned directly in the creation stories. A special society was established for the ritual sowing of the plant's seed.

The Absarokas and Kiowas were not alone in their star myths. The Pawnees of the central Plains traced their origins and the beginnings of all people to the nighttime sky. They marked their yearly cycle with ceremonial observances tied to that sky, and they knew that all on earth moved or grew only in conjunction with the movements of celestial objects. During the cold of the long winter, the earth slept. In this period the Pawnees undertook the taxing trek of bison-hunting. The men came back home prior to the celebration of spring, at which time the stars assisted the people in scheduling the appropriate moment for the ceremony to commence. In the shelter of a great earth lodge, the Pawnee priests scanned the skies, reviewing the changing positions of the stars as they perceived them through the lodge's smoke hole and entrance.

When they deemed the moment propitious, the priests signaled that they could begin the ceremonies to arouse the earth from its winter slumber. Two stars, the Swimming Ducks, heralded the advent of spring by their debut on the horizon. The ducks spoke to the animals, calling upon them to shake themselves from their winter rest. Soon thereafter, lightning in the sky presaged a type of thunder announcing that the time was at hand for the creation ceremony.

The Pawnees tied the story of creation to a collection of twelve sacred bundles, each affiliated with a specific star. The first bundle, that of the Evening Star, had been safeguarded in the earth lodge of Old Lady Lucky Leader. Now the priests carefully and reverently opened it slowly on the yellow calfskin that symbolized all the bison. Two ears of corn stood for their main crop; two owl skins represented the chiefs' alertness. The unrelenting warriors were depicted by hawk skins, while paints showed the powers of the four directions. Flint for fire and sweet grass for incense completed the contents of the Evening Star bundle. The priests joined to sing of the creation, carefully and methodically retelling how things came to be. As they did so, they brought the world back to life.

As the year progressed, the Pawnees conducted the other necessary ceremonies, particularly keyed to the spring planting, the fall harvest, and the hunting of the buffalo. The cycle regulated their actions, gave rhythm to the season, and provided continuity to the lives of the people. About five hundred years before, they had inaugurated an extraordinary ritual that may well have been derived from a Mesoamerican culture more than a thousand miles to the south. This rite involved human sacrifice, a sacrifice the Pawnees believed was required because of the demands of the Morning Star.

In the Pawnee account of creation, the Morning Star was the male figure

A Weitspek chief ("Mec-ug-gra") from a community at the juncture of the Trinity and Klamath rivers in northern California. Dressed in leather and pelts, he carries his arrows in a skin case and holds both a bow and a club.

whose heroic quest led him to the female figure, the Evening Star. From him came the creation of the sun, and from their coupling came a girl who went to earth. She joined with a boy, the son of the moon and the sun, to become the first humans. Given his creative role in their past, the Morning Star could ask the price of a girl. Periodically he appeared in the autumn as a vision to a warrior, and the warrior had to lead an expedition to an enemy camp, where the Pawnees attempted to capture a girl to fulfill the Morning Star's grim demand. The sacrifice did not occur right away. The Pawnees took the captive girl on their winter hunt for bison and conducted the ritual with her only after the successful completion of the hunt.

The captive girl endured a period of extended tribal preparation and rites. She wore ceremonial garb obtained from the Morning Star bundle: a calfskin skirt, a blouse, a buffalo robe, black moccasins, and a feather in her hair. Her body was painted red. After a four-day ceremony, she was led to an altar, her body now red on her right side for the day and the Morning Star and black on her left side for the night and the Evening Star. The people sang to the girl about the Morning Star, and she was forced to climb a ladder up to a scaffold, where she met her end. A man took out a bow and arrow and shot her through the heart. Her blood fell on the tongue and heart of a buffalo, and those parts of the animal were burned in a ceremonial fire. Men from the village eventually took the girl's body out onto the plains. The people feasted and rejoiced, for the Morning Star had been placated and the Pawnees knew he would safeguard their welfare in the days to come.

The Pawnees also increased their chances for well-being through their horticultural abilities. They grew ten varieties of corn, eight types of beans, and seven kinds of squash and pumpkins. Since they were part of a different linguistic family from the Hidatsas, they possessed different names for their crops. Beans and squash were secular crops with no religious significance, but corn was another matter. One variety of corn, called Wonderful or Holy Corn, the Pawnees grew only for religious purposes and not for consumption. They designated two ears of this corn for inclusion in sacred bundles. The Pawnees put an ear for winter in a buffalo skin and an ear for summer in another buffalo skin. They planted this corn ceremonially and annually substituted the new corn for the old in the bundles. Their success in farming allowed them to pursue a prosperous, sedentary lifestyle, augmented by the pursuit of buffalo.

People such as the Pawnees exemplified a Plains Indian world that in 1492 had already known centuries of comings and goings on foot, of adaptation, change, and experience. By that time, farther west in the Great Basin three major groupings of other native peoples had emerged: Shoshones, Utes, and Paiutes. This trio, in turn, was subdivided many times into local communities united only loosely by language and overlapping traditions. The region itself was far from insular. Influences from surrounding areas affected the peoples. Proximity to the Pacific coast encouraged the entrance of shells into trade thousands of years before Columbus. Animal skins, agricultural products, obsidian—resources perishable and otherwise—were exchanged.

In a challenging environment, trade networks made a vital difference in the quality of life. When one realizes that such exchanges took place for centuries before the horse, the range and extent of such networks become all the more impressive. Nonetheless, people obviously had to acquire or produce things before trade was possible. Great Basin residents had to survive in an especially harsh world that never provided overwhelming surpluses of food. One used what one had, made do with what existed, and sought ways of adding to what often was a meager resource base.

By the late fifteenth century, divisions of the Shoshones occupied a widespread territory in the Great Basin, ranging from western Wyoming to the border country of California and Nevada. The Shoshones were hunters and gatherers who used many different resources during the course of the year and traveled considerably to do so. Thus, the seasons dictated the movement of the people, and knowledge of the land and its bounty proved critical. To the eyes of the outsider this world appeared forbidding and barren, but to the Shoshones their homeland offered sufficient means for a good and full existence.

The Western Shoshones lived primarily in Nevada, with some communities also residing in eastern California and western Utah. They had important subsistence activities in each of the four seasons of the year. The spring offered a particularly promising opportunity to trap groundhogs and ground squirrels as these animals roused themselves from the inactivity of winter, carrying the added weight that made it more difficult for them to elude the hunters. The men used a wooden hook they had carved to trap the groundhog. Once the animal had been lured into biting the hook, it could be seized and killed. Soon thereafter it would be roasted and the meat consumed. The Shoshones also captured birds for food. At this time the sage grouse mating season occurred. The hunters crept up to the location where the birds were mating. One man assumed the appearance of an antelope to move among the sage grouse. Wrapped in an antelope skin, he stealthily gained an appropriate spot, while other men attached willow nets to the sagebrush. At just the right moment the "antelope" startled the sage grouse, which in their attempt to flee became enmeshed in the nets.

Shoshone women scoured the land to gather plants for food and medicine. They fashioned seed beaters from willows and berry bushes and employed these implements to strike loose seeds from trees, grasses, and other vegetation. In late summer and fall serviceberries, chokecherries, and currants ripened and were picked.

In the higher elevations, the ubiquitous piñon pine was often the source of bountiful harvests. The women stretched to reach the highest cones, using a pole to knock them to the ground. In good years the pine nuts were plentiful, providing in storage a bulwark against the ravages of hunger. But not all years were good ones. Because the harvest occurred in late fall, when the people congregated, they knew that the piñon nuts represented one of their final opportunities to add to their winter cache.

Yet their mood was festive as the harvest began. Their bellies were full. If the nuts proved plentiful, the winter would be bearable. The religious leader convened the people, tossing pine nuts to the north and south, the east and west, beginning a three-day dance to pray for a fine harvest.

The Shoshones ate some of the nuts right away, either raw, roasted, or ground as a kind of mush made with water. More of the cones were buried in the earth, protected and hidden by piñon branches. As the winter progressed, the people returned to their caches and withdrew the cones. In the thin days of early spring, they came again to retrieve what remained.

Berries and nuts, seeds and fish were important elements in the Shoshone diet, but the people were not vegetarians. In the autumn the men assembled to hunt the pronghorn antelope. As in the piñon harvest, religious leaders played an active role. Armed with special powers over the skittish animals, they counseled the men as to where and when to hunt. Only when they approved could the hunt begin.

In the days before horses and guns, the men had to drive the antelopes into corrals in order to capture and kill them. They constructed lengthy enclosures, as much as a mile or two long, dragging in sagebrush, piling up stones, and perhaps bracing the walls with wood. When the corral was ready, and if the sanction had been received, the hunt could proceed. The night before, a religious officer left an arrow in the sagebrush; if the arrow had antelope hair on it the next morning, the hunt surely would be successful.

The men ranged for miles into the country before attempting to drive the antelope in the direction of the corral. The antelopes were creatures of the open country. If the people were able to drive them into the corrals, the antelopes despaired. Disoriented and lacking the deer's ability to leap, they rarely escaped the makeshift enclosures. The people fell on their terrified prey, killing as many as seemed necessary, and released those that remained. The antelope,

Three baskets from Pai communities along the Colorado River in what is now northern Arizona. The large basket on the left was used for collecting seeds, and the other two were for storage. Courtesy of the Field Museum of Natural History.

like the buffalo, provided more than meat: tools, clothing, shoes, and thread were fashioned from different parts of the animal.

The children joined in the communal rabbit drives, held ideally in the autumn when the animal's fur had grown heavy. The greater the number of people who could be mustered for the drive, the better were the chances of trapping some of the rabbits in the nets that were strung along the bushes. The children scurried and yelled at the elusive animals, who could run even faster than they. Nevertheless, if enough rabbits were cornered, then not only food but clothing and blankets were in the offing.

Confronted with a more difficult quest for food, Shoshone communities in 1492 had less elaborate forms of clothing, housing, and religious ritual than those of Indians in many other parts of the Americas. A more nomadic life encouraged temporary lodging and clothing that could be transported easily. Only in some of the eastern reaches of Shoshone country did access to buffalo and to the fish and game of the mountains permit less reliance on gathering. Still, the people could know prosperity based upon their knowledge of the land.

The second major division of the Great Basin native peoples, the Utes, resided primarily in present-day Utah and western Colorado. Their environment was somewhat less stringent than that of the Shoshones. Greater precipitation afforded a more abundant plant and animal life. Most Utes had access not only to antelope and rabbits but also to buffalo, deer, elk, mountain sheep, and even moose. They picked a wider range of berries and picked more of them. In the west, Utes relied more on fishing; in the east, hunting was more important. Those who lived in the more arid portions of Utah had to rely more heavily on gathering.

The men hunted with the season. Winter snows of the high country presented an opportunity to hunt elk. Snowshoes permitted the men to make their way through the drifts. They strapped their feet into circular shoes made of wooden frames and rawhide and fur thongs. Trudging through the otherwise impassable snow, they worked together to ambush their prey. The men also organized antelope and rabbit hunts in which groups of people trapped the animals. They sought ducks and mud hens on the lakes and sage grouse near water sources. Their best chance for success came in the late spring or summer when the young birds were not yet mature and the adults were molting. In some instances the men simply crawled up and clubbed the birds, but bows and arrows were used when such direct methods were impossible.

The desert harbored other edible life. Here the people ate insects and animals that might have been ignored elsewhere. They collected ants, crickets, cicadas, and grasshoppers. They captured rattlesnakes, horned toads, and chuckwallas. These were not necessarily dietary items of choice, but helpful additions for communities that often lacked adequate access to large mammals and other consistent, reliable food sources. By drying and mixing these foods with other edibles, such as berries and seeds, they could be stored and made more palatable.

The lakes and streams in Ute country yielded as much as one-third of the people's diet in some locales. Men fished even in the cold of winter, using a time-honored method: cutting a hole in the ice and then harpooning a fish with spear or arrow. As the ice disappeared, they could add nets and traps to their repertoire. Streams obviously provided better odds for capturing fish and so the people concentrated their energies there. They relished the fresh fish and probably with some reluctance dried the leftovers for future meals.

In most areas, gathering provided at least another third of the Ute diet. In much the same fashion as the Shoshones, but with more options available, Ute women followed an annual cycle of ripening berries, seeds, and nuts. Red raspberries were consumed fresh after being picked or were dried into cakes for later consumption. The women parched the Indian ricegrass to get rid of its scales, then winnowed and ground it into meal for cakes or mush. Ute women were extraordinarily creative in devising ways to prepare and store their inventory of available foods, their inventions varying according to local resources.

The women were also skilled fashioners of buckskin, as well as creators of clothing from skins of other animals, including rabbits and sheep. The skin was scraped and soaked in order to get rid of the hair. The women applied animal brains to the hide, then left the hide out to be baked by the sun. They soaked it again, stretched it, and finally smoked it; only then was the task completed.

The demands of everyday life for cooking, transportation, and housing also spurred creative uses of land and animal resources. Elk or buffalo hides formed tipis in parts of Ute country; willow or other brush provided shelter elsewhere. Willow and squawbrush were transformed into baskets and cradles and traps. Wood, hide, and fur were combined in the making of snowshoes that assisted more rapid and effective travel in the winter months.

The final major division within the Great Basin was composed of three branches of the Paiutes, who are known today by their geographic locations—Northern, Southern, and Owens Valley (California). The Northern Paiutes occupied a wedge-shaped area from eastern Oregon through western Nevada, while the Southern Paiutes lived in southern Nevada and the southwestern Utah–northwestern Arizona region. As their name suggests, the Owens Valley Paiutes lived in a much smaller territory, centering on the Owens Valley in east-central California, on the eastern side of the Sierra Nevadas.

Northern Paiute country in 1492 encompassed distinct subregions, which respectively fostered somewhat different local economies. In places such as Walker Lake and Pyramid Lake, the people fished throughout the year. The men used nets and harpoons to catch cutthroat trout and cui-ui in the rivers

Acorn granaries of interlaced branches and grass, constructed by Miwoks of central California. The illustration shows these storage containers set in trees, on stilts, on the ground, and suspended in a cradle. This engraving accompanies *Tribes of California,* a report by journalist Stephen Powers of his travels in the mid-nineteenth century.

that fed the lakes. Small boats allowed the fishermen or duck-egg collectors to pole their way through the shallower waters near the shore. Using the tules and cattails, they created duck decoys so lifelike that ducks regularly were lured into the vicinity to be seized by the men.

One succeeded in hunting, gathering, or fishing not only by stealth and skill but through supernatural assistance. Power manifested itself in all things in the skies and on the earth. As they grew older, religious leaders, or shamans, obtained power in dreams that taught them how to use this gift for specific purposes. They aided the quest for a good piñon harvest, a fine fishing catch, or a productive antelope hunt. They led the people in prayers designed for such purposes. Hardly solemn occasions, the gatherings could be more properly seen as group celebrations, marked also by games and contests.

Illness, however, was a serious matter, often testing the full range of the shaman's healing abilities. There were so many reasons why a person might become sick. Perhaps one had made a mistake or committed some more serious indiscretion. Maybe one had been bitten by a snake. Or, without one's knowledge, a shaman or another person with power could have inflicted the

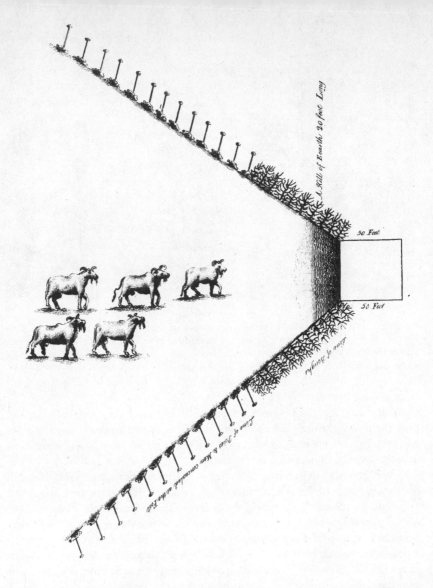

A diagram of a buffalo pound drawn by Edward Umfreville, a Canadian fur trader, in 1790. Plains hunters employed many techniques to capture bison. In the method pictured here, they built fences of brush and wood to guide bison into a corral made of trees. At the entrance to the corral, they constructed a ramp which rose to a height of twenty feet. Once the animals entered the funnel formed by the two fences, tribesmen would stampede them over the precipice and into the corral.

illness malevolently, usually by inserting a rock or other object into the sick person's body. The healer sang, chanted, or danced, trying to find out what had caused the illness. Once the cause had been discovered, the shaman could then provide the necessary cure. If a foreign object was present, the shaman sucked it out, spat it out, and got rid of it.

The Owens River allowed the Paiutes in its vicinity to practice irrigation in an otherwise dry country. Using irrigation ditches, they channeled water to plants that grew wild. By diverting water from streams flowing into the river, the people flooded the meadows to get more water to the plants, thus promoting their more rapid growth. They directed the water through temporary dams of rocks, brush, and earth. The thirsty bulbs in the swamps were thus artificially irrigated, swelling to a much larger size than they would have attained unaided.

Success with irrigation did not free the Owens Valley Paiutes from the nomadic pursuit of game and other plant resources, but it did mean they could construct more permanent and substantial structures. With a portion of their year spent residentially, they could invest their time profitably in building homes, sheds, windbreaks, ramadas, and community houses. Some of these were built in a sturdy enough fashion to last for years in this valley that offered a rare degree of stability for the people fortunate enough to reside there.

The Southern Paiutes generally lacked this degree of assurance. In their harsh surroundings they needed to cover long distances in their annual subsistence cycles. More gatherers than hunters, they traversed the country north of the Grand Canyon. Skilled basketmakers and adept at squeezing a satisfactory life out of the often meager resources of the land, they subsisted where many others could not have done so.

Despite its physical harshness and the relative poverty of its resources, the Great Basin not only was far from void in 1492 but was inhabited by peoples who, over many centuries, had become highly skilled in the management of the environment. Long before the time of Columbus, they had made many discoveries about their land and its resources that allowed them to wrest a life from their surroundings. From birth to death among the Shoshones, Utes, and Paiutes, the people created order and established meanings in the pattern of their days. With a small population and a sizable world in which to etch their destinies, each person mattered at each stage of that cycle, from the youngest infant to the most aged elder. There were roles to play all along the way and thus lessons to be learned, values to be inculcated, skills to be mastered, songs to be remembered, dreams to be recalled, and stories to be imagined and told.

The third broad subregion, the Southwest, encompassed roughly the lands that today comprise west Texas, New Mexico, Arizona, southern California, and the northern reaches of Mexico. Five hundred years ago, before the imposition of such man-made political borders, its divisions were marked by wa-

Three women in the San Joaquin Valley of California winnowing grass seeds. The woman on the right removes seed from a storage basket and grinds it briefly before placing it on the trays held by her companions. They then toss the seeds in the air, allowing the hulls to blow away.

terways and mountain ranges, valleys and seemingly limitless vistas, and by the presence of many different groups of people, some of whom had been in the area for countless generations and others who were relative newcomers and only beginning to become a part of the land.

There were clear links between many of the inhabitants of the Southwest in 1492 and those who had gone before. In both the present-day U.S. Southwest and northern Mexico, the period prior to the end of the fifteenth century had been characterized by significant change. Several major cultures north of the present-day international boundary line had either disappeared or merged into ongoing communities. People now called the Anasazis had occupied large sites of Mesa Verde (Colorado), Canyon del Muerto and Canyon de Chelly (Arizona), Betatakin and Keet Seel (Arizona), and most strikingly at Chaco Canyon in northwestern New Mexico, where a population that might have exceeded 8,000 had flourished. Then in the 1300s, within a matter of decades, the sites had been abandoned and the people had gone on to form new towns or to join existing villages, or had simply vanished. Their village architecture, their splendid turquoise jewelry, and their stunning geometric black-and-white pottery eventually became a part of Pueblo Indian culture. Still, this transition spoke to problems in the Southwest that seemed inherent or inevitable— drought, war, and illness—and that may have combined to drive the Anasazi from their homes.

Whatever caused the depopulation of the Anasazi communities reinforced a guiding principle, an overriding understanding that already has been suggested: life was fragile, and harmony was difficult to achieve and to maintain. Such a realization inspired both conservatism and innovation in the Southwest. The people lived in a world filled with fury, and the spirits of the earth and sky had to be placated. Their religious leaders were entrusted with the terrible responsibility of serving as intermediaries between the people and their gods. They had to balance the duty to live in the proper way and conserve the good of the past with the need to incorporate changes that could ensure the continuity of one's people. If they borrowed certain elements from other societies, they could make such additions their own over time. And over a still more extended period these innovations could become well enough embedded in the culture to be considered traditional.

The largest tribe in the arid west of the late-twentieth-century United States illustrates that adaptation and change. In 1492 the Navajos had arrived but recently in the Southwest. They had made their way down to the region over a great many years from an earlier residence in northwestern Canada and eastern Alaska. Their language belonged to the family called Athapaskan, so named after a lake in that portion of northern North America. They and the Apaches brought similar languages to the Southwest—languages quite unrelated to those spoken there by other Indians.

While they did not alter their language appreciably, the Navajos did alter their culture in other ways to place themselves within their new homeland. They had to belong in that environment. They had to belong to that particular land and sky. They began to do so in part through the stories they told. The old people recounted tales of emergence into the fourth or present world. Through these tales they established their separation from the Apaches and the importance of various places within their new territory. They identified Governador Knob as the site for the discovery of a baby later known as Changing Woman. Blanca Peak, Mount Taylor, the San Francisco Peaks, and the La Plata Mountains became the boundaries of their domain and became known as the four sacred mountains. The lava beds near present-day Grants, New Mexico, became the dried blood of the monster slain by the twins, sons of the Sun and Changing Woman.

At the same time, as newcomers to the Southwest, they observed and often borrowed skills or traits. They learned to be successful farmers, developing their horticultural abilities to the point that the first Spanish chroniclers of the Navajos spoke of them as the people with the great planted fields. They came to know the southwestern sky and the stars that showed them when to plant their corn. Corn became an essential symbol in Navajo thought, reflecting the growth and vitality of people. They may also have learned weaving and sand painting from their new neighbors. Eventually such origins did not matter, for their weaving and their sand painting were, in time, indisputably Navajo as well as artistic and cultural expressions of true beauty.

Their neighbors included the village dwellers of New Mexico and Arizona whom the Spaniards labeled by their housing form: the Pueblos. Some of these groups, such as the Hopis and Acomas, had occupied villages continuously for several hundred years prior to 1492; other villages were quite well established by that time. These stable towns had allowed for gradual expansion through the years, permitting development of new kivas (underground circular places for ceremonial activities) and the addition of new rooms for growing populations. The people had constructed adjacent buildings to allow passage from one unit to another without a person having to go outside, helpful both in the event of severe weather or under enemy attack. They had chosen sites high on mesas or in other positions that naturally gave the occupants advance warning of intruders from afar as well as defensive advantages against any attacks.

Such stability had been possible because of a successful economy based on agriculture. The Pueblos were able to produce abundant crops of corn, beans, squash, and cotton. Even though the high plateau country they occupied was often afflicted by short growing seasons, sandy soils, and uncertain amounts of water, Pueblo farmers had mastered the art and science needed there. While the women sometimes helped, the men did most of the farming, from initial planting to final harvesting. From their deceptively short and scraggly but deep-

The interior of a kiva in what is now western New Mexico. These underground rooms, with flagstone floors and roof supports made from cottonwood trees, were entered through a hatchway in the roof. When not in use for ceremonies, kivas served as gathering places for men, as depicted here. Before important ceremonies, priests painted ritual scenes on the kiva walls. The depressions in the walls are not windows but niches for offerings.

rooted corn, they coaxed impressive yields; their other crops furnished equally striking results.

They attributed such outcomes to knowledge, hard work, and appropriate ritual. While some of the details or emphases varied from one part of Pueblo country to another, the Pueblo villages had created a particularly rich and complex ceremonial cycle that engaged the creative and dramatic talents and energies of the people throughout the year. As agriculture was at the heart of the economy and rain was necessary for the crops to grow, it is not surprising that the people offered many prayers for rain and for good harvests. By paying proper homage, the people expected the rain and the harvests to respond to their entreaties. More generally, the ceremonies contributed the basis for social order and individual integration into the order.

Such ceremonies lasted generally more than a week, divided between time spent privately in the kivas and, later, more openly in the plaza aboveground. This combination suggested secret knowledge and ritual, not to be revealed, and public ceremony infused with celebration and, at times, frivolity. In the privacy of the underground chambers, the participants sang and prayed as well as prepared for the final dimensions of the ceremony. Ritual knowledge had

Taking Care of the Earth and Sky   **109**

to include a degree of secrecy in order to maintain its power. From initiation in Pueblo societies to growing responsibilities later in adult life, the mysteries of belief were gradually revealed.

The Pueblos believed in the emergence of the people from a previous world into this one, and they reflected that process as they came from the kiva into the full view of the plaza. There the masked figures of many forms emerged, symbolizing beings, from birds—such as eagles—to humans of various kinds, including mudheads, who appeared as an early form of man.

A full range of dramatic expression was displayed for the public, who were perched on top of the buildings or lined along their walls. There were moments of great solemnity, for the ritual had to be observed in just the right way for it to succeed. There were extraordinary figures: giants and clowns, corn maidens and butterfly dancers. There were also moments of uncontrolled hilarity, as the ritual clowns mimicked the people both within and outside the village walls. But ultimately the purpose was serious, for in the rituals the Pueblos believed they were responsible for ensuring balance and harmony in the movement of the seasons, the summoning of rain, and the maturation of the crops in the sandy soil of their windswept plateau country.

From their first days, Pueblo children learned of the world through pairs: men and women, day and night, winter and summer. They came to understand an order established because of such divisions. They were initiated into either a winter or a summer society, each responsible for rituals during one-half of the year. They learned the correct behavior, the necessary activities, the vital responsibilities of men and women. From first memory they recognized that they had been born into and were part of a community whose needs, obligations, and hopes required their full participation and allegiance. The Zunis and other Pueblo peoples spoke of a child's breath and life path being joined to one's parents and extended family. As the individual became and continued as a part of a specific community, he or she realized that one's home was rooted to a particular landscape, with the surrounding mountains, water sources, and sky having special significance.

Other Indian groups in the Southwest also had developed that sense of place. Those other Athapaskan migrants, the Apaches, were less influenced by agriculture than the Navajos, and focused more on hunting and gathering. In 1492, they were still moving southward and were first starting the process of establishing distinct branches of the people—those who are known today as Jicarilla, Lipan, Chiricahua, Mescalero, and Western Apaches. Some of them still occupied Plains country and hunted buffalo and antelope, but increasingly they hunted deer and elk as well as smaller animals. The women gathered berries, acorns, piñon nuts, and seeds in the more northern sectors. They had only partially penetrated the southern mountain and desert country of Arizona and New Mexico, but the cultural traits that would make Apaches such effective

Fishing from a tule-reed boat in what is now San Francisco Bay. The two men hold spears, preparing to fish. In this drawing, the woman in the middle of the boat wears a serape of Mexican origin. Louis Choris drew the scene when he accompanied a Russian expedition that explored the Pacific coast in 1788.

users of that rough terrain were being developed at this time through a semi-nomadic pattern that tested endurance and ability in hunting and gathering.

As the Chiricahuas were arriving in their niche along the eventual United States–Mexico border, other Indian communities had already been long settled in the surrounding area. Predecessors of the Pimas and the Tohono O'Odhams (Pagagos) had pioneered in their adaptation to the Sonoran desert. The Hohokams, centuries before the time of Columbus, had displayed sophisticated engineering skills in their construction and use of irrigation canals that had made possible farming communities where less than 10 inches of rain fell annually. Other peoples more removed from water sources such as the Gila and Santa Cruz rivers hunted mule deer and javelinas and collected the fruit from cacti, including cholla, prickly pear, and saguaro.

By the late 1400s the Pimas had established themselves as farmers of the first rank, producing cotton, corn, and other crops. They usually enjoyed a surplus from their farming, but supplemented their diet through the gathering of several dozen kinds of wild plants and, to a lesser extent, hunting. The women wove fine cotton blankets and made outstanding coiled baskets. The

Tohono O'Odhams generally had less access to dependable water sources and relied more substantially on gathering. Their residence within the heart of the Sonoran desert, however, permitted them to reap substantial harvests from the cacti and other plants in the vicinity. They were masters at harvesting the fruit of the soaring saguaros, even when it had to be retrieved from the top of the spiny cactus, two dozen or more feet above them. They used long saguaro rib poles hooked at the end to dislodge the fruit at the time it had ripened properly, sending it plummeting to the desert floor below. The Tohono O'Odhams also hunted an array of birds and animals, including mountain sheep, javelinas, deer, wild turkeys, quail, geese, and rabbits. The Pimas and Tohono O'Odhams thus could exchange food products to each other's advantage and did so on a fairly consistent basis. In the face of protracted and extreme heat in the Sonoran summer and in an especially fragile ecosystem, they had built persisting cultures.

The Yaquis, Mayos, Tarahumaras, and Seris lived southeast of the Pimas and Tohono O'Odhams in what is now northwestern Mexico. In their territory along the river bearing their name, the Yaquis used the rich lands beside the Gulf of California to establish many permanent settlements. Only the sporadic flooding of the river forced the people to move occasionally to another nearby site where they could continue to farm and reap harvests from the land and the sea. They ventured into the Gulf to gather shellfish and catch sea bass not far from the river's mouth. Organ-pipe cactus, mesquite trees, and other Sonoran desert vegetation provided fruit, beans, and seeds. With the annual overflows of the river, the Yaquis mustered two crops a year of corn, beans, and squash. The thick cane next to the Río Yaquí was hacked and whittled to produce housing and fencing, tools and implements. In this rich environment, the Yaquis could manage population densities of thirty persons per square mile. They resisted encroachments on their territory from other peoples, including the neighboring Mayos to the south.

The Mayos resided in the Sonora-Sinaloa border country, also on the Gulf of California coast. Though they were culturally similar to the Yaquis, the two groups clearly did not care for each other, and jockeyed continually for dominance of adjacent terrain. Neither people had achieved significant superiority by the late fifteenth century. One raid led to another; one death sparked a demand for retribution. Given the scattered nature of settlement, there were no massive crusades or national campaigns. Yet antipathy spurred a growing sense of local identity and loyalty, despite linguistic similarities.

Northeast of the Yaquis and the Mayos, in the valleys, foothills, and mountains of central and western Chihuahua, lived the Tarahumaras. Often using the great natural caves of the region for their homes, the people carved out their niche in craggy, pine- and oak-dotted country. Their lands received most of their precipitation in the summer, along with a dusting of snow in the

Excavated from a site along the lower Colorado River, this polychrome bowl is decorated with three figures representing Pueblo deities and a series of abstract designs. In the modern era, these figures developed into the kachinas of modern Pueblo religion. Courtesy of the Field Museum of Natural History.

winter. Hailstorms occasionally decimated the young corn plants. In this relatively remote region, the Tarahumaras enjoyed the benefits of greater isolation to fashion a culture highly resistant to change imposed from outside or new societies. Fiercely independent and locally centered, the people knew a time when little promised to be altered.

The Seris must have entertained similar thoughts about continuity. They lived north of the Yaquis along the Gulf of California coast, their territory including Isla Tiburón in the Gulf. Coastal in their orientation, they relied heavily on the sea to furnish a major portion of their food supply. Unlike nearly every other native people of the region, they were not farmers. Instead, they built one-man boats so that a Seri could go forth and harpoon sea turtles and gather shellfish and other fish. In this land of water there was little available that the people could drink. When the rain came, it arrived suddenly in torrents in the dramatic downpours of late summer, and then with equal suddenness the scorching Sonoran aridity returned. Seri life was thus marked by hunger and thirst.

Yuman-speaking communities extended from central Arizona into the Mohave Desert country of eastern California. The Yavapais, Havasupais, and Walapais occupied northern and western Arizona. Other Yuman-speaking communities, such as the Mohaves, Quechans, and Cocopas, lived near the Colorado River. The Yavapais and Walapais emphasized gathering rather than farming, ranging over millions of acres of the Arizona landscape. They traveled with the seasons as the plants ripened. If the winter allowed for a degree of settled residence, most of the rest of the year witnessed a seemingly continual migration across countless miles and thousands of feet in varying elevations. On their sandals of yucca fiber, the people made their way along rivers later to be named the Gila, Verde, Hassayampa, Santa Maria, and Bill Williams.

Their neighbors, the Havasupais, were another small group, who lived in the very shadow of the Grand Canyon. Around A.D. 100, they had moved from the Coconino Plateau into Cataract Creek Canyon, a side canyon of the abyss formed nearby by the Colorado River. This had been a transition of serious dimensions, for the canyon floor could be reached only by a narrow trail that snaked for miles downward from the plateau. If they had been pressured into the canyon by enemies, then this retreat had allowed them a true enclave in the quiet of surrounding sandstone walls. After two centuries, they started to divide their year between winter hunting and gathering on the plateau and summers with their irrigated fields on the canyon floor. They came to call themselves the people of the blue water, they who had known for centuries the pools and waterfalls, then streams and creeks, of the southern Grand Canyon rim.

The Mohaves were the largest Yuman-speaking group in the area immediately bordering the Colorado River. Like the Yaquis, they employed the river overflow to grow corn and beans. Mohave men used their hands as well as nets and baskets to catch fish from the river, and the women gathered mesquite and screwbean pods to add to the food supply. While their diet was not enormously varied, it proved adequate to permit other diversions.

In such an environment, the Mohave men had the luxury of making war a central element in their lives. For many of them, war was the most enjoyable and most valued of all activities. Fighting more for glory and honor than for territory, the men reveled in the excitement and danger. They fought the Maricopas and the Cocopas, using bows and arrows at a distance and mesquite or ironwood war clubs and screwbean-wood sticks for hand-to-hand combat. The men knew they risked scalping and death, just as they sought to inflict the same upon their enemies, but this knowledge was cushioned by their perception that they were not immortal. The Mohaves believed that, unlike the mountains and sky, the moon and the sun, they had to die at some point, and they could only die once. If it came during a particular raid or battle, so be it.

The Mohaves believed that certain of their warriors obtained special power through dreams. These individuals, whom they called kwanamis, started to have such special dreams as infants or, in some instances, while still in the womb. In their dreams, they fought mountain lions and bears, learned of the hawk's ferocity, understood how to fight and how to triumph in battle. For

A Hopi altar screen. Made of native cotton and painted with religious symbols, screens of this kind were displayed in a kiva and served as the backdrop for ritual dramas. Ears of corn border the sides of the screen, and birds and mounds of earth line the top and bottom. Male and female deities occupy the center panels. Courtesy of the Field Museum of Natural History.

others in Mohave society, dreams brought the individual's soul back to the time of creation, and one could retell the past in a stylized way before the community. Dreams also were perceived as critical to one's ability to carry out any important undertaking.

In addition to the Great Basin and Colorado River Indian groups living in southern California, other peoples occupied coastal habitats, the mountainous lands rimming the Pacific Ocean, and the desert stretches west of the present-day Arizona-Nevada border region. Most southern California Indians were united linguistically by variations of the Shoshone category of the Uto-Aztecan language family. Despite this common linguistic bond, peoples of the region possessed a strong sense of territoriality, guarding carefully the land resources that made their respective societies possible.

A prominent example of this language community were the coastal-dwelling ancestors of the Spanish-named Luiseño Indians. In addition to what the ocean provided, they harvested the acorns of oak trees. These nuts were sequestered in willow storehouses and were drawn from them as needed. While it was the principal item in the Luiseño diet, the acorn's contents presented a problem. The tannin in the acorn yielded a bitter taste that made the nut inedible in its untreated state. Thus, Luiseño women had to take the hull off the acorn, crush the nut in a mortar using a stone pestle, and then leach out the tannin by repeated pourings of warm water over the acorn meal. Afterward, the acorn meal became the primary or sole ingredient in a mush.

Despite the relative comfort of their surroundings and the comparative ease with which food could be garnered, the Luiseños through their rituals promoted strength and courage, which young initiates into their society were expected to display. Conflicts could and did arise between the people and their neighbors; men had to be willing to face adversity. Therefore, the young men, as part of their transition to adulthood, had to undergo a series of physical trials. In his late teenage years, a boy, for example, lay in a pit and permitted some of the adult men to let loose ants to meander over his body and inflict countless bites. He had to remain silent and not move for what must have seemed an interminable period of torture. Then he could rise and let the men brush off the insects, using nettles to do so.

Though not related linguistically, the Gabrielinos (of the Uto-Aztecan language group) and the Chumash (of the Hokan language family) shared common characteristics as successful, prosperous residents of the southern California coast. They were highly skilled hunters and fishermen. Both fashioned plank boats that allowed them to go well out into the Pacific. These oceangoing canoes gave their occupants the chance to harpoon sea lions, seals, and otters and catch the many different kinds of fish that passed through the channel off present-day Santa Barbara, including swordfish, sardines, halibut, and several varieties of tuna. The Chumash established additional beachheads of their culture in communities on offshore islands, extending the range of ocean territory they could exploit.

On both the islands and the mainland, the Chumash gave thanks for the different animals and fish whose existence enriched the people's lives. On the islands, the people conducted swordfish and barracuda dances, in which the participants whirled in circles, celebrating. Adorned by woodpecker or blackbird feathers, their faces painted in black, red, and white designs, the dancers were accompanied by the shrill sounds of whistles perforating the soft island air. On the mainland, the bear dance paid tribute to the most strong and powerful creature. Wearing bear paws around their necks, the dancers sang: "I am a creature of power. I stand up and begin to walk to the mountain-tops . . ."

The Chumash, in addition, were exceptionally able artisans, creating realistic figures, bowls, and other objects from a local soapstone called steatite and producing mother-of-pearl inlay on the rims and sides of stone mortars, as well as intricately designed and tightly constructed basketry. In 1492, Chumash culture was clearly in full flower, bestowing upon its people a kind of prosperity that encouraged this degree of creative and artistic evolution. No doubt the people looked to the future with a scarcely bridled optimism and confidence. In the mild climate and generous environment of the Santa Barbara area, they could have anticipated tomorrows replete with achievements and satisfactions.

The Chumash and the Navajos, the Utes and the Mandans, the Pawnees and the Mohaves—all were among the great variety of Native Americans who populated the different parts of the arid and semiarid North American West in 1492. Inheritors of long traditions from their forebears, they tried to live in harmony and balance with the earth and the sky and take care of both of them, each in their own way, for the well-being of their peoples and those who would follow them.

PETER NABOKOV with DEAN SNOW

WHEN THE HUNTING PARTY of three Penobscot River Indian families arrived at the frozen creek in the spring of 1492, the men tested the ice with their five-foot staves. It would support them today, but not much longer. The wintry season which they called "still-hunting and stalking" was ending quickly. A warm spell a few days earlier caused sticky snow to cling to their moose-hide snowshoes, slowing them down.

It was time to head downstream, following creeks to the broad river and continuing to where it widened to the sea. Other hunters and their families, whom they had not seen since autumn, would also be returning to the summer villages. The warmer evenings would offer time for recounting the past winter—all the deaths, births, hunts, and tragic, funny, and supernatural happenings of which human memory and history are made.

The hunting parties were traversing a well-watered and heavily forested landscape which white men would one day call Maine. In their own language they knew themselves as "people of the white rocks country," a phrase which Europeans would later shorten to Penobscot. They were one of six loosely organized eastern Algonquian-speaking tribes who would become known colloquially as Wabanakis, or "daybreak land people." Their territory marked

In 1724 the Jesuit priest Joseph François Lafitau published a two-volume work on the customs and beliefs of the Iroquoian people with whom he had lived. This drawing from Lafitau's *Moeurs des Sauvages Amériquains* presents a tableau of some spring food-production activities. At the top, women plant crops (presumably corn) in hills using hoes which were originally made from shells or the scapulae of large animals. Below, another group of women collect sap from maple trees and boil it to make syrup. In Lafitau's drawing the Indians appear to have recognized the greater efficiency of iron by substituting it for native materials in their hoes and kettles.

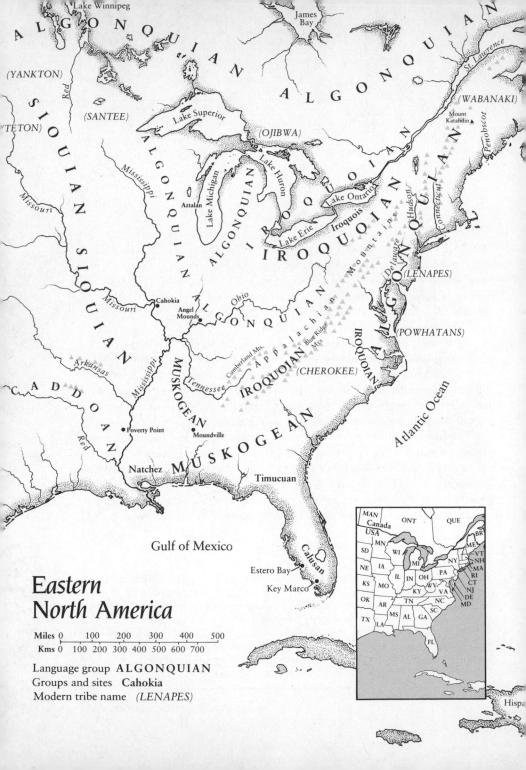

Eastern
North America

Miles 0   100   200   300   400   500

Kms 0   100 200 300 400 500 600 700

Language group **ALGONQUIAN**
Groups and sites **Cahokia**
Modern tribe name *(LENAPES)*

the northern limits of Indian farming, for late thaws and early frosts permitted them to produce only a little corn, squash, and beans.

The annual shifts between seasonal camps up and down the Penobscot River valley were determined by the time-honored habits of fishing and hunting on which their survival depended. Branching out from this great stream were innumerable tributaries that were familiar to the hunters who revisited them, usually more than once, throughout the year. Each of these natural domains was dubbed a "river," which, to the Penobscot hunting families, evoked a stretch of stream and adjoining lands on which they held relatively exclusive hunting and fishing privileges. Deep in the heart of their homeland loomed their sacred Mount Katahdin, home to the fearsome spirit known as Pamola. Few hunters ventured above the tree line to trespass on his territory.*

Waterways, and the well-trodden trails that connected them, served as the hunters' routes into the dense interior forests, where their arrows, snares, and deadfalls yielded moose, deer, beavers, muskrats, and otters in their "rivers." The central river was their highway down to the coast, where they collected clams and lobsters, speared seals, and caught porpoises.

Mobility was a necessity for the hunting life of the Penobscot. Hence, their social groups were small, and rules of residence were rather loose. Generally, it was up to the husband whether his family lived with his own or with his wife's parents. The opportunities and dictates of the hunt dominated all other concerns; social organization had to be flexible enough to let men make the most of the availability of game or shifts in the weather.

The hunters were not unhappy to leave winter behind. The "master of the animals" had blessed this group with a late-season moose cow, her unborn still in its slick, wet pouch. Their hunting had yielded enough beaver and other pelts, thick with luxuriant winter hair, to weigh down the toboggans the men dragged behind them. Their dogs also sniffed spring, and seemed happier. Ahead, everyone anticipated spearing and netting the shad, salmon, alewives, and sturgeon during their spring spawning runs.

This was also a time to harvest bark. It is hard to imagine northeastern Algonquian culture without the paper birch tree. Thin, speckled flats were peeled from the trunks at different times of year. Spring bark was thickest and was preferred for canoes, so the entire trunk would be cut down and the bark separated in the largest pieces possible. Then it would be sewn onto a canoe frame of steam-bent cedar wood and waterproofed at the seams with white-pine pitch colored with charcoal.

Summer bark was thinner, and was earmarked for roofing mats and receptacles. It could be stripped from the trunk in smaller flats without killing the tree. Then it could be folded and sewn into maple-sap buckets, baby cradleboards, and pitch-caulked cooking vessels in which heated stones were dropped to bring water to a boil. For more decorative items, floral designs were

Farmers of the Woodlands

produced by careful scraping away to the darker, inner layer of the bark. Porcupine-quill or moose-hair embroidery might also ornament the bark surfaces.

In late spring, families planted gardens before heading for the coast and the pleasures of seabird eggs, escape from blackflies, summer berry picking, flirting among the young, easier fishing along the saltwater bays, and extended twilights. At summer's end, the "going about to find something" time, the forest lured them once more.

Hunting opened in earnest with moose mating season. To entice the fat summer bulls within arrow range, hunters trumpeted through birch-bark megaphones, imitating the sounds of cow moose. Then came winter, storytelling season, when a few families collected within wigwams and lulled children to sleep with the exploits of Glooskap, the trickster figure of Wabanaki folklore.

For Penobscot Indians in 1492, this cycle of tasks and pleasures seemed as predictable and everlasting as the seasons themselves. Their way of life also made extremely efficient use of the natural resources in their river and forest world. Woodlands, waterways, and—south of Penobscot country—open fields remain the ecological hallmarks of all of the North American East. However, in 1492, there was probably far more local variation in plant and animal life than we have today.

Indeed, if we are to believe the earliest European eyewitnesses, New England, for instance, resembled a checkerboard of natural preserves with dramatically contrasting ecological features. "It did all resemble a stately Parke, wherein appeare some old trees with high withered tops, and other flourishing with living green boughs," wrote James Rosier in 1605, after walking through the forests and fields not far from Indian Island in Maine. Yet in this stroll of less than four miles, the modern-day environmental historian William Cronon pointed out, Rosier's party actually passed beneath the leafy canopies of a number of quite different micro-environments.

The sylvan paradise of northern New England, lying at the northernmost extreme of the corn-growing region, was but one section of nearly one million square miles of the eastern half of North America that is commonly called the Woodland culture area. Farther west might be added 400,000 square miles of intermixed river foliage and tallgrass prairie, where—except on strips of narrow floodplain—Indians usually were not able to sustain substantial gardening.

By 1492, the native people of this huge eastern mass of the continent occupied a world already rich and complex in human history—many different histories, in fact. At least sixty-eight mutually unintelligible tongues, representing five of the twenty known language families of North America, were spoken in the region. The net effect of over 10,000 years of adaptation by contrasting native peoples who had grown deeply tied to a great diversity of en-

A temporary fishing camp in what is now Wisconsin. Executed by a French traveler, Françis Compte de Castelnau, in 1838, the drawing shows a series of dwellings made from rush mats placed over a wooden framework, a drying fishnet, a woman tending a fish-drying rack, a small loom set before one of the lodges, and a child in a cradleboard.

vironmental regions of the eastern woodlands had produced a complex cultural mosaic.

The eastern boundary of this great region was the Atlantic coastal plain. Indian societies were complex here, and in lessening numbers also inhabited the Appalachians to the rim of the interior woodlands. Here the belly of the continent was drained by a serpentine river, the Missouri-Mississippi, that seemed a virtual sea in motion, and marked the western boundary of the woodlands.

The northern boundary of this eastern Indian world ran across northern Minnesota and Wisconsin, where it cut between the Michigan peninsulas, crossed Lake Huron and southern Ontario, and then followed the extensive St. Lawrence River system to the craggy Atlantic coast. In this corner of the Northeast the terrain turned boggy, and the northern lights shimmered over the chilly forests of what are now southeastern Canada and the Maritime Provinces.

To the south, following mountain chains so geologically old they had worn to fog-thickened dells and hollows, many smaller river drainages spread their irregular tendrils from the Cumberland and Blue Ridge chains toward the southeastern Piedmont. Past the oak and hickory forests that mantled the mountains, the landscape gradually stepped downward into the Deep South, a world of southern pine that soon reached the lowland carpet of magnolia forests along the Gulf and the humid swamps of southern Florida.

But broad characterizations of landscape "types" do disservice to the considerable diversity of "micro-habitats" through which early European visitors such as Rosier hiked. And extreme variation in plant communities was also found beyond the central Atlantic terrain. Due in large measure to this astonishing range of tree and plant life, the natural environment also nurtured a commensurate diversity and quantity of animal life. In New England, for instance, millions of passenger pigeons might blacken the sky during their spring migration. Through the weeks of the spawning runs, streams were choked with salmon, smelt, sturgeon, and alewives. Deeper in the forest, moose, caribou, deer, foxes, minks, otters, rabbits, squirrels, bears, and wolves maintained their uneasy balance of predator and prey.

Most woodland hunters adhered to special beliefs and protocols about the proper way to hunt so as to participate in this balance. The dispersed Penobscot bands actually considered themselves lineal descendants of particular animals that provided them with their identifying totem linked with the "rivers," or territories, in which they enjoyed hunting and fishing privileges. Moreover, the animals they tracked were considered to be owned by a "master of the animals," a sort of animal chief. Only by regularly propitiating this principal guardian spirit by burning tobacco, offering prayers, and displaying proper respect for their game might quarry be "given" to the deserving hunter.

By 1492 the zoological and arboreal environments of the eastern woodlands had become intentionally tailored and exploited by human beings. The parklike appearance of the New England landscape resulted from native customs of land and game management which were widespread well before the Indians' acquisition of domesticated crops. Most important was the practice of seasonal girdling and burning of trees, together with the torching of underbrush.

It has been estimated that in the northern upland forests deer populations were probably from 430 to 1,100 animals per 39 square miles. An Indian group sharing the same territory would need perhaps 340 deer hides per year, an intensity of hunting that the deer population could sustain. Purging the meadows by periodic burning and the firing of underbrush replenished the following year's grassy patches that enticed these animals. New leaves on low-lying tree limbs sprouted at an easy height for nibbling deer, keeping game visible and in the vicinity.

Favorite patches for harvesting wild blueberries, blackberries, or huckleberries were likewise set afire to replenish the soil and produce a juicier crop the following season. Along with enhancing gathering and hunting, these regular burnings gave the countryside an almost preened appearance of shaded glades and pastured vistas amid groves of variegated trees that later drew the admiration of European visitors.

It had taken time, new ideas, and experimentation for the woodland Indian peoples of 1492 to develop this annual round of land-use customs and mixed strategies of subsistence. Indian occupancy of the East is now believed to go back as far as 16,000 B.C., when Paleo-Indian foragers and hunters began settling the region in highly mobile bands. As these groups established local residency, they developed almost imperceptibly into the Indian world that archaeologists label the Archaic period, which lasted until about 700 B.C.

The domesticated dogs that accompanied the Penobscot hunters were introduced during Archaic times and were found throughout the East by 1492. Inherited from their Paleo-Indian forerunners, a principal Archaic weapon was the spear thrower. Archaic hunters improved this device to gain increased velocity during a throw by adding flexible shafts and by weighting the throwing stick with a ground stone to add leverage.

In Kentucky, the remains of cultivated squash and gourds have been uncovered dating back to before 1000 B.C. As for the diffusion of maize agriculture, however, prehistorians conjecture that this developed in the southeastern woodlands after A.D. 200, resulting very likely from the influence of Mexican Indian traders who may have also introduced to the area notions of town planning and innovative religious concepts.

By 1492, the floodplain gardens of the Mississippi Valley had been yielding crops of maize, beans, and squash for over six centuries. But gardening was not adopted by northeastern woodland peoples, initially within the southern and Laurentian lake regions, until about A.D. 1000.

By 1492, Indians in the East had been growing vegetables in two different ways for a long time. Both the Iroquoians and Algonquians practiced what is known as swidden, or slash-and-burn, horticulture. A plot of preferably well-drained land was cleared of its canopy of leaves and branches. The area was then burned and nutrient-rich ashes and organic materials were hoed into the forest floor. Seeds were dispersed within hand-formed mounds. The resulting fields did not have a very kempt appearance; generally, the corn stalks and squash vines flourished greenly amid a scatter of scorched or dead brush.

Among the semi-nomadic hunting-and-gathering Algonquian bands, who traveled relatively light and who fished, foraged, hunted, and gathered maple syrup, growing vegetables was but one subsistence activity. If a season's garden was beset by insects, or a hunt came up empty, the people generally could rely on stored foods or other options. The Iroquoians, however, who elevated swidden agriculture to their dominant means of support, might be considered true "farmers," rather than part-time "gardeners." Their sizable hillside lots were the mainstay for their matrilineal social system and for a semi-sedentary, village-based way of life.

The other important agricultural technique was floodplain farming. Practiced along the Mississippi River, it took full advantage of the natural cycle of snow melt and rain runoff each year. As the customary spring flooding subsided along the rivers, a new layer of organically rich silt was deposited on the bottomlands. These extremely fertile fields produced plentiful harvests of what the southeastern Indians hybridized into an unusually fast-growing, fat-kerneled strain of corn.

Prior to the advent of gardening, food foraging among woodland Indians had probably been the responsibility of women. The heightened importance of plant cultivation, processing, and storage steadily enhanced their role. By the time of Columbus, women were clearly the primary food producers in a number of woodland cultures whose political and religious systems reflected their status.

South of the northeastern territories of the Wabanaki peoples, the weather softened. Among the Indian groups of central and southern New England, the length of the summer allowed greater attention to gardening and so promoted a more settled village way of life. While for Penobscot hunters corn was a sometime delicacy, for the south it became a basic food staple. In present-day New Hampshire and Vermont, the western Abenakis were marginal farmers and fishermen. Among the Mahicans of eastern New York, like the Pocumtucks of the interior Connecticut River valley, work in the fields was still augmented by hunting in the woods and trapping migratory fish in local rivers.

Not surprisingly, this more temperate world had a larger native population than did the northern forests. It is estimated that the Massachusett, Wampanoag, and other Indian nations of southern New England possessed a population density of five people per square mile—ten times that of the hunters of Maine. Population densities at this high level also obtained for other eastern Algonquian-speakers farther south, the Lenapes (Delawares) and Nanticokes, and their linguistic kinfolk in coastal Delaware, Maryland, Virginia, and North Carolina. There, also, among the Powhatans and others, were permanent villages and more stable intertribal alliances.

All central and southern New England Indians spoke languages belonging to the same language family—Algonquian. Commonly, a tribesman was conversant with the words and pronunciation of his immediate neighbors, but communicated with decreasing fluency as trade, hunting, or warfare drew him farther from his home territory.

By 1492, techniques for growing and storing vegetables had been developing in the Northeast for four or five centuries. Wampanoag men cleared fields from the forests of oak, elm, ash, and chestnut. They felled the smaller

An Ottawa warrior decorated with tattoos and wearing earrings. He carries a tobacco pouch and a ceremonial pipe. The sun figure on his chest is either a metal breastplate or a tattoo. The drawing was completed by Louis Nicolas, a French Jesuit, about 1700. Nicolas was a French priest who explored the St. Lawrence and compiled a manuscript and a set of drawings known popularly today as the Codex Canadiensis.

trees and burned the thicker trunks at the base together with their branches, which left a coating of ash to enrich the soil. In Wampanoag society, rights to these cleared plots were inherited through the female line of descent.

Women broke up the ground with hoes edged with deer scapulae or clamshells. Around April, they began planting the seed corn in little mounds, often counting four kernels per hillock and perhaps adding heads of alewife fish for fertilizer. The corn came in many colors and kinds—flint, flour, dent, and pop.

By midsummer, an early crop yielded squash and beans and green corn, but the major harvest occurred in September. Apparently these crops helped each other out. The beans growing amid the corn added nitrogen, which corn consumes, while the heavy stalks offered support for the climbing bean vines. Finally, the corn provided the shade that the low-lying squash needed to reach maximum maturity.

When eaten together, beans, corn, and squash produced a greater protein intake, and Indians developed the mixed-vegetable dish which is still known by its Algonquian name, "succotash."

While garden caretakers weeded roots and protected the emerging crops from birds and pests, the majority of villagers headed for the coast to gather clams and oysters and to catch lobsters and fish. Wild greens, nuts, and fruits, which were also important to their diet, varied with season and habitat. They included blackberries, blueberries, raspberries, strawberries, and wild grapes, and walnuts, chestnuts, and acorns, which could also be dried and stored for leaner times.

In autumn, the Indians divided their time between preparing their agricultural surplus for winter storage and dispersing in hunting parties before winter set in. Deer were stalked by individuals, or were flushed into special game pens by communal drives. For warm skins as well as meat, Indians stalked moose, elk, bears, bobcats, and mountain lions in late fall, winter, and early spring. In midwinter, they dangled lines into local ponds through the ice, but dipped nets or repaired fish weirs in milder seasons.

Villages came alive in summertime, their long, mat-covered multifamily structures busy with social activity. Those villages near cultural frontiers were surrounded by a protective stockade of fire-hardened, sharpened posts. A typical settlement included storage pits, menstrual huts, and sometimes special religious structures. Plaza-like areas were used for public feasts, and for dancing performed to the accompaniment of song, drum, and rattle.

Religious specialists among the Wampanoag of present-day Massachusetts were known as "powwows." Admired and feared for their association with extraordinarily strong "manitou," or spirits, they exhibited their spirit-bestowed powers at special events to benefit hunters, control weather, prophesy the future, cure the sick, or bewitch their enemies. They also mediated between the community and the spirit world at green-corn harvest feasts and at special midwinter rituals and memorials for the dead, and they concocted war magic against tribal enemies. Among some southern New England tribes, religious specialists who behaved more like formal priests maintained temples in which bones of the chiefly class were treasured.

Exchange was lively among these different peoples, and probably bound them together in personal and group alliances. The eastern woods and riversides were laced with well-used trail systems along which goods and messages were conveyed. Individuals fortunate enough to be related to the resident "sachem," or chief, as well as powwows who were on intimate terms with them, benefited from the exchange of values and goods that moved back and forth.

In 1492, these Algonquian-speaking hunter-farmers were neighbors to more militarily powerful tribes who were representatives of another major eastern Indian language family, Iroquoian. Dwelling along the Carolina and Virginia portions of the Appalachian foothills were such Iroquoian-speaking peoples as the Nottoways, Meherrins, and Tuscaroras. The last of these would later migrate north to become the sixth member of the famous Iroquois confederacy in the eighteenth century.

Among the mountains, valleys, and flatlands that lay across what is now central New York State, the principal beacon of Iroquoian-speaking culture was positioned in the midst of a more extensive territory of Algonquian-speaking groups. What these upper Iroquoian peoples may have lost in terms of sheer acreage, however, they more than made up for in the fertility of their agricultural lands, which they utilized most efficiently.

Inhabiting the mountains of eastern Tennessee and western North Carolina were southern Iroquoians, the ancestors of the populous Cherokees. Tutelos, who lived in Virginia, were speakers of the Siouan language, while the Catawbas, farther south, possessed a language with a more distant relationship to mainstream Siouan. West of Cherokee country were the Yuchis, whose language was vaguely related to Siouan.

If the birch was the emblematic tree of Algonquian culture, it was the white pine for the Iroquoians. In their cosmology, a cosmic evergreen was believed to stand at the center of the earth. Elm served more pragmatic purposes. Slabs of its heavy bark, sewn onto stout sapling frames, shrouded their barrel-roofed longhouses, which extended up to 300 feet or more in length.

These dormitorylike buildings were also an embodiment of the Iroquois social order, for women and children under one roof were linked by membership in the same clan, which was traced through the female line. Each of the ten or so Iroquois clans took its name from a particular animal or bird that was considered to be the original ancestor of the clan's members—thus there were, for example, the Eagle, Snipe, and Heron clans. Over the door at one end of a longhouse would be a depiction of the reigning clan animal of the house's inhabitants.

The year 1492 probably found this group of woodland Indians undergoing a profound social and political transformation. Sometime between 1450 and 1550, it is believed, the five major Iroquoian-speaking tribes south of the St. Lawrence River were developing an altogether innovative form of political union—a multitribal federation with members allied for mutual defense—and were deliberating with elaborately democratic rules of order. The story of the formation of the Iroquois League provides a strong argument against the no-

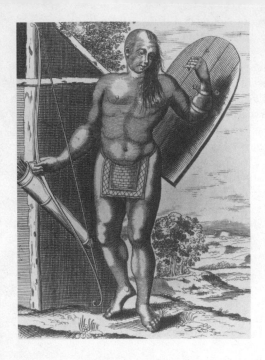

A Huron warrior carrying a shield customarily made of wood and covered with leather. His half-shaved head was probably a mark of warrior status.

tion that pre-contact Indian societies existed in a timeless vacuum and did not experience "history" until Columbus imported it.

At the dawn of this transformation, around A.D. 1450, northern Iroquoian groups were found across southern Ontario, New York, and central Pennsylvania in villages of slightly over 200 people each. As with the New England horticulturists, they practiced swidden agriculture, only to a far more intensive degree. Lacking direct access to coastal resources, they were more dependent upon gardening for survival. These tribes also appear to have been highly competitive and politically assertive.

Early Iroquoian life was divided into two domains, the clearings with their longhouses and gardens and the wider wilderness with its game and dangers. The clearings were the responsibility of women, and over each longhouse presided the oldest "clan mother." By contrast, the forests were a male domain, where the men gave offerings to the masked spirits, who responded by "giving" wild animals to respectful hunters.

Iroquois fields were cleared by hacking and burning around the base of tree trunks so that the heavier foliage died and, if necessary, the entire tree could be felled easily the following year. This also allowed sunlight to shine on the forest floor and provided ashes to energize the soil. Maize, beans, and squash were planted in hills among the fallen trees. Firewood was gathered as dead limbs dropped during the course of the year. Within a few years, however, the garden soil began to decline in productivity, and new acreage had to be opened up. Every twenty years or so, infestation from worms and other pests, plus depletion of easily available wood for fires and stockade or longhouse construction, forced relocation of the village. The entire community would rebuild not far away, often an easy walk from the old site.

For the Iroquoians, growing crops was not simply one of a number of food-gathering options; their fields were their lifeline. They were considerably more sedentary than their Algonquian neighbors. This heightened reliance upon cultigens and reliable food storage decisively elevated the prominence of women in political life. By 1492, not only was each longhouse under the authority of the eldest clan mother resident, but it was Iroquois women who handpicked candidates for the office of sachem.

However, the pattern of communities containing only a dozen or so longhouses changed by 1492, when Iroquois towns each began sheltering from 500 to 2,000 inhabitants. Perhaps a rise in intertribal warfare inspired consolidation for mutual defense, or improved farming strategies allowed for a dramatic aggregation of population. But the new social and political institutions that arose to cope with these mega-villages grew directly out of the old social fabric and residence patterns.

Traditionally, the center aisles of the Iroquoian longhouse split the buildings lengthwise. Paired family quarters faced each other like compartments in a sleeping car, with a shared cooking hearth in the central aisle. Men married "into" these longhouses—which were expanded if all existing quarters were spoken for. Although men appointed from senior households ran the affairs of the village as a council of equals, sometime around 1492 this changed. The matrilineal clans, which seem to have served originally as units that facilitated trade and exchange within the tribe, became the building blocks of a brand-new political institution. Within the century between 1450 and 1550, the Iroquois proper became known as the Five Nations, which held sway across present-day New York State. They consisted of the Seneca, Cayuga, Onondaga, Oneida, and Mohawk peoples.

According to Iroquois tradition, two legendary figures, Deganawidah and Hiawatha, conceived of a "great peace" among the incessantly feuding Iroquois peoples. They persuaded the Iroquois tribes, one by one, to accept their "good news of peace and power." Among the reforms they instituted was the abolition of cannibalism. The old social importance of the communal longhouse made it a perfect symbol for their political creation. All the member tribes talked of themselves as "fires" of an imagined "longhouse" that spanned the extent of Iroquois territory.

To its participants, this Iroquoian fraternity meant strength in numbers and

Farmers of the Woodlands

In this detail from a map drawn by Francisco Giuseppe Bressani, an Italian Jesuit who lived among the Hurons in the seventeenth century, a woman pounds corn into meal while standing before a bark-covered longhouse. Many families, all related through women, would occupy a single longhouse. Fireplaces dotted the central aisle. The building here has two smoke holes for ventilation and light.

security through allies. To outsiders such as the Hurons, neighboring Algonquians, and eventually the European powers, it meant a formidable foe. The full drama of Iroquois political destiny would actually unfold in the three centuries after 1492, but if Columbus had ventured northward, he would have witnessed a truly Native American representative government in the making.

In 1492, the areas around large bodies of inland water known today as Lakes Michigan and Huron were homeland for a cluster of central Algonquian-speaking tribes. Over time they would be known separately as the Ojibwa, or Chippewa, Ottawa, Menominee, Potawatomi, Cree, and other groups. It is difficult to reconstruct their fifteenth-century culture because of the disruptive relocations most of them experienced after 1600, and because documentation of their cultures in earlier years is limited. But one can use ethnographic accounts of their later lifeways to obtain some idea about their yearly round of food-gathering activities in 1492. Sometimes called "upstreaming," this approach to reconstructing the past employs, where possible, archaeological information as a double check. From ethnographic information of a particular historic tribe's use of excavated food caches or burial practices, for instance, one can imagine their ancestors practicing these customs and then examine occupation sites, scientifically dated at around the time of Columbus, for evidence of those practices. If one is lucky, the ethnographic and archaeological information will provide cross-references to each other.

With a variety of subsistence options open to the Algonquian-speaking tribes around the Great Lakes, the peoples' lifeways bore some resemblance to the Atlantic coast linguistic kinfolk. Nearly all were semi-nomadic, shifting each season to familiar locations to gather wild rice, cultivate small gardens, fish in streams and lakes, and hunt deeper in the woods.

In 1492, the semi-forested country that merged into prairie grasslands just west of the Great Lakes was occupied by tribes who, as migrants, had only recently carried the practice of farming into the region. Their gradual emigration west followed the long fingers of floodplain stands of deciduous trees that penetrated mid-America's grasslands. From the territory of the Crees northwest of the Great Lakes, this ragged boundary between open grassland and intermittent tree cover ran from central Minnesota to Indiana, then looped back across Illinois and Missouri before bending south toward eastern Oklahoma.

There, for the moment, the migrants stopped. This boundary zone of thinning woodlands held Plains Village peoples living near the endless grasslands that would not be fully exploited by Indians until the introduction of the horse, which Columbus and his followers brought to the Americas. The more substantial of these permanent communities were enclosed within protective palisades and dry moats. Their farming techniques probably involved more field rotation and less intensive use of river-bottom soils than was the case in the Mississippi Valley.

Here, on the edge of the Great Plains, lived other tribes as well, many seemingly poised for another gigantic move west when the opportunity (or necessity) presented itself. The prairie Algonquians included the ancestors of the Illinois, Miami, and later the Sauk, Fox, and Kickapoo. The Siouan-speakers were represented by a wide range of tribal traditions, from the more classically Great Lakes–dwelling Winnebago to the Iowa, Missouri, Omaha, Osage, and others who called the prairie lands their home, and finally to Minnesota residents like the Santee, Yankton, and Yanktonai. Other villages contained Caddoan speakers who later became the historic Wichita, Pawnee, and Arikara. For all the inhabitants of these woodland/prairie borderlands, differing ecozones as well as inherited traditions determined the specific cycle of food-gathering activities and social get-togethers that filled the tribal year.

Within the early Cheyenne earth-lodge settlements located near streams in North Dakota's grasslands, the growing of corn and periodic hunts for bison and elk divided the time as well as the responsibilities. To the Santee Sioux situated in Minnesota, however, the proximity to marshy lakes made wild rice more attractive; corn was considered only a supplement. The Santees also made more use of deer than they did of bison, which brought them into competition

Chasse Générale au Boeuf
mais a pièd .

A European depiction of a method of hunting buffalo before the acquisition of horses. Drawn in a romantic style by French chronicler Antoine Simon Le Page du Pratz, in the early eighteenth century, it presents a group of Natchez hunters closing in on a small herd of bison.

with their close neighbors, the Ojibwas. The Teton Sioux, on the other hand, were more attracted to the grasslands, surviving mainly on the hunting of bison and antelope, and relying on a middleman tribe, the Yanktonai Sioux, to trade them woodland products from the Santees and others.

Hunting was more effective if undertaken collectively. In the fall, whole villages might camp alongside or even ford the Mississippi to get closer to grazing bison. Sometimes organizing their members with the help of camp police, they would light the grass with torches to corral the frightened animals so hundreds might be easily shot by archers.

With so many different linguistic and cultural groups living practically shoulder to shoulder in this attractive transitional zone, it became important to have at least a few forms of intertribal protocol that were recognized by all. Ceremonial smoking of a pipe, or calumet, was one way to establish a time of peace, or a way to agree to support each other in war. Red stone for the pipe bowls was quarried in the rolling country of southwestern Minnesota occupied by the Yanktonai Sioux. Pipe stems were decorated with feathers, sometimes colored red if warfare was at issue, white if peace was under deliberation. It was a solemn occasion when Indians packed their bowls with tobacco—mixed with shredded cedar bark and the dried leaves of other plants—and shared words that had been sanctified with its smoke.

Throughout the western portion of these mid-American forests and rivers lay the often monumental remains of more complex cultures that had already risen and fallen by 1492. As far north as the southeastern corner of Wisconsin were the ruins of a twenty-acre fortified Indian center known as Aztalan. Nearby were laboriously formed bird- and animal-shaped earthworks lining the riverbanks. These were mute testimony to the widespread influence of ear-

Women gathering wild rice in a canoe using beaters to free the grain from the stalks. Although Captain Seth Eastman of the U.S. Army completed this drawing in Minnesota in the mid-nineteenth century, it records an important communal activity that had been a part of many Great Lakes cultures for centuries. Even though the women appear to be working in the "wild," rice fields were carefully prepared long before the harvest.

Farmers of the Woodlands   **135**

lier Native American civilizations whose heartland lay to the south and east. Aztalan reflected the importance of the second major agricultural system developed by Indians of the eastern woodlands—floodplain farming.

If Columbus had ascended the Mississippi River and gone ashore in Illinois across the great river from present-day St. Louis, he would have seen the already crumbling ruins of the greatest Indian metropolis north of Mexico. This was Cahokia, onetime capital of a highly sophisticated society which archaeologists have called Mississippian. Its refined artistic production, hierarchical social and political organization, and effective economic structure flourished in a riverine habitat.

Unlike the northerly woodland farmers, who struggled to clear their land only to enjoy a short lease on its productivity before the soil was exhausted, the Mississippian Indians knew an environment that renewed itself. Their riverine territory recharged each spring as the high waters receded, depositing fresh, fertile silt on their floodplains. Here was soft alluvial soil, free of deeply rooted grasses and easily worked by hoe or digging stick.

Advanced varieties of maize became critical to Mississippian subsistence. Earlier varieties could be grown only in the southernmost part of the East, below a line that ran roughly along the northern borders of Arkansas, Mississippi, Alabama, and Georgia. But later varieties permitted Indians to farm as far north as the Great Lakes. Of equal value were nutritious Mexican beans introduced to the Mississippians from the south. Combined with corn and squash, their protein content offset the occasional scarcity of meat.

The broad river valleys offered more than rich soil. Deer, raccoons, and wild turkeys thrived along the forest fringe of the rivers. As the Mississippi and its major tributaries swelled and shrank with the seasons, natural levees formed along the riverbanks. Swampy lands sank lower than the water level of running streams. The marshy lands attracted waterfowl in large numbers. Periodically, the rising river overflowed the levees, cutting new channels while abandoning others. They ultimately became the oxbow lakes still found throughout the Mississippi Valley.

As water levels dropped, fish were trapped in the natural holding ponds, where they continued to spawn. Between old river meanders, elongated patches of leftover earth deposits supported grassy areas, thick stands of nut- and fruit-bearing trees, and wild seed-bearing food plants. Since deer preferred to migrate daily between open grazing areas and cooler shade, the thousands of miles of Mississippi Valley lakes and marshes were a virtual game preserve for Mississippian hunters.

The relative ease of floodplain farming and the plenitude of game and wild food plants encouraged a wide dispersal of homesteads. At the peak of its development, Mississippian society probably comprised a hierarchy of settlements. Spread-out and largely undefended hamlets undoubtedly had social and

Three women from the lower Mississippi Valley, drawn by Dumont de Montigny, a French engineer who was stationed near New Orleans in the early eighteenth century. The tattooed woman on the left carries a rattle and a turkey-feather fan; in the center a companion wears a cloak made of feathers; and the third figure, a young girl, pounds corn into meal.

political ties to centralized fortified towns. Inhabitants of the countryside came to the towns, where they had recourse to arbiters to resolve local disputes, and where they congregated for certain collective rituals or sought protection during times of war and danger. It is conceivable that people even enjoyed dual residency, spending part of the year in a central town with public areas and domestic compounds made up of plastered wattle-and-daub buildings with thatched roofs, and the rest of the year in more rural settlements.

Finally, there were the major ceremonial centers—also fortified—which possessed formal plazas, pyramidal earthworks supporting temples and chiefly residences, and other domains of a civic or sacred importance. Reciprocal obligations almost certainly knit together the residents and officials of these communities. It is probable that these civic centers also exacted taxes in the form of farm produce or physical labor to maintain the fortifications and ritual structures that served the wider citizenry.

Mississippian towns and cities reached population sizes far greater than could ever have been managed by kin-based societies. The distinctions in power, wealth, and status in Mississippian society were reflected in this clustering of satellite communities around larger ceremonial centers, in variation in the quality of family residences, in the ranking of individuals during their days on earth, and in their burial treatment after death. In these Mississippian chiefdoms, high-status leaders probably transmitted their offices through inheritance.

Among the notable Mississippian ceremonial centers in present-day Illinois, Alabama, and Indiana were sites known today as Cahokia, Moundville, and Angel. Major towns like these typically contained up to twenty temple mounds surrounded by palisades and residential areas. The mounds themselves bear a striking resemblance to the terraced and stone-faced pyramids of Mexico. Flat-topped and four-sided, they were constructed by work gangs hauling earthen fill in burden baskets. Around the mounds were arrayed permanent homes of wattle and daub.

Farther out in the countryside, families maintained both summer and winter houses. During the warmer season they occupied structures with gabled thatched roofs. Some of their winter houses were semi-subterranean earth lodges similar to those which, in 1492, were common among the Siouan-speakers who had moved out to live on the prairies. One regal example of such earth-lodged construction was the "council house" at the Mississippian site of Ocmulgee, Georgia. Perhaps a ceremonial forum for leading officials, it had a diameter of more than forty feet. Opposite the door was an earthen platform shaped like a giant bird of prey with shaped-clay seats for three people, while around the circumference were positions for another forty-seven individuals— probably the local chiefdom's senior statesmen.

About three hundred years before Columbus's voyage, the central city of Cahokia reached the peak of its architectural development and political prestige. Rising above the five square miles that constituted "downtown" Cahokia was a gigantic pyramid now called Monks Mound. An artificial heap of shaped earth, its base was 1,040 feet long and 790 feet wide; it rose 100 feet high to support a wattle-and-daub-walled temple on its truncated summit. More than

A diagram of the largest urban center north of the Rio Grande in A.D. 1000. Located near the site of modern-day St. Louis, Missouri, Cahokia was founded in approximately A.D. 600 and was occupied for nearly 700 years. It contained over 100 earthen mounds, the largest of which rose 100 feet over a central plaza. While many communities lived in close proximity to the city center, members of important guilds and religious orders occupied houses within the palisades, as pictured here.

Cahokia was a planned city, aligned according to the location of a series of "woodhenges," circles of standing poles erected as observatories. In this diagram, sight lines have been drawn to show the alignments from a southern henge and distinctive mounds.

Cahokia

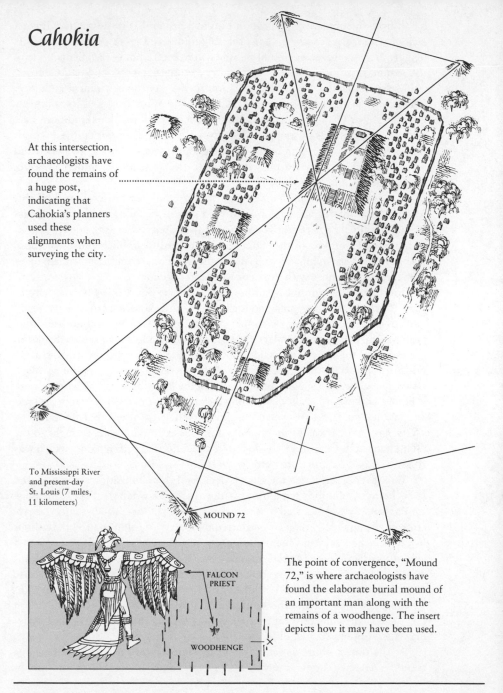

At this intersection, archaeologists have found the remains of a huge post, indicating that Cahokia's planners used these alignments when surveying the city.

To Mississippi River and present-day St. Louis (7 miles, 11 kilometers)

MOUND 72

N

FALCON PRIEST

WOODHENGE

The point of convergence, "Mound 72," is where archaeologists have found the elaborate burial mound of an important man along with the remains of a woodhenge. The insert depicts how it may have been used.

Farmers of the Woodlands   **139**

a half million cubic meters of mound fill had been piled in stages over the decades by a local population that probably numbered more than 10,000 at its height. Another 100 ceremonial mounds were erected in the immediate vicinity, geometrically arranged around plazas, ritual precincts, and ball fields.

Mississippian society was equally impressive in its geographical influence. Between its northernmost outpost of Aztalan in Wisconsin and its southerly boundary near Ocmulgee in Georgia, its economic and religious traditions held sway over thousands of square miles. From the corners of this cultural world, linked by trade rather than by any single authoritarian regime, raw goods and manufactured wares were passed trader-to-trader to the commercial, ceremonial, and political centers.

The loose collection of major and minor chiefdoms that comprised this Mississippian world was also bound by a shared set of common ritual practices. This cluster of art motifs and rituals is known today as the Southeastern Ceremonial Complex, or the "Southern Cult." Fully established by A.D. 1000, and certainly surviving beyond 1492, the religious complex blended older homegrown practices with doses of Mexican influence.

Southern Cult symbols—sunbursts, human eyes on open hands, arrows with attached lobes, weeping and forked eyes, and elaborate crosses—were engraved on shells, embossed on copper sheets, and incised on ceramics and stone tablets. The conch-shell goblets used during purification rituals also displayed these motifs, together with scenes of human figures in formal postures. During purification rituals these shell cups held a powerful emetic known as Black Drink, which was brewed from the leaves of the Yucaipa holly. Warriors drank it before embarking upon expeditions, and councilors used it before deliberating matters of state. Above all symbols was the cross motif that stood for the sacred fire, which was probably linked in Mississippian ritual thought to the divine sun itself. Certain Mississippian temples housed such a flame, which was ritually tended by appointed priests.

Whatever precipitated the abrupt decline of this civilization a few hundred years before Columbus remains a matter of scholarly debate. Perhaps Mississippian society was seduced by the blessings of its labor-and-cost-effective riverine environment. Perhaps it permitted unabated population growth without foreseeing the health problems that often accompany urbanism and lowered animal protein intake. As they lacked sanitary systems for the disposal of human waste and garbage, it is conceivable that dysentery and tuberculosis rose to epidemic proportions and mortality rates outstripped birth rates. In the absence of new blood from the hinterlands, this seems a plausible explanation for the "vacant quarter" that existed in 1492 in what had formerly been thriving Mississippian strongholds.

At the time Columbus set foot on Hispaniola, the Mississippian heritage could be detected among the various Muskogean-speaking tribes who inhabited the southeastern woodlands. Their towns still contained buildings, erected on low mounds, that served the ritual and civic side of life. Periodic rekindling of sacred fires to revitalize the entire community for another year still took place on special plazas. The ancient social system and mound-building traditions in their elaborate form survived among the Natchez, a cluster of communities along the lower course of the Mississippi, long enough to be recorded. Eyewitness accounts of Natchez lifeways by early French visitors provide an unusual glimpse into the older Mississippian world.

The Natchez had a rigidly stratified four-class society. Constituting the upper crust were the Suns, who were hereditary leaders of the chiefdom. Natchez society was also matrilineal. Since the Great Sun was always male, and his scion inherited his family status from his mother, not his father, the youth could not ascend to his father's position. To resolve the dilemma, the highest office was inherited by the Great Sun's sister's son.

To complicate matters, Natchez society possessed an asymmetrical system of marriage and kinship in which members of all three upper classes were required to "marry down." This meant that while the child of an upper-class woman inherited her class, the child of an upper-class man belonged to a class one step lower than that of his or her father. It was possible, however, to work one's way up the social ladder by individual achievement.

Along with some other Caddoan- and Muskogean-speaking groups of the Gulf Coast region, the Natchez practiced human sacrifice—more evidence of the diffusion of Mexican traits into their territories. When a Great Sun died, for instance, his wives were killed in an outpouring of public grief, and the ceremonial mounds were enlarged to accommodate their entombment.

Jutting southward from the mainland expanse of southeastern forest lands was the Florida peninsula, which, in 1492, was home to two contrasting native cultures. The northern portion was occupied by agriculturists, most prominent of whom were many semi-autonomous village groups speaking dialects of the widespread Timucuan tongue. Instead of cultivating fields, the Calusan peoples, who dominated southern Florida, hunted wildfowl and reptiles, speared and netted sharks, rays, and fish, stalked deer and foxes, harpooned whales and seals, and gathered roots, which they pulverized to make bread.

At the time of Columbus, the Timucuans, along with the neighboring Apalachees and Tocobagas, could claim long occupation of the subtropics. Archaeologists trace Timucuan culture in east and central Florida to about 500 B.C., while the early Apalachees were constructing temple mounds and adding to their shell middens along the northwestern bays and estuaries as early as A.D. 1000.

Timucuans commonly established their villages with ready access to flowing streams or freshwater lakes. Protective stockades enclosed palmetto-roofed houses, ceremonial plazas, public and family granaries on stilts, and oversized council buildings. Their dome-shaped residences probably housed individual families, who stored personal items in the ceiling area.

As with most Florida Indians, the Timucuans had a varied diet from the forests, swamps, lakes, coasts—both Gulf and ocean—and from small maize gardens on plots that they cleared from the underbrush. Venison was their principal meat, but they also gathered oysters and clams, trapped and speared fish, and snared and shot birds. Palm berries, acorns, and other natural foods augmented the food supply.

During the influential Mississippian period, many social and religious traits from the north filtered into the Florida peninsula. The totemic clans of the Timucuans, identified with the panther, buzzard, quail, bear, and other animals, were ranked. Clanship was inherited through the mother's line, and one mar-

Théodore de Bry was a Flemish engraver of the late sixteenth century who published a number of accounts of life in the Americas. His books contained illustrations, which he often altered according to the artistic and cultural ideals of his day. Here a group of five Florida Indians (probably Timucuans) transport corn and other crops in a dugout canoe from their fields to a large granary. These granaries were built of stone and earth and were covered with palm fronds.

ried outside of one's own clan. High village officials were drawn from the prestigious White Deer clan. Chiefs were easily identified by tattoos that covered their bodies, and by such regalia as copper breastplates, beaded anklets and armbands, and turkey-spur earplugs. They often had more than one wife, and wives were likewise marked by special tattoos and bead jewelry. On special occasions all might be carried on litters borne on the backs of commoners. Ordinary villagers turned over a portion of their garden produce to the chiefs, who stored this tax in a central granary.

The Calusan tribes of southwestern Florida devised complex economic strategies that provided subsistence backup when one or another food source temporarily failed. If villagers were unlucky with their fishing along the southwestern coast, for example, they sent word for dried palm berries or root flour to be transported by canoe from the interior lakes via the river system. Conversely, if inland Calusan communities desired smoked fish or oysters, a supply was rapidly brought in from the bay shore.

Although they were still hunter-gatherers, the Calusans developed a complex sociopolitical organization, thanks, in part, to the practice of arranged marriages to cement alliances between tribes. It is also believed that a single chief was based in a central settlement located on Mound Key in Estero Bay; in Columbus's day he reigned over the Calusan world of more than fifty villages. Perhaps such centralized authority was necessary to muster the work force that constructed the massive "shellworks" whose remains still dot the landscape—mounds, platforms, embankments, and walkways with façades that were often ornamented with decorative shell facings.

From the archaeological site of Key Marco, wooden goods, preserved in thick mud after one Calusan village was struck by a hurricane, testify to the perfection of their manual arts. Finely carved wooden deer heads and painted masks illustrating local animals, such as alligators, had shell-inset eyes that made them appear alive. Realistically portrayed dolphins and stylized woodpeckers were carved on ceremonial standards.

Calusan society proper was composed of two classes: the nobility, comprising the "king," as early Spanish accounts dubbed him, and his retinue and principal advisers and officials; and commoners. There were also slaves, people taken in warfare from other tribes. Upon the death of a high-ranking person, his servants were sacrificed. According to the Calusan worldview, every man had multiple souls. One remained alive with the body, to counsel surviving tribespeople, while another soul entered the soul of an animal. When that animal died or was killed, however, the soul was absorbed into the body of a smaller beast, and subsequently one still smaller, and through this diminishing process it eventually vanished.

In retrospect, this belief seems like a metaphor for the fate of the Calusan nation—indeed, for all the aboriginal peoples of the Florida peninsula. They

Saturiova

Saturiova Re della Florida nell'America Serrentionale
in atto di andare alla Guerra

"Saturiova, King of Florida," a portrait by Jacques Lemoyne de Morgues, an artist who accompanied a French expedition to the Southeast in the 1550s. Decorated with tattoos, adorned with a pelt, and carrying a spear, the Timucua leader is shown here ready for war. The cup in his left hand probably contains Black Drink, a ritual beverage often used as a war medicine. Courtesy of the Peabody Museum, Harvard.

had the disadvantage of living but a few hundred miles from the islands on which Columbus made his landings. In the wake of his explorations, this region shortly became the supply center for the Spanish pacification of Florida. The Calusans and Timucuans suffered the incursions of Ponce de León in 1513, Pánfilo de Narváez in 1529, and Hernando de Soto in 1539. After Spain established its foothold in St. Augustine in 1565, permanent colonies brought smallpox and other diseases. Between these devastating epidemics and fearsome warfare with the Spaniards, the Timucuan and Calusan peoples were virtually destroyed by 1710.

In 1492, dozens of Indian nations in the North American East stood at the threshold of what might have been. Unable to step back and envisage their potential, they were also unaware of the sadder fate that lay in store. Contrary to modern stereotypes of a monolithic woodland Indian, their forested and riverine world nurtured a dynamic cultural diversity. We can only guess at the barely documented tribal societies that vanished or were absorbed during the millennium before 1492 or through the chaos of colonialization that followed that signal year.

The final version of this essay
was prepared by Peter Nabokov
from a draft by Dean Snow.

MIGUEL LEÓN-PORTILLA

"ISLANDS WITH LOFTY MOUNTAINS ... most beautiful and of a thousand shapes . . . filled with trees of many kinds and tall, and they seem to touch the sky. Some were flowering and some bearing fruit. And the nightingale was singing and other birds of a thousand kinds. There are six or eight kinds of palms which are a wonder to behold . . ."

So wrote Columbus in 1492 about the islands of the Caribbean. Lush gardens of exuberance, they extended in countless number from the Bahamas to the Lesser Antilles like a green belt across the sea east of the even more wondrous Mesoamerica, the nuclear part of the hemisphere's mainland and the hearth of great Indian civilizations—today's Mexico and Central America.

The first inhabitants of the Caribbean islands, arriving thousands of years before the time of Columbus, had come almost certainly from the north, from the peninsula of Florida and beyond. In 1492, remnants of these true discoverers of the seabound paradise, the Guanahatabeys, called also Ciboneys, still lived in extreme western Cuba. Elsewhere in the Greater Antilles, in Cuba, Haiti (which the Spaniards named Hispaniola), Jamaica, and Borinquén (renamed Puerto Rico), as well as in the Bahamas, were peoples of the Arawakan language family, most of them known as Taínos, but also referred to as Arawaks. They had originally entered the islands from northern South America, where numerous other Arawakan-speaking groups still remained. Later, they had been followed onto the islands by Caribs from northeastern South America, who had spread through the Lesser Antilles, clashing with the Arawaks

The Codex Barbonicus was one of several descriptions of Aztec life compiled by native scribes in the early years of Spanish rule. Housed today in the Library of the French Chamber of Deputies, the Codex Barbonicus contains a singular description of Aztec ritual life. In this drawing, an Aztec priest wears the costume of the Corn Spirit Chicomecoatl-Tlazolteotl.

Mexico, Central America, the Caribbean

Miles	0	100	200	300	400
Kms	0	200	400	600	

Language group   MAYAN
Groups and sites   **La Venta**
Modern tribe name   *(KUNA)*

HOKAN

UTO-AZTECAN

Pacific Ocean

Rio Grande

Mississippi

COME-CRUDEN

Gulf of Mexico

Chichimecs

UTO-AZTECAN

OTOMIAN

MAYAN

Teotihuacán

Chichén Itzá

Uxmal

Tenoch-titlán

La Venta

Yucatan

Tikal

M A Y A N

Mixtecs

Tonalá

Palenque

Oaxaca
(ZAPOTECS)

Quiche

Copán

Tehuacán Valley

Gulf of Mexico

Mexico

Cuba

Haiti

Dominican Republic

Belize

Honduras

Nicaragua

Guatemala

El Salvador

Costa Rica

Panama

Venezuela

Colombia

Bahamas

Lucayos

Ciboneys

Cuba

Tainos

MAYAN

A R A W A K A N

A R A W A K A N

C A R I B A N

Hispaniola

Caribbean

Pacific Ocean

C H I B C H A N

P A E Z A N

A R A W A K A N

C A R I B A N

(KUNA)

and driving them to the more westerly islands. Altogether, on the eve of Columbus's voyage, upward of four million people—Ciboneys, Arawaks, and Caribs—are estimated to have occupied the different islands.

In time, a canoe-borne commerce and peaceful cultural contacts had burgeoned between the Arawakan islanders and Mesoamerica, and many elements of the high cultures of central Mexico, the Yucatan peninsula, and various areas of Central America had filtered into the ways of life of the Arawaks. By 1492, the Arawak groups of the Greater Antilles were the most culturally advanced of all the island peoples. In Cuba, Jamaica, Puerto Rico, and, above all, on the island of Haiti, a long period of internal development, together with influences from the outside, mainly from Mesoamerica, had led to the existence of flourishing Arawakan chiefdoms with complex forms of social organization.

At the top of the social strata of each of the various chiefdoms was a cacique, an Arawak word that Columbus understood to mean "ruler" or "governor." The caciques, moreover, were members of an elite, or dominant, class, known as the Tainos, a term that meant "people of high rank." The term "Taino" can be confusing. Because of their importance and stature, many of the Arawakan groups, particularly in the eastern part of the Greater Antilles, became known as Tainos, rather than Arawaks. Among all the Arawakan groups, however, the Tainos, as an elite nobility, were closely attached to the cacique, who had come from their ranks and enjoyed many rights and privileges. Together with the cacique, Taino elites controlled the production and distribution of most of the necessities of life, including food, utensils for farming, fishing, and domestic needs, and the little clothing that the people wore in the warm, humid islands. In times of warfare, they also led the chiefdom's fighting men.

Those who knew about the supernatural, who cured the sick and advised the people on important matters, also came from the Taino elite. It was not difficult, moreover, to identify the Tainos. Their personal ornaments and radiant diadems of feathers and gold made them stand out above others. They sat in special chairs and were often carried on litters. Living together in their own compounds, the families of Taino rank dwelled in large, conical-shaped homes facing an open space, or plaza, used for public ceremonies and meetings. Close to the plaza was also a batey, or ball-game court.

Obedient to their cacique and the other members of the Taino "nobility" were two lower social strata. The first can be described as that of the commoners, or ordinary people, who supported the Tainos with tribute. They resided in the villages surrounding the large dwelling compounds of the Tainos, or in the open country near fields that they cultivated, or, if they were fishermen, near the shore. The second group, comprising the lowest social stratum, was that of completely dispossessed people, whom the early Spanish chroni-

A Caribbean house with open sides and sturdy posts designed to withstand hurricanes. Here men rest in hammocks and smoke pipes, conveying an idyllic image to match the European idea of a paradise in the New World.

clers called by the Arawak term "Naboria." Although not slaves, the destitute Naborias were servants of the Tainos, often having closer and more intimate day-to-day relations with them than the ordinary commoners.

The social organization prevailing in the Greater Antilles (which also existed on the Bahama Islands, where the Arawakan speakers were known as Lucayos) echoed in several respects that of Mesoamerica. In all probability, such stratification of society on the islands, which Columbus and his men "discovered" intact and thriving in 1492, had been the result of prolonged contact between the Arawakan groups and people like the Mayas on the Central American isthmus.

In the Greater Antilles, settlement patterns and the routines of daily life also reflected the region's tendency toward social stratification. Villages and towns were of all sizes, but sometimes were quite large and contained several hundred dwellings. Some of the towns were independent and each was ruled by its own cacique. But others were joined together in large chiefdoms, or cacicazgos, headed by a single authoritarian cacique from one particular town whose Taino group was acknowledged by the others as supreme. Within the towns, rank distinctions were emphasized by the variations and locations of the homes, from the sumptuous dwellings of the Taino element around the plaza to the less pretentious surrounding homes of the commoners and the rude huts of the Naborias on the outskirts, or even farther away among the fields or along the small streams.

To a visitor in an Arawak village, there were numerous other signs of social divisions. Near the richly appointed dwelling of the cacique, one would see many of the prominent Tainos, wearing fine woven textiles, golden ear and nose pieces, and brightly colored feathers in their hair. These members of the elite, as well as their families, would be visited by the commoners, who brought to their dwellings, as tribute, the results of their hunting, gathering, or fishing, or the products of the cultivated fields which each town and village possessed. Typical of the Tainos' favorite foods were specially baked cassava cakes, made from the roots of yucca plants, and the savory meat of iguanas, the small lizards native to the Caribbean islands and parts of Mexico and Central America.

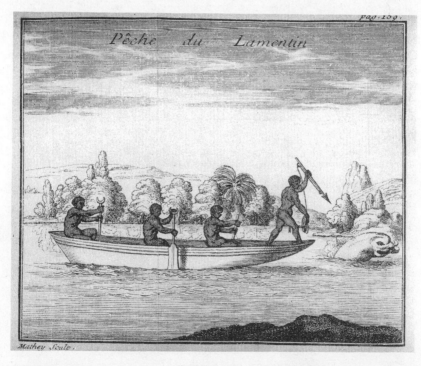

A crew of natives harpoon a manatee, or sea cow, as fancifully depicted in René Barrère's *Nouvelle Relations,* published in 1743. Despite the Mediterranean landscape (and possibly "modern" harpoon), Barrère depicts an important cooperative activity. Courtesy of the Regenstein Library Rare Book Room, University of Chicago.

The commoners, who comprised the basic farming element, were practiced agriculturists, using the slash-and-burn process to prepare the land and employing tools like the digging stick, or coa. In all of this, the Arawaks' methods and customs were, again, similar to those of Mesoamericans on the mainland.

As might be expected, the Arawaks were accomplished seamen. They fashioned dugout canoes of all sizes, many of them able to make long-distance voyages on the open sea, and some large enough to hold more than thirty men. The Taino lords, accompanied by commoners, made frequent trips from island to island—and sometimes to settlements on the mainland—conducting trade, carrying out peaceful missions, and occasionally attacking an enemy.

A magic, marvelous universe of beliefs and ceremonies was at the core of everything these island people did and thought. Friar Ramón Pané, who arrived in the Greater Antilles in 1494 and learned the Arawak language as it was spoken on Haiti, spent several years studying what he described as "the beliefs and idolatries of the Indians and how they worship their gods." Listening to the behiques, the native sages and "medicine men," he recorded information about the supernatural universe of the Tainos, the group name by which all the Arawaks were known in the eastern part of the Greater Antilles.

"I have conversed in special with those of high rank, as they are the ones who preserve more firmly their traditions," he wrote. "And the same as the Moors, they have the essence of their law in ancient songs . . . And whenever they want to sing their compositions, they use a certain instrument they call mayohabao [a sort of kettledrum] made of wood, hollow and strong . . . Accompanied by its music, they intone their songs which they have learned by heart . . ."

Friar Ramón preserved the essence of some of the ancient traditions, sung at feasts the Tainos called areytos, a term related to a word meaning "remembrance" or "to recall"—suggesting that the main purpose of the feast, with its songs and dances, was to bring back to mind and heart everything that gave the people their roots on the earth. One sacred song described the Tainos' supreme zemí, or god:

> He is in the heaven,
> he is immortal;
> nobody can contemplate him.
> He has a mother
> but he has no beginning.
> His name is Yocahu, Bagua, Maorocoti,
> and the name of his mother
> is Atabey, Yermao, Bagua, Maorocoti . . .

Yocahu, probably meaning "Being of the Yucca," one of the principal agricultural staples, would have affirmed the supreme god's attribute of being the ultimate source of subsistence. He was also named Bagua, "Sea," the other immense source of life. From the sea that surrounded the islands, the people obtained a great variety of fish, as well as crabs, lobsters, turtles, and manatees, these last being large aquatic mammals whose delicious flesh was highly favored. The third name, Maorocoti, "Fatherless," reflected the Tainos' conception of a celestial and immense womb, the divine form of Atabey, the mother of the "Being of Yucca, Sea, Fatherless." Derived from atte, "mother," and beira, "water," Atabey meant "Mother of the Waters," those of the heavens, the sea, the lakes, and the rivers.

Friar Ramón also preserved the Taino tradition concerning the origin of man:

> There is a province called Caonao,
> in which there is a mountain,
> whose name is Cauta.
> It has two caves.
> Cacibajagua and Amayaúna
> are their names.
> From them
> came the people
> who inhabit the island . . .

The names of the caves had significant meaning for the Tainos. Cacibajagua apparently referred to the Cave of the Jagua Tree, the cosmic tree of the elite Taino lineage. Amayaúna probably meant "the place [of origin] of those without merit," the commoners and Naborias. The belief about man's origins thus served to give divine authority to the social stratification of the group.

Another Spanish chronicler, Gonzalo Fernández de Oviedo y Valdés, told of the key role of the areytos, in which the songs that Friar Ramón had heard were chanted. "Their songs, in those they called their areytos," Oviedo wrote, "are their books and memorials, transmitted from generation to generation, from fathers to sons, and from those who are alive today to those who will arrive . . . Thanks to their areytos they could recall things of their past . . . They had their areytos in their principal feasts or to celebrate a victory over their enemies, or when a cacique was married, or at any occasion in which one looked for pleasure."

With great detail, Oviedo also described some of the areytos. One feast was organized by the female cacique Anacaona, the widow of the cacique Caonabo. "There," said Oviedo, "more than three hundred young girls took part in the dance, all of them virgins, as she [Anacaona] did not want that any man or married woman participated . . . And up to now they keep alive their areytos as they do not want to forget their own stories, in particular to celebrate their victories in battle . . ."

The samples of the Tainos' spiritual life that have been quoted all came from just one island, Haiti. But, wrote Father Bartolomé de Las Casas, the early-sixteenth-century Dominican missionary, "one has to know that the people of this Hispaniola, and of Cuba, and of the island we call San Juan [Puerto Rico], and of Jamaica, and all the islands of the Lucayos [the Bahamas], and of those which extend from Florida to the point of Paria [in Venezuela] . . . have almost one and the same religion." It was a religion of the songs and dances in the areytos and beliefs about the origins of gods and man, but it also included the worship of the zemís that were carved in stone or wood, ceremonial fasts, the offerings of flowers, and reverence for the behiques, the sages and "medicine men," whose words of wisdom, listened to and obeyed, helped attune the people to their spiritual universe, the source of all meaning to them.

That wonderful world of the areytos died quickly and tragically, along with the Taino chiefdoms, after the invasion of the Europeans. According to Friar Ramón, two caciques knew what was coming. After they had engaged in a prolonged fast, the supreme "Being of the Yucca" revealed to them that "they would enjoy their domain for only a brief time because dressed people, very different, will come to their land and will impose themselves [upon the Tainos]." The caciques thought at first that the "Being of the Yucca" was referring to their enemies the Caribs, but then, realizing that those people usually came to rob them and then fled, they concluded that a different people was meant. "Now," said Friar Ramón, "they believe the revelation referred to the Admiral [Columbus] and the men he brought with him."

The inquiries and reports of a few early chroniclers like Friar Ramón and Oviedo have provided most of what we know about the spiritual universe of the Tainos. At the same time, dozens of words of these first Native Americans whom the Europeans met passed permanently into Spanish, and then into English and other languages, conveying something, at least, of the Arawakan people's material culture, which they left as a legacy to all mankind.

Canoe, tobacco (originally the pipe or tube in which they smoked the plant), and barbecue (a framework for cooking, smoking, or drying food) were all Taino words that evoke images of their everyday life. Hammock came from the Taino hamaca, which the islanders used as a bed or couch. The flora of the islands was rich and magnificent, and many of the enduring words referred to plants and trees that provided edible or useful products to the Taino communities. Preeminent among them was maize, the Taino name for the great staple crop of the islands and elsewhere in the Americas. But maguey, yucca, pawpaw (papaya), mammee (the mamey apple of the tropics), tuna (the edible fruit of the cactus), and guaiacum (a tree whose resin is used medicinally or in varnishes) were also Taino words, as were manatee, cayman (the crocodile that

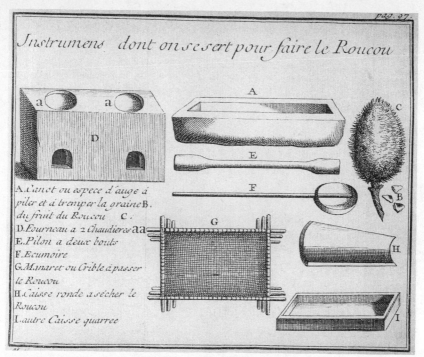

Instrumens dont on se sert pour faire le Roucou

A. Canot ou espece d'auge à
piler et à tremper la graine B.
du fruit du Roucou   C.
D. Fourneau a 2 Chaudieres a a
E. Pilon a deux bouts
F. Ecumoire
G. Manaret ou Crible à passer
le Roucou
H. Caisse ronde a sécher le
Roucou
I. autre Caisse quarree

These instruments were used for the production of an orange-red dye, called roucou (from the Tupi word urucú). Production began with the anatta fruit and used a crusher (A, E), heater (D), ladle (F), sieve (G), spout (H), and mold (I). The tools appear as part of a scene from Guiana, contained in a collection of descriptions of America, published in Paris in 1796.

lived in the islands' waters), savanna (an open, treeless plain), and hurricane, whose extraordinary force of winds and storm led the Tainos to regard it as a divine being dwelling in the heavens and the waters of the Caribbean. Thanks to the god Huracán, who was both feared and revered, the storms brought life because they kept the islands green. Through the influence of Taino sea-traders, who at times reached the Mayas on the Guatemalan coast, the deity also entered the Quiche Mayan pantheon of gods. In the *Popol Vuh,* the great Book of Counsel of the Quiche Mayan, Hurakan appears as one of the creator gods, to whom, in particular, the wind of life was owed.

One Taino word, Carib, referring to their enemies, the ethnic group that inhabited the Lesser Antilles, has a particular interest, because the Europeans corrupted it into the term "cannibal" as a synonym for the Caribs. For five centuries, much has been expressed about the ferocity, real or imagined, of these people. It is time to bring them into focus.

From the very beginning, Columbus heard about the Cannibals (pronounced sometimes by his Arawak informants as Cariba or Caniba) as the islanders who ate human flesh. On November 23, 1492, he wrote in his diary: "The [Tainos] named Cannibals those other Indians they feared so much . . . They said that the Cannibals wanted to devour them." Several later accounts described surprise raids by the Carib people against the Tainos of the Greater Antilles to obtain booty, maize, yucca, pieces of worked metal, weapons, and, mainly, captives. In the Tainos' collective memory was the recollection of how the Caribs, coming from South America, had forced them out of the Lesser Antilles, disposing of captive Taino males by what has been described as their "cannibalistic" practices and incorporating the female Taino prisoners into their own groups, adopting through them many Arawak cultural traits.

Through the years, the extent and motivations of the cannibalism of the Caribs have been the subject of controversy. While several early Spanish accounts contained numerous references to it, there were other writings, like those of Father Bartolomé de Las Casas, that were inclined to dismiss them as false or exaggerated. But repetitions of the original lurid accounts and widely disseminated drawings like the often-reprinted works of the engraver Théodore de Bry, which depicted Caribs eating human arms and other parts of the body, firmly implanted the idea of the Caribs as barbarous, flesh-hungry cannibals.

At the same time, two parallel images developed in Europe concerning the Caribbean Indians. On the one hand, the Taino ways of life were pictured as a paradigm of what could have been man's existence in the Garden of Eden. On the other, the ferocity of the Caribs and their cannibalism were seen as clear proof of the Devil's influence on man. Both were unreal, stereotypical depictions that have persisted in the popular mind until today. The controversy about the Caribs may never be resolved, but it may be worth remembering that history's judgment of them has come largely through the prism of their fearful enemies, the Tainos.

WEST OF THE ISLANDS, on the Mesoamerican mainland, meanwhile, lay another Indian world—not Asia, as Columbus imagined, but Mayan chiefdoms on the riverless, scrub-covered peninsula of Yucatan; sophisticated cultures and resplendent civilizations on the Mexican Gulf Coast and in the highlands of central Mexico; and the domains of other advanced societies stretching south from Guatemala to Panama. It was a land of many different climates and geographical features, distinct ecological provinces, and various forms of vegetal and animal life. It was also a world of many different ethnic groups and speakers of a multitude of languages and dialects. But despite the fragmentation, there existed throughout the huge region a basic cultural unity.

The Codex Mendoza was prepared during the rule of the first Spanish viceroy of New Spain. Intended as a gift to King Charles, the book is a history and description of Aztec life. The page shown here described events from the time of the founding of Tenochtitlán (A.D. 1325) to the death of the ruler Tenochtli, fifty-one years later. Each year of his reign is represented by one of the boxes bordering the page. The fire-drill image in the lower right marks the end of a fifty-two-year cycle. The eagle, perched on a cactus growing on an island, marked the spot where the Aztecs were to found their capital. The emperor Tenochtli sits to the left of the cactus and is surrounded by important officials. The warriors at the bottom of the page depict the expansion of the empire in later years. André Thevet, the French geographer, once owned this codex and signed his name at the top.

This detail from the Codex Mendoza shows an Aztec boy netting fish in a lake.

As a term, Mesoamerica was devised to designate the geographical area of that extraordinary unity.

The principal attributes of what was essentially one high culture were the following: the existence of urbanism, large populated centers with spaces reserved for temples, palaces, schools, marketplaces, storehouses, and army headquarters, and also for the ordinary people's houses that were built along well-planned streets and alleys; the same complex patterns of social, economic, and political organization; similar religious beliefs and practices; extremely precise calendars; glyphic systems of writing; concern for the preservation of the memory of the past; identical forms of cultivating the soil and similar patterns of subsistence; use of the same utensils; guilds of merchants and artisans; and, above all, basically one and the same worldview.

The development of this high culture occurred over centuries, and must be reviewed briefly to understand the rich heritage and complex reality of Mesoamerica in 1492.

It is generally agreed that it was a people known as the Olmecs who gave birth to the culture around 1500 B.C. Olmec means a native of Olman, or "Rubber Land," a reflection of the vegetation in their homeland, situated close to the Gulf of Mexico along both sides of the present-day Veracruz–Tabasco state border in Mexico. Archaeological excavations have revealed that great cultural changes began to take place there during the last centuries of the second millennium B.C. At sites known today as La Venta, Tres Zapotes, and San Lorenzo, as well as several others, the most ancient form of proto-urbanism in the Americas began to develop. In that Olmec area, the old agriculturalist villagers, who for the previous three thousand years had cultivated maize, squash, chili, beans, tomatoes, and other crops, were experiencing substantial transformations in their socioeconomic, political, and religious organizations.

The remains of the proto-urban center of La Venta provide, at least in part, knowledge of some of the changes that occurred. Built on a small island in a swampy region near the Tonalá River, ten miles above its mouth on the coast of the Gulf of Mexico, La Venta was skillfully planned. There archaeologists have unearthed several pyramidal structures, long and circular mounds, stone-carved altars, rows of basalt columns, sarcophagi, upright stone slabs (stelae) with incised symbols on their surfaces, colossal heads of basalt, and many jade figurines and other sculptures. Evidence exists that outdoor religious ceremonies were performed in large plazas, and it can be inferred that a division of labor already marked Olmec society. While a large part of the population was still engaged in farming, fishing, and the other traditional activities of subsistence, others were already specializing in different arts and crafts or had the task of providing for the defense of the group. Both the government and a cult of the gods were probably the concern of the religious leaders.

For years, many scholars have maintained that a god with feline features was the principal deity of the Olmecs. A careful study of the iconography of the god, however, contradicts that view. The supreme Olmec god is, indeed, the very early manifestation of the Rain God, later worshipped universally in Mesoamerica. But his face is by no means what has been asserted to be a stylized transformation of that of a jaguar. The god's face, instead, is shaped by the convergence of the bodies of two serpents which form his nose, plus two serpents' eyes and two serpents' fangs which complete his countenance. The serpent—in sharp contrast to the Judeo-Christian tradition—thus became, from the days of the Olmecs, the omnipresent symbol of Mesoamerican religiosity.

Olmec culture, through commerce and perhaps also by a sort of missionary activity by some of its religious leaders, spread across Mesoamerica. Clear signs of its influence are visible in many archaeological sites along the Gulf Coast, in the central highlands, in western Mexico (mainly the present-day state of Guerrero), in the Oaxaca region, in the land of the Mayas—Chiapas, the Yucatan peninsula, and Guatemala—and even in more distant places, in Honduras, El Salvador, Nicaragua, and Costa Rica. The basic unity of pluralistic Mesoamerica is thus understood: Olmec culture exists at the roots of the later magnificent outgrowths.

The earliest extant evidence of Mesoamerican writing and of precise calendric computations, although linked to the Olmecs, was not found in Olmec country. Stelae with inscriptions carved around 600 B.C.—the oldest yet discovered, and strongly influenced by the Olmecs—were unearthed at a site far from the original Olmec homeland. That place is Monte Albán, close to the modern city of Oaxaca. There, beside a religious center constructed in different stages on top of a hill, numerous structures visible on the slopes provide evidence of an urban center that began to develop about 700 or 800 B.C. and whose inhabitants were the ancestors of the present-day Zapotec people. On the rather large number of stelae—known as "stelae of the dancers," because of the dancelike postures of the human figures carved on their surfaces—can be seen the very oldest extant forms of writing anywhere in the hemisphere. The glyphs are for the most part ideograms: dates, places, and persons' names. Some of the signs include representations of hands—as in the case of the writing developed later by the Mayas—probably denoting various types of action, as "to conquer" or "to be installed as ruler."

Olmec influence was also quite pronounced in Central Mexico, where, about 100 or 200 B.C., a small town, Teotihuacán, the future "metropolis of the gods," began to develop. With its growth and expansion, authentic urbanism became a reality in Mesoamerica. It took several centuries and generations of priests, architects, and sages to plan, construct, and enlarge that magnificent city, the Mesoamerican paradigm conceived to exist forever. The capital of a chiefdom, Teotihuacán left vestiges of its widespread cultural influence and political and economic dominance in several places in central and southern Mexico.

The metropolis itself was a marvelous achievement. Two great pyramids towering toward the sky, the enclosure of Quetzalcoatl's temple, and many other structures, including palaces decorated with mural paintings, schools, marketplaces, and religious monuments, were designed, engineered, sculpted, and painted by master artisans and craftsmen. There were also large suburbs where the commoners had their homes. At its zenith, about the end of the fifth century A.D., the American Indian metropolis of Teotihuacan was larger than Rome, with a population of probably 50,000 and covering an area of about fifteen square miles.

In texts of the indigenous tradition transcribed at the time of the Spanish invasion of Mexico, the ancient inhabitants of Teotihuacán are described as "sage and religious people." They worshipped Tlaloc and Chalchiuhtlicue, Lord and Lady of the Waters; Xiuhtecuhtli, Lord of Fire; Xochipilli, Prince of Flowers; and Quetzalcoatl, Feathered Serpent. In various forms, Teotihuacan's religion, as well as its arts and urbanism, were to influence a long progression of other Mesoamerican peoples, including those who had succeeded to dominant positions in 1492.

It is known that, probably through commercial contacts, Teotihuacan's influences reached the Mayas, providing a new ferment that fostered local processes of change among people already affected by the earlier Olmec cultural penetration. But in the end, the splendid Mayan cultural outgrowth that began to consolidate about the third century A.D. has to be attributed to the Mayas themselves. In the centuries that followed, the period of their classic grandeur, which lasted until the ninth century, more than fifty Mayan centers of prime importance were born. Among them were Tikal, Uaxactún, and Piedras Ne-

Kuna men of the area of present-day Panama meet in a sparsely furnished house to talk while sharing a cigar passed to each of them by a child. Tobacco, domesticated in the New World long before the arrival of Europeans, was used in many ritual and social settings. This drawing is from a description of the New World written by the English traveler Lionel Wafer, published in London in 1699.

gras in Guatemala; Copán and Quiriquá in Honduras; Nakum in Belize; Yaxchilán, Palenque, and Bonampak in Chiapas; and Dzibilchaltún, Sayil, Coba, Labná, Uxmal, and Chichén Itzá on the Yucatan peninsula.

As in the case of the people of Teotihuacán, different social strata coexisted among the Mayas. The commoners, who lived on the outskirts of the Mayan centers, engaged in agriculture and provided services in a variety of everyday affairs, including commerce and the production of utensils and other goods. In contrast to them were those of lineage, from whose ranks came the captains of the army, the priests, and the rulers. The sages, making use of their inheritance of Olmec achievements in the fields of writing and time computation, developed calendars of great precision, as well as a sophisticated form of hieroglyphic writing. Several hundred years before the Hindus and the rest of the world, they discovered the concept and use of zero and had a symbol for it. Their astronomical observations led them, also, to attain a year-count one-ten-thousandth more exact than the Europeans' calendar after the Gregorian correction.

Mayan hieroglyphic texts are preserved in abundance, inscribed on stone stelae, lintels, stairways, mural paintings, bones, ceramics, and in a few surviving books, or codices, of a later period made from amate tree bark processed into a sort of thick paper. Scholars have made considerable progress in deciphering Mayan writing, although the task is not yet completed. Hiero-

El Castillo, a Mayan ruin at Chichén Itzá in the Yucatan. This lithograph, based on a drawing by the English artist Frederick Catherwood, was one of the first accurate depictions of
ancient American monuments. The base of the pyramid pictured here measured about 200
feet on each side, and the temple at its peak covered more than 1,600 square feet. Catherwood also noted that the temple doorways were covered with hieroglyphic writing and
carvings. His rendering conveys the scale and splendor of a people who contributed to the
cultural history of America in 1492.

glyphs related to the calendar, the gods, religious ceremonies, places, humans,
and objects, but, also, happenings and forms of action, have been identified.
Even more important, much has been learned about the nature of Mayan writing. Today, scholars know that it was a well-developed system to express not
merely isolated ideas but textual sequences by the use of ideograms and pho-
nograms in which a nucleus is complemented by affixes and other relation-
markers that correspond to the linguistic patterns of an ancient Mayan variant
known as the Chol language.

From what has already been deciphered, something is now known about
the contents of the classic Mayan inscriptions. While some of the texts related
particularly significant events, such as the enthronement of a ruler, an alliance
between two or more chiefdoms, a victory, or the death of a dignitary, others
conveyed astronomical and time-oriented information. Among such texts were
correlations of destinies attributed to various calendric periods or the tables of

eclipses. Indications have also been found of hymns, prayers, and various kinds of accounts relative to the universe of the divine realities.

The comparison of the Mayan inscriptions with the texts of oral traditions, transcribed much later during the early colonial period, is particularly revealing. In the *Chilam Balam Books* (texts attributed to high-ranking priests, or chilams) and the *Popol Vuh* of the Quiche Mayas of Guatemala, both transcribed after the arrival of the Spaniards, the continued existence of a widespread Mesoamerican cultural base is clear. The religion and worldview of the Mayas, as well as of the other Mesoamericans, in 1492 were still essentially similar, still deeply rooted in a common cultural universe. That universe, moreover, had endured many ups and downs, even the collapse of the period of classical splendor.

Whatever the causes may have been (and there is no agreement on the matter), between A.D. 650 and 950, there was a downfall of classical civilization in Mesoamerica. It occurred first at Teotihuacán, where archaeological evidence indicates a sudden collapse. Was the city burned, as some of the buildings' walls and beams suggest? Was such a fire the result of an assault from the outside, or of an internal political and/or religious struggle? Or was the metropolis abandoned because the large population had overused the land and deforested the countryside, causing climatic and ecological changes so serious that the people could no longer feed and support themselves?

The city of Monte Albán and other Zapotec settlements prolonged their existence during a period of growing decadence, but they too were eventually abandoned. Playing out a sort of fatal destiny, the many Mayan centers, one by one, were deserted. There are no signs among any of them of external attacks or internal revolts. Palenque, Tikal, Uaxactún, Copán, Yaxchilán were simply abandoned. For Mesoamerican man and society, this was a first great experience of almost total downfall. The Mayas would recall it in many of their prophetic texts, which would also prophesy the coming of another time in which a more radical collapse of their culture would take place. For the moment, however, the breakdown in classical Mesoamerica did not mean the death of the high culture.

Ironically, one of the main consequences of that first cultural collapse of classical Mesoamerica was the wide diffusion of ideas by those who fled the old centers of civilization. Nahuatl-speaking groups who had lived north of Teotihuacán, Totonacs of the Puebla-Veracruz area, Mixtecs of Oaxaca, and Quiche, Cakchiquel, and other Mayan groups of Guatemala all received the influences of Teotihuacáns who migrated into their areas from their declining metropolis. In the complex migratory movements of the time, groups of Pipils (Nahuas of the ancient Teotihuacán nobility) settled at many different sites in Guatemala, El Salvador, Honduras, Nicaragua, and the neighboring regions of Costa Rica, bringing elements of their culture with them. Some of the

Mayas established new cities and, in several instances, returned to their old ones, erecting new buildings and giving another life to the centers they had previously abandoned. Even in the distant north, as far away as the American Southwest and, perhaps, the Southeast of the present-day United States, other ethnic groups profited from the spread of traits of the Mesoamerican high culture. In what are today's New Mexico and Arizona, Pueblo Indians assimilated elements of Mesoamerican origin, and can thus be viewed as having lived in the northern outskirts of the area of high culture.

Among the many Nahuatl-speaking groups who became the inheritors and, in various ways, augmenters of the glory that was Teotihuacán, two above all stand out. Both of them had probably been subject to the Teotihuacáns and had lived in the north as sort of advanced outposts, protecting the frontier against bands of barbarian Chichimecs, people of the bow and arrow, who were hunters and gatherers in an arid region. Both also, when the collapse of Teotihuacán became known to them, made the decision to "come back," as the indigenous texts put it, to central Mexico, the land of their origin. They did so at different times.

The first to return were the Toltecs, a people whose great guide and culture hero was the high priest Quetzalcoatl, the one who had taken as his own name that of the benevolent god. The second, moving south later, were the Aztecs, or Mexicas. Each of them would enjoy a span of grandeur. The Toltec descent from the northern plains occurred around the middle of the tenth century A.D. The Mexicas entered the Valley of Mexico three centuries later.

The Toltecs established themselves at Tollan, a place of renown about fifty miles north of present-day Mexico City. Tollan means "metropolis," which is what the Toltecs built on the site. Ruled by the sage high priest Quetzalcoatl, they initiated a new golden age, which the indigenous texts describe with profound admiration:

> The vassals of Quetzalcoatl were highly skillful. To them nothing was difficult: they cut the green stone and cast gold, and produced still other works of the craftsman, of the feather art . . . indeed, all these arts,
> started, proceeded from Quetzalcoatl, the arts and wisdom . . .
> The Toltecs were very rich. They lacked nothing
> in their homes. Never was there famine . . . The Toltec priests
> took their manner of conduct from the life of Quetzalcoatl.
> By it they established the law of Tollan and, later, the
> same law became also established in Mexico . . .

Although the splendor and predominance of the Toltecs were short-lived, they propagated their culture—in large part the legacy of Teotihuacán—among many distant peoples, including the Zapotecs and Mixtecs of Oaxaca. The Mayas, too, who had been in a state of decline after the downfall of their classic culture, experienced a resurgence under the influence of the Toltecs. Thus, a new ethnic and cultural fusion developed in Mesoamerica.

The golden age of the Toltecs ended after less than two centuries. But the wisdom of their high priest Quetzalcoatl, and all that they had achieved as creators of culture (called Toltecayotl, the essence and plenitude of whatever belongs to the Toltecs), were inherited as a precious legacy by the Aztecs, or Mexicas. Those people entered central Mexico around the middle of the thirteenth century.

According to their ancient books and traditions, the Mexicas came from the north, from a place named Aztlán, Chicomoztoc, "At the place of herons" and "Where the Seven Caves are." There, Tezcatlipoca, "Smoking Mirror," their patron deity, had spoken to them and promised them a country that they should look after as their own. In that land, their priest Huitzilopochtli promised, also, the Mexicas would become rich and powerful. While still living in the north as tributaries to those who ruled in Aztlán, they were known as Aztecs. Later on, their god ordered them to change their name to Mexicas, in anticipation of the place name of the metropolis they were to found, Mexico-Tenochtitlán. This explains why at times they also called themselves Mexica-Tenochcas.

After a long pilgrimage in search of the promised country, the Mexicas reached the region of the lakes in the Valley of Mexico. There, on a small island, they saw what their god had told them would be a sign of where to stop: a powerful eagle, standing on a prickly pear cactus, devouring a serpent. It was a symbol that their god—already identified with the sun (the one who makes the day, the years, and the ages, radiant "Eagle of Fire")—had once more manifested himself. From then on, the eagle on a cactus devouring a serpent became the symbol of the Mexica nation, and is today the central element in the coat of arms of modern Mexico.

With the settlement of the Mexicas on the small island, where they grew in strength and expanded, the ancient tree of culture, so deeply rooted in the Olmec and Teotihuacán traditions, flourished again. The material achievements and spiritual universe that in the early sixteenth century would arouse both the admiration and the hatred of the Spanish invaders were the Mexica, or Aztec (for Aztlán, their northern place of origin), version and summing up of Mesoamerican high culture.

That universe was replete with original sacred connotations. The world had been established and reestablished several times. The ancient texts, inherited from the Toltecs, who had probably derived them from the Teotihuacáns, spoke of four "Suns," or ages, that had existed and vanished through the will of the gods. The present age, the fifth (although the Mayas believed it

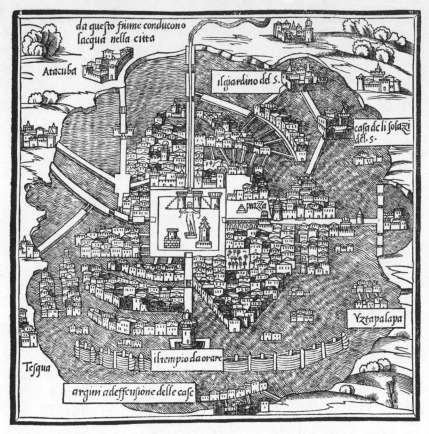

da questo fiume conducono
lacqua nella citta

Atacuba

il giardino del s.

casa de li solazi
del s.

plaza

Yztapalapa

il tempio da orare

Tesqua

argini a deffensione delle case

Completed less than a decade after the fall of the Aztec capital, Tenochtitlán, this map represents a highly Europeanized version of the city. Houses and temple pyramids are depicted as castles and churches, while parks and causeways look Mediterranean rather than Mexican. Nevertheless, it accurately portrays many distinctive features of Tenochtitlán: the highways connecting the metropolis to the shores of Lake Texcoco, the central ceremonial plaza, and the city's distinctive neighborhoods.

was the fourth), was the one ruled by the "Sun of Movement." The gods had reestablished the sun, moon, earth, and man. By their own sacrifices, they had "deserved" this age.

The Nahuatl word "tlamacehua," "to deserve," is rich in meanings, for it refers to "being worthy" as well as signifying "to do penance" and "to practice sacrifice." In the ancient books, it was said that the gods had to do tlamacehua in order to restore the sun, moon, earth, and man. They did it for four days in a celestial and primeval Teotihuacán and, at the end, cast themselves into an enormous fire, the teotexcalli, "divine hearth." With their sacrifice, the sun, moon, and earth were restored. Quetzalcoatl, the wise god, was asked to restore man. He descended to the "Place of the Dead" in search of the precious bones of men who had existed in the previous cosmic ages. Rescuing the bones, he took them to the "Place of Our Origin," the abode of the supreme Dual God, Ometeotl.

Quetzalcoatl himself and Cihuacoatl, the "Feminine Twin" or "Female Serpent," were actually no other than the supreme Ometeotl, or He-She, Our Father–Our Mother, invoked by all the Mesoamericans, using several names. These terms also described deities with His-Her attributes and forms of action. To transmit life to the precious bones, Cihuacoatl placed them in a precious vessel, i.e., her womb. The old sacred text said that "because the gods did penance, deserved [tlamacehua] us with their blood, we men are macehualtin [the deserved by the divine sacrifice]."

To be macehualtin ("to be deserved by sacrifice") denoted the primary and essential relation of human beings to the divine realm. Man was "deserved" by blood—the liquid conveyor of life—because man was needed by gods. They needed him to keep the universe alive. To be useful, men too had to perform tlamacehua, "the act of deserving through penance and sacrifice," including the bloody sacrifice of human beings. By performing tlamacehua, men reenacted the primeval divine action, giving life in exchange for creation, and restoring the order of the universe. In this way only was the flow of life maintained on the earth, in the heavens, and in the shadows of the underworld. Ometeotl himself, the supreme Dual God, was the one who caused man to perform this kind of observance on earth:

> He causes us to merit, to deserve, virility, the
> eagle's
> warriorhood, the tiger's warriorhood . . . In our hands
> he
> places the eagle-vessel, the eagle-tube, the
> instruments
> for the sacrifice.
> And the macehualli [man, the deserved] now becomes
> father
> and mother of the Sun [sustainer through sacrifice].
> He
> provides drink, he makes offerings to the one Who is
> Above
> us, and in the Region of the Dead.

Thus, this cosmic age of the "Sun of Movement" continued alive. Man had to realize that everything in his life had "to be deserved": to be born, to grow,

An Aztec stone sculpture from Texcoco representing Chicomecoatl, the Corn Spirit. The figure holds ears of corn in her hands. Courtesy of the Field Museum of Natural History.

to enter school, to become a warrior, to gain possession of a piece of land, to cultivate it, to obtain water and food, to win a war, to elect a good ruler, and, above all, to approach and appease the gods.

The supreme Dual God, Ometeotl, was also invoked with the names of Tezcatlipoca, "Smoking Mirror," and Tezcatlanextia, "Mirror Which Illuminates Everything." In fact, in the guise of Tezcatlipoca, He-She was present in the four quadrants of the world, and in the ancient books there is not one but four Tezcatlipocas, painted in the corresponding cosmic colors of the quadrants, yellow, black, red, and bluish-green. It will be recalled that it was Tezcatlipoca, the great god, who summoned the Mexicas while they were still in the north to obey and follow him to a privileged place he had reserved for them. The priest through whom Tezcatlipoca spoke to the people was later deified. His name was Huitzilopochtli, "the Hummingbird of the Left." In the Mexicas' iconography, the attributes of the god Huitzilopochtli, prime protector of the Mexica nation, show a great similarity to those of Tezcatlipoca, and it appears evident that Huitzilopochtli was the Mexicas' interpretation of Tezcatlipoca, himself the manifestation of the supreme god.

On the island in the swamp, the Mexicas built Tenochtitlan—the heart of today's Mexico City—gradually enlarging and enriching it under a succession of high rulers who established dominance over the region. At the same time, they began to worship the supreme duality in a new manner. On top of twin pyramids were shrines with the images of both Huitzilopochtli and Tlaloc, the Mesoamerican Rain God. By placing the two deities side by side, the Mexicas introduced a new version of the duality. Huitzilopochtli, their own Tezcatlipoca, was now also the sun; Tlaloc, closer to the earth, provided the vital liquid without which all that provided sustenance could not germinate.

In accordance with their calendric systems, which they had inherited from other Mesoamericans, the Mexicas worshipped their gods and celebrated their feasts. Time—and, with it, the earth, the heavens, the underworld, and everything that existed—had been deserved by virtue of Huitzilopochtli, the Sun, the "One Who Makes the Day." He ruled upon all the cycles of time. There were nine hours of the day, and as many of the night. The days were counted in groups of 13, 20, 260, and 360, plus five ominous ones at the end of the year.

The 260-day count, divided into twenty groups of 13 days each, constituted a complex system that was used to provide knowledge of man's destinies. Thanks to it, one could anticipate, propitiate, and placate the gods, who were the bearers of the destinies along the counts of the days, years, and cycles of years. There were special books, the tonalamatl, books of the days-destinies—some of which are still preserved—that were consulted frequently to do time computations and to learn when acts of tlamacehua (deserving) should be performed. Fear and anxiety often accompanied the "readings" of these books, but because of them man could become attuned to the rhythms of the divine universe from which the destinies flowed. Indeed, the count of 260 days and the 365-day solar calendar, with their various moments and sums of the periods, could only be interpreted by means of the ancient books. They were the sources from which were derived the norms and counsel for any specific circumstance, from birth to death.

Lord Ahuitzotl, who ruled the Mexicas, or Aztecs, from A.D. 1486 to 1502—the time during which Columbus and the Spaniards arrived in the Caribbean—rebuilt and consecrated the main temple in Tenochtitlán, enriched the city with great public works, and expanded commerce and the power of the Mexicas over other peoples. At the end of his reign, the Mexica domain embraced most of the Nahuatl-speaking chiefdoms of central Mexico; the Mixtec and Zapotec regions of Oaxaca; parts of Chiapas, Ayotla and Mazatlán in present-day Guatemala; and a large part of the Huastec and Totonac countries along the Gulf of Mexico. To the southeast, the Mayan chiefdoms, though agreeing to trade with the Mexicas, managed to preserve their political independence. Altogether, the Mexicas in 1492 ruled over several million people.

Tenochtitlan itself, the largest metropolis in Mesoamerica if not in the world at that time, had a population of perhaps a quarter of a million. Archaeological evidence, which has been brought to light from time to time in modern-day Mexico City, together with surviving indigenous codices and texts in the Nahuatl language, provide vivid images of some of the glories of the great Mexica city. Surrounded by Lake Texcoco and other, smaller "water mirrors," the metropolis covered almost five square miles. Three large causeways linked it to the lands of the valley. One led toward the south, to the towns of Iztapalapa, Coyoacán, and Xochimilco, the flowery garden. Another connected the city with the northern shore of the lake, with Tepeyacac, "the nose of the mountains," and with a famous sanctuary dedicated to Tonantzin, "Our Mother," which stood on the site of the present-day shrine to Our Lady of Guadalupe. The third causeway led toward the west, to Tlacopan, an old indigenous town whose name was corrupted into Tacuba. A branch of this third causeway, with a double aqueduct built upon it, went directly to the fountain of Chapultepec, where a beautiful forest existed, antedating the present park which, in the same location, is a main attraction of modern Mexico City.

On the eve of the Spaniards' invasion, Tenochtitlan was a most magnificent abode of men and gods. There, one would see numerous tall-rearing temples, topped with awesome shrines and sculptured images of the gods, painted in a flowery gamut of colors; monumental palaces where the supreme ruler and his council met and where judges administered justice; a variety of schools—the calmecac, which were centers of high learning, the telpochcalli, or houses for the youth, and the cuicacalli, "houses of songs"—and marketplaces, especially the famous one of Tlatelolco, where every product of the land could be found; zoological and botanical gardens, a Native American innovation; the neighborhoods where the different artists and craftsmen lived and worked—the silversmiths and goldsmiths, the ceramicists, the feather workers, the sculptors, painters, embroiderers, and many others; the houses of the common people with their small vegetable gardens; the channels that crossed the city and the streets and pathways lined with fragrant trees and plants; and, above all, the large plaza in the center of the city bordered by the majestic palaces of Kings Axayacatl and Moctezuma, and fronting on the Main Temple, the most splendid Aztec achievement, with seventy-eight sacred monuments, all surrounded by the coatepantli, or "wall of the serpents."

When, in 1519, the invader Hernando Cortes and his men first gazed upon these temples and palaces, the schools and causeways, and marketplaces, they thought the wonders they saw must be a dream. As the chronicler Bernal Díaz del Castillo put it:

> Some of the soldiers among us who had been in many parts of the world, in Constantinople, and all over Italy and Rome, said that so large a market place and so full of people, and so well regulated and arranged, they had never beheld before.

The teeming multitudes in the city constituted a highly stratified society. Ruling over all was the king or tlahtoani, the "Great Speaker," who, although not thought of as a god, was treated and obeyed as if he were one. With authority and power "beyond what can be imagined," he was a member of the Mexicas' aristocracy, or highest class, the pipiltin, "those of lineage." To be of lineage meant having a Toltec ancestry with a link to the sage lord Quetzalcoatl. The pipiltin filled all important positions. They were assistants to the high ruler, the chiefs and captains of the army, the religious leaders, the judges, and all others who directed and led the everyday affairs of the state. The pipiltin were entitled to possess lands, which commoners cultivated for them, and their children attended the centers of high education, the calmecac.

The commoners, known as the macehualtin, "the deserved by the gods' penance," were grouped in basic socioeconomic units called calpulli. Originally, the members of a calpulli were linked by kinship. But in Tenochtitlan and some other towns, calpullis had become geographic units as well, composed of all the families living in a certain place. As an institution, the calpulli had existed in Mesoamerica since at least the days of the Toltecs. In the countryside, and in domains over which the Mexicas spread their authority, many small settlements of farming peoples had been founded by, or organized into, calpullis, with their own local councils of family leaders and protective deities. At times, a number of calpullis were "entrusted" to a Mexica administrator, or to a member of the pipiltin class, who could exact tribute and personal services from them.

Many of the commoners, members of the calpullis, worked communal "lands of the calpulli," producing agricultural products that filled markets like those in Tenochtitlan. But other calpullis were without lands, and their members had to hire themselves out to work for the pipiltin, or for the commoners of other calpullis. These people were known as mayequeh, "those whose possession was their own arms."

In difficult times, like those of famines, epidemics, or wars, the poorest of the landless commoners often sold themselves or their children as slaves. They became tlatlacotin, literally "those cut or reduced." But their period of slavery was not necessarily for the rest of their lives, for by their labor they could regain their freedom.

Merchants and artisans belonged to the commoner class, but by 1492 they had gained great social and economic importance. They had their own legal codes, guilds, and religious practices. The god Quetzalcoatl, invoked as Tlacatecuhtli, "the Lord of the Nose" (i.e., the One Who Guides), had become the patron deity of the merchants, who, although busy at local marketplaces, also conducted long-range commerce, carrying on a substantial trade with many different peoples, some living in far-distant places. One of their principal

86

The Florentine Codex—another compendium assembled by native scribes to illustrate Aztec life before the conquest—was distinctive for its extensive native-language commentary. This drawing of an Aztec feather worker presents the many activities of this specialized guild. After cleaning, feathers were stored in baskets until woven or layered into shields, banners, and headdresses. Courtesy of University of Utah Press.

routes ran to Tuxtepec, an important trading center in northern Oaxaca, then divided into two branches, one continuing toward the Pacific coast in Chiapas and Guatemala and the other, the more important, reaching Xicalanco on the Gulf Coast at the western base of the Yucatan peninsula. By maintaining contact with people of Mayan languages, the Mexica traveling merchants, known as pochtecah, played an important role as "cultural exchangers." They disseminated cultural traits of central Mexico and brought back utilitarian objects and elements of the worldview of the Mayas.

Through the Mayas, the Mexica merchants established indirect contact with the peoples of the Caribbean islands, which explains why in some of its aspects the socioeconomic organization of the Tainos resembled not only that of the Mayas but also that of the Mexicas. Many similarities can be seen between the high-ranking caciques of certain islands and the tlahtoani, or rulers, of some of the small and middle-sized chiefdoms in central Mexico that came under the domination of the Mexicas. Although more research is necessary to be certain of the connection, the Taino elite may also be compared to the pipiltin. Both were "distinguished" people, with many special privileges. At the same time, the commoners on the islands and in central Mexico had similar obligations. They had to obey and do the work, often for the benefit of those who governed them.

During the years of the Mexicas' greatest splendor, the merchants, who brought the goods of Mesoamerica to Tenochtitlan, played a key role in the socioeconomic life of their nation. Thanks to them, as the ancient text said, "the Mexica were great." But they were only one part of a busy society. Ten million or more people, most of them under the rule of the Mexicas, lived in central Mexico and worked hard. A division of labor existed: men were in charge of agricultural tasks, commerce, military affairs, and most of craft production; women were assigned household duties, including spinning, weaving, and preparing dough for tortillas, which required long hours of arduous work over a grinding stone.

The arts and crafts, mainly the work of males, flourished. Artisans produced wooden objects, ranging from digging sticks and spoons to canoes; paper from amate tree bark; luxury items for the pipiltin, including gold and silver necklaces, bracelets, and pectorals; and magnificent feathered headdresses, capes, and insignia. A most honored specialized art was that known as tlahcuilolli, "book painting and inscribing," a skill practiced by both men and women, as evidenced in pages of several amate-paper books that depict painters and scribes of both sexes doing their work.

Commerce, the various subsistence activities, and the arts and crafts all contributed to the flourishing of the Mexica culture, its religious cult, and the prestige of the rulers and those of lineage. Conversely, the religious, political, and institutional foundations exerted a profound influence on Mexica society as a whole, including its economy. Great, indeed, as a result, were the achievements of those who had become the rulers of the Mesoamerican Cemanahuac, "the lands encircled by the waters" (the known world). Those of lineage, the Mexica supreme high ruler, priests, sages, captains, ambassadors, artists, merchants, farmers, fishermen, hunters, soldiers, all the many commoners, including slaves, comprised that rich, complex society which on the eve of 1492 was still expanding toward the four quadrants of the world and which history would one day call the Aztec empire.

For the moment, in 1492, life continued uninterruptedly in the Mexicas' domains. In Tenochtitlan, solemn feasts were held as usual, worshipping Huitzilopochtli, the Mexicas' manifestation of the supreme god, Tezcatlipoca, "Smoking Mirror." There were music and dances, and the priests continued to sing their religious chants, praising the sun—Huitzilopochtli—as their own patron god:

> *You live in heaven,*
> *you uphold the mountain,*
> *Anahuac, the land surrounded by water,*
> *is in your hands.*
> *Awaited, you are always everywhere;*
> *you are invoked, you are prayed to.*
> *Your glory, your fame is sought.*
> *You live in heaven,*
> *Anahuac is in your hands.*

Many other Mexica chants, as well as poems, discourses, and historical texts, have come down to us. Together with the surviving pre-Hispanic and early colonial indigenous books, they comprise a rich body of literature of the Nahuatl-speaking peoples. Many are literary treasures, like the following composition left by an indigenous sage:

> *Where is the road*
> *that leads to the Land of the Dead,*
> *the place of the downfall,*
> *the region of the fleshless?*
> *Is it true perhaps that one lives,*
> *there, where we all shall go?*
> *Does your heart believe this?*
> *He hides us*
> *in a chest, in a coffer,*
> *the Giver of Life,*
> *He who shrouds people forever.*
> *Will I be able to look upon,*
> *able to see perhaps the face*
> *of my mother, my father?*
> *Will they sing me*
> *a few songs, a few words . . . ?*

When Columbus landed in the year 13-Flint, according to their native calendar, the Mexicas had reached their cultural apogee. Human sacrifices and the ritual communion of small pieces of the victims' flesh, offered "to deserve the god's existence"—a sacrament vividly anticipating one that would soon be preached by Christian missionaries—were inseparable ingredients of a culture which, with all its contrasts, was a summing up of Mesoamerica's grandeur.

In the native calendars of the Mexicas, as well as of the Mayas, the year that corresponded to 1492 was an ominous one. Listen to what the chronicler Chimalpahin recorded for the year 13-Flint:

13-Flint, there was disease, the Sun was devoured [there was an eclipse], there was hunger . . . A mountain between the volcanoes Iztaccihuatl and Popocatepetl split. Water sprang from the interior of it, and many
ferocious beasts devoured the children . . .

Other ancient texts in Nahuatl corroborate these dire happenings in 13-Flint. For their part, the Mayan sages left in their prophecies words of sorrow concerning a 4-Ahau Katun, the count of twenty years that corresponded to 1477–97:

This twenty-year period is established, rules at Chichén Itzá . . . The quetzal bird shall come, the green bird shall come. Kukulkan [Quetzalcoatl] shall come. Blood vomit shall come. It is the word of God. The Itzá shall come . . .

The Mexicas, Mayas, Zapotecs, Mixtecs, Quiche Mayas, and many others—all men of maize, children of a New World—were to experience in a few years the consequences of that landing, "when the sun was devoured, the mountain split, famine and blood vomit infested the Cemanahuac, the Lands-Surrounded-by-the-Waters, the world. It was the invasion, onslaught and destruction, the time in which, as a native sage exclaimed in pain: 'Our heritage became a net made of holes . . . when our cries of grief rose up and our tears rained down . . .' "

In abasement, magnificent Mesoamerica hid its face. But the people whose soul and culture were so gravely endangered—the surviving Mesoamericans—learned how to endure and persist. Now their voices are once more being heard. Five hundred years after the time when the Sun was devoured, Mesoamerica has not disappeared. Some will say it is a miracle of history that its languages, peoples, and cultural heritage are alive. Mesoamericans believe it is their destiny for them to *be,* as long as this cosmic age will continue to exist and this Sun will shine. This is what Our Father, Our Mother, the Giver of Life, the One Who Is Close, the One Who Is Near, has deserved for them here on the earth.

LOUIS C. FARON

ALONG THE PACIFIC OCEAN in the country of the Mapuche Indians of central Chile, there are forest- and swamp-hemmed beaches of black volcanic sand. I stood on one once, watching the angry ocean, seemingly also black, pound into a great white surf that churned up onto the beach and spent itself in foam at my feet. This was an ageless coastline that had seen human passersby since the time of the Ice Age. As my footprints disappeared in the frothy water, I wondered at the prints of others that had washed away during the distant millennia.

In 1492, man, indeed, was an ancient resident of South America. In the narrow corridor of the Mapuche lands, where streams come rushing down through forests from the ramparts of the southern Andes only fifty or so miles inland from the surging Pacific, archaeologists found a 15,000-year-old human footprint and also—well preserved in a peat bog—the evidence of occupation by semi-nomadic bands of hunting and gathering peoples of that remote period. Among the discovered remains at the site, called Monte Verde, were the wooden foundations of living quarters, fireplaces, stone-knapping workshops, and specialized stone tools for fleshing the bones of gigantic game animals.

These Ice Age predecessors of the Mapuche also hunted deer, llamas, guanacos, and various rodents, using clubs, spears tipped with sharp, flaked stones, and bolas. Made of two or three grooved stones about the size of golf balls tied to leather thongs, the bolas, or balls (still in use today among Ar-

Johann von Staden, a native of Hamburg, lived as a captive among the Tupinambas of eastern Brazil from 1547 to 1555. Upon his return to Europe, Staden published an account of his travels. This illustration from that book presents various aspects of Tupi life. We see a group of longhouses arranged around a central plaza and protected by a wooden palisade. Nearby, people fish with arrows from a canoe while companions stand at the edge of a weir gathering their catch with nets.

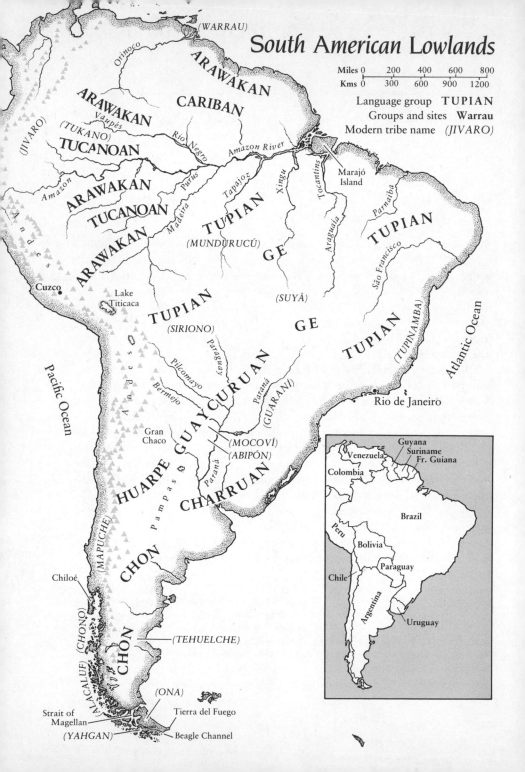

South American Lowlands

Miles 0   200   400   600   800
Kms 0   300   600   900   1200

Language group **TUPIAN**
Groups and sites **Warrau**
Modern tribe name *(JIVARO)*

(WARRAU)

ARAWAKAN

ARAWAKAN

CARIBAN

(JIVARO)

(TUKANO)
TUCANOAN

Orinoco

Rio Negro

Amazon River

Marajó Island

ARAWAKAN

Amazon

Purus

Madeira

Tapajoz

TUCANOAN

TUPIAN

Xingu

GE

TUPIAN

(MUNDURUCÚ)

Araguaia

Tocantins

São Francisco

Parnaíba

ARAWAKAN

Cuzco

Lake Titicaca

TUPIAN

(SIRIONO)

(SUYÁ)

GE

TUPIAN

(TUPINAMBA)

Atlantic Ocean

Paraguay

Pilcomayo

Paraná

Bermejo

GUAYCURUAN

(GUARANÍ)

Pacific Ocean

Gran Chaco

HUARPE

(MOCOVÍ)
(ABIPÓN)

Paraná

Rio de Janeiro

Pampas

CHARRUAN

(MAPUCHE)

CHON

Chiloé

(CHONO)

(ALACALUF)

CHON

(TEHUELCHE)

(ONA)

Tierra del Fuego

Strait of Magellan

(YAHGAN)

Beagle Channel

Guyana
Venezuela
Suriname
Fr. Guiana
Colombia
Brazil
Peru
Bolivia
Paraguay
Chile
Argentina
Uruguay

gentine gauchos), were twirled around the head, then hurled at animals or large birds so that the thongs wrapped about their legs, trapping and immobilizing them. But the largest of the hunters' prey was the hairy, long-tusked mastodon, itself on the move southward on its own food quest as a result of life-threatening environmental changes at the end of the Paleolithic era.

At Monte Verde, archaeologists also uncovered the bones of seven mastodons, as well as the remains of marine animals, roots, berries, seeds, and varieties of medicinal plants, providing evidence of the life of an Ice Age band of about fifty people who had had enough food to continue to live in one place for a year or more. There were indications, too, that these early hunters and gatherers had been part of a trade network that extended up and down the coast and between the coast and the interior, for some of the artifacts they left behind had come from a much wider region than they themselves had occupied.

Before the end of the last Ice Age, countless generations of hunters like them made innumerable and remarkable adjustments to the many different natural environments through which they passed. The route of Ice Age peoples between the western flanks of the Andes and the Pacific Ocean was a natural funnel for the migration of man and animals, and it is certainly the best documented to date. But early man, coming south from North America, had also spread down the continent along the Caribbean and Atlantic coastlines. Taking paths of least resistance and eschewing mountain ranges and dense jungles, they and those along the Pacific followed the resource-rich coasts and river systems in slow, sporadic advances, refining their skills in hunting and gathering until by 7000 B.C. some of them reached the Strait of Magellan and Tierra del Fuego at the southern tip of the continent. Then, as the mastodon vanished, life for the hunters became an unceasing search for small animals, forcing them to move constantly as nomads.

With the Ice Age hunters and gatherers having provided a base for new cultural periods, South America became a continent on the move. Venturing into new areas, borrowing ideas from other peoples, developing and spreading new techniques, and adapting by invention, numerous groups crisscrossed the forests and plains, fashioning mythologies of their origin and of life and death to create a skein of beliefs that even transcended continents, joining North and South American peoples in their mystical appreciation of the lands in which they lived. By the time of the European invasion, basic and elaborate native technologies, social organizations, and religious and moral systems had been in existence throughout South America for millennia, and myriad languages had evolved.

Omitting the area of the central Andes, whose stupendous, high-civilization achievements by the Incas and their predecessors will be discussed in the next chapter in this volume, our look at the lowland native societies in South America in 1492 begins not with the Mapuche (to whom we will return later) but at the top of the continent. There, an agricultural revolution that had originated 7,000 years earlier in both Mexico and Peru had extended its influence and added farming as a source of livelihood to groups that had once been only hunters and gatherers of wild foods.

Among the beneficiaries of this horticultural revolution were almost all the peoples inhabiting the humid tropical forests of the Amazon Basin. One of them, who called themselves Shuara, "human beings," distinguishing themselves from their neighbors, but who became known to history as Jivaro, lived in a natural stronghold in the northwestern part of the basin. Isolated from surrounding peoples, whom from time immemorial they considered enemies and subhuman, they defeated all who tried to enter their lands—which began on the Andes' eastern slopes, where cascading waterfalls tumbled over the most precipitous escarpment in all of South America, and ended where rivulets and streams cut through saturated jungle to the smooth, lowland waters of navigable tributaries of the Amazon.

Testifying to their long background of isolation was their language, which differed from that of any of their neighbors and which scholars have included tentatively in a catchall category, the Andean Equatorial language family. Their isolation placed them in a cultural backwater. Although geographically close to the central Andes, a major location of New World civilization, they lacked even canoe transportation. At the same time, they stood outside the paths of diffusion of the almost ubiquitous bitter manioc, the staple food of the tropical forests.

Not surprisingly, the history of the Jivaro is that of a warlike people who were jealous of their identity and land, who had a reputation as warriors and mutilators of victims' bodies, and who were known especially for their unique skill in shrinking human heads, a custom that sent shudders throughout the northwestern Amazon. Some decades before the Spanish conquest, the Inca emperor Huayna Capac felt the full force of Jivaro hostility when he tried to conquer and absorb them as tribute payers. His highland army was fiercely repulsed, and the expedition ended in the Incas' disorderly retreat. Early Spanish accounts also tell of the bellicosity and isolation of the Jivaro. It was not until the early nineteenth century, in fact, that they began to make the two-week trek out of their home country to a highland frontier town to trade for machetes for easier cultivation and for shotguns to upgrade their defenses and hunting efficiency.

In 1492, some 4,000 Jivaro occupied and defended an area of about 2,000 square miles. They lived in large, polygynous, extended-family households in a scattered pattern, without the villages or central plazas that were so common among many of the other tropical forest peoples. Their sense of being Jivaro, or humans, was reinforced more by their antagonism toward other peoples, whom they raided to obtain trophy heads and bones, than by feelings of unity with their own Jivaro neighbors. They built their houses a half mile or so apart on rises that afforded defensive views of the surrounding jungle, and also of the cultivated fields that encircled their communities. Their houses were constructed solidly of heavy posts and beams, lashed together with vines and covered with thatch in a hip-roof style that enabled a runoff of water from tropical downpours. The roofs also had outlets for smoke from the cooking braziers and from a central fireplace that illuminated the large dwellings. In fact, these were extraordinarily large houses for the estimated average of ten persons per household, but size was dictated by the needs of social and recreational events—dancing with relatives and guests—that were held indoors, sheltered from the heavy rains, as well as from raiding enemies. The idea, so characteristic of other village horticulturalists, of a central plaza as a gathering place for all households, was foreign to the Jivaro. Never would they place themselves in jeopardy of being caught unawares and unprotected outdoors.

The Jivaro were sophisticated farmers and also productive hunters and gatherers. A timeworn dichotomy existed: men hunted, women gathered. Men cleared the jungle growth; women and children seeded, cultivated, and, with the help of husbands, fathers, and big brothers, harvested.

At first light, the head of the Jivaro household quietly awakened brothers, sons, nephews, and uncles, and all set forth, tool in one hand, club or bow in the other, to begin the day's agricultural work. The Jivaro, like other tropical forest people, practiced slash-and-burn horticulture. It was an ancient technique. Designating an area for clearing, the head of the household strode about in a cloak of reeds and leaves to ward off annoying insects and directed the others to girdle the large trees with their stone axes, slashing the bark deeply enough so that the generative sap would not rise. The huge trees would soon shed their leaves, allowing sunlight to reach down to the forest floor. Smaller trees were cut down and burned, along with the brush undercover. The ashes contained potash fertilizer that had a soil-restorative effect but which, nevertheless, leached out rather easily when the rains came. Soil depletion, plus the rapid takeover of weeds, necessitated the abandonment of fields after a few years, and cultivation would shift to another area. The cycle was repeated over and over, despite the arduous efforts of women cultivators to battle against the stifling undergrowth.

Once the new plot was prepared, it was time for the women to plant sweet manioc, the basic starch of the Jivaro and a versatile tuber that could be left in the ground for many months after it matured. It could be harvested as the need arose, to be made into flour or boiled with other vegetables and meat in a pepper-pot stew. Today, we know one of its end products as tapioca; the Jivaro knew another as beer, which they drank in great amounts.

In addition to sweet manioc, bananas (or plantains), and sweet potatoes,

Jean de Léry was a Huguenot minister who traveled to Brazil in the sixteenth century. His descriptions of Tupinamba life are considered valuable because they are generally free from stereotypes. In this illustration from Léry's *Histoire d'une Voyage,* Tupinamba dancers wear leg rattles and feathers. The man in front has his head shaved, presumably to show off his battle scars. Léry added the parrot and monkey to illustrate these unique South American creatures.

the women of the tropical forest planted tomatoes, onions, maize, pineapples, varieties of squash, hot peppers, sugarcane, tobacco, gourds, and cotton—all part of the New World's gift to the Old.

The men, once freed from the task of preparing plots, had time for other, more congenial activities: getting ready for fishing by damming ponds and streams, gathering special drugs to stun the fish, and whittling palm tree slivers into darts for their blowguns. They spent many days making the blowgun itself, and taught the young men all their skills. The elders also told the young stories about the creation of the universe and of animals, plants, and especially mankind, the Jivaro, and about the spirits of the forest. From the older men adolescent boys learned how to hunt the jaguar, deer, peccary, and other large game, not only the mechanical skills of tracking, stalking, and killing but the magical and ritual perfection necessary for a successful hunting way of life.

In another drawing from Jean de Léry's account of Tupinamba life, a family is depicted with a hammock and another unique American plant: the pineapple. The figures are not accurate depictions of Native Americans; they conform to European ideals of shape and form.

The capture of smaller game, lizards, frogs, and such, they learned as little children, as they toddled along with their mothers on root-digging and berry- and fruit-picking expeditions. Thus, hunting, gathering, and horticulture were the mainstays of a mixed economy long before the Spanish conquest disturbed the ecological basis of Native American lifeways. Long after the coming of the white man the pepper pot still boiled and the barbecue cooked their food, so ingrained and successfully adaptive were Jivaro lifeways.

Besides drinking manioc beer, the Jivaro chewed datura, a strong hallucinogen that resulted in visions and in the supposed acquisition of greater ability to perform life's tasks, such as creating bountiful harvests and raising healthy children, winning in battle, and receiving help from supernatural beings. There was an equation between the use of datura and one's eternal soul that had to do with the fear of death and measures, like a hallucinogenic vision-

Born in 1501, André Thevet was cosmographer to the King of France. Thevet took advantage of his position to study and report on the Western Hemisphere, which was becoming known to Europeans during his lifetime. His interest took him to both Canada and Brazil. In this illustration from Thevet's *Le Vrais Portrait des Hommes Illustres,* published in 1584, we see Quoniambec, a Tupinamba leader, dressed in his finery and wearing labret plugs in his cheeks and chin. While the ornaments seem accurate, the warrior's profile and musculature rely heavily on European ideals.

quest, to prevent death. The religious aspects of this practice were complex, and involved the necessity of killing one's enemy. Indeed, these beliefs fomented an urge to kill, which led a young man to join a killing party, usually accompanied by his father and patrilineal kinsmen. He went forth knowing that with the use of drugs he had achieved an immortal soul which could only be killed by supernatural, not physical, means. Death came only when the vision failed, when the community's shaman-curer lost his own battle between Jivaro good and the evil powers associated with the Jivaro enemies.

The Jivaro concept of bush spirits, their use of alcohol and other drugs to induce spiritual experiences, and their belief in spirit helpers and human practitioners gifted in the art of curing were age-old in the world and differed from the beliefs of others only in cultural particulars. Some of these beliefs must have been transported across the Bering Strait from Asia 35,000 years ago and found their way south all the way to the Strait of Magellan and land's end many thousands of years later. By 1492 they were part of the cultural inventory of most South American societies.

Although the majority of tropical forest peoples other than the Jivaro depended on canoes for transportation, the Warrau, "boat people," of the Orinoco Delta in what is now Venezuela could not have survived without them. Canoes were essential to life in the inundated lower delta, with its shorelines of drowned stands of mangrove, few habitable beaches, and no overland trails.

Had the Warrau been confined to the rich intermediate delta with some higher and drier locales, their life would have been drastically limited and difficult to preserve. A family spent most of its waking hours in canoes on fishing, hunting, and gathering trips, even cooking, eating, and sleeping in them on long-distance ventures.

The Warrau built their houses on the rare beaches along the shorelines, seeking the highest ground available. Rectangular pole-and-thatch structures were raised above the water level on pilings laboriously forced through the mud. Tall forked posts held up the ridgepoles. Both ends of the houses were open, but the gabled, palm-thatched roofs sloped down to floor level. Sometimes, several houses were built on a huge platform made of two layers of tree trunks covered with a thickness of clay and set on pilings. These villages, unique in South America, were an engineering marvel created by people who possessed only the simplest tools.

Warrau furnishings were sparse, consisting of hammocks made from palm fiber and little wooden stools, sometimes carved to resemble animals. Hanging from the pole rafters were numerous objects crafted by men and women according to a sexual division of labor that was not always rigidly observed. Men wove hammocks, some of the baskets, and the tipiti (a "finger catcher" press for squeezing poisonous prussic acid from bitter manioc), using palm fiber and leaves. Women wove most of the other household goods: containers, circular trays, special fans to blow into flame the continually smoldering embers of the cooking fires on the clay floors, and other fans to chase off the ever-present swarms of insects. Smoke from the fires held down the mosquitoes inside the houses, but fans were the only defense against them outside. The Warrau did not wear protective capes against their bites, like those of palm fiber used by the Cubeo, Witoto, and other peoples, or those of leaves and reeds worn by the Jivaro.

In addition to building the houses, the Warrau men performed the intricate and arduous task of constructing two kinds of canoes used by their people. The simpler was a small, flat-bottomed skiff of bark that held two or three men. It had a very shallow draft and was designed to penetrate the waters of the flooded jungle where many different kinds of game and fish were sought. The other, a dugout canoe holding fifty or more people and capable of making long voyages, even out to the Caribbean Sea, was constructed from a giant hardwood tree. This large craft was used as a war canoe in raids against neighboring Arawak and Carib settlements and served also as a carryall for an entire village in its move to a new site.

The Warrau employed many age-old skills and procedures in manufacturing the large canoes. Looking in on a village would make clear the grand and protracted scale of the enterprise. The old, much-repaired canoe, it would be seen, had become too small for the growing population. The male family heads had known that this day would come, and for the past year had been looking for the most suitable tree from which to fashion a new communal craft. The search had become part of their daily lives, and as each candidate was spotted on fishing and hunting trips or during the clearing of distant garden plots, its use was suggested. Later, around the fire at night, as the men wove hammocks, fashioned fishhooks from palm spines, or played with their sons in the hammocks, the tree's potential was discussed more thoroughly. It was mainly at night that the Warrau men talked over serious things, while still performing sedentary chores. A consensus was finally reached in a most informal manner, for there was no chief to consult or give orders. Since social organization was based on close kinship ties among the men who shared a household or a cluster of houses, each male participated in the decision, which was reached democratically, though with deference to age and the acquired wisdom of a natural leader.

At the arrival of the dry season, when the waters receded from the highest ground, the tree was slashed so it would die. At the end of the dry season, fire after fire was built around the huge base of the tree, charring into the trunk bit by bit while the men cut away the burned wood with treasured stone celts acquired from a trade network that extended back to a source in the far-distant mountains. Some men used an adze made locally of Caribbean conch shell. After the tree was felled there were weeks of charring, chipping, and scraping still ahead. The top of the tree was removed at just the proper length for the canoe, no more, no less. At last, the trunk could be skinned of its bark and then floated into place at the village.

It was then that a thousand-year-old tradition of craftsmanship came into play. Charring and scraping were repeated—carefully controlled by a specialist, who was sometimes from another village—in a process continuing for almost a year of hollowing the trunk into a dugout or canoe form. When the log was roughly in final shape, it was widened by fire, water, and steam and its sides braced apart in the midsection. The hull was thinned to an inch or so and bowed from stem to stern. The final result was a specialist's delight, and it was no wonder that the men capable of directing this marvel not only were accorded great prestige but were considered supernaturally endowed by the Serpent Spirit who called them to her side after death.

By 1492, the Warrau were practicing horticulture, having acquired the knowledge from neighboring Arawaks and others to the east and west of the Orinoco Delta. Still, they subsisted mainly by fishing the labyrinthine waters of the delta and by collecting the abundant fruits of the jungle. The Mauritia (moriche) palm was their mainstay, products of which they ate, wove, wore, slept in, sat on, and lodged under. Although they had learned about bitter manioc from contact with coastal Arawakans, the pith of the Mauritia palm provided their basic starch. This palm tree was fundamental to the land side of Warrau life and was an integral part of their religious ritual, a symbolic link between the boat people and the deified culture heroes who had provided them with the tree. During the harvest season, the Mauritia was sacrificed to the gods. Even rotting palms gave life in death, providing the white grubs that the Warrau prized highly.

As the people fished and traveled about, their eyes were always alert for something to gather—larvae from rotting trees, iguanas and their eggs, crabs that scurried along the banks and hid among the mangrove roots, snails from the still waters, and leathery turtle eggs, abundant in their shallow incubation pits on the river edges. In moving about, the people made mental notes of stands of fruit trees and conferred on the different ripening times, deciding when to come back for a harvest. They anticipated feasting on pineapples, papayas, guavas, cherimoyas, and cherries, or drinking their juice. These were only some of the delicacies and natural riches of their territory, which they had to defend against invading Caribs, who occasionally plied their seagoing canoes in the estuaries of the Orinoco Delta, trying to reap what they did not have in their own lands.

In July and August, whole communities galvanized into action. It was crab season, and the men of the villages departed en masse to hunt them in the endless mangrove stands, setting up temporary shelters along the Caribbean coastline and back into the broader estuaries of the delta. Crabs were gathered by the thousands, and the men loaded up their canoes and paddled home, blowing conch shells to announce their success. Women boiled the crabs, and the feasting began.

If the Mauritia palm provided an inexhaustible source of starch, the innumerable species of fish supplied all the protein the Warrau needed. Methods and devices used to catch fish were nearly as varied as the species themselves, some techniques dating from the end of the Pleistocene. They ranged from fishing in narrow, rocky gorges with plaited baskets tied to long poles to employing bare hands to pull fish from the mud of shallow pools where they became stranded in the dry season. More efficient for large hauls was the weir, made of palm fiber mats and placed across a small stream at high tide. The men waited; then as the tide receded, they sprang into motion, spearing the fish or using multipronged arrows or harpoons. These last were also used from a canoe to secure large fish that were attracted to the surface by a baited line. After a good catch, Warrau fishermen placed the fish bones in the thatch of their roofs to propitiate the spirit Owner of the Fish and ensure continued success.

Hunting was done with some reluctance, for the Warrau considered the game "people of the forest" and refused to kill the large animals of the jungle, many of which were tabooed. They had a simple cuisine of roasted rodents, birds, baked and boiled fish, toasted palm meal, and raw food. Apart from crab feasts, they ate sparingly twice a day.

Houses built on stilts along waterways of the Amazon, with women engaged in house-keeping while men return in a canoe.

In contrast to the Jivaro, the Warrau felt as one with others who spoke the same language but, aside from that, had no strong feeling of tribal membership. They fought trespassers, even other Warrau, on their fishing grounds or in their traditional harvest areas of the jungle. Their villages were composed of clusters of related males, each of whom might have several wives. Indeed, the Warrau were considered the most polygynous society in what is now the eastern Venezuela and Guiana region.

Despite the absence of ceremony, marriages were arranged at an early age, with a girl's parents selecting her future husband and making a contractual agreement with his family. At puberty, the boy moved in with his bride's parents for several years; thus the older males worked not with their sons, as was common elsewhere in the tropical forest, but with their sons-in-law, who remained until each had children. After a few children were born, the son-in-law built his own house, setting up his own cycle as household head, arranging marriages, and receiving bride service from sons-in-law of his own. He also took other wives, usually younger sisters or cousins of his first wife, for whom he paid bride-price, the belief being that wives got along better if they were blood relatives.

When a woman was ready to deliver her child, she went to a special little hut to await its arrival. Unless the birth was difficult, no one attended her, and she bit through the umbilical cord and tied it off with an ordinary piece of string. After burying the afterbirth, she returned to the house with the baby and resumed a normal routine. Not so the husband, for he began to observe a ceremony common in the tropical forest and known as the couvade. For days, even weeks, he spent nearly all his time in his hammock, abstaining from work and from sexual intercourse with any of his wives, and observing eating taboos. By refraining from eating certain kinds of meat and fish, he ensured the well-being of the new infant. Depending on the fertility of his wives, he might observe couvade more than once a year.

Puberty and torture went hand in hand, as both boys and girls had to undergo an ant ordeal to prove their courage and worthiness for adulthood. They were ceremonially placed in a hammock and covered with stinging ants. For hours they had to endure this painful test of fortitude with calm silence. Some did it better than others, but the stoic ideal was always approximated and all adolescents attained full majority.

Death was handled ritually by members of the village, although relatives from other settlements might visit to mourn. If a person died in a village other than his or her own, relatives who lived there acted as hosts, for, by custom, the deceased was buried in the spot on which he or she died. A person lived and died within this wide network of relatives, and although he or she might not work with them every day, as with members of his or her own village, there was a feeling of community and friendship. Only relatives were friends, and only relatives were married. All outsiders were suspect.

The ritual of the burial itself had to be carried out perfectly and with the utmost attention to detail and moral concerns. Since all death was attributed to evil spirits that could linger in the vicinity and cause harm or death to others, the entire group felt threatened. The group called upon their shaman to perform acts that would ensure the deceased's safe passage to the afterworld and protect the mourners. When an important kinship elder died, his house was vacated and his body allowed to putrify until most of the flesh fell off the skeleton. Then the skeleton was adorned with personal ornaments and placed in a corner of the house. Sometimes the corpse was lowered into the river until fish picked the bones clean. Later, the skeletal remains were put in a basket with the skull on top of the rest of the bones. Sometimes the basket was hung in the house; at other times, it was placed in a canoe. Eventually, it was buried deep in the earth. If the death was particularly traumatic, the entire village was burned, the large canoes were loaded with people and the village's possessions, and a new site was sought. Perhaps the group split up, some moving in with relatives in another village, others striking off to establish a new community. And so the life cycle ended, with widows wailing, the shaman performing, and the spirit of the departed speeding onward to the afterworld.

Inland, about 2,000 miles from the Warrau, through thick jungles, cascading rivers, mountains, and savannas, the lands of the Carib-speaking Pariagoto, Macusi, Waiwai, and Bonari, and across the Amazon River, was the territory of the Mundurucú, fierce, tattooed headhunters, who occupied the very center of Brazil, in the drainage of the Tapajos River, a great southern tributary of the Amazon.

Relative latecomers to this region, these Tupian speakers moved into the Brazilian Matto Grosso late in pre-Columbian times as one spur of a great Tupian migration across the face of the continent. Linguistic and mythological evidence confirms the path of their wanderings and indicates a previous existence limited to hunting and gathering. For example, their language lacked certain words for tropical forest agricultural crops, and their myths dwelled on hunting prowess to the exclusion of horticultural knowledge. There was nothing, moreover, to indicate a former fierceness. Once in the region, however, they acquired the knowledge of building canoes and the skills of river transportation and, in one of the most profound cultural adjustments ever made, traveled far and wide in a quest for enemy heads. Their rapacity was recorded in the oral histories of the equally fierce Nambicuara, Parintintin, and other peoples who stood in their path in various parts of the Tapajos Basin.

The Mundurucú lived in gallery forests, not choking jungle, at an altitude of 2,000 feet on the northern slopes of a watershed that drained north into the Amazon Basin. They built their villages on high, grassy knolls that afforded good views of their surrounding agricultural fields, of the rivers and streams they fished, and of the jungles in which they hunted—the jungles that separated them from neighboring Mundurucú villages, with whom they were always at peace, and the jungles that sometimes harbored attacking Nambicuara, Parintintin, and other hostile peoples.

Several pole-and-thatch houses were grouped in a circle around a central plaza in which was a structure special but not unique to the Mundurucú, the men's house, forbidden to women. Close kinship ties bound the village into gratifying social interaction in their daily individual and cooperative activities, as they went about hunting, gathering, fishing, and gardening, the mixed economy typical of most of the tropical forest peoples. Each village was headed

Despite the fact that this illustration of the interior of a Galibi longhouse is from the report of a nineteenth-century French explorer, it contains many elements of traditional technology that would have been present in 1492. Carefully arranged from left to right under the hammock are examples of pottery, weaving, a club, a paddle, stools, arrows, a manioc strainer, and a string of pod rattles.

by a chief and was politically independent. Important intervillage activities, warfare, and large-scale hunting and fishing expeditions were arranged and directed by a council of village elders and the chief, who was usually a shaman.

In their new environment, the former hunters and gatherers became prosperous horticulturalists, and their numbers swelled to about 20,000 by Columbus's time, enabling them to maintain a powerful fighting force. There also came about a change in cultural values: the prowess of the great hunter of animals of the field was superseded by that of the great hunter of human heads, and this became a fundamental part of their religious beliefs.

The Mundurucú achieved eminence not only as warriors but as hunting strategists and sharpshooters with the bow and arrow. Their exhilaration during these activities was the source of folktales and religious mythology, regularly reinforced by nightly tales told in the men's house. This was a male-dominated society, symbolized by the presence of this special hut from which women were barred. Built off to one side of the plaza, its precincts were sacred. Bows and arrows were fashioned there and traditional lore was recounted for

the benefit of adolescent boys' ears. The cardinal myth, shared with other patrilineal tropical forest societies, told of a time when women were the leaders.
It described how the men made a bull-roarer, a piece of flat wood fixed to a
string and twirled around the head to make a rushing, humming, or roaring
noise. Upon hearing it, the women thought it was the sound of a supernatural
being and were frightened into submission to the men who controlled it. In this
way, men outsmarted women, proving male superiority and supremacy. In
mythical fashion, this story explained the evaluation of men and women in
society.

The most prized targets of the Mundurucú arrows were wild boars, after
which came jaguars, tapirs, deer, monkeys, varieties of birds, and the reptiles
and rodents that women and children killed while on foraging outings or when
they cultivated the crops. Mundurucú craved meat, or so the hunters claimed.
Without meat, people felt hungry. Actually, there was no shortage of food.
The gardens produced an abundance of both sweet and bitter manioc, as well
as the usual inventory of tropical crops. But the people also needed meat.

Only men hunted, but both men and women fished during the several weeks
of the dry season. Camps were set up along the banks of large rivers some distance from the villages. Sites were chosen where there were shallows and lagoons in which fish could be drugged with a poison grown in the gardens
especially for that purpose. The roots were chopped up and carried in bundles
upstream by the men. There they beat the roots to a pulp so that the poisonous
sap flowed downstream with the current. Women and children waited below
at a place where the water eddied into a fairly still pool and there collected the
stupefied fish as they floated to the surface. It was a noisy and exciting time for
the women, who cried out with delight as they scrambled in knee-deep water
to harvest the thousands of small fish with their scoop nets. The men now
joined the women and used their spears to catch the larger fish. Sometimes
small streams were dammed with branches to prevent any of the fish from es-
caping. As much as a ton of fish might be taken back to the village to be
smoked, salted, sun-dried, and shared with the entire village. The products of
the fish kill, the hunt, and the garden belonged to those who worked for them
and were regarded as personal property. However, any food that came into
the household was shared by all, and surplus was freely distributed. No one
went hungry. It was the rule.

As did other Native American societies, the Mundurucú thought that their
land was the most beautiful and that they were the only real people. Each
group, bounded by its regional surroundings, knew almost nothing of what
lay beyond. Their real world was minuscule and unvaried; their supernatural
world was encircled by demonic spirits and by flesh-and-blood enemies who,
since they did not speak the same language, were less than human and deserved to be killed, to lose their heads. This tropical forest concern with bodies

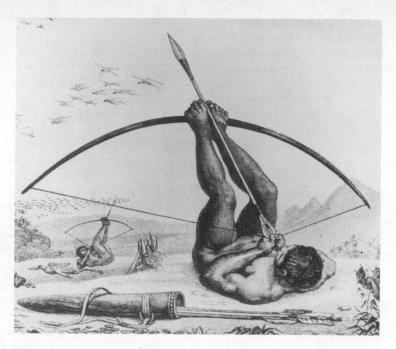

These archers, who lived near modern-day Rio de Janeiro, assembled along flyways to shoot large migrating birds. The hunters had to use their feet to take advantage of the full power of these oversized bows.

alien in language, thought, and appearance who were taken in warfare ranged from the exotic mutilation of shrinking heads to eating parts of the corpse. The Mundurucú took enemy heads and impaled them on posts in the villages, a practice that occurred, also, in Queen Mary Tudor's sixteenth-century London and in seventeenth-century European colonies, like New Amsterdam in North America, probably without the same mystical overtones.

The Mundurucú maintained their way of life by their aggressiveness. Hostilities took place in the dry season, when war parties were on the march, attacking settlements at random. The raids were motivated by the concept of blood vengeance, as well as by a desire to frighten enemies and injure their warriors. It was not a trivial affair, cutting off a head, especially if enemies were around to try to prevent one from doing it. Enough heads were taken, however, to make all the settlements along the Tapajos River quake when confronting these fierce warriors, or even upon learning that they were on the warpath. At the onset of the rainy season, the successful headhunters returned to their village to begin a lengthy series of ceremonies, some continuing for three years. These religious rituals underscored the supernatural power of the trophy head and were occasions of ecstatic revelry.

When a head was taken, its preparation was begun immediately. Long before the men's return to the village, the brains were removed and the teeth were knocked out and retained. The head was then parboiled and dried, making the skin like parchment. A cord was strung through the mouth and out one of the nostrils. The gaping eyes were closed with beeswax. Soon after his return to the village, the taker of the head sponsored the first ritual act, "Decorating the Ears." Feathered pendants from five species of birds, each of which had a ceremonial association with a particular clan and its eponymous clan spirit, were hung from both ears.

This was only the first of the duties of the successful headhunter, who was now considered an awesome hero with a sacred status. He had to abstain from everyday activities, including sexual relations with his wife or any other woman, which under normal conditions might have occurred once or twice a week. He took a ritual bath in the early morning so as to avoid the sight of a woman. Spending most of his days in his hammock in the men's house, he talked sparingly and only on serious subjects. He did not eat with the men, but went to his wife's house, where he and she sat back to back. The list of complex and extraordinary observances was almost endless, but all served to shelter his eminent person and spirit from worldly contamination. A spiritual force, his very presence on a game hunt, even though he took no part, was enough to ensure success.

When the next rainy season began and the village was at full strength, the "hero" hosted the second step in the ceremony, "Stripping the Skin from the Head." People from other villages were invited to the ceremony, and there was much feasting, singing, and dancing. The head was skinned and the skull hung in the men's house. At the onset of the third rainy season, the high point of the rituals was reached during a ceremony called "Hanging the Teeth." The teeth that had been knocked out and saved were now strung together and placed in a basket in the hero's house. Most important in this ceremony was the all-night singing by the men's society, which included all Mundurucú warriors from surrounding villages. After the feasting was over and the songs sung in honor of these warriors, they returned to their own villages. With that, the supernatural powers of the hero evaporated. After three years of exalted status as "Taker of the Head," he once more resumed normal participation in the daily life of his village, although he remained an honored person for life. It was possible to conceive of complications during the three-year period. For example, if his three wives had borne children during the time of his exalted status, he would have had to play the conflicting roles of father-in-couvade, perhaps cuckold, and valiant warrior.

Let us now sample another slice of South American life in 1492, along the

Atlantic coast of Brazil. From the island of Marajó at the mouth of the Amazon River to the site of present-day Rio de Janeiro, in a coastal corridor of some 2,200 miles, lived groups of Tupi-speaking peoples whom anthropologists called Tupinamba. They were newcomers to this region, having migrated from somewhere deep in Amazonia to the Atlantic seaboard in a religious pilgrimage to the promised land of their grandfathers. Each of their horticultural villages was made up of from four to eight huge communal houses, encircling a plaza that supported a rich schedule of social and religious activities, including cannibalism.

The Tupinamba thrived on great size and scale. Their houses were 500 feet long and up to 100 feet wide. As many as thirty nuclear families, or between 100 and 200 people, related by blood and marriage, occupied each dwelling. The populations of these villages dwarfed those of the Jivaro, Warrau, and Mundurucú and were commensurate with the complexity of the political, military, and religious life of the Tupinamba. One wonders what it was like to live in a house with 200 other people of all ages. Certainly, social visibility was great and efforts at privacy were mostly symbolic. Only two wall posts separated each family unit, which had its own fire that was always smoldering. Family hammocks were hung in a way that served as another symbolic division of space.

A center aisle led to openings at both ends of each house for easy entry and exit. The houses were well ordered, with domestic items hung from the rafters, and small tables, carved benches, and many kinds of pottery containers neatly placed on the hard-packed dirt floor.

Living and sleeping arrangements in the house said much about the social organization of the Tupinamba, as well as about their ethnic bias. First, the head of this segment of the village patrilineal-descent group had a special place to live. He slept there with one or more of his wives and with his captive female slaves and a young boy or two who performed various services. This proven and still virile warrior, wearing no more than his two-foot-long penis sheath, sat on a carved stool surveying his extended family and waiting to be bathed, pampered, and fed. He did not wonder about what he would eat, for the meal was traditional tropical forest fare—manioc soup, perhaps mangara leaves as a green, and boiled fish in its broth—all seasoned with several varieties of hot peppers ground up with sea salt. He sat in silence, his meal served in bowls, cups, and plates by his eldest wife. The rest of the family helped themselves from a common pot. Later, slaves ate the leavings.

For most of the year, the Tupinamba cultivated their gardens, but during oyster-gathering months entire villages emptied out to camp by the seashore. Even the little children pitched in and were taught the different species, what magic spells brought good fortune, where to harvest, and how to smoke the oysters. More than that, they learned the joy of communal collection and working in concert. The Tupinamba enjoyed traveling in extended-family groups whether it was to collect oysters, cultivate distant fields, gather honey, or for whatever reason. But the oyster collection brought special pleasure, as their huge mounds of shells—now archaeological laboratories—testify. Perhaps because this coastal area was so poor in game, their hunting activities existed for the most part in their mythical accounts of the animal-rich jungles of their ancestors. Fish scoops, drugs, and weirs replaced the bow and arrow, and fishing was also a collective activity enjoyed by all ages of the extended-family group.

Despite the peaceful aspects of their society, the Tupinamba are remembered mainly for their ferocity in warfare and for their cannibalism. In later years, Europeans wrote of these activities in lurid detail, much of it imaginative, secondhand reporting. The Tupinamba and others, like the Caribs and Cubeos, considered the eating of human flesh a ritual act, part of their belief in consubstantiation. The consumption of human flesh was an act of supernatural importance and, like the headhunting of the Mundurucú, was believed by all to be necessary to ensure the survival of the race and the blessing of the ancestral spirits. It was said that in addition to eating war captives, they ate their own people who had been guilty of some heinous breach of social interaction. By so doing, these offenders had become subhuman and had to be expunged from society by ritually placating the supernatural. The Tupinamba thus not only achieved power and prestige from ceremonial killing and the consumption of human flesh, but maintained their consonance with the universe, personalized by the supernatural beings who lived invisibly within the precincts of each village and who, when properly propitiated, helped "humans" ward off the evil spirits inhabiting the jungles and gain success over their enemies.

Even warfare began with a spiritual imprimatur. A number of warriors set out to avenge the death of, and cannibalistic act against, a member of their own lineage group. The Tupinamba reckoned the division of time by the appearance and waning of the Pleiades on the horizon, and thus had some astronomical orientation in their most important activities. As horticulturalists, this cosmic event had both practical and supernatural meaning for them. Similarly, the time for avenging the murder of one's lineage brother was regulated by the position of the stars in the sky, for Earth and Sky were one. At the proper celestial moment, the day of vengeance was set. Warriors were greased, feathered, ceremonially admonished, and readied to kill. Dancing was finished. No bad omens had been seen. The parrot had not spoken ill.

In anticipation of revenge, the war implements had been prepared: the broadsword, a hardwood club with a razor-sharp edge; the shield of tapir skin blessed by the shaman. The young men set forth stealthily by night, having forgone sexual activity, establishing an aura of ritual purity. The warriors were accompanied by their women, but no children were allowed to come

A fanciful engraving based on a depiction by Johann von Staden of an attack on a palisaded Tupinamba village. Women and children flee while men defend the town. Attackers wear feathers and a few use shields. Canoes fill the lower right corner.

along. If the people had to travel far, they went by canoe. There might be a whole fleet setting forth if the number of victims to be taken was large. The number depended on the enormity of the outrage to be avenged.

Secrets were poorly kept in their area, and the attack was foreseen. Because of the frequency of such assaults, villages were palisaded, with holes in the walls for shooting arrows. Some even had moats. Trumpets were blown on both sides, and the battle was joined. If the attackers could not scale the palisaded walls and overwhelm the village, they built a hedge of thorny bushes and placed the village under siege. They shot incendiary arrows at the houses and at the palisades. If they were successful in storming the village, the heads and genitals of the slain enemies were cut off and carried back to the village, along with the captives. The testicles were then reduced to fat and eaten

A Continent on the Move

by the headman. A time for torturing and eating the captives was set, but until then there was no harsh treatment of the prisoners.

Chicha, beer made from maize, was prepared for the drinking bout which took place at the time of sacrifice. Portions of the victims' flesh were allotted to people in advance. The captives were decorated and made to join the villagers in singing and dancing. Then they were killed with a special club, but not before being permitted to throw missiles at their captors. Blood from the victims was drunk, and the flesh was eaten by all except the executioner. After the sacrifice, he took a new name and underwent ritual purification so the ghosts of the victims could not seek him out and do him harm. The Tupinamba had similar rites for a slain jaguar, a man-killer, who was the most powerful and ferocious animal they hunted. It was evident that both of these ceremonies centered on a belief that to consume one's enemy was to incorporate his power. Taking part in these rituals was obligatory.

Despite their success in establishing themselves on the coastline, many groups of Tupinamba eventually migrated inland on their quest for the "Land of the Grandfather," promised to them in a shamanistic revelation many generations before. Their migrations took some to the edge of the Paraguay River, where they became known as the Guaraní, and others to the eastern slopes of the Andes. One such group of Tupian pilgrims, who eked out a fingertip existence into the twentieth century, was the Siriono of eastern Bolivia. Exactly what route they followed from their Tupinamba homeland, what cultural attributes they left behind, and whether they were pushed into the inaccessible high forests by more aggressive peoples are not known, but they were an example of a society caught midway between tropical forest horticulturalists and nomadic hunters and gatherers. There were enclaves of numerous other peoples in the tropical forest regions of South America who, like the Siriono, knew rudimentary cultivation but depended almost entirely on hunting and gathering. The Guayakí, Southern Cayapo, Shiriana, Guahibo, Guaitaca, Moro, Purí-Coroado, Waica (Yanomano), Macú, Chiricoa, Guarahibo, and Yaruro were examples of such peoples who occupied parts of the continent in 1492.

The Siriono, or Mbia, "people," as they called themselves, differed greatly from their more powerful horticultural neighbors, the Arawakan-speaking Mojos and Chiquitos. Almost always on the move, the Siriono lived in temporary settlements in rudely built lean-tos of poles tied to trees and covered with palm leaves for protection against the incessant rain. The shelters were remarkably large, housing an entire matrilineally related band of 40 to 100 people. Like their far-distant Tupinamba forebears, they did not like to live apart in elementary-family units.

Every three or four days, they packed up their meager possessions and set out on foot, for the rivers were not deep enough for canoes. Men carried their bows and arrows; women took their digging sticks, infants, family hammocks, net bags, and smoldering embers wrapped in green palm fronds for the night's fire. Fire-making was not known, and they had to carry live coals or borrow fire from another group. When they did plant, they searched out natural clearings because they lacked the stone tools necessary for slash-and-burn cultivation. They gave little care to the small amounts of sweet manioc, sweet potatoes, and tobacco that they planted, and consequently suffered skimpy harvests. The Siriono followed the game in a manner that brought them back to their gardens in time for harvest. But most vegetables and fruits in their diet were wild products gathered by the women on the day's trek.

Instead of wearing clothing, the Siriono painted their bodies with urucú for decoration and to ward off insect bites. They also wore necklaces of animal teeth to which was added the penis bone of the coati or gristle from the ankle of a harpy eagle as a magical charm against supernaturally induced illness or death.

During the course of his life, a man might take several wives. The first wife's hammock was hung to the right of her husband's, the second to the left, the third at his head, and the fourth (if any) at his feet. Since residence was matrilocal and the wives tended to be close matrilineal relatives, domestic friction was usually kept within bounds. The household leader was the head of this localized lineage, containing six or seven families, which constituted the hunting band. The Siriono exploited a large hunting area, but they did not fight with each other over territory and withdrew from an area when threatened by more aggressive neighbors. Simple beliefs in bush spirits directed their daily hunt, and they had few myths—their past forgotten in the all-absorbing present, in which fear of starvation invaded their nightly dreams.

Heading southward with the rivers, through the very middle of the continent, we continue on to enter a huge depressed plain known as the Gran Chaco, the great hunting ground, where all the world was on the move. To the east, the Paraguay River was its boundary, separating Chaco people from yet one more group of Tupian-speaking pilgrims, the Guaraní of Paraguay, who were tropical forest village horticulturalists. On the west, the plain reached the Andean foothills, homeland of the horticultural Chiriguano and Chané. On the south it merged with the pampas. It was a cultural and ecological cul-de-sac in which customs from the Andean and tropical forest peoples had reached a dead end, surviving only in a severely attenuated form. In the northern Chaco there was a desultory type of horticulture of the sort described among the Siriono, but this gave way entirely to hunting and gathering as one moved south.

Many small societies of different language families lived in the Chaco, but the most prominent group of its central and southern sections comprised those speaking Guaycuruan dialects. The name Guaycurú, used by the Guaraní, referred to the warlike Abipón, Mocoví, Caduveo, Lule, Mascoi, Toba, Pilagá, Mbaya, and others. The environment was markedly different from that of the tropical forest. Part of the year the Chaco was a very dry country, recording some of the highest temperatures in South America. If it were not for the seasonal overflow of rivers that formed huge lagoons, the land would have become an uninhabitable, dry, cracked crust. When these lagoons dried up unexpectedly, people were forced to migrate to the rivers, where they vied for territorial rights, much as they did during the fishing season.

Although it was by turns arid plain and impenetrable swamp, the Chaco provided its peoples with more wild plants and food trees than were found in the tropical forest. The algarroba tree, an evergreen producing large fleshy pods (carob, St. John's bread), supplied food that could be dried and eaten year-round. Many varieties of food-producing palms were available in the swamplands and along the major rivers. The region teemed with game, and the rivers were filled with fish in season. To outsiders like the Guaraní and Chiriguano, the Chaco was a forbidding place. To the Guaycuruans, it was a homeland of abundance which they exploited very successfully. The successive yields of varieties of edible plants during different seasons, and their irregular distribution, caused the Chaco people to migrate from place to place in an annual gathering cycle. Detaching from the main band and then reattaching to it, small extended-family groups foraged at times on their own, giving a pulsating aspect to the size and composition of the hunting and gathering bands. Social organization and activities were determined by the gathering cycle, and at no time was this more evident than during the harvest of the algarroba, when related bands came together. This was the time to renew kinship bonds, to feast, to arrange betrothals and stage marriages, to hold ritual performances with the shaman—in short, to rejoice and reaffirm belief in their uniqueness as "the people." Wet times, dry times, weariness, and rejoicing—this was the rhythm of Chaco life.

For two months of every year all Chaco peoples, even those from the far interior, left their habitats and semi-permanent houses and headed for the Pilcomayo, Bermejo, and Paraguay rivers. Risking trespass and consequent hostilities, bands rushed to the rivers for the fish runs. If possible, peaceful access was arranged by negotiation and payments of food to those groups already in place, but if not, there was open hostility. Some fished collectively in bands, like the Mataco, Pilagá, and Ashluslay. Others, the Abipón, Mocoví, and Toba among them, worked in extended-family groups. Two types of nets, one firm, one flexible, were used in the swifter rivers. Occasionally bows and arrows or bare hands were the weapons when fish were especially thick. Hooks and fish poisons were unknown.

Except during the fishing season, at least one man in each extended family hunted on a daily basis. When the entire band changed campsites, all the men immediately fanned out, killing as many animals as possible, while the women moved along behind, carrying their heavy loads of domestic goods and infants.

Yet they never missed a chance to forage for wild roots, lizards, seeds, and edible insects. After establishing a camp, men set up a variety of traps for the women to tend while they again went forth, with bows and arrows, spears, clubs, and bolas, to hunt the prized jaguars, peccaries, rheas, deer, and waterfowl. They were certain to find anteaters, armadillos, foxes, and iguanas on their quest, and even tapirs and caymans were not uncommon kills.

The men entered new hunting grounds and swept them clean by burning the grassland, scaring the large game out of their lairs. Smaller animals, springing out of the fire, were clubbed to death and those roasted in the conflagration were gathered up and eaten on the spot or piled up and carried back to the settlement. Now the men encircled the large game, moving ever and ever closer to their targets. Less dangerous game such as the rhea and the deer were clubbed, but it took many sharpshooters to bring down the peccary and the jaguar, with the bowmen shooting in a cross-fire pattern. After a successful hunt, the men returned laden to the settlement, where they remained until the meat supply ran low again.

The Chaco Indians had other ways of hunting game. A stalking pattern was used for taking rheas. Hunters camouflaged their heads and shoulders with grass, sneaking up within arrow or bola range. The Pilcomayo River peoples glued rhea feathers to their heads and arms and imitated the movements of the birds, hoping to approach unnoticed for the kill. They wore charms around their necks made of rhea feathers and the grass and leaves eaten by those birds. Some hunters painted themselves black, believing that this made them invisible to the bird. Others rubbed their bodies with magical plants. Since they thought that the special qualities of an animal were incorporated into the person who ate it, they preferred to consume animals they respected and whom they feared for their ferocity, like the jaguar, peccary, and tapir. But whatever the animal, it was eaten entirely, including the contents of the intestines.

Even when the Chaco Indians settled down for a month or more, their shelters were flimsy. They were constructed by the women, who used digging sticks to make a circular or elliptical set of holes in the ground deep enough to support stout branches, whose slender tips they interlaced to form a domed roof. Related families built long communal shelters consisting of a series of individual small huts. Sites for these shelters were selected with an eye to available water, at the edge of copses of trees or heavy brush, so that in case of surprise attack, people could retreat into a more easily defended hideaway.

Intricate body-painting and tattooing took the place of clothing. At most, people wore hide capes in very cold weather, crude moccasins to ease travel across vast sunbaked stretches, and decorative belts of knitted and dyed caraguata string. Adornment of the body, rather than full clothing, was a source of pride to the Guaycuruans, especially the use of ostentatious lip and ear plugs. These were inserted and enlarged from childhood on, so that an older person's

This drawing of a Camacan woman, who lived along the southeastern coast of present-day Brazil, is by Jean Baptiste Drebet, a French artist who lived in the region from 1816 to 1831. She is adorned with crescent-moon designs painted on her chest, a series of necklaces, and fresh flowers inserted in her headband.

earlobes might reach to the shoulders and the lower lip look like a protruding tongue. One group carried this to such extremes that the Spaniards called the tribe the Lengua. The Mocoví stuck feathers through their cheeks, and others shaved their heads, creating a tonsure effect or a bald patch running from forehead to crown. Pilagá, Abipón, and Mocoví women were heavily tattooed with intricate patterns that were begun in early childhood and completed just before marriage. Elaborate designs were painted on all parts of the body with genipa and urucú dyes, soot, ashes, and minerals that provided shades of black. Body painting was more than cosmetic artistry. It was of great symbolic importance in protecting warriors.

These Guaycuruan peoples earned themselves a reputation for fierce hostility throughout the Chaco, as well as among their Guaraní neighbors. Their main motives for fighting were familiar: to avenge the death of a band member, to prevent trespass on hunting or fishing grounds, to capture women and children of enemies. Traditional antagonisms pitted Toba against Pilagá, Mataco against Toba, Abipón against Mocoví, and so forth. And of course, all the Chaco peoples living along the Paraguay River, even those coming there seasonally, fought the Guaraní, who lived on the other side. In addition, the northern Chaco Mbaya fought with the Caduveo and Guaná of the Brazilian tropical forest. These blood feuds were conducted like hunting expeditions, carried out by a relatively small group of warriors who stalked the enemy with great stealth.

"It is time," said the lineage elder, "to avenge the death of our kinsman." With these words, he put the pattern of war in motion. Word had just come back to him from his own hunting party that a small extended-family group was separated from the main enemy band and was camped in the open and hence vulnerable to attack. Related males from other households were invited to take part and to discuss and agree upon tactics. Preparations for the raid and drinking and dancing to shore up courage often lasted for several days. Men danced, but women and children also participated in the festivities, drinking the chicha and listening to the lineage historian build up confidence by reciting past military exploits and also teach the young about the high points of bravery. The warriors themselves observed certain sexual and food taboos in order not to sap their strength. They painted their bodies with black and red dyes and donned ornaments that constituted their military regalia. Abipón, Mocoví, and Mbaya wore toucan beaks or deer antlers on their headbands. Enemy scalps and heads taken in previous battles were displayed during the dances, which were accompanied by pipes and whistles made from the leg bones of slain enemies.

Since stealth and surprise were essential, the raid began in the predawn hours, and if not successful or if one of the warriors was killed, they beat a quick retreat. The same cautious tactics were used by all Chaco societies, and there were actually few fatal casualties, for there was no glory in death. But this war party was victorious and returned to camp with its trophies: heads, scalps, and captive women and children. The heads were impaled on stakes; the scalps were given to women who had lost a husband in warfare; and the enemy women and children were incorporated into the band as drudge labor, some of the women later becoming wives or concubines. The festivities then began. To the beating of drums, the warriors' wives danced with the newly taken trophies, whooping their joy and singing vituperative songs about the enemy. The lineage genealogist and historian again participated in the activities, recounting stories of past blood feuding and promising future victories. After that, the band prepared for an anticipated counterattack. If none came immediately, the band moved out to establish a new settlement at a safe distance—a tactical withdrawal.

If the raiding party brought back its own dead, there was no victory feast, and funeral observances took precedence. When a person died, whether in war or from illness, the corpse was buried quickly but with elaborate ceremony. All members of the band assembled, some of the scattered segments notified by smoke signals. The lineage elders and shaman conducted the ceremony, which ensured that the deceased's spirit would not linger about but depart speedily for the afterworld. Certain precautions were taken if it was decided that the person died as a result of witchcraft. The Abipón took out both the heart and the tongue, boiled them, and buried them separately from the body. The Mocoví piled straw on the corpse and burned it. The Lengua made a cut where the evil spirit was said to have entered the body and put a hot coal, an armadillo's claw, and red ants into the wound. All of these actions helped to defeat the sorcerer.

After burial, the band began its mourning rites. Sometimes the whole settlement was burned as part of the ceremony. Often all the possessions of the deceased were burned. As a result, the ghost could not find a way back to the surviving group and, therefore, could not haunt them. Abipón funeral rites were most spectacular, lasting a week or more. All the women of the band chanted and demanded revenge, leaping about and waving their arms in a frenzy. Naked, with their hair hanging disheveled on their shoulders, they danced to beating drums and shrilling whistles, hissing and wailing. When they rested, the shaman took over and sang mournful songs. After a week, it was time to begin festivities to celebrate the departure of the deceased's soul to its final resting place, the land of the spirits. No longer did the ghost linger about the camp, and the group was now spiritually clean and rejuvenated. The Mataco and Lengua believed the dead lived in families and bands in an underworld where they continued to carry out a pale reflection of their earthly activities. The Toba believed that the afterworld was in the sky, where the sun always shone. Whatever the belief, and whether borrowed from Andean or tropical forest peoples or a product of their own speculations, their concepts of morality and proper handling of the dead served to bind the people together in a common ritual that gave solace and strength to the living.

We leave these hunters and gatherers of the Gran Chaco to their constant quest for new hunting territory, knowing that their hour of historical greatness came later, after they acquired horses from the Spaniards, learned their cavalry techniques, and became the scourge of a much vaster region than they occupied in 1492. The acquisition and military use of the horse radically changed Guaycuruan economic, political, military, and religious organization, culminating in one of the most dramatic cultural-ecological adaptations resulting from contact with Europeans in all of South America.

The southern Chaco blended into the Argentine pampas, a vast, dry, treeless plain of shoulder-high, saw-toothed grasslands. Anthropologists have recently begun to call this elongated triangle of the continent the Southern Cone, a usefully descriptive geographical reference. Along the northern tier of the Cone, between the Atlantic Ocean and the foothills of the Andes, were the Charrua, Querandí, and Puelche—all hunting and gathering in the grassy pampas. The southern, narrower part of the Cone was much more arid than the pampas and lacked abundant grass. It was a land of large, sandy, rocky

A Patagonian woman as depicted in the report of the Charles Wilkes U.S. Exploring Expedition, published in 1845. She was painted across her cheeks and lips, and wore little more than this cape of guanaco skin.

wastes with thorny scrubland and very little surface water. This was the home of the Tehuelche, who ranged over their hunting territories as far south as the Strait of Magellan. This region is called Patagonia (Land of the Big-Footed People), because Magellan's sailors thought that these rather tall Indians had especially outsized feet. In fact, their moccasins were stuffed with straw to ward off the cold, and therefore their feet seemed huge only to the unpracticed European eye.

The inhabitants of this harsh, treeless wilderness dearly loved it, understood it, and exploited it successfully by ingenious hunting and gathering techniques, with the help of beneficent supernatural forces. They did not live in huts but built themselves toldos, or windbreaks of guanaco skins tied to two or three poles embedded in the ground. Wood was hard to come by and, when found, was shaped into poles with stone adzes. So precious were those poles that they were used for many years and carried from one campsite to the next by women on their almost daily treks. Wind was fierce in the Southern Cone. Cold and damp gales from the raw Atlantic and Antarctic water swept across the steppes. The Patagonians protected themselves by draping over their otherwise naked bodies the skins of guanaco, fox, wildcat, and jaguar, stitching the smaller skins into a capelike garment. Both sexes wore pubic coverings of skin, adorned their bodies with painted designs, and ornamented themselves with bone jewelry. Tattooing was also common. Men were fastidious about pulling out their sparse facial hair.

Twenty or more toldos, each with its own cooking fire, comprised the camp of a patrilineal hunting band. If game was plentiful, the people stayed in one site for two or three days before moving on. If not, they broke camp the following day and trekked to the vicinity of another water hole, with the hope of stalking the game that came to drink. Because of the absence of rivers and lakes, both the people and the animals they hunted depended heavily on water holes that were scattered across the countryside. The hunters were thoroughly familiar with the location of the water holes and the habits of the game.

Each hunting band maintained friendly relations with its neighbors, even though each one guarded its own well-defined territory against trespass. If a neighboring band needed to hunt in another's territory, it had to obtain permission or run the risk of hostile retaliation. Good relationships were necessary among bands, because they were the basis of marriage alliances. Each patrilineal band was an exogamous social entity, meaning that men had to seek wives from other bands; marriage with a female of one's own band would have been considered incest. During the seasonal period of drought, two or more bands might be forced to congregate at one of the few water holes that had not dried up, sharing this scarce resource. It was at just such a time that marriages between members of two bands were negotiated and the terms of bride-price and dowry spelled out. Likewise, interband religious ceremonies, puberty rites for both boys and girls, and the celebration of births took place. But first, a large collective hunt had to be undertaken to provide abundant food for the festivities and a long respite from the usual migratory hunting and gathering pattern. Death, too, was a multilineage affair, since the deceased necessarily had relatives in several bands, and formal mourning ceremonies were postponed until joint band participation was possible.

The Tehuelche were the only people we have met so far who believed in a Supreme Deity. He was an otiose god who remained aloof from human affairs. His evil counterpart, however, was very active and was blamed for all misfortunes. Most public religious activity was designed to placate this evil god. The Supreme Deity was offered individual and spontaneous prayer. He was "Lord of the Dead," residing far beyond the stars, whom the souls of the dead joined if the people had properly buried and mourned for their bodies. That is what happened when an old man or woman died. The young who died went to an underworld, where they stayed until they became old. Their souls then entered a newly born child of their lineage—a form of reincarnation distinctive of the Tehuelche.

Just south of Patagonia, across the stormy Strait of Magellan, lived the Ona, who occupied most of the island of Tierra del Fuego, land's end. They had a lifestyle and a religious and moral order similar to that of the Tehuelche, with whom they maintained contact, despite the fact that neither possessed canoes. The shellfishing Yahgan, who occupied the archipelago on the fringe of Tierra del Fuego, and depended upon canoes in their daily food quest, occasionally ferried the Ona and Tehuelche across the treacherous waters of the strait.

The people of the Southern Cone, as well as the Ona, occupied game-rich environments that supported multifamily patrilineal bands and required collective hunting techniques. In contrast, the Yahgan and their neighbors on the archipelago, the Alacaluf, lived in independent elementary families that exploited scarce resources that did not support or require the collective activities of a large group.

The Yahgan, who called themselves Yamana, "human beings," inhabited many small islands, the peaks of submerged mountains at the southern end of Tierra del Fuego, where mean temperatures reached 50 degrees only in summer. These islands sometimes rose to a height of 1,500 feet and were heavily forested, strewn with decaying logs and thick underbrush. Since overland travel was nearly impossible, the Yahgan world was bound up in the surrounding stormy seas. A range of rugged mountains between them and the plains-dwelling Ona served to isolate them further, and since neither the Ona nor the Yahgan understood each other's environment, they had neither the desire nor the technology to exploit one another's territory.

Each day, despite the howling winds, sleet, and rain, the Yahgan family, naked except for small capes of sewn seal or fox skins, set out in its leaky canoe on a search for food. Mother, father, and children each had specific jobs to carry out. Arriving on the beach of a tiny island, the mother and children collected mussels, the mainstay of their diet. If the beach was crawling with crabs, everybody gathered them. Then if someone discovered that there was also an abundance of sea urchins in the shallow surf, attention turned to them. Even toddlers used pointed sticks to catch the crabs and sea urchins, while the mother and father employed three-pronged spears in a much more efficient manner. Sooner or later, the mother and older children set up a beehive-shaped hut and started to boil the catch of the day. Meanwhile, the father took the canoe into deep water to try his luck at fishing.

The canoe was the only means of family transport. In it were carried all the family's possessions, the spears and clubs and fishing lines, and many small netted bags and extra clothing, as well as the skins and poles used to make the night's shelter. It might also have contained a raised hearth of mud on which the Yahgan family preserved the ever-burning coals for their fires, shell cooking utensils, and all the other family paraphernalia.

Occasionally, the father repaired his canoe by replacing broken pieces or tightening some of the lashings in order to halt some of the leakage. It was a

Among the myriad peoples of the Amazon Basin, the Cubeos are distinctive because they have maintained an elaborate mourning ritual designed to dismiss the souls of deceased community members. This costume of bark cloth, collected in the twentieth century, indicates the complexity and persistence of ceremonial life in the region. Courtesy of the Field Museum of Natural History.

noteworthy creation, anywhere from twelve to twenty feet long with a center beam of three feet, narrowing to blunt ends. The outer skin was made of inch-thick tree bark stripped from a special evergreen with bone chisels and mussel-shell knives. The bottom and side pieces were sewn together with strips of whalebone and caulked with grasses mixed with mud. This supporting skeleton was then lashed to the bark skin and hardwood struts inserted and secured to the gunwales. It required the joint efforts of the men of several families to make a canoe. This interrupted the hunting and gathering schedule for several days, which meant that a temporary surplus of food had to be put aside. Even more important, the activity depended on the chance proximity of several related families.

Although the Yahgan family's way of life was a chancy one, fraught with grave physical dangers, there was always food to eat. They had made a remarkable adjustment to their harsh environment. A most important reason for their success was the idea, deeply embedded in their cultural value system, of never using up the natural resources in any given area. Their protection of the environment assured them that months later, in their migratory food quest, they might return to the same beaches or hunt seals and birds on the same rocky islets.

Individual families remained isolated from each other for most of the year, although they might have passed one another at a distance, or come into brief contact during their erratic movements in search of food. They went where the food was. Each family pursued its own way, regardless of where other families went. Since the location of resources varied from month to month and year to year, they had no fixed migratory routes, such as the Ona, the Tehuelche, and other hunter-gatherers of the Southern Cone had.

It was chance that enabled a number of elementary families to meet and remain together for any length of time. The amount of time depended on a temporary and unpredictable surplus of food, such as a dead or dying beached whale, a herd of seals trapped in the shallow waters of a lagoon, or the sighting of thousands of nesting birds on a tiny island. The people who first spotted such a windfall immediately sent up smoke signals to gather other families for the kill and for the celebrations that followed. It is unlikely that the same group of families participated in this cooperative effort on two consecutive occasions.

When an island of nesting birds was the target, all the available males assembled on the shore of an adjacent island, which might have been no more than fifty yards away, and waited there until dark, when all the birds had roosted for the night. They eased across the channel in their canoes, landing as quietly as possible. Then they fanned out along the shore and worked inland to surround the nesting ground. At a given signal, they lit their torches and rushed pell-mell toward the center of the circle, clubbing the birds that were blinded and confused by the lights.

Beached whales were another matter. No stealth was required, just very hard work. Men, women, and children attacked the beast with all the sharp tools at their disposal. It was difficult and time-consuming to cut through the thick hide of the twelve- to fifteen-foot-long animals. As each hole was made, it was enlarged until blubber and meat were removed in sufficient quantity. Like the birds, the meat was roasted over an open fire, since there were no pots in which to boil it. Some of the meat was eaten raw, sometimes after it had spoiled.

It was at these times that group ceremonies expressing the richness of Yahgan religious and moral beliefs took place. Besides whales, birds, and seals, many mussels, crabs, sea urchins, and fish were gathered, which provided enough food for families to hold the ciexaus, a puberty ritual that marked the passage from childhood to nubile status and without the observance of which a person could not marry. Part of this formal recognition of puberty involved the instruction of the initiates by elders in the mysteries of life, death, and religious morality that underscored life's responsibilities and perils.

During the period that food was being prepared, others began to build a large house of branches, which they covered as best they could with the skins used for their own individual beehive huts. The main branches that supported the roof were painted red, white, and black, the same colors used on decorative symbolic boards hung inside the house. Although ciexaus was held for pubescent boys and girls, all the adults participated in it as sponsors of the initiates. Each boy and girl wore a feathered headdress and carried a painted walking stick. They sat cross-legged in the middle of the house and listened respectfully while their sponsors instructed them in moral values, which included the obligations of working hard, sharing freely with other Yahgan, and being peaceful and mature, as well as a long schedule of do's and don't's. They were warned that failure to observe these traditions would anger the Supreme Being, who might punish them with an early death. The ceremonies were highlighted with singing, dancing, and feasting that extended this occasion of joy until the food ran out. This was the only communal activity.

Just to the north of the Yahgan, across the Beagle Channel, the Alacaluf carried on a very similar way of life and ritual activity. Like the Ona and the Yahgan, the Alacaluf staged their rituals only in time of plenty, sending up smoke signals to gather their nearest relatives, who in turn announced the event to others in the same way. The gatherings, then, were often extraordinarily large, and it was understood that the closest relatives would help out. The Alacaluf also used smoke signals to warn of hostile attacks by the Yahgan from the south or the Chono from the north, as well as of threats from other Alacaluf resulting from their own internal blood feuds.

To the north of the Alacaluf lived the Chono, who used canoes in an almost identical, dangerous environment. Squeezed in between the Alacaluf and the southernmost Mapuche people, who occupied the island of Chiloé off the southern Chilean coast, the Chono were the receivers of many different cultural ideas and ways of life. Despite the fact that their terrain was as difficult as that of the Alacaluf, there were small sectors in which horticulture was possible, and the Chono had stolen the simplest techniques of farming from the Mapuche. They grew potatoes, which they stored for surplus, providing a buffer to the exigencies of hunting and gathering. Yet in most aspects of their culture and social organization, they were like their aquatic nomad neighbors of the southern archipelago.

Heading north of Chono territory, past the island of Chiloé, and into the

This illustration from the memoirs of an Anglican missionary, H. J. Bernau, presents the method employed by the natives of the Berbice River to gather fish when the water level is low. Tribesmen prepare a poison by pounding vines and scattering them over an area which they have fenced off from the main course of the river. After the fish have been stupefied, they are gathered into dugout canoes. Larger fish were taken with a bow and arrow.

hilly forests of the mainland Mapuche, we arrive back at our starting point near the site of the Ice Age mastodon hunters who left clear evidence of human occupation 15,000 years ago.

By 1492, parts of South America had experienced an agricultural revolution that made it possible for people to grow food surpluses which could support large populations in relatively permanent settlements. The central Andes saw the culmination of this development and the rise of states and empires. But the Mapuche also benefited from agricultural and other inventions as they spread south into their territory from Peru.

When Columbus arrived in the Caribbean, the Mapuche had a thriving agriculture that included eight or nine varieties of maize, over thirty kinds of potatoes, and chili peppers galore. Other roots and grains were cultivated, as well as an assortment of fruits. In all, they raised more than sixty different kinds of crops in great abundance. Besides this, they gathered numerous kinds of wild plants, adding as many as seventy-five more species to the plants they cultivated. Although they killed guanacos and many kinds of birds, such as doves, ducks, and geese, hunting was not important and, because of the dense forests, was difficult and unrewarding. Fishing and shellfishing were done only by the coastal Mapuche. Porgies, silversides, flounder, and mullet were usually netted or speared. Sea urchins, crabs, mussels, and clams were gathered by both men and women.

Cultivation was the main subsistence activity and differed from the tropical forest slash-and-burn horticulture. The Mapuche cleared land for their gardens by burning down trees that they had killed by slashing, but similarity with the methods of the tropical forest people ended there, because the Mapuche were able to cultivate the same parcel of land over and over again. The fact that they usually left a parcel fallow for a year, so that it could replenish itself, indicated an entirely different agricultural technology. This meant that Mapuche were able to remain in their homesteads for a lifetime. In the drier, northern part of their territory, they practiced irrigation, digging a network of canals through which water was regularly distributed. This freed them from a dependency on rainfall.

For all the Mapuche, northern, southern, Andean, and coastal, the main crop was maize. Beans were grown in the same field, and after the maize was harvested, the stalks served as bean poles. On the first clearing, they were able to clean out all the underbrush, which they used as fuel. The larger trees were cut into planks and employed as walls for their houses. Stout branches were made into fences to corral the domesticated llamas that served as pack animals, as the source of wool to be woven into clothing, and, in special ceremonies, as food.

The soil, softened over the years, was cultivated with a wooden shovel and a three-pronged stick. A simple digging stick was all that was needed to make holes for the seeds. Men did the heaviest work. Women and children planted the seeds, weeded, and took part in the harvest. Neighborhoods performed farm work on a communal basis, each household assisting the others until the work was done. Harvests, however, belonged to the family that owned the field. Each phase of the work—planting, cultivating, and harvesting—was followed by a feast.

The Mapuche did not live in villages, but in large, patrilineal, extended-family houses that formed dispersed settlements of kinsmen. The houses, each on its own farmland, were in view of one another, but set apart at considerable distances. The settlements were established on the best farmlands, in valleys, on level stretches, and near the streams and rivers that were abundant in the Mapuche country. The hillsides were forested, providing logs for house-building, for "forts" serving as lookouts, and occasionally for palisades erected around small fortresses where the people gathered for protection in times of attack. The Mapuche raided each other's settlements regularly in a blood-feuding pattern similar to that of the tropical forest peoples.

In the more northern part of their extensive territory, the Mapuche made good use of the palisaded redoubts when Inca armies marched down from the central Andes and tried to establish work colonies among them. The Incas were partially successful in subduing the northernmost Mapuche, known as Picunche, but were repelled by the huge population in the heartland of the Mapuche territory. The Mapuche lacked tribal organization and peacetime military leaders. But in a time of large-scale hostilities, they were able to muster large fighting forces by the custom of "passing the arrow." This was a rallying symbol passed from one lineage group to another over a wide area. Temporary military leaders were chosen from among the best and wisest lineage elders. Less than a generation after the Inca failure to conquer the Mapuche, the Spanish army of Pedro de Valdivia suffered the same fate. Indeed, the Mapuche held off white armies and settlers until 1882, when they finally sued for peace and accepted life on reservations.

Since Columbus's time, many native societies have disappeared in South America as a result of contact with Europeans and centuries of maltreatment by their descendants. Yet a fair number of them have survived, if not prospered. Among them are the Mapuche. Over a million strong in modern-day Chile, they are one of the largest indigenous populations that retain their cultural and moral identity.

The most traditional of their values may be seen in their religious observances, for they have resisted Christian proselytization almost completely. Although their attendance at observances such as the agricultural fertility ceremony is many times what it was in the fifteenth century, and different crops and animals are part of today's ritual, the old-time gods, a pantheon of nature deities headed by an anthropomorphic Supreme Being, are still adored through animal sacrifice and the burning of food offerings. Evil spirits are still kept away from the ceremonial field by masked dancers, while the priests, all elders of the patrilineal-descent groups, make ritual incantations to the Supreme Being and to certain of the nature deities such as the god and goddess of the west wind and the god and goddess of abundance. They give thanks for the good harvest, for the increase in animals, for human well-being, and still petition the gods to shower future blessings on the Mapuche, the ancient "People of the Land."

GOVERNADOR·DELOSPVENTESDESTER.

CHACASVIOIOGACOSINGA

GVAMBOCHACA

uedor de puente   puentes

In the Realm of the Four Quarters 8

ALAN KOLATA

IN THE FALL OF 1492, as the fleet of Christopher Columbus approached landfall in the Caribbean, far to the southwest a native lord of the Andes was preparing to take dominion over the largest empire ever forged in the Americas. In that year, the Inca Huayna Capac, the last independent heir to a remarkable Andean social tradition grounded in aggressive religious and cultural proselytism, found himself on the verge of coronation as the supreme lord of a domain of startling proportions. The Incas' name for their empire reflected their own belief that they had conquered the Andean world: Tawantinsuyu, the Realm of the Four Quarters.

The lands of this realm incorporated a dazzling and sharply juxtaposed series of physical landscapes that ranged over the territories of five modern Andean republics: Peru, Bolivia, Chile, Argentina, and Ecuador. The world of the Inca contained an astonishing array of radically different environmental zones, replete with brusque contrasts in climate, vegetation, topography, soil, and other more subtle biological and physical associations.

The wild diversity of terrain, and therefore of ecological potential, represented a significant impediment to the achievement of regional political integration. Nevertheless, Incan armies were able to extend the power of their lords

On New Year's Day, 1613, an elderly Peruvian Christian named Don Felipe Guaman Poma de Ayala completed "A First New Chronicle on Good Government," and sent it off to the King of Spain. A large portion of this plea for imperial reform described life in the Andes prior to the Spanish conquest in 1532. Because the author was Native American, and because he belonged to a family which had served the Inca regime, his "Chronicle" is considered a unique source for the study of ancient Peru, even though we have no evidence that the King of Spain ever read it. Here an Inca governor stands before a suspension bridge along the royal road which ran the length of the mountain kingdom. Note the governor's sandals, formal tunic, and ear spools—all marks of high status.

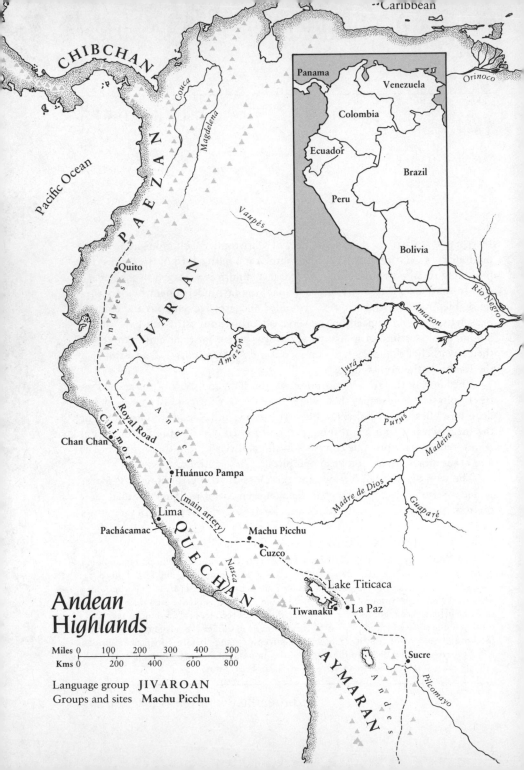

Caribbean

Orinoco

Inset map
Panama
Venezuela
Colombia
Ecuador
Peru
Brazil
Bolivia

CHIBCHAN

Pacific Ocean

Cauca

Magdalena

PAEZAN

Andes

Quito

JIVAROAN

Vaupés

Amazon

Amazon

Rio Negro

Jurá

Purús

Madeira

Royal Road

Chimor

Chan Chan

Andes

Huánuco Pampa

(main artery)

Madre de Dios

Guaporé

Lima

Pachácamac

Machu Picchu

Cuzco

QUECHAN

Nasca

Lake Titicaca

Tiwanaku

La Paz

Andean Highlands

Miles 0   100   200   300   400   500
Kms 0   200   400   600   800

Language group   **JIVAROAN**
Groups and sites   **Machu Picchu**

AYMARAN

Andes

Sucre

Pilcomayo

from the tortuous, dissected mountain slopes and valleys of highland Peru to the perpetually arid coasts strung along the western margins of the South American continent, and from the humid, subtropical enclaves encrusted in the great eastern flanks of the Andean massif to the cold, austere, and seemingly endless high plains of the Titicaca Basin.

The social obstacles that confronted the Inca political, economic, and military apparatus in its drive to conquest were no less bewildering in their diversity or daunting in their complexity and power. The Inca empire, at its apogee, incorporated over 200 separate ethnic groups, most speaking mutually unintelligible languages. The imperial bureaucracy strained to conquer, and then to administer, societies that covered the entire spectrum of human organization from small, dispersed bands of hunters and gatherers who inhabited isolated areas in the densely forested selva regions of eastern Ecuador and Peru to the powerful, immensely wealthy indigenous states of the Pacific coast and the Andean altiplano, such as the kingdoms of the Chimor, Chinca, Lupaca, and Colla peoples.

Despite these formidable environmental and social barriers to empire, within the evanescent space of three generations—during the fifteenth and early sixteenth centuries—the Incas succeeded in transforming themselves from a small tribal group jockeying for power in the circumscribed, relatively peripheral mountainous region around Cuzco in the southern highlands of Peru into the greatest single Indian political entity. Extending their authority over an area of some 3,000 miles in length from north to south, they ruled approximately seven million people.

Throughout the Andes, public works ordained by the emperors of the Incas dominated, and at times transformed, the natural landscape. Monumental cities, temples and fortresses of stone, marvelously engineered roads cut through granite mountain slopes, and, most especially, massive agricultural terraces and hydraulic works were emblematic of Inca power and productive capacity. Yet it is not so much these awesome products of the Inca empire that claim our curiosity but, rather, the processes that brought them into being.

What, for instance, were the cultural institutions that structured and gave impetus to the Incas' imperial ambition? What form of power did the Incas exercise over their conquered provinces far from their imperial capital of Cuzco? How did they mobilize the staggering labor force that was required to sustain their war machine while simultaneously erecting and maintaining the extensive and monumental public works? What kind of perceptions, thought processes, and beliefs informed the Inca worldview, confirming in their own minds that right to rule other nations? And what impact did the radical social transformation that the Incas experienced in their evolution toward statehood and imperial power have on the structure of the Inca nation itself and on other ethnic groups that they subjugated?

This molded pottery water jar decorated with a cat is from the Chimu region of what is now northern Peru. The Incas annexed the Chimus around 1470 and made them a distinct province within a rapidly expanding empire. Objects like this were subsequently traded widely throughout the Andes. Courtesy of the Field Museum of Natural History.

Answering these questions engages us in an exploration of the social history and the dynamics of the evolution of civilization throughout the Andes. The imperial achievements of Tawantinsuyu were not simply the brilliant invention of the kings of Cuzco, as Inca court propagandists, in a virtuoso display of self-aggrandizement, would have had us believe. They had not occurred in a cultural vacuum. The roots of the Incas' civilization, much like that of their Mesoamerican counterparts, the Aztecs, were firmly planted in the deep bedrock of earlier cultural traditions. Before the Incas, the political history of the Andes had been marked dramatically by the ebb and flow of other, more ancient city-states and empires. The Wari and Tiwanaku states of the Andean highlands had left an enduring legacy of aggressive imperial expansion in the same regions that the Incas would conquer some 700 years later. Many of the organizational tools that the Incas used to bind local populations to the yoke of their central government had been devised and elaborated in the centuries before them by these early predatory states, and they had long been common currency in the pan-Andean repertoire of state formation.

Similarly, on the desert coast of northern Peru, the kingdom of Chimor had been ruled by a dynasty of divine kings who had forcefully commanded the resources and the obeisance of a vast population for generations before the Incas even had pretensions to imperial rule. The richly decorated palaces and royal sepulchers at Chan Chan, the remarkable capital city of Chimor, had been the scenes of unimaginable exhibitions of kingly power and wealth when the first leaders of the Incas had been nothing more than a chaotic collection of competing warlords living in crude fortified compounds. The ideology and practice of divine kingship, like other institutions that became indelibly associated with the Incas, were clearly not exclusive to the lords of Cuzco. A long, rich stream of extant cultural beliefs, social institutions, and economic systems shaped the essential contours, if not the precise course, of Inca state history.

Thus, the story of the Incas, who in 1492 were in the midst of extending their domain in the Andes, was the final pre-Columbian chapter of an exceedingly complex, vibrant saga of human adaptation over several millennia within a setting of formidable environmental extremes. The process of successful cultural adaptation to the harsh physical realities of the Andean world had elicited similar organizational and institutional responses from a broad range of cultures in this important region, one of only two that witnessed the evolution of a pristine civilization in the New World. To understand the historical underpinnings of the Inca state, we must first grasp the intimate relationship between the economy and the environment in the Andean world.

Overall, a singular and most striking aspect of the Andean natural environment is that it is banded, both horizontally and vertically. Proceeding roughly north-south along the Pacific coast, the horizontal bands are formed by coastal rivers piercing the monotonous gray-brown desert, one of the most forbidding tracts of land on earth. These rivers, yielding a series of fertile belts in an otherwise sterile and hostile environment, over the millennia became oases for coastal peoples.

The vertical bands are the product of the Andean range. "Who," wrote Herman Melville in *Moby Dick,* "could show a cheek like Queequeg, which, barred with various tints, seemed like the Andes' western slope, to show forth in one array, contrasting climates, zone by zone?" This climatic stratification that inspired Melville is the result of changes in altitude, correlated with variation in precipitation and topographic relief. Altogether, we can visualize the Andean natural environment as a grid in which changes along the coastal end of the valleys alternate sharply between fertile and sterile zones, while vertical zonal changes are formed by a gradual increase in available moisture. Changes in the grid are stark horizontally but subtle vertically, with different microenvironments grading one into the other.

Because of these manifold bands, each providing access to a different suite of natural resources, it is not surprising that in the ancient Andean world, environment and economic systems were inextricably linked. The linkage was most dramatic in the highland zones—the Andean intermontane basins, mountainous eastern slopes, and altiplano—that were the core regions of the Inca empire. Here the irregular spatial distribution and temporal availability of subsistence resources profoundly influenced the structure of native Andean populations.

Most of the indigenous peoples incorporated by the Incas into Tawantin-

Terraced fields near Cuzco. Andean farmers built these plots along the sides of the Uru-
bamba Valley to make maximum use of their mountainous environment. Courtesy of the
American Museum of Natural History.

suyu were relatively self-sufficient agriculturalists, generally capable of producing enough food to satisfy their basic caloric requirements. The inhabitants of the highland basins above 9,000 feet in elevation, however, were severely constrained by the kinds of food crops they could cultivate. Agriculture at high altitudes in the Andes is inherently risky, prone to debilitating frosts, hail, wind, droughts, and floods. Only the hardy, high-altitude-adapted tubers such as potatoes, oca, ullucu, and mashwa and the unique chenopod grains, quinoa and cañiwa, grow in that dour environment. In starkest numerical terms, approximately 95 percent of the principal Andean food crops can be cultivated below 3,000 feet, but only 20 percent reproduce readily above 9,000 feet.

The implication of this contrasting resource distribution is clear. In order to enlarge the variety and quantity of their foodstuffs and reduce the risk of subsistence agriculture, people living at high altitudes sought access to the products of lower, warmer climatic zones. The most highly prized of the temperate-land crops were maize and coca. Maize was important both as a bulk food product and as the principal ingredient of chicha, or maize beer, an essential component of ceremonial feasts that were hosted by political leaders throughout the ancient Andean world. Coca was the preeminent ritual plant of the Andes, indispensable for the entire panoply of formal communal ceremonies related to agricultural and animal fertility and transitions in the human life cycle, and for a multiplicity of informal rites performed by individuals and households.

In most of the pre-industrial world, the problem of different resource distribution is resolved by long-distance trade carried on through an institutionalized complex of merchants and markets. These mechanisms result in the flow of desired commodities through relatively long, indirect chains of barter over which the end consumer exercises little control. Although highland Andean peoples participated in such merchant-mediated networks, they relied more heavily on the direct appropriation of desired resources by a strategy of maintaining autonomous production forces in as many ecological zones as possible. The distinct commodities produced in these various zones were extracted, processed, and transported entirely by members of a single group. This economic strategy enhanced community self-sufficiency by directly ensuring the diversification of production and by eliminating the uncertainty engendered by potentially fragile trading relationships and the manipulations of merchant brokers.

Since the principal axis of environmental and natural resource variation in the Andes derives from altitudinal change, the strategy of direct access to a maximum number of ecological zones by a single group has been called "verticality," or vertical economy. Even today, one can see rural communities, particularly along the eastern slopes of the great Andean cordillera, maintaining use rights simultaneously to pasturelands for llama and alpaca in the high, cold meadows of the mountains above 12,000 feet, to potato, oca, and quinoa fields in the mountainous basins over 9,000 feet, and to plots of maize, coca, and other warm-land crops in regions well below 6,000 feet.

The exploitation of altitudinally stratified resources in the Andes takes many specialized forms, but we can identify two principal variations that capture the essence of this remarkable economic practice. The first is what may be referred to as compressed verticality, in which a single village or ethnic group resides in a physical setting that permits easy access to contiguous or closely located ecological zones.

Different crop zones, pasturelands, or other localized resources such as sources of salt, honey, or fruit trees are within one or two days' walk of the parent community. Generally, the parent community is situated above 6,000 feet in an agriculturally productive mountain basin. Individual members of the community or, at times, the entire village may reside temporarily in one of the lower ecological zones to manage the extraction of products unavailable in the high-altitude homeland. The village maintains temporary dwellings on a number of ecological "floors" and rotates residence among them in accordance with the agricultural and pastoral cycle of the seasons. The efficiency of this system relies heavily on group solidarity and the sharing of reciprocal obligations. Communities engaged in this form of verticality are characterized by strong bonds of kinship and by an ethic of self-help.

The second variation resembles compressed verticality in that a single group maintains residences in multiple, altitudinally stratified environmental zones. But in this stratagem, which has been called the vertical archipelago, the ethnic group or village exploits resources in zones that are noncontiguous and widely dispersed, constituting a series of independent "islands" of production. In some villages engaged in this strategy, community members must trek up to ten to fourteen days from their home base in the mountains to reach distant fields in the tropical lowlands.

Although examples of the vertical archipelago economy still exist in the Andes, this form of land use was most highly developed in the pre-Columbian world by complex societies such as the indigenous Aymara kingdoms of the Titicaca Basin. In these kingdoms, the vertical archipelago was transformed into a formal, specialized system of production in which satellite communities from the home territory were sent to reside permanently as colonists in distant tropical forest and Pacific coastal locations. There, the colonists grew crops and extracted products for their own consumption and for transshipment back to their high-altitude compatriots. By establishing this policy of permanent colonization, these polities enhanced the efficiency of their economic system by producing crops and other goods in multiple ecological zones. In this system, food crops, raw products, and other commodities, rather than people, circulated through the archipelago.

The colonists from the highlands frequently shared the resources of the foreign territories in which they were resettled with the indigenous inhabitants, at times adopting the dress and customs of the local people. The colonists, however, maintained basic rights to marriage, residence, familial lands, and property in their communities of origin in the distant highlands. The number and kind of colonists maintained by the altiplano kingdoms in the various islands of production were highly variable, but could range from single extended families of a few people to entire village communities.

Rather than dismantle the native tradition of the vertical archipelago when they began to reorganize populations and production in their nascent empire, the Incas expanded and intensified this uniquely Andean economic strategy. This trait of co-opting and adapting local institutions, beliefs, and patterns of economic and political behavior to the needs of their empire distinguished the Incas. The success of their imperial expansion owed more to the Inca elite's perceptive manipulation of ancient pan-Andean values, economic strategies, and political concepts concerning the reciprocal relationship of rights and obligations between community leaders and their people than to brute superiority in force of arms. The adoption and further development of the vertical archipelago is one example. But to understand the Incas better, we must first gain a more specific vision of the basic economic and political institutions that formed the organizational armature of their state.

Perhaps the most intriguing questions regarding the Incas concern the social and political means they employed to create rapidly and rule successfully an empire of enormous ethnic, linguistic, and geographic diversity. We can derive at least partial answers by exploring the various organizational tools they used when incorporating a new valley or province into their political orbit.

One of their first steps after absorbing a new territory was to reorganize the prevailing system of land tenure to suit their empire's economic needs. The great Spanish cleric and chronicler of the Incas, Bernabé Cobo, writing in the mid-seventeenth century, provided a thorough account of how the reorganization of productive land was undertaken. When the Incas, he said, "settled a town, or reduced one to obedience, he set up markers in its boundaries and divided the fields and arable land within its territory into three parts. . . . One part he assigned to religion and the cult of his false gods, another he took for himself, and the third he left for the common use of the people. . . . In some provinces the part assigned to religion was greater; in others that belonging to the Inca; and in some regions there were entire towns which, with their territory and all that it produced, belonged to the Sun and the other gods . . . in other provinces (and this was more usual), the king's share was the largest. . . . In the lands assigned to religion and to the crown, the Inca kept overseers and administrators who took great care in supervising their cultivation, harvesting the products and putting them in the storehouses."

Cobo was fascinated by the manner of disposition of the third division of arable land that was to be allocated to the local inhabitants in the nature of commons. "These lands," he remarked, "were distributed each year among the subjects by the chief [the local ethnic lord], not in equal parts, but proportionate to the number of children and relatives that each man had; and, as the family grew or decreased, its share was enlarged or restricted. No man was granted more than just enough to support him, be he noble or citizen, even though a great deal of land was left over to lie fallow . . ."

This brief passage encapsulates a number of fundamental insights into the nature of ancient Andean rural society. It makes clear that productive lands were held in common by the local communities and ethnic groups. Beyond the level of individual nuclear families, these communities and ethnic groups were organized into social groupings known as ayllus. Generally, the Andean ayllu was a group of related families who held land in common and traced their descent from a common ancestor. There was no concentration of arable land or pasturage in the hands of a few wealthy private owners. Individuals as heads of households only held the usufruct, or use right, to parcels of land, and the amount of land that could be exploited for the benefit of the household was not permanently fixed. The political leaders of the community, called curacas in the Andes, determined on a periodic basis the subsistence needs of each household, and readjusted the size of the designated land allotment to conform with changes in the composition of these households. This system of communal disposition of productive lands reflected the age-old Andean ethic of mutual aid: no individuals were allowed to claim basic natural resources as their personal property, but at the same time members of each household retained the right of assured access to sufficient community farmland or pastureland to support themselves and their family.

The system of communal land tenure also played a significant role in maintaining an ecological equilibrium in the sometimes fragile agricultural environment of the Andean highlands. Since individuals were not permitted to acquire land as personal property, they had no opportunity to enrich themselves in the short term by continuously cultivating the greatest amount of land possible and then selling off surplus agricultural products at a profit. This built-in constraint on the potential for entrepreneurship and monopolization of natural resources by individuals ensured that the community as a whole would always have enough productive lands to guarantee its survival. Cobo's bemused observation that this system resulted in large sectors of land left fallow underscored this equilibrating effect of traditional Andean concepts of communal property holding and decision making.

The Incas understood and respected these native notions of community autonomy and self-determination. Although when the Incas absorbed a new province they expropriated substantial tracts of land for the purposes of the state, they made certain at the same time that sufficient land was allotted for the support of the local communities. More importantly, they chose shrewdly not to usurp the traditional prerogative of the curacas in deciding how this land would be allocated among their members.

Elsewhere in his commentary, Cobo hit upon the true key to the tremendous productive capacity of the Incan state. After the Incas expropriated a certain portion of arable lands in newly conquered provinces for the support of the state cults and the central bureaucracy, "the labor of sowing and cultivating these lands and harvesting their products formed a large part of the tribute which the taxpayer paid to the king." In addition to carving out lands from the conquered provinces for themselves, the Incas also exacted an annual tax from villagers and townspeople in the form of agricultural labor. The local inhabitants were required to prepare, plant, weed, and harvest the state fields. As Cobo described it, the products of these fields were then processed and stored under the watchful eyes of Inca overseers in immense state granaries.

In a world where money was not a principal feature of economic transactions, taxation took the form of labor service for the state. Although payments in kind, such as designated quantities of tropical forest bird feathers, honey, salt, dried fish, mollusks, and other raw products, were assessed by Inca administrators in some provinces, the principal form of taxation and source of revenue for the Inca state was the agricultural labor tax. This intense emphasis on discharging obligations to the state by labor service rather than by payments of currency, standardized manufactured goods, or other forms of primitive money, separates the Andes from other centers of early civilization such as Mesoamerica.

The agricultural labor tax was not an invention of the Incas, but was another ancient feature of the Andean social landscape. Throughout the Andes, local political leaders and ethnic lords had extracted surplus labor in community-owned fields from their subjects for generations before the coming of the Incas. The Incas, operating within an idiom familiar to any pre-Columbian Andean farmer to whom work rather than money was the essential means of discharging economic and social debts, simply assessed additional labor obligations on the local communities.

Although Inca provincial administrators set quotas for the labor tax in each village and province and supervised the accounting of agricultural goods that flowed into the state storehouses, it was the responsibility of the local curacas to give individual work assignments to the heads of households, who then distributed the tasks among their members, including all able-bodied men, women, and children. With the onset of the highland planting season in August and September, the two classes of fields that belonged to the state—those reserved for the support of the state religious cults and the central bureaucracy—were worked first, followed by the fields that remained for the support

TRAVAXA
CHACRAMÃTAPISCO

A farmer keeping birds away from his crops. In October (spring in the Andes), when seedlings began to appear, farmers took their slings to the fields to drive away birds and other predators.

of the local populations. The fields were divided into long strips or sections, called suyu by the Incas, and each section became the responsibility of an individual household, or group of related households. By incorporating the local leaders into the supervision of the agricultural labor tax, the Incas reduced their own administrative costs. More importantly, however, they minimized their intrusion into the daily life of the provincial villages and towns, permitting them to maintain the politically valuable illusion that these communities retained local autonomy.

Apart from the agricultural tax assessed at the level of the community, the Incas also demanded a second form of annual labor service from taxpayers. This obligation, called the mit'a, varied greatly in kind and length of service. The mit'a was used by the Incas to provide temporary work gangs for the construction of huge public monuments, for filling the ranks of the Inca army during its frequent campaigns in the provinces, for cultivating the private estates of the Inca elite, for extracting precious metals from state mines, and for many other services for the state that required heavy manual labor. The scale of some mit'a operations was truly astonishing. Spanish chroniclers related that over 30,000 men at a time were mobilized for the construction of Sacsahuamán, the great fortress-shrine of the Incas perched on the mountain slopes above the imperial capital of Cuzco.

The Inca mit'a labor tax system possessed a number of uniquely Andean features that distinguished it from corvée, or other forms of forced labor routinely employed by empires elsewhere in the ancient world. Much like the agricultural tax, the mit'a system was administered principally through local officials of the various ethnic groups subject to the Incas. When a draft of men was required for a military campaign, or to construct a bridge or an irrigation canal, the Inca governor in the affected province would call upon the heads of the various villages, towns, and ethnic groups, who would each be obliged to supply a designated number of taxpayers to complete the task. These local officials would then select from among the pool of eligible taxpayers (married heads of households) in their community on a rotational basis to supply their quota. In this way, the labor obligation was distributed equitably both among the different local ethnic groups in the province and within the groups themselves. No individual taxpayer was forced to serve the mit'a more frequently than another, and, apart from some special exemptions, all communities and ethnic groups participated in the system, contributing labor service according to the size of their population.

Local autonomy in implementing the mit'a labor tax was one of the special characteristics of the system that enhanced its efficiency and flexibility. But there was another principle in this system of taxation that reveals its character as a quintessential native Andean institution. To the indigenous peoples of the Andes, the mit'a was not perceived as a simple, one-sided tax debt assessed by their political superiors. Rather they viewed the mit'a as a complex skein of reciprocal obligations. If the government compelled them to contribute labor on public projects, or on the private estates of the ruling elite, the state, in turn, had the obligation during the period of labor service to provide the taxpayer with food, drink, clothing, tools, and housing if the project was distant from the home community.

To commoners, the Incan mit'a was a variant of an ancient pattern of reciprocity among family, kinsmen, and neighbors that, even today, remains a vital principle of social relations in rural Andean communities. In this system, for instance, a newly married couple, with the aid of local officials, may call on their relatives and friends to help them build their first house. In return for this donated labor, the couple, and perhaps their immediate family, provide food, drink, and hospitality while the job is completed. They also incur a future obligation to contribute some equivalent service to those who participated in the house raising. This mix of mutual labor service and hospitality permits individuals to mobilize labor beyond that available in their households and contributes to community solidarity.

When the Incas assessed the mit'a labor tax, they acknowledged the reciprocal nature of the social obligation by holding large-scale ceremonial banquets in the principal administrative centers of the province. Local political leaders and commoners were feted with great quantities of maize beer and food drawn from the imperial warehouses. At times on these occasions, the Inca administrators would also distribute clothing and sandals to the mit'a work gangs. Of course, if one compared the relative economic value of the labor service contributed by commoners with that of the hospitality and occasional suit of clothes contributed by the central government, there was no equivalency. The purpose and heart of the system, however, was not to exchange work for an equivalent value in goods, but to reaffirm symbolically the fundamental social principle of reciprocity.

That symbolism was projected vividly by a telling ritual convention. Theoretically, the Incas were obliged to "request" mit'a work crews from the local curacas; they could not compel them directly by fiat. In practice, this convention was little more than a fiction. At any time the Incas had sufficient coercive power to force subject communities into compliance. By engaging in this symbolic gesture of reciprocity and ritualized state generosity, the Incas confirmed, in at least a fictive sense, the authority and autonomy of local leaders and their communities, achieving in the process an enormous propaganda coup. The Incas, like any imperial state, held the power to rule by force and intimidation. But whenever possible, they chose instead to govern by persuasion through the local chain of command, respecting at least in name the basic institutions that formed the foundations of traditional Andean societies.

Although the agricultural tax and the mit'a labor service were the two principal sources of generalized revenue for the Incas, there were several specialized institutions that contributed substantially to the productive energy of the Inca state. In addition to their function as tools of production, these institutions performed strategic roles in Inca statecraft, emphasizing the intimate nexus between economic and political behavior in the Inca regime.

The first, known as the mitimae, held special fascination for the Spaniards, possibly because they recognized certain elements embedded in the institution that echoed their own traditions of statecraft. The contemporary Spanish chronicler and soldier Pedro de Cieza de León left a detailed description of the mitimae that portrayed the essence of the institution. "As soon as one of these large provinces was conquered," he wrote, "ten or twelve thousand of the men and their wives, or six thousand, or the number decided upon, were ordered to leave and remove themselves from it. These were transferred to another town or province of the same climate and nature as that which they left . . . and these were called mitimaes, which means Indians come from one land to another. They were given land to work and sites on which to build their houses. And these mitimaes were ordered by the Incas to be always obedient to what their governors and captains ordered, so that if the natives should rebel, and

Peruvian goldsmiths at work. This engraving from Girolamo Benzoni's 1565 account of travels in Spain's American colonies shows a group of Peruvian craftsmen working before a house that displays the adaptation of Incan stonework to European house design. While the workers on the left melt gold ingots, the craftsman on the right hammers sheets into goblets.

they supported the governor, the natives would be punished and reduced to the service of the Incas. Likewise if the mitimaes stirred up disorder, they were put down by the natives. In this way these rulers had their empire assured against revolts and the provinces well supplied with food, for most of the people, as I have said, had been moved from one land to another."

In a passage remarkable for its analytical perceptiveness, Cieza de León went on to distinguish three classes of mitimaes—military, political, and economic. The military mitimae served an important function as border guards, populating and commanding army garrisons on the fringes of the expanding Inca state. These were essentially groups of soldier-citizens who maintained a military profile on behalf of the Incas, as well as reclaiming and cultivating lands and herding llama and alpaca on the border zones of the empire. In many respects, these mitimaes fulfilled roles similar to those of the army garrisons and civilian colonists who were established in frontier areas of the Roman Empire. Frequently, rudimentary army camps on the Roman frontier were transformed over time into colonial "new towns" through the actions of the legionnaires who remained for many years, establishing farms, roads, markets, and smithies, and engaging in a host of other urban occupations.

The second class of transplanted colonists, the political mitimae, also served security functions. They were more numerous than the military mitimae and were found in every province of the empire. These mitimae had been forcibly removed from their homelands and resettled in other provinces, where they were required to retain their distinctive ethnic costume, headdress, customs, and forms of social organization. The strategic goal underlying the Incas' implantation of political mitimae was to reduce the chances for rebellion in conquered provinces by shattering traditional patterns of shared ethnic identity among large contiguous populations. By intermixing local inhabitants with pockets of foreigners in self-contained colonies, the Incas substantially inhibited the potential for subversive political coalitions. "In this way," observed Cieza de León, "all was quiet, and the mitimaes feared the natives, and the natives feared the mitimaes, and all occupied themselves only in obeying and serving."

Cieza de León characterized the third use of mitimae colonists as "stranger" than the others. He went on to describe these economic mitimae in the following terms: ". . . if, perchance, they had conquered territory in the highlands or plains or on a slope suitable for plowing and sowing, which was fertile and had a good climate . . . they quickly ordered that from nearby provinces that had the same climate as these . . . enough people come in to settle it, and to these lands were given, and flocks, and all the provisions they needed until they could harvest what they planted . . . For a number of years no tribute was exacted of these new settlers, but on the contrary they were given women, coca, and food so that they would carry out the work of settlement with better will."

To Cieza de León and other Spanish military men the use of frontier garrisons and colonial outposts was entirely familiar. But the Inca principle of economic mitimae was alien to these representatives of an essentially feudal, medieval European tradition. First, the institution incorporated the unfamiliar Andean ideal of reciprocity. In transplanting populations to reclaim productive lands in a new province, the state was obligated to provide the colonists with a "grubstake": food, coca, and women. Second, these mitimae colonists were exempted from taxation until they could reclaim enough land to sustain themselves and produce a surplus for the state. Finally, and perhaps most importantly, few Spanish chroniclers or administrators grasped the significance of the economic mitimae as state expressions of the Andean vertical archipelago economy. The principal intent of the economic mitimae was to enhance the productive capacity of the Inca state by reclaiming marginal land and, in some cases, by focusing the labor of thousands of transplanted colonists on the production of a single prestige crop, maize.

One of the most remarkable and well-documented uses of economic mitimae occurred during the reign of Huayna Capac (1493–1527). This last independent emperor of the Incas expelled the native populations of the Cochabamba Valley, one of the richest and most fertile in Bolivia, in order to install 14,000 new colonists from a variety of ethnic groups, who were placed there under the direct control of two Inca governors. These multiethnic colonists were brought to Cochabamba explicitly to produce maize for the state. The vast quantities of maize that flowed into the imperial storehouses in Cochabamba were eventually shipped to Cuzco for ultimate consumption by the Inca army. Huayna Capac completely reorganized the system of land tenure in Cochabamba to accommodate this grand scheme of repopulation and intensive state maize production. He divided the entire valley into 77 long strips, or suyu, and then assigned individual ethnic groups to work the suyus or fractional parts of suyus, depending on the topographic context of the designated strip and the population size of each colonizing ethnic group. Only 7 of these strips of land, interspersed among the other 70 suyus, were allotted to the 14,000 colonists for their own subsistence. The remaining portion, more than 90 percent of the arable land in the valley, was given over to intensive production of maize for the state.

As was the case with other multiethnic mitimae colonization schemes, the work assignments and other internal affairs of each ethnic group were governed by the group's own political leaders. These persons were then responsible to the two Inca governors who headed up the political hierarchy. In return for their service to the Incas, the various ethnic curacas were rewarded with small plots of land within the valley, as well as with some Inca prestige goods such as cotton mantles, and occasionally with women for secondary wives. By Inca governmental decree, each group maintained its own ethnic costume, headdress, and way of life.

It is clear that the Cochabamba economic mitimae served multiple purposes for the Inca state. Primarily, they were a tremendous economic engine, capable of producing massive quantities of maize for the state in at least two annual crops. More than 2,000 preserved Inca stone storehouses on the hillslopes of the Cochabamba Valley attest to the productive capacity of these transplanted colonists. Secondarily, of course, these colonists performed an important security function. A series of transplanted, fragmented ethnic groups working side by side in Cochabamba presented less of a threat to the state than the potentially unified indigenous inhabitants of the valley deported by the Incas.

The three categories of Inca mitimae, then, crosscut each other. Political mitimae frequently served economic functions; military mitimae were, almost by definition, also political mitimae; and large-scale economic mitimae colonization schemes such as in the Cochabamba Valley, by their organization and multiethnic composition, became simultaneously effective security devices. Although the principal colonization projects organized by the Incas focused on agricultural development schemes, mitimae colonists were also established to exploit specific concentrated natural resources such as salt, gold, silver, timber, clay for pottery, semiprecious stones for jewelry, hard stone for construction, and the like. The number of colonists relocated in these projects varied greatly, ranging from extended families to entire villages and ethnic groups reaching into the thousands, as in the case of Huayna Capac's reorganization of the Cochabamba Valley. We have no precise information on the total number of people removed from their homelands and resettled elsewhere. But all sources indicate that it was a substantial portion of the population. Such massive transfers of communities and villages as mitimae, who became directly dependent upon the Inca state bureaucracy for political security and for the potential of enhancing their own social position and economic well-being, resulted in a gradual dissemination of Inca language, values, expectations, and cultural beliefs. Under the impact of this program of population mixing on an imperial scale, old ethnic identities, loyalties, and beliefs began slowly to transform themselves in conformity with the new Inca ideal, enhancing the unification of the empire itself.

The Incas assiduously promoted identification with the central government through three other forms of labor relations: the yanacona, camayo, and aclla institutions, which were, in essence, Inca names for special status relationships between individuals and the state. The yanacona have been interpreted as everything from a true slave class of the state responsible for the heaviest manual labor to domestic servants for the Inca elite. Perhaps the single most satisfactory definition of the term yanacona is "personal retainer." In many respects, the yanacona were much like vassals in a feudal state. They were attached to the households of individual Inca lords and owed personal fealty to them. In return for personal service to their liege lords, the yanacona were generally exempted from the agricultural and mit'a labor tax obligations assessed against the ordinary citizens of the realm.

The rich variety of services that they performed for their Inca overlords implies that there were many kinds of yanacona situated within a complex hierarchy of status. Some yanacona cultivated the private estates of the Inca elite, others gathered firewood, cooked, managed private llama herds, or served as skilled artisans in the private households of their lord, or in the temples of the state cults. Like some powerful officials of pharaonic Egypt who were originally of commoner status, many yanacona also held privileged and responsible positions in the governance of the empire. They served as petty officials on the staffs of Inca provincial governors, frequently overseeing the labor of transplanted mitimae colonists. In return for faithful service and personal loyalty, these yanacona were rewarded with gifts of land, women, food, clothing, and emblems of their special status in the eyes of the Inca state, such as a particularly fine cotton mantle, or perhaps a copper cup, armband, ring, or other adornment. Since the yanacona, particularly those who served in the royal households of the Incas, owed their relatively high status to personal relationships with the Inca elite, their bond of traditional loyalty to ethnic groups or villages of origin was weakened in favor of their service to the Inca government. Through time the yanacona became essential players in the daily administration of the empire and, like the mitimae colonists, pivotal elements in the Inca strategy of domination and governance in the conquered territories.

The special civic status of camayos was similar to that of the yanacona. They labored full-time on behalf of individual Inca lords in the royal households in Cuzco and in the provinces; they were exempt from the otherwise universal labor tribute; and, as with the yanacona, their status was inherited, handed down from generation to generation through the male line. Unlike the highest-status yanacona, however, who could hold positions of trust and moderate power as petty managers and enjoy some upward mobility through the social hierarchy of the Inca state, the camayos held specific, fixed occupations that they discharged for the Inca elite throughout their lifetime. Documents of the early sixteenth century preserve for us an expansive list of specialized occupations of people identified as camayos. They were miners of precious metals, stonemasons, carpenters, weavers of fine textiles, potters, dye makers, feather, wood, bone, and shell workers, goldsmiths, hunters, herders, honey gatherers, herbalists, coca cultivators, porters, litterbearers, gladiators, and bodyguards.

Often, entire villages containing one or two hundred people specialized in a particular craft occupation, such as weaving, woodworking, or potting. These villages of camayos supported their daily subsistence needs by cultivating land given to them by the Inca state for that purpose, or by exchanging their craft products for food. Certain camayo groups such as salt miners and silversmiths exploited, or depended upon, concentrated natural resources for their products. Frequently, these groups were moved from their villages of origin by the Inca state to new sources of essential raw materials. Like the more numerous transplanted mitimae colonists engaged in agrarian and pastoral pursuits, these craft-specialized camayos became a strategic part of the state-managed, vertical archipelago economy by providing a constant flow of desired commodities to the Inca elite.

Many of the products of the craft camayos were essential for the massive public demonstrations of generosity and for the private gifts given to assure the loyalty of local curacas, who were the key to Inca political patronage and the control of newly conquered provinces. Some of the finest artisans of the craft camayos achieved wide repute, honor, and prestige within the royal households of Cuzco, and were materially rewarded for their virtuosity in creating exquisite objects of display. But despite the possibility of improving their economic status, the camayos could not aspire to, or attain, an elevated social position. In the Inca state, vertical movement in the hierarchy of power was strictly controlled.

To the modern mind, perhaps the most exotic of the specialized forms of labor relations created by the Inca state was the aclla, or "chosen women." The Inca rulers selected young females to live communally in special residential compounds, referred to as the acllahuasi (house of the chosen women), in the larger cities of the empire. There the women performed a variety of services for the state, spinning cotton and wool for the clothing of the Inca elite, weaving particularly luxurious textiles, cooking delicacies and brewing maize beer

Left: Guaman Poma's depiction of Incan granaries. According to Guaman Poma, these storehouses were built throughout the Inca empire to hold tribute that included dehydrated potatoes, dried meat, cotton, chilies, coca, and manioc. A scribe records contributions by means of the quipu. *Right:* Major Incan shrines were attended by groups of virgins, or "chosen women." Some members of these orders worked in the fields, played instruments, or wove fine cloth, but Guaman Poma's drawing shows a group performing what was considered the most prestigious activity: spinning and weaving cloth for religious figures in the shrine.

in great quantities for public ceremonies, and tending to the daily chores of maintaining the principal shrines of the state cults. Some of the aclla were drawn from the families of the highest nobility, and these frequently served as concubines to the emperor himself. Others were distributed by the Inca ruler and his generals as secondary wives to warriors who had distinguished themselves in battle, or to local kings and curacas who had demonstrated loyalty to the Inca cause.

In essence, the aclla were sources of concentrated skilled labor for the state, as well as precious commodities for the conduct of diplomacy. Like most monarchies throughout the world, the Incas relied on strategic marriages to strengthen political ties with the provincial nobility. Of course, females who were direct descendants of the royal household in Cuzco were the most desirable marriage partners for the highest-status native lords of the provinces. These marriages constituted true dynastic alliances and resulted frequently in heirs with aspirations to high positions in the central governmental bureaucracy, or even with pretensions to the throne itself.

But the genius of Inca statecraft was to apply this somewhat circumscribed notion of dynastic alliances among the princes and princesses of royal households to virtually every rung in the social hierarchy of control. The tremendous concentration of unencumbered aclla in the provincial capitals of the Inca state was the key to this institutionalization of strategic marriages. Because of their elevated status as "chosen women" of the Incas, the aclla were seen as desirable marriage partners, endowed with the prestige of the state, and promising the provincial nobility identification with the power and authority of the central government. It is not surprising that the acllahuasi in the principal cities of the empire were jealously guarded by the Incas, and that the violation of a "chosen woman" was designated a capital crime in the state's criminal code. All of these strategic forms of political and economic relations, the mit'a and mitimae, the aclla, camayo, and yanacona, generated an enormous flow of goods and services for the Inca empire, truly an economic engine of staggering proportions. But how did the Inca manage this economy?

Again, the words of Cieza de León, written in frank admiration of the audacity of Inca imperial organization, offer us vital clues: ". . . in more than 1,200 leagues of coast they ruled they have their representatives and governors, and many lodgings and great storehouses filled with all necessary supplies. This was to provide for their soldiers, for in one of these storehouses there were lances, and in another, darts, and in others, sandals, and in others, the different arms they employed. Likewise certain buildings were filled with fine clothing, others with coarser garments, and others with food and every kind of victuals. When the lord was lodged in his dwellings and his soldiers garrisoned there, nothing, from the most important to the most trifling, but could be provided. . . ." Perhaps more than any other native state of the ancient Americas, the Incas were justly renowned for the scale and efficiency of their elaborate commodity warehousing system. The progress of the Spanish conquest of the Andes, in fact, would have been slowed substantially had it not been for the endless ranks of Incan storehouses, known in the Quechua language as qollqa—filled with food, clothing, arms, and supplies—that the conquistadors found arrayed on the outskirts of Inca towns.

Bernabé Cobo, like Cieza de León, described the Incan storage system, and provides us with intriguing insights into its internal organization. "The storehouses of the Crown and of Religion were different," he wrote, "although they were always together, like the owners of what was stored in them and the uses to which it was put. The storehouses of the Incas were much bigger and longer than those of Religion; this implies that the Incas' share of lands and animals was greater than that which was given to the gods." This perceptive passage suggests that when the Incas incorporated a new province into their empire, they linked the construction of massive storehouses with the reorganization of the land-tenure system, which, as we have seen, partitioned territories into three principal divisions—central government, state cult, and autochthonous landholdings. Products from the state's two territorial partitions flowed into separate, spatially segregated qollqa. One set of storerooms was designated for the state cults and another for the use of the central government. If Cobo was right, the governmental qollqa were larger and more numerous and contained a wider variety of raw and manufactured goods than those designated for the support of the religious cults.

The qollqa themselves were substantial circular and rectangular structures built of fieldstone, wood, and thatch, and provided frequently with elaborate ventilation systems to assist the preservation of bulk food supplies like potatoes and maize. At the Inca provincial capital of Huánuco Pampa in the north-central highlands of Peru, archaeological investigation has revealed that circular qollqa were used for maize storage, while rectangular qollqa seem to have been assigned to tuber storage.

To control the flow of bulk foodstuffs and manufactured products through the warehousing system, the Incas maintained a corps of civil servants, the "representatives" and "governors" Cieza de León mentioned, who accounted for the collection and transshipment of these valued goods. One class of civil servant that was particularly important to the accounting system was the quipucamayoc, or keeper of the quipu. Quipu were ingenious mnemonic devices that encoded, through a series of complex, recursive patterns of knotted and colored cords, a wide array of economic, political, social, and ritual information critical to the smooth functioning of the state bureaucracy. The quipucamayoc were a hereditary, occupationally specialized (camayo) class of men in the Inca state who recorded on the knotted cords essential information regarding the amount of goods circulating into and out of state storehouses and performed tasks analogous to those of scribes in other archaic states. The quipucamayoc reported directly to the higher echelons of the state bureaucracy, to the provincial or territorial governors, and ultimately to the Inca emperor himself.

The vast bulk of state storage facilities were constructed in the imperial capital of Cuzco and near important towns and provincial capitals along the qhapaq ñan, or royal road of the Incas. The qhapaq ñan was formed by two north-south routes, one in the highlands and the other along the Pacific coast, bound together by a series of east-west lateral linkages through the principal mountain passes of the western mountain chain of the Andes, the Cordillera Negra. The highland route of the qhapag ñan extended over 3,000 miles, from

GOVERNADOR DE LOS CAMINOS REALES
CAPAC NAN TOCRICOC AUTA
INGA

hoc lle cochan nan

Gucasquani capac nan

ue dor de los camines
capac

CORE ON MAIOR I MENOR
HATVN CHASQVICHVRV
MVLLO CHAS QVI CVRACA ~

core on

Yan tun

Left: An Incan highway under construction. A laborer holds what appears to be a measuring stick while a governor of the royal road gives instructions. Markers like modern milestones indicate distances between major points. Befitting his high station, the governor wears sandals, a tunic, a small crown, and ear spools. *Right:* Announcing his arrival with his conchshell horn, an Inca messenger wears a white feather sun hat and carries a stick and sling to protect himself. A container holds food from a nearby granary. Guaman Poma reported that the messengers who traveled along the Incan highways had the speed of "sparrow hawks."

Chile to Ecuador, while the entire Incan road system may have integrated as much as 25,000 miles of disparate, seemingly intractable landscapes, including the deserts of the Pacific coast, the highland pocket basins of Peru and Ecuador, the vertiginous, knotted mountain slopes of the great Cordillera Blanca's eastern flanks, and the trackless high plains of Bolivia and Chile. Radiating out from Cuzco, the various branches of the qhapaq ñan united the four principal geographic segments of the Incan realm—Chinchaysuyu, Antisuyu, Collasuyu, and Contisuyu, the northern, eastern, southern, and western quarters, respectively.

The Incan road system, particularly in the broken, tortuous terrain of the Andean highlands, was an audacious engineering achievement of the first magnitude and, quite likely, the largest single construction project ever attempted in the ancient Americas. The qhapaq ñan together with its lateral feeders was a powerful tool of political integration for the Incan central government. Messages could be sent along the royal road between Cuzco and its far-flung provincial capitals with incredible speed, using a system of relay runners, called chasqui, who were stationed along designated segments of the road. The developed road system also greatly facilitated the efficient movement of bulk and manufactured goods, mitimae colonists, provincial officials, and, of course, Inca armies throughout the empire.

Provincial capitals, such as Jauja, Cajamarca, and Pachácamac, were established along the length of both the highland and coastal routes of the qhapaq ñan to coordinate local administration and the economic exploitation of natural and human resources. In regions where there was no local settlement that could serve as an appropriate provincial capital, the Incas created cities, such as Huánuco Pampa, building them frequently on a symmetrical grid plan, or modeling large segments of them after the core area of the imperial capital of Cuzco. In conquered territories that already possessed substantial urban centers, the Incas simply absorbed the native town into the network of cities that formed the centralized focus of Inca administration. As at the ancient coastal settlement of Pachácamac near modern Lima, Inca rulers often constructed a few important administrative buildings, such as a temple for the state's solar cult, storerooms, residential compounds for the Inca elite, and perhaps an acllahuasi, placing them in prominent locations within the towns to mark and symbolize their incorporation into the Inca empire.

Along the royal road in the provinces between these principal cities, towns, and capitals, the Inca state maintained a series of "inns," or way stations, called tampu. Each tampu offered basic temporary accommodations and meals for traveling Inca officials and could provide food for the army during military campaigns. Tampu usually consisted of a series of large rectangular structures arrayed around a central plaza intended as residence halls for travelers, communal kitchens, and banks of storehouses that were stocked with food. More elaborate tampu close to the provincial capitals frequently included stone baths and shrines for the state cults. These way stations along the royal road were constructed, maintained, provisioned, and most likely staffed permanently with local mit'a labor from the surrounding region. They were essential links in the chain of command and communication that bound the Inca provinces with the imperial capital of Cuzco.

The network of provincial cities, towns, and tampu, centralized clusters of state storehouses, and a highly developed road system, all constructed and maintained through the coordinated efforts of local mit'a labor forces, constituted an effective physical infrastructure for the Inca imperial enterprise. But the organizational system they devised for administering the empire was no less impressive than these more visible physical artifacts. One fundamental principle of Inca statecraft in the imperial provinces, reflecting the remarkable shrewdness and political pragmatism of the Inca ruling elite, was to confirm the traditional authority of the local political leaders, or curacas, in dealing with their own communities. Cieza de León, among other Spanish commentators intrigued by Inca principles of command, described this phenomenon in his wondrous chronicle of Peru: "And they had another device to keep the natives from hating them, and this was that they never divested the natural chieftains of their power. If it so happened that one of them . . . in some way deserved to be stripped of his power, it was vested in his sons or brothers, and all were ordered to obey them."

This system of preserving the local mandate of the native elite has been aptly termed indirect rule. For an empire that was rapidly, almost frenetically expanding, and only in the nascent stages of generating formal principles of colonial governance, this system of indirect rule was simple to implement, relatively efficient, and the least intrusive in altering the daily rhythms and decision-making autonomy of potentially hostile local communities. The key to the success of indirect rule was the ability to secure the cooperation and at least the overt political loyalty of the local curacas. As we have seen, one strategy for co-opting these local lords was worked out through marriage alliances with the Inca elite which established irrevocable bonds of kinship. The ritualized exchange of daughters as marriage partners between the Incas and the local elite created powerful incentives for the provincial political leaders to "buy into" the Inca system. The network of real and fictive kinship ties engendered by these alliances provided rich opportunities to local lords for the strategic manipulation of the resulting patron-client relationship.

Of course, this strategy of enticing the local curacas into the patronage system by holding out the promise of wealth and enhanced social prestige was effective only as long as the curacas were able to deliver the labor and productive capacity of their people. The Incas realized this critical linkage and helped the local curacas resolve potential conflict by massive displays of state generosity: "and so, making the people joyful and giving them solemn banquets and drinking feasts, great taquis, and other celebrations that they use, completely different from ours, in which the Incas show their splendor, and all the feasting is at their expense . . ." Like the Romans' policy of "bread and circuses," intended to defuse the potentially explosive problem of a malcontent underclass by occasional distribution of free staples and the staging of massive public entertainments, the Inca practice of periodically redistributing warehoused food, drink, and clothing to commoners during state-sponsored festivals was designed to dissipate social tensions and to incorporate commoners into the new economic and social order of the Inca world.

At the same time that the Incas were governing newly absorbed provinces through the practice of indirect rule, their statesmen were gradually fashioning more formal, centralized channels of tribute and labor recruitment based on a decimal system of administration. In this system, labor obligations were assessed on an ascending numerical series of tributary households that began with a minimal unit of 10 households (termed chunka) and terminated with the maximal unit of 10,000 households (hunu). Between these limits, there were decimal groupings for 50, 100, 500, 1,000, and 5,000 tributary households. The Incas periodically took a census to account for fluctuations in the size and residential patterns of the empire's population. On the basis of the census figures recorded on imperial quipu, they adjusted membership in these decimal groupings of tributary households to reflect changing demographic realities.

Each decimal unit was headed by an official who, at the lower levels of the household groupings at least, was drawn from the local communities. Officers of the various decimal units were ranked in a formal, pyramidlike hierarchy. Some officials were appointed to their offices by higher-ranking decimal administrators, while others appear to have inherited their positions. The chain of command and reporting responsibility began with the basal chunka leader and proceeded upward progressively to the hunu officials. Above the rank of the hunu heads of 10,000 households, administrative responsibility was vested in individuals with direct consanguineal or political ties to the royal households of Cuzco. These were the surrogates of the emperor himself, serving as provincial governors, or as members of the imperial council, which included extremely high-ranking representatives from each of the four quarters of the realm.

As the Incas began to consolidate their authority in a conquered province, they gradually attempted to streamline the complicated political mosaic of local lords' claims to power and traditional prerogatives by imposing the uniform decimal system of administration. This system had clear benefits for the Inca central government, permitting the state to operate with a relatively homogeneous form of political organization and labor recruitment in a pluralistic social landscape characterized by extreme ethnic, linguistic, and cultural divisions. The advantage to local curacas was not as readily apparent. With the emergence of what was essentially an imperial class system of favored officials, those curacas who were not designated as decimal officers saw many of their social prerogatives and their traditional access to local labor pools begin to dissolve. The resulting tensions generated by the imposition of the decimal system were substantial, and there are numerous stories in the chronicles of resentful "natural lords" of the provinces promulgating massive rebellions against Inca rule at every opportunity.

Despite the inability of the Incas to consolidate their rule completely and permanently in all provinces of the empire, the organizational infrastructure and facilities that they established ensured a continuous flow of commodities, information, and people along the qhapaq ñan to the imperial capital of Cuzco.

Cuzco, of course, was the principal seat of the Inca ruling caste, the locus of both the royal court and the holiest shrines of the imperial religion.

For the Inca people, Cuzco was a regal, mythic city, redolent with the symbolism of power. The royal city was both an icon of Inca rule and a cosmogram that displayed in the spatial arrangement of its public architecture the structure that framed the natural and social orders. It was conceived as the axis mundi, the city at the center of the empire that bound together the complementary universe of the sacred and the secular. It was the origin point for the royal road extending out into the four quarters of the realm, and the administrative city par excellence. It was, in short, the ultimate nexus and arbiter of wealth and power, social identity, and prestige, cult, and command.

The conquistador Pedro Sancho de la Hoz recorded one of the first European impressions of the Inca royal city: "Cuzco, because it is the capital city and the residence of the Inca nobles, is large enough and handsome enough to compare with any Spanish city," he wrote. "It is full of the palaces of the magnates, for in it reside no poor folk. . . . The streets, all stone-paved and straight, cross each other at right angles and have each a stone-lined water channel running down the middle . . . there are many houses on the hillsides and others below on the plain . . . and in the valley in the middle there are more than a hundred thousand houses surrounded by hills . . . including storehouses." The more taciturn Pedro Pizarro simply noted: "It was astonishing to see the people in Cuzco." Although these fragmentary comments give us few clues to the actual size and social composition of Inca Cuzco, all historical and archaeological sources indicate clearly that the city, befitting its status as the capital of the largest and most pluralistic empire of the ancient Americas, embraced a large, heterogeneous population engaged in a variety of specialized occupations for the Inca state.

We do know that Cuzco was the principal residence of the royal court and of the elite of highest status in Inca society. The physical setting and architectural design of the core metropolitan zone dramatically reflected that reality. This central area was composed of an elegant ensemble of expansive public plazas, palatial residences built of finely cut ashlar masonry, and rich temples all set between the confluence of two great rivers, the Tullumayo and Huatanay, which the Incas artificially canalized within the city.

By the end of the fifteenth century, the Inca elite in Cuzco were organized into twenty distinct social groups, or royal ayllus. These ayllus maintained separate residential compounds constructed on a grand scale in the heart of the city. Ten of the royal ayllus were invested with supreme status as direct descendants by blood of former kings, and were called panaqas. Panaqa members, as consanguineal relatives of former kings, controlled vast wealth, including enormous agricultural estates, pasture lands, llama and alpaca herds, hundreds of yanacona and camayos, and access to a huge mit'a labor force.

A stylized illustration of an Inca temple devoted to sun worship. Benzoni was a critic of Spanish imperial policy who wanted his readers to appreciate native religion.

These resources represented the wealth that had been accumulated during the reign of the monarch who in life was the founder and, in death, the divine ancestor of the panaqa that bore his name. Male members of the panaqa were assured high governmental positions during the lifetime of their kingly relative. After the death of the reigning king, his patrimonial estate passed under the control of his principal male heirs, who became the political leaders of the panaqa.

It was the obligation of the panaqa members to perpetuate the memory of the deceased king who had originally founded the panaqa. Ancestor worship was the fundamental bedrock of indigenous Andean religion, the basis of ritual activity in the ancient social unit of the ayllu. Among the elite of Cuzco it took the form of an elaborate cult of the royal mummies, which both fascinated and repelled Spanish chroniclers who vividly recorded this key element of Inca spirituality. The Incas, wrote Pedro Pizarro, "had the law and custom that when one of their rulers died, they embalmed him and wrapped him in many fine garments. They allotted these lords all the service that they had in life, so that their mummy bundles might be served in death as if they were still alive . . ." The panaqa members, Cobo related further, "brought [the royal mummies], lavishly escorted, to all their most important ceremonies. They sat them all down in the plaza in a row, in order of seniority, and the servants who looked after them ate and drank there. . . . In front of the mummies they also placed large vessels like pitchers, called vilques, made of gold and silver. They filled these vessels with maize beer and toasted the dead with it, after first showing it to them. The dead toasted one another, and they drank to the living . . . this was done by their ministers in their names. When the vilques were full, they poured them over a circular stone set up as an idol in the middle of the plaza. There was a small channel around the stone, and the beer ran off through drains and hidden pipes."

This lurid spectacle of the descendants of dead kings ministering to their ancestors' elaborately costumed, desiccated corpses with offerings of food, drink, and toasts in the plazas of Cuzco obscures the subtle political and religious nuances embedded in the cult of the royal mummies. Although grounded in the pan-Andean religious practice of ancestor worship, the elite cult was something more than the simple veneration of a dead lineage ancestor.

In the first instance, the elaborate feasting of the dead royals was organized around, and intended as, ceremonies of agricultural fertility. "When there was need for water for the cultivated fields," Cobo made clear, "they usually brought out [the dead king's] body, richly dressed, with his face covered, carrying it in a procession through the fields and punas, and they were convinced that this was largely responsible for bringing rain." Dead kings, furthermore, were frequently addressed in the protocols of panaqa toasts as Illapa, the weather deity who personified the atmospheric forces of wind, rain, hail, lightning, and thunder—all the meteorological phenomena responsible for the growth or destruction of agricultural crops.

In another important meaning, the public display of the royal mummies in the principal plazas of Cuzco during state occasions, arranged in "order of seniority," was a graphic affirmation of the legitimacy of Incan dynastic rule. On these occasions, the reigning king would participate in ceremonial processionals throughout Cuzco quite literally in company with the complete line of his royal ancestors, who were physically represented by their richly adorned, revictual bundles. Who could contest the legitimacy of the Incas when the entire dynasty, the distilled history of their ruling mandate, was constantly visible and present to the nation? By these ritual actions, the deceased monarchs and the living emperor symbolically became one—embodiments of legitimate power, emblems of agricultural fertility and abundance, and powerful icons of national identity.

The cult of the royal mummies was an intense expression of social and ritual solidarity within the Inca ruling caste, particularly among the ten panaqas that exploited and benefited materially from the patrimony of their kingly ancestors. Other cults and esoteric beliefs promoted this same sense of solidarity and imperial destiny among the Inca peoples as a whole. One such cult focused on the sun deity, called Inti. The Inca kings identified themselves as descendants of Inti, thereby appropriating symbolically the life-giving essence of the

A fanciful depiction of llamas transporting cargo in the Andes. This illustration from Pierre Vander Aa's sixty-six-volume *Galerie Agréable du Monde,* published in 1729, reflects Europe's fascination with exotic animals. Nevertheless, as the largest domesticated draft animal in the Americas, llamas played a crucial role in the Incan imperial system.

sun. A golden idol of Inti in human form was maintained in the Qorikancha, or "Golden Compound," perhaps the single most important structure in Cuzco. The idol was reputed to contain in its hollow stomach a paste made of gold dust and the ashes of the ritually cremated hearts of former Inca kings.

The great temple of Qorikancha contained many other idols of the state cults, and incorporated in its interior precincts niches for the sacred mummy bundles of Inca royalty. More importantly, it was from the Qorikancha that a symbolic, sacred landscape of Cuzco, and by extension the Inca empire itself, was organized in an incredibly complex, but logically ordered system of shrines arrayed along lines of sight. This sacred landscape was central to the Inca people's notions of their own identity as an ethnic group, and to their belief in their right to rule other nations.

Bernabé Cobo's description of this sacred landscape of Cuzco provides us with an entrée into this fascinating aspect of Incan political and religious belief: "From the Qorikancha, as from the center, there went out certain lines which the Indians call ceques," he wrote. "They formed four parts corresponding to the four royal roads that went out from Cuzco. On each one of those ceques were arranged in order the shrines which there were in Cuzco and its district, like stations of holy places, the veneration of which was common to all. Each ceque was the responsibility of the parcialidades [the Spanish name for groups of people who formed related parts of a larger ethnic whole] and families of the city of Cuzco, from within which came the attendants and servants who cared for the shrines of their ceque and saw to offering the established sacrifices at the proper times."

This remarkable conceptual organization of Cuzco and its near environs incorporated a total of 41 directional sight lines, or ceques, radiating out from the origin point at Qorikancha, along which the Inca recognized 328 individual huacas, places or objects imbued with sacred power. As Cobo noted, different sets of related families (ayllus), or larger social groups (parcialidades), were charged with the responsibility of maintaining the huacas along the ceque line designated to that group. Responsibility for the ceque line included the obligation of offering periodic, ritually prescribed sacrifices at these sacred shrines.

The ceque system of Cuzco carried multiple layers of significance that bound Inca concepts of geographic and symbolic space, time, history, and social organization. Perhaps the most important meaning embedded in the ceque system was reflected in its role as the physical expression of the Incas' sidereal-lunar calendar. Each of the 328 huacas represented one day in this agricultural calendar. Throughout the agricultural cycle of the seasons, members of at least one of the Inca parcialidades resident in Cuzco were engaged in daily communal rituals designed to ensure abundant harvests and the fertility of camelid herds. These increase ceremonies, organized according to the principles of the ceque lines, served as a trenchant reminder to the Incan classes of Cuzco that their success as a people destined to rule other nations hinged on group solidarity, and on their ability to sustain a symbolic concordance between the social and natural orders.

Cuzco, as the political and symbolic center of the Inca world, was, above all else, a monumental representation of power. Here the Inca elite self-consciously designed and audaciously displayed their own conception of themselves as lords of the Andean world. They invested Cuzco with the powerful resonances of constructed public images: the image of the secular power of the empire, suffused with the vast, differentiated wealth of its many subject nations; the image of the sacred power of the Inca ruling classes who appropriated for themselves the essential role of ritually mediating between society and the forces of nature; and the image of dynastic power, the city as seat of a long lineage of divine emperors, both living and dead, engaged in the exercise of legitimate authority. Incan Cuzco was, in short, the image of concentrated imperial power, a representation of an ideal social order, and a publicly projected cognitive map that related this social order to the perceived physical order of the universe.

Although we can reconstruct the nature of Incan society at its apogee in the late fifteenth century with reasonable accuracy, our sources on the early Incas are veiled in the ambiguity of orally transmitted origin myths and obscured in the self-serving, custom-made pseudohistory of an originally marginal people newly come to power. The Inca elite routinely recast accounts of their origins and place in the Andean world to accommodate emerging imperial ambitions. Ethnic propaganda became easily transformed into official history, the "true" record of Inca rule. In this context, individual identities, actions, and actual historical events merge ineluctably with myth, metaphor, symbolism, and allegory.

With the Spanish conquest, the Incas' own vision of themselves, as transcribed by the chroniclers, was distorted again, but in a different way, through European misconceptions concerning the content and meaning of indigenous narratives. For instance, the presumed roster of thirteen or fourteen Inca kings given to us in the chronicles may not reflect the process of a linear, chronological succession to the throne at all. The Spaniards naturally assumed that the native king list elicited from their Inca informants implied principles of monarchial rule and succession analogous to those in operation in European courts. There is a compelling argument, however, that the concept of sovereignty in the Inca state entailed a system of dual kingship. Many traditional Andean cultures, including the Inca, possessed a system of social organization, called the moiety, in which societies were divided into two complementary halves. The capital of the Incas was itself partitioned into two major sectors, termed Hanan and Hurin (or upper and lower) Cuzco, each of which may have been ruled by a king. In other words, the king list, as well as many other elements of Inca "history," may actually replicate symbolically fundamental organizational principles or religious beliefs of Andean societies. To the Incan mind, history was not necessarily an ordered, chronological narrative, but rather a complex mélange of belief, myth, and remembered fact.

Given this situation, scholars of the Incas have turned to a coordinated approach, integrating archaeological research with critical interpretation of textual material. As a result of their efforts, the character of Inca society, economy, and politics has begun to emerge from the ambiguity of fragmentary texts, and from the confusing jumble of decayed cities slumped in ruin. Only in the recent past have we begun to appreciate fully the subtlety of Incan statecraft and the manner in which the Incas formed the largest empire in the Western Hemisphere by the perceptive adaption and manipulation of institutions and social relations that were basic to the ancient Andean world. The mit'a and mitimae, aclla, camayo, and yanacona, all betray their origins as specialized forms of labor and status relations that had been worked out by native Andeans over centuries. But the peculiar genius of the Incas was to take this fundamental institutional substratum, transform and magnify it in scale through the shrewd application of political principles such as indirect rule and ritualized state reciprocity, and employ it on a massive scale as a technique of empire-building. Even if the Incas built upon the experiences, innovations, and adaptive skills of their cultural predecessors, their achievements in the arena of politics and statecraft stand unparalleled in the New World.

Through the rapidly clarifying looking glass of Inca society, we can also hope to glimpse a broader reality that underscores the incredible tenacity, ingenuity, and self-reliance with which the ancient peoples of the Andes adapted themselves to their intensely beautiful but demanding environment. This process of adaptation by Andean people to their unforgiving physical landscape continues today, although now framed in the context of increasing integration with national and global economic markets and social trends. Even under the pervasive impact of national assimilation, the lifeways of the native inhabitants of isolated rural Andean enclaves still generate powerful cultural resonances that echo the strategies for survival, beliefs, and structures for communal action that were shaped so successfully by their ancestors in the centuries before the imposition of Western colonial rule.

Part Two

AMERICAN CIVILIZATION, 1492

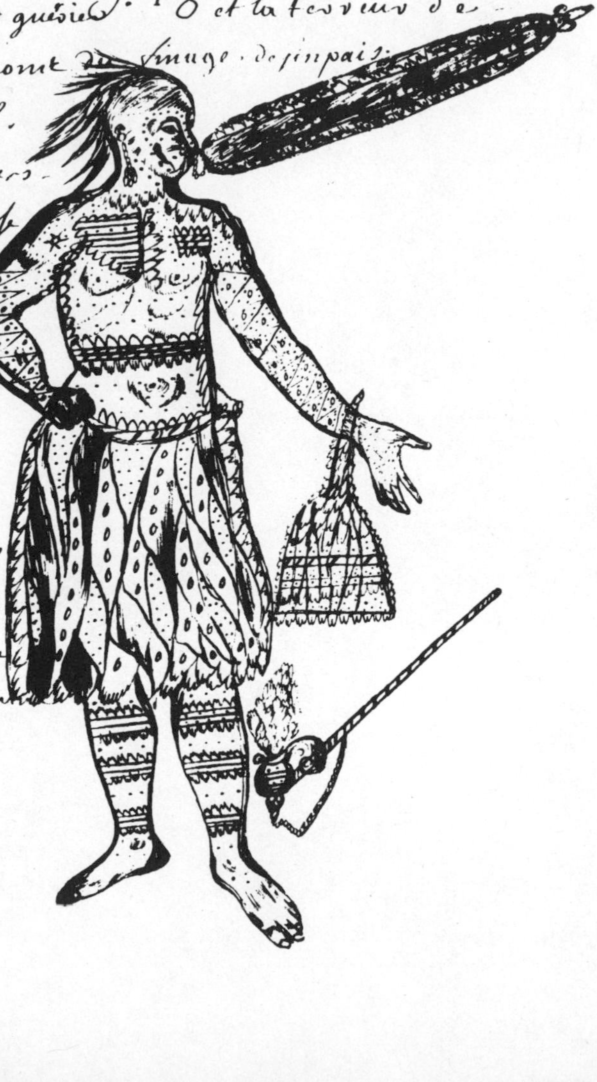

JOEL SHERZER

ON THE EVE of Columbus's voyages, Native America possessed an astounding diversity of languages, greater by far than all of Europe. In 1492, as many as 2,000 separate, mutually unintelligible languages were spoken by the many different peoples inhabiting the Western Hemisphere. Of these, approximately 250 were spoken in North America, some 350 in Mexico and Central America, and 1,450 more throughout South America. This diversity was manifested in many ways—in the sounds of the languages, the ways in which they were pronounced, in their grammatical patterns and structures, in vocabularies, in historical relationships, and in the place of language in the different cultures and societies.

Although a common origin for all American Indian languages cannot be ruled out, there is little contemporary evidence for it. In fact, the remarkable diversity of the languages argues rather for multiple and divergent histories, making quite clear that there was not only no such thing as *the* American Indian language but no way in which a single general or common language was ever used by all Native Americans. In addition, there was no sense in which American Indian languages could be characterized as primitive. All languages in the Americas were as complex and rich as any language spoken anywhere in the world. With regard to specific characteristics, just about every major feature of language could be found on the American continents.

At the same time, certain linguistic features were relatively rare in the Americas, while others were more common in America than elsewhere and

This drawing of Tessouat, known to the French as Le Borgne de l'Isle (One Eye of the Island), an Algonquin leader from Alumette Island in the Ottawa River, is attributed to Louis Nicolas and was completed at the end of the seventeenth century. Here Borgne addresses his assembled warriors through a speaking tube.

Phrases from 1492

PRESENT INDIAN LANGUAGES

Okanogan

təl iscpəx̣pəx̣twiʼlx
*from the time I became
aware of things . . .*

kən pəx̣pəx̣twiʼlx
. . . I became aware of things . . .

Flathead Salish

təl iscpəx̣pəx̣twiʼlš̌
*from the time I became
aware of things . . .*

čən pəx̣pəx̣twiʼlš̌
. . . I became aware of things . . .

1492 LANGUAGE RECONSTRUCTIONS

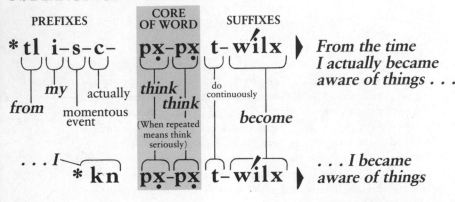

PREFIXES   CORE OF WORD   SUFFIXES

*tl i-s-c- px̣-px̣ t-wiʼlx ▶ *From the time I actually became aware of things . . .*

- *from* — tl
- *my* — i
- momentous event — s
- actually — c
- *think* / *think* — px̣-px̣ (When repeated means think seriously)
- do continuously — t
- *become* — wilx

. . . I ***kn px̣-px̣ t-wiʼlx** ▶ *. . . I became aware of things*

ABOVE: Shown in familiar left-to-right reading lines

BELOW: Shown in concentric patternings of native traditions

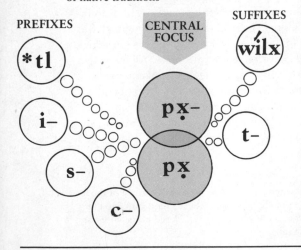

PREFIXES   CENTRAL FOCUS   SUFFIXES

*tl   **i-**   **s-**   **c-**   **px̣-**   **px̣**   **t-**   **wiʼlx**

SOUND UNITS (Phonemes)

- boundary
- č ch in church
- x French r
- x̣ German ch in ich
- š sh in shoe
- ə a in sofa
- ʼ throat catch (glottalization)

MEANING UNITS (Morphemes)

kən/čən	I
tl	from
i	my
s	momentous event
c	actuality
px̣ px̣	reduplication of think, root is px̣
t	continuously, persistency
wiʼlx/wiʼlš̌	developmental, becoming
*	reconstructed or hypothetical form

distinguished Native American languages as a whole from those in other regions of the world. Rare among Indian languages, for instance, was the employment of suffixes on nouns to express such cases as nominative, accusative, and dative (as in Latin), or of nominal and pronominal gender references (like the English "he" and "she" or the Spanish "el" and "la"—a feature in America limited almost entirely to the Chinookan languages of present-day Oregon and Washington). On the other hand, special features of many Indian languages conveyed sharp distinctions between animate and inanimate nouns and between objects one possessed by definition (such as kin relations and body parts) and those that were incidentally owned (such as a knife or other tool). Native languages also frequently expressed location, such as within, above, below, or beside an object, by means of suffixes on nouns or elements placed after nouns.

The pronunciation of Indian languages—often characterized by the presence of more consonants than were typically found in European languages—was also marked by many sounds and distinctions of sounds that were relatively rare in European languages. They included: glottal stops (an interruption of breath produced by suddenly closing the vocal cords, as in the pause between uh and oh in the English uh-oh); a distinction between two types of sounds made with the back of the tongue—a k similar to the English k and a uvular q, produced farther back in the mouth; sounds similar to the ts of hats in English, but occurring anywhere in a word, particularly at the beginning; glottalized consonants, produced by a closure and reopening of the vocal cords simultaneously with the pronunciation of the consonant; and various laterals, or l-like sounds.

Since many sounds could be expressed voiceless and voiced, glottalized and nonglottalized in various Indian languages, there was a much larger number of distinct, contrasting consonants than exists in European languages. In addition, in languages with many consonants and consonantal contrasts, it was possible to have words with a large number of consonants clustering together in combination with very few vowels, sometimes only one, or even none. Among the Bella Coola Indians of the Northwest Coast, for example, the word for "animal" was nmnmk' (the apostrophe indicating that the k was pronounced as a glottalized consonant).

This diagram illustrates the grammatical features of a language spoken by interior Salish people at the time of Columbus. In the fifteenth century, the ancestors of the native people living in eastern Washington, Idaho, and western Montana had yet to divide into separate though related linguistic groups. The techniques of historical linguistics allow us to posit an ancestral form from modern-day examples. The drawing indicates how the meaningful core of a Salishan word becomes elaborated into different grammatical phrases. The diagram also illustrates the differences between linear written English and the concentric constructions emphasized in native formations.

Indian languages also shared many grammatical features in common, affecting both morphology (the structure of words) and syntax (the structure of sentences). Particularly prevalent was the use of reduplication, the repetition or doubling of all or part of a word, in order to change its meaning in particular ways. With nouns, reduplication was often used to indicate a special kind of plurality, the distribution of an object here and there in space. Among the Washo Indians of North America's Great Basin, gusu meant "buffalo," while gususu indicated "buffalo here and there." The reduplication of verbs served a variety of functions. Frequently it was used to express different aspects of the way an action was conceived. One of the most elaborate systems of verbal reduplication was that of the Nootkas of Vancouver Island. With a single verb stem meaning "to turn," or "make a circuit," and by reduplicating it and a verbal suffix in various ways, the Nootkas could convey "turning about, circling," "to start turning about," "to start turning to turn about," "turning round and round," "to start making a circuit," and "to start in on a spaced series of circuits."

Other grammatical features in the Americas included sound symbolism, the regular, systematic alternation of consonants or vowels in order to indicate that an object or activity was either small, affectionate, or endearing on the one hand, or large, ugly, or depreciated on the other; the distinction between inclusive and exclusive first person plural pronouns, distinguishing we (including the hearer: you and I) from we (not including the hearer: I and someone other than you); the addition of tense and aspect markers as suffixes to verbs to convey the time of the action and the way the action was conceived (among the Kunas of Panama, taksa meant "he saw," takkoe meant "he will see," taktappi meant "he went there to see," and taksokkali meant "he is about to see"); and the incorporation of a verb's object as a prefix of the verb, as in a Nahuatl word that meant "I eat meat" or "I am a meat-eater," but was literally expressed: "I-meat-eat."

Indian languages distinguished inalienable (one's grandparents, for instance) from alienable possessions (a bowl) by the obligatory addition of a possessive expression (my) to the noun, as well as suffixed elements indicating such positions as in, under, on top of, toward, and among. Many used verbal prefixes to express the instrument by which an action was performed; evidential markers, usually suffixed to verbs, to indicate the type of validity of the information reported, whether what was described in the verb was known to speakers because it was hearsay or gossip, or because they had witnessed it, dreamed it, or heard about it in a myth; and sound changes or the addition of grammatical elements to call attention to individuals with particular physical characteristics or to distinguish men from women, adults from children, and respected individuals from depreciated persons.

Many American Indian languages were characterized, also, by what has been called polysynthesis—the joining of many forms with distinct meanings and functions into a single word, so that what in European languages would be stated in a sentence containing several or even many words was expressed in one quite complicated word, including compounds and affixes. In the following examples, hyphens are placed between meaningful elements within a native word, which is then translated both literally, element by element, and finally more freely:

In Fox, an Algonquian language of the Mississippi Valley, the word eh-kiwi-n-a-m-oht-ati-wa-ch(i) was translated literally "then-indefinite movement round about-connective-flee-causality with reference to an animate object-activity done for the subject-one another-plural-animate" or, freely, "Then they together here and there kept him in flight from them."

In Hupa, an Athapaskan language in California, the word te-s-e-ya-te (literally, "here and there in space in-progress-I-go-future") is translated freely as "I will be going here and there."

These and many other grammatical features reveal Indian languages to have been anything but primitive. Quite the contrary, they exhibited an incredible complexity, albeit of types sometimes strikingly different from those of European languages. Like all languages, they mirrored the speakers' view of the universe and especially the world around them. Among the Indians, this view included fine attention to details of position, direction, motion, form, shape, and texture, all frequently encoded in and expressed through highly wrought words imaginative and poetic in form.

As with all the world's languages, the vocabularies of American Indian languages reflected universal concerns (words for parts of the body, immediate kin, celestial bodies), the local ecology (plants and animals, mountains, bodies of water), and the particularities of the belief systems and cultural practices of the individual peoples. Often there was an elaboration of vocabulary to express a focus of cultural tradition or ecological need. The Eskimos and other Arctic and Subarctic groups had distinct and independent words for types of snow, thus making possible a necessary precision unmatched in the languages of Europe. Central Alaskan Yupik Eskimos, for example, had different single words for "snow on the ground," "light snow," "soft, deep snow," "drifting snow," "snow cornice or snow ready to avalanche," "clinging snow," "fresh snow," "snowflakes on the ground," "snowbank," and "snow carved in a block." In addition, words were often adapted to fit new and changing environments. When the Athapaskan-speaking Navajos migrated south to the Plains and the present-day U.S. Southwest from their original Subarctic homeland, they used the Athapaskan word for snowflake to express a newly acquired cultural item, seed.

Native beliefs and practices were also reflected in the ways words were grouped together into classes and categories. The Panama Kunas grouped words for plants and fruits into various classes according to a gradient system of ownership that took into account their economic value and significance in the diet rather than the actual private garden or tree ownership (which did exist among the Kunas), the food's place in the structure of the meal (e.g., as fruit, salad, or vegetable), or its size or shape (bush, tree, or shrub). Plantains, which were considered the equivalent of food (the word masi meant both plantain and food in general), and coconuts, which were regarded as the equivalent of money, were the most privately owned and, like staple crops such as potatoes, could never be taken or borrowed from another person. Mangoes and avocados when on the tree were also thought of as privately owned, but could be picked up and eaten by a hungry person when they fell to the ground. On the other hand, various kinds of nuts were regarded as belonging to the Supreme Being, or God, and could be taken in any quantity at any time without asking permission of the land's owner.

Another important feature of native vocabularies was the metaphor—the use of words or groups of words that related one realm of meaning to another. To students, they provide a window into American Indian philosophies, worldviews, and cultural symbolism, as well as poetic sensibility. In many Mesoamerican languages, vocabularies consist of a relatively small number of root words (perhaps as few as 1,000) plus a much greater number of derivatives from the root words. The relationship between the root and the derived words was often metaphorical. For example, in classical Quiché, one of the languages of the ancient Mayas, precise positional relationships (the equivalent of such English prepositions as "in front of," "behind," and "on top of") were expressed by following nouns with words derived from those referring to parts of the body. Thus the word for "mouth" was used to express "before," that for eye or face became "in front of," head became "on top of," back became "behind," and belly or womb became "inside."

A number of Mesoamerican languages used parts of the body by metaphorical extension to denote other objects. In most Mayan languages, the bark of a tree was called the "skin" of the tree, a door was called the "mouth" of the house, and fruit was referred to as a tree's "eye." Conversely, aspects of the local environment would be applied to the body, as when human veins were known as "paths of blood." Body parts could also be used metaphorically in relation to one another. The thumb was called the "mother of the hand"—a metaphor that related kin terms and body parts.

Similarly, color terms were often derived metaphorically from other words or objects. In Nahuatl, the language of the Aztec civilization, the word for the color white was derived from that for salt; red from the word for blood; black from ink; green from vegetal greens; yellow from the word for the metal gold; and colored from the word for chili. Sometimes metaphorical derivations had a playful or humorous aspect. The Nahuatl word for "govern" was derived

In this page from the Codex Mendoza, Aztec children are taught by adults, as indicated by speech scrolls near each mouth. In each panel dots indicate the ages of the children—eleven at the top to fourteen at the bottom. In the top two tiers (boys are on the left and girls on the right), children are punished according to their age. In the lower two, boys learn to gather reeds and fish, while girls learn to grind corn and to weave. Daily rations of food are one and a half tortillas at ages eleven and twelve, then two tortillas at ages thirteen and fourteen.

A Richness of Voices

from the words for nose and lead, and thus meant literally "to lead someone by the nose."

In the verbally artistic language of ceremony and ritual, metaphors were often developed and expanded in creative and imaginative ways. The Tzotzil Mayan-speaking Chamula of Chiapas, Mexico, used the sun and its heat as metaphors for types of talk and ways of speaking. The more ritual, traditional, and ancient forms of speech were, the more they were considered to be heated, while the more colloquial, ordinary, and modern they were, the less they were regarded as heated. Thus, metaphorically, the age of the classical Mayas is still conceived of by contemporary Chamula as the age of the heat of the sun. At the same time, in the chants and speeches of Kuna chiefs, the various parts of a Kuna house were used as metaphors for the Kuna social and political structure. The central pole represented the chief, secondary poles represented the chief's assistants or spokesmen, and the side bamboo walls symbolized the ordinary villagers. In contrast, the word for flower was used to represent the women of the village.

Attention to the diversity and typology of the many Native American languages in 1492 raises a number of questions. How were all the languages related to one another? What was their history and what can knowledge of their history reveal about the history of the people who spoke the languages? Also, how was the diversity of language structure related to the diversity of culture, worldview, and the perception of experience?

Sorting out the languages into classifications of relationships to one another helps provide us with information and answers. Of the various ways in which languages can be classified, two have proven particularly useful: (1) genetic classification and (2) areal-diffusional classification. Genetic classification groups together all languages which can be shown to have had a single common origin. Languages related in this way are said to belong to the same language family and to be descended, or to have evolved, from a single parent language. Thus, within Europe, the Romance languages—French, Italian, Spanish, Portuguese, etc.—constitute a language family, being all descended from the parent language of Latin. At a deeper level of relatedness, the Romance, Germanic, Slavic, and Celtic languages respectively constitute branches of the Indo-European language family, being all descended ultimately from a single Indo-European "proto-language."

In the Americas of 1492, there were (and still are) many different language families, including, to name just a few, the Algonquian, Arawakan, Athapaskan, Iroquoian, Mayan, Quechuan, Siouan, and Uto-Aztecan. Each included a number of separate but genetically related languages. Some of the languages within the Algonquian family were Blackfoot, Cree, Delaware, Fox, and Ojibwa; some within the Athapaskan family were Apache, Chipewyan, Dogrib, and Navajo; some within the Iroquoian family were Cherokee, Mohawk,

Oneida, and Seneca; and some within the Uto-Aztecan family were Comanche, Hopi, Huichol, Nahuatl, Northern and Southern Paiute, and Papago. (An extended list of language families and the related languages that each encompassed appears as an Appendix at the end of this volume.)

Some language families were quite widespread and included many languages covering large and sometimes geographically separated and environmentally different areas. Others were smaller and more compact geographically. Whatever the extent of distribution among them, if the languages were genetically related to one another, it can usually be assumed that the ancestors of their speakers had a common homeland where the original proto-language was spoken. Knowledge of such relationships thus enables us to reconstruct original homelands and paths of migration.

Genetic classifications are of two kinds. Narrow classifications group languages that are closely related and whose existence goes back in time only 3,000 to 5,000 years. Broad classifications, which are much more speculative, attempt to relate the narrow genetic families to one another in larger groupings, often called phyla. They provide a vastly greater time depth and concern possible linguistic divisions that occurred from 5,000 to 10,000 years ago and beyond, among ancient ancestors of groups of language families.

The method of proving and establishing genetic relationships is by inspecting both the grammatical structures and the vocabularies of languages. Related—especially closely related—languages have quite similar grammatical structures. The longer that languages are separated from one another, the more their grammatical structures diverge, especially when they are influenced by neighboring languages with different structures. The vocabularies of genetically related languages also show similarities, and when the sounds of words differ, they do so according to regular correspondences, in which the words remain generally similar despite the change of sounds. Such related words, descended from an original parent language, are called cognates, and their study has provided much information about the past of different Native American groups. The examination of cognates from within the large Uto-Aztecan family, for instance, has illuminated earlier stages of Uto-Aztecan culture, giving evidence—through the divergence of horticulturally related words descended from an original proto-Uto-Aztecan language, spoken about 5,000 years ago—that Uto-Aztecan people were already agriculturalists, using planting sticks and grinding corn. The existence of cognate words for bow and arrow and acorn has also provided evidence of a hunting and gathering stage of early Uto-Aztecan culture.

By looking at maps and comparing the genetic classifications with the geographic locations of the groups speaking related languages, one can also suggest interpretations concerning original homelands and migrations. Generally speaking, the geographic center of gravity of a genetically related group of languages (the area in which there is the greatest variety of related dialects and languages within it) can be suggested as the original homeland, the center from which the various related language groups dispersed. Studies of the geographic range of the Uto-Aztecan languages, for instance, indicate that the probable homeland of this group, which eventually included Shoshones, Aztecs, and many other peoples of North America and Mesoamerica, was within what is currently northwestern Mexico.

In North America, similarly, the concentration of Eskimo-Aleut languages in the Arctic indicates that the very last arrivals to the New World spoke some kind of Eskimo-like language. The concentration of Athapaskan languages in the western Subarctic indicates that the immediate predecessors of the Eskimos spoke some kind of Athapaskan-like language. The speakers of the proto-language that was the ancestor of Athapaskan, Eyak, and Tlingit also possibly lived in Asia.

The gradual easterly movement of American Indians over time can be deduced from the fact that fewer language families, each with wide geographic distributions, were found in the East than in the West. Of the 57 postulated North American Indian language families, 37 were located west of the Rocky Mountains and 20 in California alone. The Northwest Coast and California were densely populated with different genetic groups. These were probably among the most recent groups to arrive in the Americas, and in 1492 they were still struggling with one another for the most attractive locations. On the other hand, peoples farther east had been pushed there by the increasing population pressure from other groups. A good example of a geographic distribution that reflected a gradual eastward movement from a western homeland was that of the Algonquian family. Indeed, if Algonquian is related to Wiyot and Yurok (both located in California), as is generally believed, we can locate the center of gravity of Algonquian on the Pacific coast and identify "family members" who had migrated to the Atlantic.

Other genetic relationships reflect a gradual north-to-south movement of Native American groups. The Athapaskan case is particularly striking. Since modern Apache and Navajo are relatively closely related to one another and also to the large number of distinct Athapaskan languages in Alaska and Canada, we have evidence of the quite recent (not long before 1492) movement of the Apache and Navajo south to their present locations in the U.S. Southwest from a more northerly homeland on the continent. At the same time, the very great time depth reflected in the proposed Hokan and Penutian phyla (from each of which various language families evolved) indicates not only a north-to-south movement but, given the relatively recent arrival of American Indians in the Western Hemisphere and the great age of these phyla, a possible Asian homeland for these groups as well.

A knowledge of genetic relationships among the languages of Mesoamerica and South America makes possible the following interpretations: The original homeland of the diversified and populous Mayas was in the highlands of Guatemala. The classical Mayas probably spoke two or three different Mayan languages. Apart from the language of the Huastecs, who were separated from other Mayan speakers by 1,000 miles and migrated away from the rest of the family more than 2,500 years ago—thus before the time of the classical Mayan civilization—the Mayan languages were clustered together geographically. This was a linguistic reflection of, and evidence for, the fact that the Mayan peoples, as distinct from Uto-Aztecan-speaking groups, were never expansionist.

In South America, the very great number and diversification of languages can be attributed to the longer period of time that elapsed after the South American groups migrated south from the north and lost contact among themselves. In particular, the many nomadic hunters and gatherers who lived in true refuge areas of South America—areas too harsh for either the typical highland or the typical lowland dweller—spoke languages usually classified as isolates, not related obviously or closely to any of the larger language families, thus reflecting early migration into the continent's hinterlands. At the same time the wide distribution of Quechua, with relatively slight linguistic differentiation, indicates the expansion of the Inca empire and of Quechua-speaking peoples and the fact that many conquered groups of those who were influenced culturally by the Incas learned Quechua as a second language or even replaced their own native languages with Quechua.

In contrast to genetic classifications, areal-diffusional classifications group languages on the basis of linguistic features they share, not necessarily from a common origin, but from contacts between and among speakers. Reflecting trade, intermarriages, bilingualism, and other intense interrelationships, the evidence of areal diffusion enhances and enriches our cultural-historical interpretations at different time depths. In 1492 the Pacific Northwest, for example, was characterized by a large number of linguistic features that cut across at least six distinct language families, comprising many different languages. The widespread distribution of these features reflected high densities of population in which peoples with different languages met one another frequently at trade and fishing centers, intermixed in feasting, storytelling, dancing, and other social events, and often intermarried. Similarly, in Mesoamerica, many common linguistic features reflected a long period of contact among the various peoples, as well as a widespread influence of the languages of several high civilizations on neighboring languages, in particular the influence of Mixe-Zoquean languages, which were probably spoken by the Olmecs.

Given the diversity of the languages of the Americas and the remarkably different ways they structured and organized reality—when compared with one another and with European languages, at the time of their first contact with one another—it is natural to wonder about the relationship between these languages and their speakers' perceptions of reality. There is no question that the grammars respectively of Hopi, Navajo, Mayan, and Nahuatl enabled their speakers to conceive of their universe in unique ways. Whether their languages conditioned or compelled them to think and perceive in particular ways is a much more controversial question.

The Hopi language of Arizona, while it distinguished tense—present, past, and future time—was much more attentive to verbal aspect, the ways in which actions were conceived of as occurring. This provided speakers of Hopi with a quite different perspective on the physical world than that of speakers of Western European languages. The difference between this southwestern tribe's view of the world and that of, say, early Franciscan priests would have a profound effect on each group's view of the other.

Traditionally, Western European languages encoded a basic semantic contrast in the distinction between nouns and verbs. Nouns label persons, places, things, and events of long and infinite duration, while verbs label actions and processes. The Hopi language, on the other hand, classified things of short duration, such as lightning, wave, flame, storm, and cycle, as verbs, and actions and experiences of longer and steadier duration as nouns. In addition, the fine-grained attention to aspect distinguished the relative length of time an event or action lasted, whether it was completed, ongoing, expected, or predictable, and its relation to other events and actions, as earlier, later, or simultaneous.

It is easy and perhaps dangerous to exaggerate the significance of these differences between Hopi and European languages. But there is no question that the Hopi language (like other Native American languages, each in its own way), by being so attentive to the manner in which actions and events occurred in minute and explicit detail, provided its speakers with a distinct perspective—with the possibility of expressing a view of nature and of the social and cultural world around them that would be attuned to ambiguity, and that would make them uncomfortable with "simple" declarative sentences such as: "In the beginning, God created the heavens and the earth."

Just as the Hopi language was extremely sensitive to the ways actions and events occurred, other Native American languages paid close heed to the forms and shapes of objects. The Navajo language related attention to the form and shape of objects with regard to the movements, motions, and distributions in space of the events and actions in which objects were involved. Navajo verbs which referred to states or conditions did not distinguish tense or aspect, but, rather, specified withdrawal or absence of motion and whether the object being described was in a given position at a point in space and time. Thus, a mountain was "a round solid object lies at rest," a mountain range was "round solid objects lie in a row," and a slender stone pointing upward was "a rigid object has extension from a fixed point." On the other hand, Navajo verbs which referred to events were conceived concretely in terms of movements of corporeal bodies or entities metaphorically linked with corporeal bodies. Movement was reported in painstaking detail that included attention to the forms and shapes of objects and their distribution in space. The English sentence "he picks something up" must be translated into Navajo twelve different ways, according to whether the object is round and solid, long and slender, animate, fabric-like, bulky, wool-like, rope-like, or mud-like, or is in a set or is a rigid container. And it was not verbs alone that were conceived of in terms of motion. Nouns also were often framed as motion. Thus, "full moon" in Navajo was expressed as "hoop-like object has rolled out."

The Navajo language's emphasis on movement and direction provides a picture of the worldview of this nomadic people that comes through clearly in their myths, legends, and folktales. In Navajo verbal tradition, subjects did not perform actions. Rather, they were included in actions already defined by means of the set of objects to which they belonged. And they related themselves to objects through motions or positions. In this sense, nature was more powerful than human beings.

The place of human beings in nature was addressed in interesting ways, as well, in languages in which the noun-verb distinction was ambiguous, as was the case in several Native American languages and language families. In Lacandón, one of the Mayan languages, particularly in intransitive, present-tense forms, there was no real distinction between nouns and verbs. The same Lacandón word was used to mean "my food" and "I eat." In the Mayan languages more generally, human beings were not conceived of as acting on nature and the world around them, so much as being in place within nature and the world. This orientation was expressed linguistically within the ancient Mayan literary classic, the *Popol Vuh,* in which the gods didn't just act, but considered, "How should this be done?"

Sometimes it is not grammar that provides a window on reality and cultural organization, but grammar in combination with vocabulary and, specifically, networks of words which work together to provide a particular organization of the world. The languages of Mesoamerica provide some fascinating examples, especially given the poetic, metaphorical bent of the processes of word creation and derivation in this area.

In Mesoamerica, certain key words had a polyvalence which served to relate various concepts in a web of symbolic associations. Thus, the ancient Mayan word kinh (which had closely related cognates in all the Mayan languages spoken in 1492) associated day, time, the sun, heat, festival, and destiny, all basic Mayan concepts. This web of associations encoded and expressed the central and significant roles of the sun and the heat in Mayan life, both for everyday and ritual purposes. For the Aztecs, Mayas, and other peoples of Mesoamerica, this web of words relating the sun, heat, and the cycle of time did not constitute a set of abstract symbols, but rather a concrete reality enmeshed in the world of myths, glyphs, and religion, which governed all aspects of human and natural life.

Another symbolic association encoded in and expressed through derivations between words was the intimate relationship between power and language ability and mastery. Thus, the Aztec word for "ruler" was literally "he who possesses speech."

The metaphorical and symbolic thrust of Aztec and Mayan language and thought was reflected in another characteristic of the classical Nahuatl and Mayan languages—dualistic metaphors. In classical Nahuatl, for example, single ideas were often expressed by a combination of two words. These dualistic metaphors were used both in everyday language and in the poetic language of Aztec ritual, which was pervaded by dualism. Here are some Aztec dualistic metaphors:

> the skirt the blouse = a woman
> water hill = a town
> flower song = poetry
> jade quetzal plumes = beauty

Nonetheless, since any concept can be translated, however cumbersomely, from one language to another, it is hard to argue that Hopi, Navajo, Nahuatl, or Mayan speakers were actually imprisoned by their languages and forced to perceive the world around them in particular ways, and only those ways, that were encoded in the grammars, vocabularies, and metaphors of the languages they spoke. Furthermore, there are cases in the Americas, such as in northern California and in the northwestern Amazon region, in which whole geographic areas were characterized by remarkable uniformity in culture coupled with radical diversity in the languages spoken. On the other hand, there is no doubt that the examples presented here provide insights into the ways American Indians perceived the world around them and their understanding of and their feeling for time, space, form, shape, motion, and movement, which constituted a poetic imagination inherent in the languages they spoke. This poetic imagination becomes all the more clear in actual poetry, the rich verbal art of American Indians, which in 1492—and continuing into the present—was a central element in the many rituals and ceremonies of Native America.

Many observers have pointed to the power and the sacredness of the word in Native America. This was often expressed in the words of Native Americans themselves, as in the passage from Munro S. Edmonson's translation of the classical Mayan *Popol Vuh,* in which the act of creation is described as an act of speech:

> The Mother said this,
>   And the father:
> "Should it only be still,
>   Or should it not be silent
> Under the trees
>   And shrubs?
> Indeed it would be good if there were
>   Guardians for them," they said.
> And when they thought
>   And spoke,
> At a stroke there came to be
>   And were created
> Deer
>   And birds.

It is evident that language and speech were, and are, central in the politics, religion, curing, and magic of American Indians. And language and speech were not only sacred and powerful but, in addition, poetic and verbally artistic. In fact, poetry and verbal art were usually essential, often in quasi-magical ways, to the power and sacredness of the word. At the same time, there was tremendous diversity in the ways in which the word—language and speech—entered into the social and cultural life of Native Americans. In some societies, silence and laconism were valued; in others, verbal effusiveness. In some societies, talk was omnipresent, as an essential ingredient in everything one did; in others, it was instrumental, a part, but not a defining feature, of such activities as hunting, farming, and warfare. In some societies, individuals were judged and chosen for leadership roles on the basis of their verbal abilities; in others, it was their skills as a warrior or hunter which counted most, and speaking abilities were secondary.

Oratory, formal speechmaking, was an important aspect of many Native American societies in relation to leadership qualities and as a necessary feature of rituals and ceremonies of many kinds. Among the various Iroquoian groups of New York and Canada—particularly within the famous Iroquois League that was coming into existence in 1492—there was an ancient oratorical tradition which entered into all facets of traditional religious and political life, including death, curing, and agricultural ceremonies. Most Iroquois ceremonies involved many speakers, representing families, clans, or whole nations, making formal speeches. In these speeches, as well as in dances and songs which took place in the Iroquois longhouse, speakers, with what might have seemed to Europeans to have been great repetition, told their audiences that their welfare derived from the spirit forces. This oratory was a central feature of ritual and kept the Iroquois world spiritually alive and well. Iroquoian and other Native American speechmaking involved an interplay of fixed elements and flexible adaptability, memorization and individual creativity, in addition to the use of a clear speaking voice, balanced content, and discretion.

While speaking well and often for long periods of time was a much-noted feature of Native American life, it contrasted strikingly with another frequent use of language, especially in North America: the selective *absence* of speech—silence and laconic pithiness. Apaches and other groups living in the present-day U.S. Southwest observed silence in certain moments—when meeting strangers, during the initial stages of courtship, between relatives and friends after a long period of separation, in response to shouted insults and criticism, in the company of someone whose spouse or kinsman had just died, and during the performance of a curing ritual. In addition, many North American In-

In this drawing from Joseph François Lafitau's *Moeurs des Sauvages Amériquains,* published in 1724, an Iroquois council is depicted as resembling a gathering of Roman senators meeting in a spartan landscape. Despite this distortion, the drawing accurately portrays the role of wampum in public oratory and diplomacy. The belt in the speaker's hand enables him to speak with authority. The two other belts at the speaker's feet will be used in turn. Each band of wampum was made of shell beads arranged in unique designs that served as both documents and memory aides. Lafitau inserted an example of a wampum belt at the bottom of the drawing.

dians, including the Apaches, were celebrated for their pithy, laconic humor, often directed at outsiders or engaged in at their expense. North American Indians have often been stereotyped as taciturn. But the stereotype of the silent Indian is clearly incorrect and is no doubt based in part on a misunderstanding of Native American rules of verbal and nonverbal etiquette. Just as wrong would be to interpret Iroquoian orators as long-winded when, in fact, the length of their speeches was often foreordained by the occasion at hand and intricately bound up with their ritual function.

Speaking ability, especially in the sense of oratorical skills, was important all over Native America. Verbal practices were so important to the Aztecs that they called themselves "people who explain themselves and speak clearly." The great sixteenth-century Spanish chronicler of the Aztecs, Fray Bernardino de Sahagún, reported that priests, judges, and royal dignitaries were taught in schools to speak well. "The thirteenth rule was to teach the boys to speak well, to bow and curtsy, and anyone who did not speak correctly or did not bow to whomever he met, or remained seated, they pricked with the points of maguey leaves." Aztec fathers, according to Sahagún, counseled their sons on how to speak: "Thou art to speak very slowly, very deliberately; thou art not to speak hurriedly, not to pant, nor to squeak, lest it be said to thee that thou art a groaner, a growler, a squeaker."

Among the ancient Mayas, oratory was also important and was related to prophecy. Future Mayan leaders were chosen by means of a procedure which included a trial by riddles—they had to interpret certain metaphorical expressions, known as the language of Zuyua. The Aztecs also used riddles ritually. Those provided by Sahagún offer a view of both the metaphorical worldview and the humor of the Aztecs:

What are the ten broad stones which one bears on the back? One can see from our little riddle that they are our fingernails.

What is that which is a small mirror in a house made of fir branches? Our eye.

What is that which follows along the gorge, going clapping its hands? The butterfly.

Farther south, among the Incas in the Andes, oratory was similarly important. Here, in a modern translation by Harold V. Livermore, is what the Inca historian Garcilaso de la Vega said about the importance of verbal art and tradition, especially its preservation, in the Inca society of 1492:

> Another method too was used for keeping alive in the memory
> of the people their deeds. . . . The amautas who were their phi-
> losophers and sages took the trouble to turn them into stories,
> no longer than fables, suitable for telling to children, young peo-
> ple, and the rustics of the countryside: they were thus passed

from hand to hand and age to age, and preserved in the memories of all. Their stories were also recounted in the form of fables of an allegorical nature, some of which we have mentioned, while others will be referred to later. . . . But as the Incas had no knowledge of writing, they had to use what devices they could . . . they chose historians and accountants . . . to write down and preserve the tradition of their deeds by means of the knots, strings, and colored threads, using their stories and poems as an aid. This was the method of writing the Incas employed in their republic.

In the Central and South American lowlands, oratory continues to be esteemed to this day. Among the Kuna Indians of Panama, speechmaking ability was highly valued and was a major criterion in the selection of leaders. Chiefs and their spokesmen regularly chanted and spoke myths, legends, folktales, personal experiences, and counsel, typically in the evenings, to audiences of men and women gathered in a centrally located meeting house. The language of Kuna oratory was highly metaphorical and, like oratory elsewhere in the Americas, involved the creative and individual manipulation of traditional forms and themes.

In addition to political ritual, which centered on oratory and involved communication among humans, there was magical ritual, often the basis of curing, which focused on communication between the human and spirit worlds. Among the Kunas, magical rituals were elaborate, and language was essential to them. The centerpiece of Kuna magic was a memorized chant, performed by a specialist in a ritual, secret language to representatives of the spirit world. There were many such chants, which lasted from several hours to several days. Some were aimed directly at curing diseases or ailments—high fever, severe headache, epilepsy, madness, malaria, difficulty in childbirth, or snakebite. Others provided the performer or another person with special powers to carry out a successful hunt, to hold a hot iron rod, or to grab a dangerous snake and raise it in the air. These chants were esoteric and not intelligible to ordinary people. They were translatable, however, word by word from the spirit language into everyday Kuna, and both specialists and spirits understood them and appreciated their aesthetic qualities. In fact, it was in large part because of their aesthetic properties that the spirits were convinced by these chants to carry out the specialist's bidding. The chants were narratives; they told stories of battles in which good spirits won out over evil spirits.

Music or musicality was common in lowland South American magical and curing language. As among the Kunas, magical musical chants played a major role in the curing rituals of the Suyá Indians of the Matto Grosso, Brazil. For the Suyás, as for the Kunas, curing chants were more important than herbal

A Kuna leader with his family and attendants, as depicted by an English traveler, Lionel Waffer, in 1699. The leader's station is indicated by his earrings and adornment. The leader's attendants and retinue are identified by nose rings of varying sizes.

medicines. Suyá curing chants were performed very quietly, almost whispered, and in an intelligible but highly metaphorical language. Metaphor was crucial to the magical functioning of the chant. For example, the chant for a child with a high fever named the white cayman. This was because the cayman, according to the Suyás, lay very still in the water without a tremor and never got hot. The chant imparted to the feverish child the quietness and coolness of the cayman.

The Kuna and Suyá curing chants were semantically meaningful, in the sense that it is possible to translate them into English. In other South American societies, the ritual language was either so ancient or so transformed from everyday language that it had no specific meaning. Its power resided in the efficacy of the general mood and tone created by its musicality and rhythm.

Magical curing chants were also used in North America. In the present-day U.S. Southwest, these were called "ways" and were performed in the context of curing rituals. Among the Apaches, they began early at night and ended shortly before dawn the following day. Illnesses were believed to be caused by supernatural powers. In curing rituals, one or more medicine men chanted and made use of ritual paraphernalia in order to neutralize the sickness-causing power and thus cure the illness.

A Richness of Voices   **269**

These Ojibwa pictographs were reproduced in the nineteenth century by Henry School-craft, an Indian agent who married into the tribe. They indicate the sequence for invocations, offerings, and songs during a particular ritual. Numbers were added to the original figures to assist explanation.

Navajo curing chants, which were a central feature of curing rites, reenacted the creation of the world and placed the patient in this re-created world. The patient was identified with the good and power of various deities and removed from the effect of the dangerous and evil sources that caused the disease. The chant was the verbal performance of a myth that described a culture hero's diseased condition and cure through identification with, and control of, deities. The patient was thereby identified with the culture hero and thus came to be similarly restored to good health.

There were a large number of distinct Navajo curing chants, with many variants and special features. Most chants had two- or three-night forms and five-night forms. The choice of the appropriate chant was determined by means of divination. The performance of the chant was accompanied by other ritual procedures, including dances, the making of prayer sticks, ash blowing, and sand-painting. The chants were classified according to mythological association, ritual association, and relation to the cause of the disease. The Holy Way group of chants dealt with problems related to lightning, thunder, the winds, snakes, various animals, and other Holy People. Enemy Way was performed for sickness caused by the ghosts of foreigners. One of the most frequently performed chants was Blessing Way, which placed the Navajos in tune with the Holy People and ensured health, prosperity, and general well-being. It was precautionary and protecting. Navajo curing chants were extremely powerful and dangerous at the same time. The chants and the symbols within them had to be memorized and their power derived from their perfect and exact performance, sound for sound and word for word.

Although American Indian speeches, myths, legends, folktales, and magical chants were finely integrated with the social and cultural lives of the speakers of the languages and played a central role in politics, religion, curing, and recreation, they were also appreciated in and for themselves as creative, imaginative, artistic, and humorous. Various principles and features characterized the verbal art. Primary among them were repetition and parallelism, metaphorical language, and the dramatization of the voice in oral performance.

Many forms of verbal art in Native America, especially those used in ritual and ceremonial contexts, were structured through the repetition of sounds, words, phrases, lines, and verses. This structure moved the texts along, provided an incantatory tone, and aided in the memorization of fixed verbal forms as well as the creative performance of those that were flexible or adaptable. In parallelism, the repetition, such as in this small portion of the Navajo Blessing Way (derived from the work of Gary Witherspoon), was of a frame, within which there was variation:

> Earth's feet have become my feet
> by means of these I shall live on.
> Earth's legs have become my legs
> by means of these I shall live on.
> Earth's body has become my body
> by means of these I shall live on.
> Earth's mind has become my mind
> by means of these I shall live on.
> Earth's voice has become my voice
> by means of these I shall live on.
> Earth's headplume has become my headplume
> by means of these I shall live on.

In Mesoamerica, a common form of parallelism was the metaphorical couplet, which was a major organizing principle of the verbal art of the classical Aztec and Mayan civilizations and is one more linguistic reflection of the dualistic mode of thinking that has been noted for these civilizations. Couplets, as well as triplets, were characteristic of the poetic structure of the Mayan epic, the *Popol Vuh*. Here is an example from a speech (from the work of Dennis Tedlock) in which the gods who were the makers and modelers of humankind called upon older gods, who were diviners and artisans, to help them:

So be it, fulfill your names:

Hunahpu Possum, Hunahpu Coyote,
Bearer twice over, Begetter twice over,
Great Peccary, Great Tapir,
lapidary, jeweler,
sawyer, carpenter,
Maker of the Blue-Green Plate,
Maker of the Blue-Green Bowl,
incense maker, master craftsman,
Grandmother of Day, Grandmother of Light.

Metaphorical language pervaded the verbal art of the Americas in 1492, in part because of the closeness Native Americans had always felt to the natural world around them and their social, cultural, aesthetic, and personal identification with it and in part because of their faith in the immediacy of a spirit world whose presence could be made manifest in discourse.

Metaphor was often a powerful force in the verbal art of curing and magical rituals. The case of the Brazilian Suyá was typical, especially of lowland South America. Just as the Suyá curing chant for a child with high fever metaphorically names the cool white cayman, the curing chant for a toothache named the wild pig, since it ate roots and its teeth did not hurt. The curing chant for an easy birth named a small fish that slips easily out of the hands.

Metaphorical language also often entered into political rhetoric. Kuna political speeches and chants abounded in metaphor. A particularly rich area in this regard was the language which described Kuna social and political structure itself. Chiefs and other political leaders were symbolically represented as trees in the jungle, as animals of various kinds, and as poles used in the construction of a Kuna house.

The metaphorical and symbolic bent of Mesoamerica was reflected in the grammars, vocabularies, and verbal art of that region. The sacred literature of the Mayas expressed a refined and sensitive aesthetic in which plants, animals, objects from nature, agricultural products, cardinal directions, and colors formed a web of metaphorical associations. A beautiful illustration is this hymn from one of the Yucatec Mayan books of the *Chilam Balam,* which recorded ancient Mayan history in oral poetry. Metaphors and repetition and parallelism provide the intersecting organizational basis of this text, published by Miguel León-Portilla in his *Pre-Columbian Literatures of Mexico:*

The red flint
is the sacred stone
of Ah Chac Mucen Cab

[the red spirit hidden in the earth].
The red mother silk-cotton tree
is his arbor in the east,
the red chacalpucté is also his tree,
the red zapote and the red mushrooms. . . .
The red turkeys with the yellow crest
are his turkeys.
The light brown and red maize are his maize.

The white flint
is the sacred stone of the north.
The white mother silk-cotton tree
is the arbor of the white Mucen Cab
[the white spirit hidden in the earth].
The white turkeys are his turkeys.
The white beans are his beans,
The white maize is his maize.

The black flint
is the stone of the west.
The black mother silk-cotton tree
is his arbor.
The purple and black maize is his maize.
The yam with the black stalk is his yam.
The black turkeys are his turkeys.
The black maize is his living maize.
The black kidney bean is his kidney bean.
The black bean is his bean.

The yellow flint
is the stone of the south.
The yellow mother silk-cotton tree
is his arbor.
The yellow pucté is his tree.
Yellow is his yam.
The yellow maize is his living maize.
The kidney bean with the yellow shoulder is his kidney bean.

Nahuatl dualistic metaphors were the generating principle underlying the couplets and triplets of Nahuatl poetry, thus doubly reifying the expression through verbal art of the dualistic worldview. The following triplet is based on the dualistic metaphor "jade and quetzal plumes," which symbolized beauty in Aztec thought:

> *Yet the jade is broken.*
> *Yet the gold is smashed.*
> *Yet the quetzel plumes are scratched.*

Since Native American verbal art was orally performed, much of its aesthetic fascination and appeal derived from the dramatization of the voice in performance. Indian performers were masters of the voice. Modulations of the voice included alternating fast and slow and loud and soft speech, and creating rhythmic and pitch patterns in both spoken and chanted forms. Interactions with other performers and the audience also contributed to the oral structure of verbal art, as in the ritual dialogue widespread in lowland South America. The use of pauses, integrated with the patterned repetition of words and grammatical elements, created lines and verses analogous to the lines and verses of Western European poetry. In this passage from the *Popol Vuh,* the ancient Book of Counsel, the voice moves in an orally diagonal fashion, simultaneously vertically and horizontally, as lexical doublets, parallel line structure, and what has been reconstructed by Dennis Tedlock as the original performance pause-pattern work together:

> *the   maker*
> *modeler,   mother of,*
> *father of   that which is alive,*
> *that which is human,*
> *with breath,*
> *with heartbeat*

Language is intimately related to our view of the world and to our place in it. In fact, it is often by means of language that culture and belief are conceived, created, and transmitted. There is no better way, then, than through language to enter the American Indian world as it was in 1492.

It is often claimed that language is the most conservative aspect of culture. What this means is that for the most part language changes at an extremely slow pace and that relations between and among languages remain evident for centuries, even millennia. This fact about language places us in a most fortunate situation with regard to trying to imagine what languages were like in the Americas in 1492. In many ways, an examination of commentaries of the time, in comparison with contemporary research, attests that what we find today is much as it was in 1492.

Investigation of language in Native America reveals a creative and dynamic imagination in which language, from grammar to metaphor, was central and integral to relationships among individuals, cultures, societies, history, and the environment. Every day and night on the eve of Columbus's voyage, native people throughout the Americas, from the highlands of Guatemala to the lowlands of Brazil, from the populous Pacific Northwest to the isolated South American Gran Chaco, created and performed a remarkable diversity of verbal forms characterized by metaphorical richness, complex poetic and rhetorical processes, and intensely personal styles, all of which were an intimate part of the replication and transmission of their cultural and aesthetic traditions.

SAM D. GILL

ODD BALLOON SHAPES, spotted and blotched with grayish-white paint, hung in bunches about the dimly lit interior of the qasgiq, or community lodge. A feathered image of a bird was suspended from the roof in such a way that it glided up and down as if in flight. At the back of the room, to the rear of the bird, stood a pole, ten feet in height, painted red and white at top and bottom and bound with bundles of wild celery stalks. This was the setting for the several-day-long Bladder Festival, celebrated by many Inuit (Eskimo) peoples of the Arctic.

A wooden tub, placed in a hole in the center of the lodge, represented a seal's breathing hole, an entryway into the sea beneath the ice. Drums beat loudly as a young man called in the voice of the eider duck. The headman sang a song; all present—men, women, and children—joined in the refrains. As the singing progressed, the people began to dance, portraying the familiar activities of some of the creatures they knew—loons, murres, and beavers.

When the dance concluded, a man carrying a tray entered the lodge and offered food to the keepers of the game and to the life-forms (shades or souls) of the animals slain during the hunts of the past year. These animals' life-forms were represented by their bladders, which dangled like balloons about the qasgiq. In preparation for the dance of the following day, an inflated sealskin was hung from a stake. It had gull wing feathers attached to its flippers. To a drum accompaniment, the dance, performed by several groups of four men and a young girl, imitated seals and walruses. When the dance ended, hunters amused

Tsimshian mask, with movable eyes and jaw, portraying the spirit of cold. Such masks were used in elaborate winter ceremonial dances during which families dramatized spiritual ties between their ancestors and particular supernatural beings. Courtesy of Field Museum of Natural History.

everyone with humorous speeches. Late at night, the leader extinguished all the lights and from the roof made a speech to the bladders. Responses from the seals could be heard. Torches of wild celery were used to purify the qasgiq. At the finish of a song sung by all, the hunters rushed to their bundle of bladders hanging from the ceiling. They attached the bladders to the shafts of their spears and passed them up through the smoke hole to the man standing on the roof.

In the climactic event of the festival, the hunters then ran to a hole that had been cut in the ice. Their way was lighted by a huge wild celery torch. Each hunter ripped open his animal bladders and, walking around the hole, dipped the bladders and a kayak paddle into the sea. Finally, each bladder was pushed beneath the surface with the paddle. The rising bubbles marked the path of the disappearing bladder. The life-forms had begun their journey home.

What did this festival event accomplish? Why was it performed? Can we understand it as *religious* in any sense? Although there are certain elements of the Bladder Festival that seem to bear obvious religious themes—such as the bladders representing the souls of animals—rarely do we see such events as fully religious. Since the time of Columbus, Native American "religion" has been understood by non-natives primarily from the perspective of Western religious traditions. Religion is defined in terms of churchlike institutions, the presence of scripture, and belief in god or gods. It is rare to find anywhere in the Americas institutions that parallel the ecclesia of Western religions. Although Native American cultures are rich in story traditions, the peoples—with the exception of Mesoamericans—did not write their languages; thus, at least in the technical sense, they have no histories, philosophies, scriptures, or doctrines. Although spiritual entities, divinities, and rich story figures are known among virtually every culture native to the Americas, the theological assumptions of people from Western monotheistic traditions have often overshadowed or markedly skewed these figures. So to see the Inuit Bladder Festival as religious requires some reflection on what is signified by the term "religion."

The Bladder Festival was based on the belief that every living thing had within it, or associated with it, a life-form or what might be called a soul (inua to the Bering Strait Inuits). This soul was invisible, though conceived of and sometimes represented in humanlike form. Because it bore the identity of any living thing—human or animal—it permitted the outer visible form to be changed without loss of identity. Animals and humans that changed their appearance were very common in Inuit stories. The origin of human beings was told in a story about Raven. By removing his raven appearance to reveal the human form lying beneath, Raven gave origin to the human lineage. This belief underlay the extensive use of masks by the Inuits which portrayed this relationship between a human or an animal and its inua. Likewise, in the Bladder Festival, the bladders of all of the animals killed throughout the hunting sea-

From the tops of their earth lodges, people view the climax of the four-day Okeepa Ceremony of the Missouri River Mandans. During this ritual, young men were initiated into manhood and the tribal world was renewed. To the left, four poles hold cloth offerings, while in the center, an enclosure shelters a sacred pole and commemorates the group's rescue from an ancient flood. There is evidence that this ceremony took place centuries before 1492, even though this scene was recorded by the American artist George Catlin in the 1830s.

son were saved, for they represented the inua of these animals. The Bladder Festival honored the inua of the animals and performed a ceremonial act of sending them back to their homes. The leader of the Bladder Festival was a person of special spiritual qualities, known by the Siberian term "shaman." In some performances of the festival, the shaman actually conducted the bladders/inua to their home by entering the sea through the ice hole, reemerging after a considerable time. Properly treated and returned to their homes, the inua would indwell flesh-and-blood animals to become available once again to the Inuit hunters. Thus, although the Bladder Festival may not meet our conventional expectations as a religious event, there is no question that it has a religious character, that it bears important religious forms and themes.

The Bladder Festival is but one of thousands of actions or events having religious forms and themes that were probably performed in the late fifteenth century by native peoples throughout the Americas. In a consideration of the

Religious Forms and Themes   **279**

A romantic portrait of an Iroquois curer, shrouded, cloaked, and wearing earrings. He holds a bag of herbs and a rattle; a tobacco plant grows at the lower right. While most Iroquois curing was performed by masked members of medicine societies, specialists in the community offered herbal cures for specific illnesses.

religions of these cultures as they existed in 1492, we must keep several things in mind.

The hundreds of cultures native to the Americas have come to be known only gradually during the centuries. Records of their festivals and rituals as well as their worldviews are sparse. Often the best records of the aspects of culture that carried religious themes and forms were not made until the late-nineteenth or even the twentieth century. By that time even cultures that appeared to be traditional, that seemed not to have changed, had nonetheless experienced extensive alteration during the preceding several centuries. Unfortunately, we can often do little more than guess at the measure of this change. The religions of only a few cultures can be accurately described as they were in the late fifteenth century. We will present examples of religious forms and themes that probably existed at that time, but came to be known only later. These themes and forms were incorporated into religions that were in many respects distinct from tribe to tribe. There were hundreds of religions in the Americas. We will use the past tense throughout—not to deny that many of the examples we discuss are present today, but only to indicate that the theme or form was probably important at the time of Columbus.

We will understand religion in terms that can encompass both Native American and Western religious traditions, although they often contrast strikingly. Religion is made up of those forms and themes that both express and define the extent and character of the world, especially those that provide the cosmic framework in which human life finds meaning and the terms of its fulfillment.

Stories of many kinds were told by Native Americans. Many recounted the creation of the world. Others told of heroes who showed humans how to live their lives. The basic traits of the human character were explained in story. Stories kept track of history, of tradition, of great and not so great human beings. There were stories of buffoons and fools who challenged every system of order, every semblance of stability, yet ironically seemed to vitalize the world by their wily actions.

Stories of creation and origin are those most often termed "myth." Because they are often fanciful in character and because they are at odds with the modern scientific understanding of world and universal origins, we have often dismissed these stories or relegated them to the domain of entertainment. Even worse, we have seen them as evidence of a primitive naïveté. But we must appreciate these stories, set in the beginning, as describing that which was most fundamental to a people at the time they were told. These stories established truth and meaning.

The Achomawi Indians of California attributed the power of cosmic creation to speech. In Navajo creation stories, both thought and speech were personified as male and female figures inseparable from the vital forces of all the world. In Acoma Pueblo creation accounts in the present-day U.S. Southwest, thought is personified as a creatress. The creator deity, Moma, was a major figure in the stories of the Witotoan tribes, who lived along the Putumayo River, which borders Colombia and Peru. The name Moma means "father," and Moma, identified with the moon and perhaps in another form with the sun, is both creator and culture hero. The Witoto considered that "the word" preceded Moma and even gave origin to him. Moma was understood as the personification of the power of the word. As hero, he transmitted this power to the first human beings. For the Witotos, as for many peoples throughout the Americas, the word was identified as a creative force. The Amassalik Inuits of eastern Greenland reflected this belief in their language, in which the word "to breathe" also meant "to make poetry" and stemmed from the word referring to the life force. With the power of the word held to be of such creative potency, all speech acts—especially prayer, song, and story—had creative potential.

All over the Americas tribes told about the creation of the world in stories that said that in the beginning there was nothing but an expanse of water. The first beings were perched on the back of a water turtle. Among these beings were animals who took turns diving into the water to try to swim to the bottom, where they might get a bit of soil to use in creating the earth. Animal after animal attempted the task. Each was gone longer and longer. Each returned exhausted, almost dead, and without any soil. One animal was finally able to bring up just a tiny bit of soil beneath its claw. The earth maker took this bit of dirt and made the earth out of it. But the whole earth still rested on the back of the turtle.

Some tribes told stories about how the creation was accomplished by the sexual union of a man and a woman, although these were rarely, if ever, identified as the earth and the sky. Common to all Andean peoples in South America was the worship of the sun and moon as a fructifying pair. In Peruvian art the sun and moon appeared as god and goddess in humanlike form accompanied by two-headed serpents that represented rain and lightning. This pair was attended by plants and animals known for their fertility, such as carob and monkeys.

Rather than relating stories of world creation, some tribes, such as those in what is now the southwestern United States, told of journeying through subterranean worlds leading to emergence on the earth's surface. The world and peoples already existed in the beginning of these stories. The peoples lived far below the present earth's surface. Heroic guides were sent to lead them through the lower worlds. Not all those within the earth emerged, but those who did, usually the human beings, were known as the daylight people or as hard- or dry-food people. Those who did not emerge, who remained beneath the earth's surface, often the supernaturals, were green or, as the Tewa called them, the "Dry Food Who Never Did Become."

Culture heroes were central to stories told throughout the Americas. The Apachean peoples (Apaches and Navajos) had migrated from western Canada to the southwestern United States by the end of the fifteenth century. They brought stories of hunter heroes, often a younger and older brother (sometimes sisters), who lived in the interim period following creation but before the beginning of the human era. The newly created Navajo world was a world of rules and restrictions, a place of order. But it was a world without experience. What would happen if the rules were broken, or how to repair the broken order if it occurred, was not known. Yet life could scarcely proceed without breaking rules or violating restrictions. The heroes of these stories had the courage to live even if they had to suffer the consequences. The suffering they experienced as a result of their courage opened them to the knowledge and powers of healing and re-creation. These heroes gave origin to the Navajo way of life, including the bulk of the ritual processes that distinguished Navajo religion.

Culture heroes were frequently twins. The Iroquoian peoples of eastern North America told stories of twin brothers who appeared in the last group of episodes in a long and complicated creation narrative. The narrative began in a sky world, a world of perfection that was soon tainted by the introduction of human emotions, the love shared by a young woman and man. Their love, as is so often the case, was accompanied by pain and suffering. To resolve their suffering, the woman was pushed through a hole in the sky, thus separated from her lover. Although banished from the sky world, she was to help create the human world below. An earth-diver episode established terra firma. The woman, impregnated by the wind, gave birth to a daughter, who, in turn, impregnated by the water, gave birth to twin boys. One of the twins was born from its mother in the normal fashion; the other, impatiently unable to await this process, ripped open his mother's side, through which he was born. The manner of their births corresponded with the characters of the respective twin brothers. The good twin set out on the earth to establish a world ideal for human habitation. The bad twin set out not only to nullify the good but to introduce the bad. The struggle of the twins characterized the nature of the Iroquoian world. The meaning of life was bound up in the never-ending struggle between positive and negative forces.

The Warraus, or "boat people," of the Orinoco Delta and adjacent swampy regions of northern South America, whose dugout canoes served them not only as a means of travel but as a place to sleep, cook, eat, and play, told stories of the first man, Haburi. Haburi wandered about the earth seeking food. With him was his son, who was not born of woman. Haburi found the house of a woman, but he was unable to get her to share her food with him until he showed her his child. Later the woman made a canoe of wax, in which she and Haburi departed, leaving the child behind. Now alone, the child carved a male child from wood as a companion. The image, however, transformed into a female and came to life. This boy and girl became the ancestors of the Warrau people. Other Warrau stories attributed the creation of the canoe to Haburi. Long bound under the influence of Frog, a woman who claimed to be his mother, Haburi eventually learned the identity of his real mother and resolved to escape from Frog. He built a canoe, but it was stolen by a duck. Time and again he built canoes, each time losing them to various ducks (accounting for the origin of their buoyancy). Finally he built one that was not stolen, and in it he and his mother escaped. He foiled Frog by telling her to enter into a hollow tree to suck honey from a beehive. When she did so, the opening closed around her. Imprisoned in the tree, she became a tree frog.

A wily, robust, sexually promiscuous, selfish, gluttonous kind of character appeared in the stories of cultures all over the Americas. The character took many forms—mink, raccoon, raven, hare, spider, jay, old man—but none so common as the coyote, who was the inspiration for the present-day popular coyote and roadrunner cartoons. While Coyote was ruthless and cruel, he could be kind, thoughtful, and heroic; he was grossly sexual and erotic, but he could be prudish and finicky; he was destructive and dangerous, but he could also be a creator.

In one widely told incident, Coyote (or another of these figures) came upon someone who could send his eyes out of his head to the limb of a tree and call them back by saying, "Eyes hang upon a branch; eyes come back." Coyote wanted desperately to be able to do this. The eye-juggler refused again and again to tell him how to do it, but Coyote's pathetic appeals finally wore him down. Coyote ignored the warning that he must never perform the trick more than four times in one day. When he sent his eyes up for the fifth time, they did not return. No matter how hard he tried, they would not come back. Shortly they began to swell and spoil. Flies crawled upon them. But Coyote was not easily defeated. He lay quietly in the grass until a mouse came along and tried to cut a hair from Coyote's fur for his nest. Coyote leapt upon the mouse and made it trade one of its eyes for its freedom. With mouse vision Coyote was able to locate a buffalo. He tricked it into giving him one of its eyes. Coyote thus regained vision, but he was a ludicrous fellow with one tiny eye rolling about in one eye socket and one eye so large it mostly protruded from the other.

Such characters as Coyote were known throughout the Americas for their powers of transformation. They were able to change their appearance to any form so that they might satisfy their sexual appetite by tricking a woman into marrying them. They often changed their appearance to trick someone into providing them with a meal. Sex and food were the basic interests of these figures wherever their stories were told. Yet they were fooled as often as they fooled others. Fox, a character in the stories of the Toba tribe in Argentina, met Jaguar. Jaguar liked Fox's rattle. To trick him, Fox persuaded Jaguar that the rattle was actually his heart and that Jaguar had one too. Jaguar permitted Fox to extract his heart so that he too might have a rattle. Fox removed Jaguar's heart through his anus, as befitting his foxy character, thereby killing Jaguar. Fox cut up Jaguar and began to roast the meat. While waiting, he grew thirsty. Chunga, a bird, showed Fox where there was water. She also agreed to swim with him. But while Fox thought she was swimming with him, she sneaked off and stole the roasted Jaguar meat. Fox pursued Chunga and, disguised as her friend, was able to get some of the meat back. However, Pigeon, who had red eyes that Fox admired, ended up with even this meat by tricking Fox into rubbing red pepper into his eyes so that they too might become red.

Erotic, gluttonous, untrustworthy story characters such as Coyote and Fox seem far from religious, yet most Native American cultures have valued them highly. In one respect, at least, the stories of these characters showed powerfully how not to act. Children could learn, and adults could reconfirm, proper behavior through these exciting and entertaining tales. Through their telling, touchy subjects like selfishness and sexual behavior could be addressed. More

An Oneida man, elaborately tattooed, smokes a long pipe and carries tobacco pouches, as drawn by Louis Nicolas. According to the artist's caption, the figure is honoring the sun, which he worships as personal guardian. Tobacco was used to communicate with the supernatural throughout the Americas.

profoundly, the incongruence, even the broaching of the unthinkable that the stories often dallied with, raised for people the question of meaning itself. That is, in their way, they showed that order and rules were in some sense linked with the creation of meaning, in contrast with the shock of chaos experienced through the sometimes unrestrained violation of order by these characters. Laughter and religion were at one in these stories.

While stories from the late-fifteenth-century Americas have not survived except through the lineages in which they existed, other cultural forms had such gross physicality that at least some traces endured even the destructive forces of conquest. With the aid of archaeological excavation and reconstruction techniques, cities and villages can be reconstructed from the rubble of conflict and the ravages of time. Architectural forms—from enormous pyramids and temples to modest houses—leave a lasting impression upon the landscape. Acting conjointly as cultural beings, Native Americans constructed houses and temples, laid out villages and cities. In doing so, they designated places that corresponded with a variety of domestic, political, and ceremonial activities. These architectural forms reflected the hierarchies and structures of their religions and societies.

The Aztec capital city, Tenochtitlan, whose site is within present-day Mexico City, was one of the grandest cities in the Americas at the time of Columbus. The Aztec universe consisted of thirteen celestial layers and nine underworlds. Each of these regions, characterized by color and attributes, was the domain of a deity. The horizontal structure of the world was conceived of as a four-petaled flower or a cross with a jade bead in the center. Each of the four regions was distinguished by a tree with a bird perched in its top and by a deity who held up the celestial regions. Both vertically and horizontally the Aztec understanding of the cosmos focused upon a central place, the capital city. The city was thus a microcosmic model of the universe. At its center was a huge ceremonial complex containing schools, administration buildings, a ceremonial ball court, and skull racks, holding the skulls of scores of sacrificial victims. In the center of the ceremonial complex stood a temple built upon a great pyramidal base. This ceremonial center was surrounded by a ten-foot wall. The city was divided into four regions by major roads that crossed at the great temple in the ceremonial center. Even these four regions were subdivided into microcosmic patterns oriented upon secondary centers. Tenochtitlán was not only the center of the Aztec world; it bore the imprint of the order of the whole Aztec universe.

Along the Rio Grande in New Mexico is a long-existing Tewa Pueblo village currently known as San Juan. The boundaries of the Tewa world were marked by mountains up to sixty miles from the village of San Juan, one standing in each of the four cardinal directions identified by name and color. When the Tewa people emerged from their primordial domain beneath Sandy Place Lake, far to the north of San Juan, some of those who stayed behind were recognized as deities. The Tewa considered their residence to be in lakes corresponding with the four mountains. Closer to the village in each of the cardinal directions are flat-topped hills. Each of these hills, regarded as dark and foreboding, has a cave or tunnel, the domain of supernaturals who serve a mediating function between humans and the spiritual world. Still closer to the village in all of the four directions were shrines, known as "Souls-dwelling Middle places," each one associated with a specific supernatural figure. The village itself, in the arrangement of pueblos (house complexes) and dance plazas where the public rituals have long been performed, replicated this structure of religious significance. Interacting with these many designations within the Tewa landscape, the Tewa people have participated in an ongoing process of creating and maintaining order. That order sustained and gave meaning to the social, political, economic, and ceremonial dimensions of their community activity. In this way religion permeated every dimension of Tewa life. Religion was inseparable from the Tewa conception of the land. The orientation and design of architectural structures throughout the Americas, even those without obvious religious purpose, bear the imprint of religious significance.

Religion is a human activity, a way of creating and discovering worlds of meaning. This attribute of religion is reflected in many ritual objects whose physical design is inseparable from the use made of them. Such objects often survive to tell the story of their religious importance. Pipes are intended to be smoked. Masks are carved and prepared so as to be worn, flutes to be played, and bull-roarers to be whirled. In Mesoamerica the picture books that survived the conquest or were prepared shortly afterward often depict religious activities. Petroglyphs and pictographs, earth mounds and etchings, leave reminders of human activities, sometimes religious in character, although the meanings of so many of these are extraordinarily opaque. Some of the mounds and etchings are spread so hugely across the landscape that they cannot be fully appreciated except by viewing them from high in the air, a view obviously not possible until quite recently. The Nasca lines that stretch for miles across the Ingenio Valley in Peru were created at a time long before the arrival of Columbus. Some of these lines, as do many mounds, take the form of animal and mythical figures, probably corresponding with the story and religious traditions.

The Aztecs and Mayas lived in highly developed material cultures and possessed glyphic writing systems. Many objects of religious importance to them have survived. Found in a drainage ditch, a discard of the conquest of Mexico, was the famous circular disk known as the Aztec Calendar Stone. This disk apparently lay in a temple at Tenochtitlán, where it played a major role in the ceremonies of human sacrifice. The glyphs on the stone document not only the fifty-two-year calendar cycle but the ages through which the world passes. The stone reflects the centrality of the sun and the belief that the strength of the sun was dependent upon its being fed human blood and hearts. The Aztecs used this huge stone disk to keep their place in history and in the solar, celestial, and cosmic cycles in which they lived. According to the stone, they fed the sun by the sacrifice of human beings in order to enact their responsibility for maintaining the continuity of life.

At the completion of each fifty-two-year cycle a major ceremonial event assured the initiation for a new cycle. In preparation for this ritual renewal all fires in Tenochtitlán were extinguished. Cooking vessels and eating utensils were destroyed. Houses and temples were swept clean. Atop a hill outside of

This painted stone figure, found in a crypt in the floor of a kiva in eastern Arizona, suggests a female earth deity still important in the mythology of modern Pueblo Indians. Painted in stripes of red, black, yellow, and white suggestive of the colored layers of the Pueblo underworld, this figure perhaps represented a creative force. Courtesy of the Field Museum of Natural History.

the city, a victim was sacrificed. Within his chest a new fire was quickly ignited. The new fire was carried by torch into the city to the Great Temple and from there to other temples throughout Tenochtitlán. From these temples the new fire was borne to households and to outlying towns within the empire. All that survives of this ceremonial are the bones of the victims, the architectural ruins of the setting, and storybook depictions of it, yet the dramatic performance in blood and fire gave power to the ongoing progression of Aztec time.

The convex shape of the back of a mask and the eyeholes are evidence that a mask is intended to be worn upon the human face. Masks are for performances; they are to effect the presence of the beings they represent. Masks are powerful religious objects found throughout the Americas. The Inuits of Alaska fashioned from driftwood some of the most complex and creative masks to be found anywhere in the world. The Iroquoian tribes carved faces into living basswood trees, splitting them off in such a way that the tree remained alive. These were the faces of spirits to be used primarily in healing rites. Perhaps the best known of the faces represented the power of the malevolent brother in the Iroquois creation story. When the good and malevolent brothers met at the end of the era of creation to determine the stronger—so the story related—they held a mountain-moving contest. The bad brother succeeded in moving the mountain a little. As he turned to measure the reaction of his brother, the good brother moved the mountain right against the back of his boastful brother. When the bad brother turned back around, he permanently bent his nose and mouth on the mountain. As the loser of the contest, he begged to be allowed to utilize his powers to cure the diseases for which he was the cause. Iroquois people wore masks with bent noses and mouths to embody the healing power of the malevolent brother. The healing power of this masked figure demonstrated the belief that even malevolent power could be used to good effect.

Tribes along the Pacific Northwest Coast in North America carved elaborate masks to represent the animal ancestors of human lineages. Most distinctive among them were those that opened and shut to reveal multiple identities. These transformation masks corresponded with the stories of the origins of human lineages. Originally all beings were animals, but some removed their animal appearances to reveal their inner human forms. In masked performances outer animal forms represented by the outer layer of the mask were opened mechanically to reveal an inner human face, thus replicating the events of the lineage origin. The Pueblo tribes in the southwestern United States, too, have long used elaborate masks in complex ceremonial cycles.

In the fire-lit interior of a plank longhouse, Kwakiutl men dressed as wolves and bears dance to the accompaniment of drummers beating on a hollow log. Scenes like this displayed family privileges during long, wet winter nights along the Northwest Coast.

Religious Forms and Themes   **289**

In South America, masks representing animal and bird spirits and figures, told of in story, were used by many tribes in association with hunting. Knee-length hooded costumes made of bark cloth and painted with geometrical designs were used as masks by the Cubeo and Cauá of the Vaupés region of the northwestern Amazon. Humanlike faces with distinctive animal features that appeared in these costumes represented spirits of animals. These mask-costumes were used in rites intended to control the enemies of the hunters.

Wind instruments—trumpets, flutes, and megaphones—were used widely in tropical South America to present the voices of the deities. North of the Amazon the instruments were associated with vegetation deities; south of the Amazon they were played in esoteric men's rites. The Tucano of the upper Amazon had a wooden megaphone (toki), said to be invented by the culture hero, Dyoi, to serve as the voice of spirits who would enter two carved wooden figures. A bark trumpet (bu-bu) was played to accompany the spirit voices.

Bull-roarers are simple sound-producing instruments constructed by attaching a string to a flat piece of wood through which a hole has been pierced. A roaring or whirring sound is created by whirling the wooden piece at the end of the string. Bull-roarers are known among cultures throughout the world. In eastern Brazil, the bull-roarer sounds were considered to be the voices of the dead. The Bacairi, a tribe in central Brazil, had fish-shaped bull-roarers that originated, according to their stories, as a gift from the dogfish. Called yélo or iyelo, the words for thunder and lightning, these bull-roarers were used in rituals to bring rain.

Native Americans often expressed their conception of the life cycle as a movement across the landscape, as a road, a road of life. Many things, from houses to ceremonial dance circuits, were made religiously meaningful by this orientation. The Piman peoples of the southwestern United States represented the road of life as a circular, single-path labyrinth that wove in and out, eventually reaching the center. Pimans understood that by following their culture hero, I'i'toi, along this path they would reach their life goal.

Throughout the Native American life cycle, many transitions, many new beginnings, were celebrated and effected by religious ritual. Rites of passage that initiated the formal religious life and that conducted a child into adulthood were widely practiced. As children reached the age of reason, they were often initiated into religious societies or into an adult status in their cultures. Puberty rites for girls usually correlated with their biological maturity—the onset of menstruation. Isolated from their communities, these girls had to observe many personal restrictions, such as not touching their own flesh lest they mar their beauty; drinking only through a straw to prevent causing an excess of rain; avoiding the food and belongings of men, especially hunters, lest they weaken them; and practicing benevolence, humility, and proper demeanor. In their isolation, the girls were attended by exemplary women who taught them the ways of womanhood, including the responsibilities of a wife and a mother. Boys achieved manhood more commonly by their accomplishments in hunting and warfare or in vision-fasting.

One approach used to initiate children into their religious lives was to disenchant them out of their child's point of view. Children were encouraged to accept a naïve realism, to hold the view that the world was as it appeared to them. Among the Hopis of the southwestern United States, such an approach is still used. The children are encouraged to view the masked spirit beings, kachinas, as the spirits themselves. The children never see the personators without masks, or masks that are not being worn. It is integral to the initiation process that the children witness for the first time the masked figures costumed but without their masks. Recognizing the kachinas as their male relatives, they are sorely disenchanted. Many cry and feel that they can never again trust adults. The long-term effect of this approach to the initiation of the religious life is striking. To truly appreciate the spiritual world, to see the fuller dimensions of reality, they learn that the world is more than it appears to be. The Hopi and other American tribal cultures use a technique of creating a naïve view only to destroy it, utilizing the power of disenchantment that accompanies loss of naïveté to initiate deeper inquiry and insight.

The Onas of Tierra del Fuego at the southern tip of South America made similar use of masks in the male initiation rites. The initiated males entered the village appearing as spirits, with their bodies painted in patterns of pink, black, and white and wearing masks made of skin and bark. They quickly frightened away the women, then turned to the initiation of the youths, which centered on the revelation that the spirits, as they appeared, were masked humans.

Isolation and vision-fasting were widely practiced in the Americas. Among the Ojibwas and other tribes in the woodlands of the Great Lakes region in North America, boys were led into the woods in the spring to fast for a dream or vision. In the branches of a red pine an elder built a platform from ten to twenty feet above the ground. Here the youth remained without eating or drinking until he had the dream or vision. If he had a bad experience, the lad returned home; he would try again another year. The vision experiences were remembered, and served the recipient as a guide for life, revealing vocation and destiny. Power objects revealed in visions were acquired as tokens by which to recall the visions and their powers. The quest for vision was also conducted by some tribes at times of grief, as a vehicle to acquire shamanic powers, and as fulfillment of vows.

Dreams and visions, though seen worldwide as access to the spiritual world, were so important to Iroquoian tribes that they were incorporated into ritual. The Iroquois held that some aspect of the human life form could leave the body during sleep to have spiritual experiences remembered as dreams. To fulfill dream wishes was therefore religiously important and often led to the

Burial ceremonies for a chief. Engraved by Théodore de Bry and published in 1590, this illustration presents several aspects of the funeral rites held for Timucuan leaders in Florida. The bereaved gather around a mound erected over the departed's grave. His arrows circle the structure and his drinking cup rests at its peak. Three mourners are at the upper right; in the lower left a man has his hair cut as a sign of grief. Finally, the grieving community places the dead chief's belongings in his house and sets it ablaze (upper left).

expenditure of remarkable effort. During the Midwinter Ceremonies, various dreamers posed riddles of their dream wishes to be guessed—and often acted out—by the whole community.

Though rare in North America, hallucinogens were widely used among peoples in South America. Tribes of the northwestern Amazon commonly drank hallucinogenic beverages in conjunction with initiation rites for youths, funeral ceremonies, and a rite of the new year known as yurupari, which commemorated the act of incest which the Sun Father committed with his own daughter at the time of creation. In the ritual, painted and adorned men were seated on stools on one side of a large room, women on the opposite side. A large torch lighted the room from its central location. The ceremony began with the recitation of the creation story, the origins of humanity and the phratries. Throughout the night the men repeatedly drank a hallucinogenic beverage and sang and danced. The women kept the men happy with their laughter and they severely chastised those who failed to continue drinking and dancing.

"Shaman" is a word widely used to designate every sort of priest, healer, ritual specialist, and sorcerer. The term, in its original Siberian meaning, referred to religious specialists who used ecstatic techniques. If taken in this restricted sense, "shaman" would accurately designate individuals in but a few American cultures, yet, with caution, the term may be used more broadly to designate those who had access to extraordinary spiritual powers and employed those powers to influence the human world. Shamans had spirit allies, often an animal spirit, a mythical figure, or a deity. Distinctive of the shaman profession was the ability and technique necessary to call upon these spirit allies, techniques that involved entrancement, the use of power objects, and the use of songs or chants.

Shamans acquired their powers by inheritance, personal quest, purchase, election by society or by a spirit being, or through an experience of affliction treated by a shaman or shamanic society. In South America hallucinogens were used to acquire and access spiritual powers. Isolation and fasting were more common in North America.

Shamans served their communities in many capacities, such as calling game animals, interceding with a spiritual chief or keeper of game animals, clairvoyance, divination, and weather control, but the most common and widely practiced activity of shamans was healing. By one reckoning, illness was caused by the intrusion of an object into the body of the sufferer by some malevolent power or witch. Shamans, empowered by a spirit ally or by medicine, located the object in the sufferer's body by clairvoyance and cured the resultant illness by sucking the malevolent object from the body of the sufferer. Another reckoning attributed illness to the loss of life force or vitality due to its theft by a malevolent force. To treat this illness the shaman journeyed spiritually to the home of the malevolent being to recover—often by combat—the life force of the sufferer. Some dramatically enacted the journey and struggle. Among them were the Coastal Salish of the Pacific Northwest, whose shamans used canoes in healing lodges in which they dramatically played out the journey in search of the life force of a sufferer. Some shamans performed spirit flight by entering into a state of trance. Others, the Inuits, for example, entered the sea through holes in the ice, to emerge only after an extended time.

Throughout the Americas religion has served as an important binding and ordering element in society. In the simplest sense, most religious actions were societal in that they established or enacted the societal order. But, also, social actions were performed either under the guise of ritual or under the mandate of religious tradition. The Zunis were the first group north of the Rio Grande contacted by Europeans. At that time there were apparently seven Zuni villages. The Zuni world was divided into seven domains—the four cardinal directions, zenith, nadir, and center—a structure that pervaded all of Zuni life, including clan, ceremonial, and calendrical organizations, and remains largely intact today. Zuni clans were organized into seven groups, each corresponding with one of the directional designations. Each group, especially those that corresponded with the four cardinal directions, had social roles defined in the temporal and spatial terms associated with the corresponding direction. The Crane, Grouse, and Evergreen Oak clans were clans of the north. They were associated with winter and with yellow, the color of morning and evening light in the winter, as well as the color of the northern auroral lights; with wind, air, and breath; and with activities that centered on war and destruction. The clan symbols were appropriate to the place and its attributes: the crane's flight announces coming winter, the grouse changes its color to white in winter, and the evergreen oak stays as green in winter as other trees do in summer. The clan that controlled the priesthood was located at the center, the intersection of all other regions, apart from, yet at one with all. Joined at this center place, Zuni society was unified and each division given equality with every other. Even the powerful Zuni priesthood was integrated into Zuni society by the basic religious principles of Zuni. As time progressed through the calendar, Zuni life cycled around centers in time and space. Standing in the center of the world, a Zuni village is called itiwana, which means "the middle place."

Quite in contrast to the Zuni were the Aztec, Mayan, and Incan cultures. Their religious organizations rested on various levels of priesthoods that were integrated with secular authorities. As reflected in the architecture of temples perched on pyramids rising high above the cities, these cultures were radically hierarchical in structure. The Incas maintained an extensive priestly organization integral to their political structure. The priestly caste, headed by a high priest who was a near relative of the emperor, itself constituted a hierarchy with various levels of priests specializing in such tasks as divination, sacrifice, temple service, and hearing confessions. While the priests were the center of Inca religion, particularly as it functioned officially for the state, there were still many religious figures—shamans and healers—outside of this hierarchy. A counterpart to the priests, though not hereditary, was the *aclla,* the "chosen women" or "Virgins of the Sun," who were recruited at the age of ten and prepared for roles that ranged from temple service to sacrificial victims (see page 233). The Virgins of the Sun were led by a high priestess considered to be the consort of the sun god.

Among the Aztecs, Mayas, and Incas, priestly power was maintained by the avoidance of salt, meat, and sexual intercourse. Priestly duties included making sacrifice (from food offerings to human sacrifices), hearing the confessions of the people, conducting initiation ceremonies for young priests and nobles, and conducting ceremonies both on a regular calendrical basis and on special occasions such as harvests. In these cultures, religious life was sanctioned by the state; the power of priests and rulers reinforced one another.

The Midewiwin, or Great Medicine Society, was a religious shamanic so-

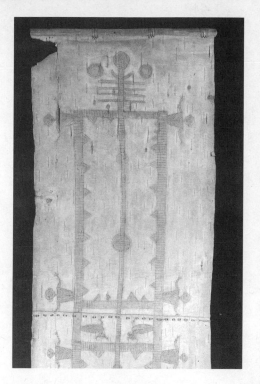

These etched birch-bark Midewiwin scrolls served as memory aids during ceremonies of the Midewiwin, or shamans' society, of the Great Lakes. The diagram indicates the proper seating arrangement within the medicine lodge for a particular ritual. Courtesy of the Field Museum of Natural History.

ciety that stood at the core of the central Algonquian cultures in the Great Lakes region of North America. Upon election, individuals were initiated into the Midewiwin by being symbolically killed. Revived from this ritual death, the initiate became a newly born member of the society. The influence of the Midewiwin pervaded social, political, and economic life.

Religion was involved even in war and in other violent ways by which Native American cultures distinguished and protected themselves from their neighbors. The Aztecs provide a dramatic example of this aspect of religion. Rooted in the Aztec belief that human blood and the human heart contained the vital energy for the sun's continued motions and subsequently the continuing creation of the cosmos, Aztec rulers sought sacrificial victims by waging war against surrounding towns and cities. The power of the Aztecs spread during the fifteenth century as they conquered neighboring peoples, bringing back captives to Tenochtitlan to use as sacrificial victims. At the height of this activity, many thousands of captives from surrounding cultures were sacrificed, integrating both the religious importance of sacrifice for the renewal of time and human life and the importance of conquering neighboring peoples to ex-

The people of the Great Lakes region usually called this specially constructed lodge a shaking tent. When a shaman stationed inside went into a trance, the lodge began to shake violently as various spirits, often led by Turtle, entered. When all were gathered inside, members of the community sitting outside would ask questions. They inquired about events in other places and in other spiritual realms and asked for information concerning their future.

tend the Aztec domain of power. The increased influence of the Aztec culture was itself considered evidence of the energizing potency of human sacrifice.

Hunting, gathering, fishing, and agricultural activities provided nutrition for Native Americans, but, equally important, they were activities that reflected and enacted Native American religions. One of the oldest of Native American religious actions was bear hunting as practiced by circumpolar cultures. Bears, as well as other animal species, were understood to reside in a home or region under the control of a chief or master/mistress who protected them and sent them out to be hunted. A successful hunt depended upon proper communication with the master/mistress of animals, often done by a shaman.

Among the Naskapis of the Labrador peninsula, the shaman talked with the animal master by means of entranced drumming and singing. Parallel to the shaman communicating with the master/mistress of the species, the hunter communicated with the actual game animals in the hunt. The hunt was often thought of, if not actually conducted, in a ritual manner. Before the hunter killed the bear, he was supposed to address it, using a ritual, and often a kinship, name. He was to apologize to the animal and to explain that the kill was essential to the sustenance of the hunter and his family. The hunter was to plead with the bear not to be angry and to assure the animal that its body would be treated with respect. The manner of the kill was ritually prescribed, as was treatment of the carcass. Some hunters gave offerings of tobacco to the dead animal. Others dressed it in fine garments. The carcass was butchered in a prescribed manner, with some parts, understood as representing the life force of the animal, placed on display or ritually disposed of so that the animal spirit or life force would return to its home, regenerate flesh, and return the next hunting season. The Jivaros of Ecuador attended particularly to the skull of game animals, believing that the display of a skull would attract living animals of the same species. The distribution of meat reflected the hierarchy and interrelationships in the hunters' community.

The religious notion of the master/mistress of animals was known among hunting peoples all over the Americas, although there were varying understandings of the character, role, and appearance of this type of figure. The Tupinambas of eastern Brazil knew a figure they called Korupira, who was the owner of the forest and all of the animals of the forest. Korupira seems to have overseen human actions related to the forest animals and punished hunters who wantonly killed the animals. While the guardian of animals commonly took

Two deer dancers painted by the early-twentieth-century San Ildefonso Pueblo artist Awa Tsireh (Alfonso Roybal). Evoking themes of health and fertility, such dances were ancient in the Southwest. Versions of the antlered headgear, cotton clothes, open-work leggings, and woven kilts could have been in use in 1492.

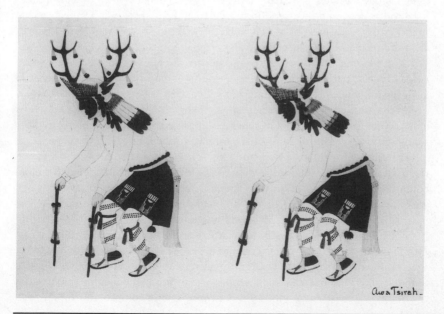

an animal form, often very large or even grotesquely misshapen, Korupira's appearance was very different. He was a little, bald-headed, one-eyed, green-toothed, large-eared, hair-covered man whose legs were jointless and whose feet turned backward. From a hollow tree deep in the forest, he controlled the interactions of hunters and animals.

The religion of the Kwakiutls of the Pacific Northwest coast of North America centered on the interdependence of human beings and animals, articulated through the imagery of eating, digestion, and regurgitation. Because the people believed that humans and animals had been the same at the time of creation, they thought of animals as primordial kin and they believed that particular animals were the ancient ancestors of human lineages. During the hunting season the Kwakiutls killed and ate the game animals. During the winter, the ceremonial season, humans donned the masks of their animal ancestors and danced as the animals. Kwakiutl rituals often included cannibal themes, enacting the reciprocal phase of the human-animal interdependence. In the winter, humans were ritually consumed by the animals and by the great mythic cannibals, returning in kind the summer human consumption of game animals. Through their ceremonies and stories, the Kwakiutls enacted their vital interdependence with animals.

Fishing and whaling were forms of hunting and often resembled, in their ritual dimensions, the hunting of land animals. The Quileute-Hos of the Olympic Peninsula in the present-day state of Washington hunted whales from light canoes. Whales provided many things needed by the Quileute-Hos—food, oil, sinew, and a variety of implements. The whale was a figure central to their story traditions, playing a role even in the creation of the world. Whalers were trained in the lore and rites of the whale as fully as in the physical skills of whaling. In addition, to initiate his career, a harpooner underwent ritual ordeals. The whale hunt was prepared for and conducted with song, and a successful whale hunt culminated in a giveaway feast dance or potlatch.

At the southern tip of the Americas the Yahgan shamans of Tierra del Fuego invoked the spirits that ruled beaches and marine animals, beseeching them to send fish, crabs, seabirds, and other animals to the hunters and fishers.

Hunting constituted a rich body of action by which cultures sustained themselves not only as nutrition-demanding entities but as meaningful human communities in a complex world. The language of the hunt, the relationships with animals, the activities of the hunt, and the rituals of hunting were the means by which hunting peoples were religious beings.

For centuries, sun watchers have stood at the edge of the Hopi village of Oraibi in present-day Arizona to locate the rising sun among the land features that silhouette the horizon at dawn. The ceremonial calendar corresponded with the sun's seasonal movement from north to south and south to north upon the horizon. Those ceremonials did not simply commemorate the passing seasons; they effected the passing of time and were the basis for a meaningful way of life known as Hopi. The performance of ceremonials is how the Hopis have enacted their responsibility for the continuing creation of a meaningful world.

Religion is often reflected in the agriculturalists' concern for the cycle of seasons, the weather, and fertility. Maize was the principal crop of agriculturalists in the vast region from roughly the U.S.–Canadian border all the way south through Mesoamerica to deep into South America. Gradually domesticated for cultivation as early as 4000 B.C. in the southern part of Puebla, Mexico, maize eventually became central to hundreds of Native American cultures. Many agriculturalists also hunted at least on a seasonal basis. Thereby, animal and hunting themes were often coexistent with vegetable and agricultural themes in their religious expressions.

In eastern portions of North America, particularly in the southeastern United States, a corn woman figure was important to the story traditions. The Cherokees told stories of Selu, Corn Woman, who mysteriously produced corn for her family. Curious as to how she produced this food, her sons followed her to the corncrib and secretly observed that she produced the corn by rubbing it from her body or by defecating it. Believing this to be evil, the boys plotted to kill their mother. With foreknowledge of her death, Selu requested that upon killing her, the boys clear a piece of ground and drag her bleeding body over it. Where her blood touched the soil, corn grew. The story relates the origin of the cultivation of corn, for upon the death of Corn Woman the production of corn required human labor. The story also shows the vital interconnection between life and death, between the blood of death and blood as the source of life, a connection that suggests continuity with the kind of imagery often used by hunting peoples. Blood, which among hunters was often associated with the killing of game necessary for human life, is in this story of corn associated with feminine fertility, with waste and elimination (particularly female), and with soil. The paradoxical identity of life and death seems in this story to have been transformed and expanded into the paradoxical identity of waste and food.

Other renderings of these life-and-death interdependencies expressed through the active medium of blood took various forms of sacrifice, even human sacrifice, practiced in a region that extended from the plains in North America, where the Pawnee sacrificed a young girl to Morning Star, into Central and South America, where human sacrifice played a major religious role.

Manioc, sweet potatoes, and peanuts, the food that sustained the Jivaros of Ecuador, came from their gardens. Each household had a large garden or several smaller ones. The women tended the gardens. The Jivaros connected the fruitfulness of their gardens with Nunui, who was conceived apparently either as a goddess living within the earth or as a group of plant fairies. Influ-

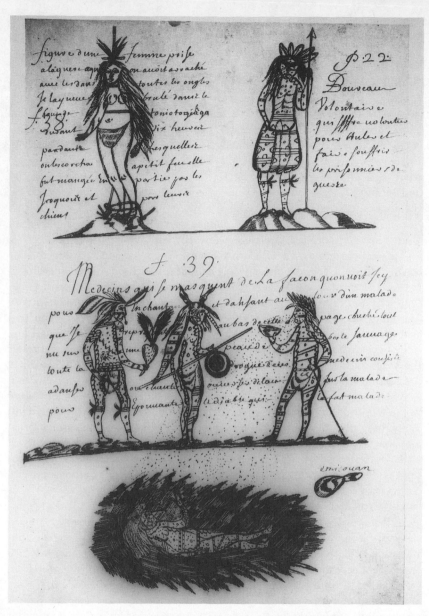

A curing scene by Louis Nicolas. Men with a rattle, a drum, and a bowl of medicine stand ready to cure the patient resting on an animal hide below. During the cure, medicine was sprayed over the patient to dislodge the disease, to the accompaniment of singing and dancing.

enced by hallucinogens, Jivaro women saw Nunui as a very fat woman only three feet tall, dressed in black. During the day she resided under the soil, where she encouraged the growth of the crops. At night she emerged to dance in their gardens. The crops depended on providing Nunui with a place to dance, a well-cared-for garden, and with "babies," three red stones placed under an overturned serving bowl in the center of the garden. The Jivaros believed that if a garden was not properly weeded, Nunui withdrew deep underground, taking the plants with her. Nunui had to be provided with babies because, according to the story, long ago Nunui gave the Jivaros her baby, a plump female child. This baby provided anything that the Jivaros asked of it. However, the Jivaro children mistreated her to the extent that she withdrew everything she had given the Jivaros. The only way the Jivaros could appease Nunui was to provide her with "babies."

An agricultural way of life seems to have correlated with an emphasis upon feminine fertility and goddess figures. Corn women, corn maidens, and fertility goddesses were undoubtedly common figures throughout the agricultural region. However, an agricultural way of life did not necessitate an emphasis upon the feminine. The Caua and Cubeo tribes of the Vaupés region of the northwestern Amazon associated agricultural fertility with male potency. They enacted this interconnection by performing masked phallic dances. The masked dancers wore large phalluses made of bast and used red cones from trees to represent testicles. The dance movements imitated coitus. The culmination of the dance occurred when the dancers spewed semenlike material throughout the village, houses, and fields. The dancers chased groups of women and girls, spurting "semen" among them. The hilarity and good humor of such dances did not dampen their importance in producing fertility for the community.

In the late fall or winter of A.D. 1064–65, a volcano in what is now northern Arizona spewed lava and ash for miles. The Hisatsinom, "the ancient people," who lived in the area anticipated the eruption and moved, taking even the roof beams of their houses with them. When the crater cooled, the remaining cinder cone was distinguished by having a reddish coloration near the top of the west-facing side, appearing to be always cast in the light of sunset. It became known as Sunset Crater.

By the fifteenth century, a dynamic period for the peoples in this southwestern United States region, the Hisatsinom had merged into the Hopi. Apachean hunters were entering the area, having migrated from the far north. Contact had been established with plains tribes and tribes along the west coast. On the eve of the contact with Europeans, during this period of great cultural creativity, a story was told about the eruption of Sunset Crater that had occurred some four centuries earlier. It was the story of Ka'naskatsina, or Sunset Crater kachina. This story has been recently recorded from a Hopi, Michael Lomatuway'ma, by Ekkehart Malotki. It is exemplary of the creativity and continuity of religions all over the Americas. It is a story of a spiritual figure that continues to dance at Hopi, still vital after many centuries.

In the story, an unwilling or uninterested bride in the Hopi village of Musangnuvi ground corn every day without stopping. Girls often interrupted their grinding to entertain suitors. This girl never stopped. Her family worried, for she was of marriageable age. The family grew hopeful when they heard the daughter stop grinding now and then. Tactfully they inquired about the identity of the suitor. He brought gifts of food, foods out of season: baked corn when there were no crops in the fields and dried rabbit meat when rabbits were not easily hunted. The family was baffled, but any Hopi would have known that the suitor was a kachina, because kachinas live in a world opposite the human world. The suitor's gifts reflected this.

Consistent with Hopi courting practices, the man arranged to take his prospective bride to visit his family. The suitor, Ka'nas, or Sunset Crater kachina, used a rainbow as a vehicle to carry them to his home, not in the Hopi world. Four times he extended the rainbow. On the third stop, the girl needed to defecate. Her urge was caused by Old Spider Woman. While she attended to this, Old Spider Woman spoke to her, foretelling the difficult trials the girl would have to undergo in the kachina's home. Old Spider Woman sat upon the girl's ear and promised to serve as her powerful ally.

In the kachina home, with the help of Old Spider Woman, the girl successfully passed four trials. For one trial she ground ice into water that was stored by the kachinas to provide rain for the Hopi people. The girl delighted the kachinas by cooking a huge feast. They reciprocated, as a satisfied groom's family would, by returning to the girl's home to give gifts, to feast her family, and to entertain them with dance. The groom's family dressed the girl as a bride. All went well and the two were married. The kachinas returned to their home, leaving the couple to reside at Musangnuvi. Thanks to the power of Ka'nas, the Hopis enjoyed abundance.

But this is not a story of "they lived happily ever after." No good story would end here. In the village there lived a group of sorcerers, notably called "turds," who were jealous of Ka'nas. They plotted against him. One of the "turds" made a mask resembling Ka'nas's, planning to seduce his wife by assuming his identity. The plan worked. Although both Ka'nas and the other Hopis seemed to know immediately what had occurred, the wife realized what had happened only when her husband returned. She felt ruined and Ka'nas concluded that he could no longer live with her or the Hopis. "Since you yielded to those sorcerers," he told his wife, ". . . you are theirs now."

With his departure went the prosperity of the Hopis, but Ka'nas was not satisfied. He wanted revenge. Ka'nas dug a hole on a hilltop (Sunset Crater, of course) in which he started a fire and enticed the wind to fan the fire. But the hole was dug too deeply and the ground fire merged with the fires under the earth. The result was an enormous explosion, creating a holocaust that spread nearly to Hopi, many miles away. The people were terrified, but this did not satisfy Ka'nas.

There followed years of drought, wind, and hail that left the Hopis destitute. All of the "turds" eventually died. Ka'nas's wife's family were the only ones spared the suffering, being provided with a secret supply of food. After years of watching this suffering, Ka'nas finally relented.

In reconciliation, a group of Ka'nas kachinas and many other kinds of kachinas went to the Hopi people bearing food, and they danced to entertain them. Asked by the Hopis to stay, the kachinas declined, but they took residence in a shrine near the village where the Hopi people could honor them by depositing prayer feathers.

This wonderful story utilizes ancient geological history in a portrayal of a way of life and the difficulties of living it. The story encompasses such important issues as family and marriage, the problems of jealousy, the responsibility to reject sorcery and evil, the importance of food, the necessity of rain, and the interdependence of human beings and the spiritual world. The story raises complex and difficult issues as well. Why did Ka'nas and the people interpret the deception of Ka'nas's wife as an act of adultery? Why did this woman have to bear the brunt of both the trials of Ka'nas's family and the shame and consequences of being tricked? Why did the wife's family secrete away the food given them by Ka'nas rather than share it with their friends and relatives? Why did Ka'nas make all the people suffer when it was only the sorcerers that offended him? What does the story say about disguise and impersonation?

These questions cannot be simply answered now, probably because this is not a story that provides answers. The story, likely throughout its long tradition, has presented for contemplation the concerns of the peoples who told and heard it, peoples whose world was complicated and sometimes difficult to live in, yet rich in meaning. The story, though thoroughly entertaining, is remarkably complex and provocative. It is in the telling and retelling of such stories and in the singing and dancing of such figures as Ka'nas kachina that cultures all over the Americas have enjoyed religious vitality.

JAY MILLER

LOOKING DOWN from a hill, an old woman reflects on her life and surroundings. She sees her land and people as a united whole, bound together by bonds going back to the creation of the world, when only the immortal spirits existed. Since that distant time, other people came into being, leaving traces on the landscape before her. She sees their campsites, the places where her ancestors and relatives were born, lived, died, and were buried. On a hillside, she sees a den where generations of cougars have lived, and a pond where a family dog drowned.

She sees much more—the cavern where ancestors of her family came out of the ground, the crag where Raven turned a selfish lady into stone, the deep pool where Beaver has a home, and the locale where barren women go to leave offerings and pray to have children. All of these places have been hallowed by stories about spirits and ancestors whose experiences justified the beliefs appropriate to this landscape. All of these people, places, and memories constituted her society, one of many in the Western Hemisphere of 1492.

To most native inhabitants of the Americas on the eve of the sustained contact with Europeans, society was, characteristically, an all-encompassing moral order whose members were "people" of many species and kinds, *only some of whom were human.* Composed of innumerable beings from many generations, each society was thoroughly "grounded" within a particular homeland. Moreover, dominant features of the landscape, believed to be inhabited by powerful spirits, were associated with predominant families, which

A war dance performed inside a Kansa earth lodge, as depicted by Samuel Seymour, the artist who accompanied the Stephen Long expedition across the plains to the Rocky Mountains in 1819–20. For Kansa people, warfare was a highly ritualized activity designed to protect the community from outside threats, both physical and spiritual; it was only one aspect of social life.

often formed a regional elite. Known as "real" people, members of such elite families, relying on the security of their strong ties to a particular landscape, were connected by obligation, ritual, trade, or marriage. Every terrain was saturated with memories, which compressed generations of experience—ranging from daily routines to great crises—into useful knowledge. Because of this retold past, the world was familiar in all of its extremes, full of hope or warnings about people's long-term involvement with the total environment.

The touchstone for all interactions was the human community, whose members were regarded, not as masters of nature, but as mediators of complex relationships among all "people," human and otherwise. Humans acted as the nexus or link in the interplay of immortals (the supernaturals of a locale) and mortals (all of the species that lived, died, and were reborn in that habitat). Through special relationships, renewed generation after generation, particular immortals and members of special human families worked together to maintain the spiritual and ecological balance of a region. These families knew the proper prayers, offerings, procedures, and rituals needed to compensate the appropriate immortals for the use of local resources.

Humans occupied a pivotal position in creation because, unlike other "people," they could not change shape. Humans were limited to a bipedal body, upright posture, manual dexterity, and set genders. The other "people," both immortals and mortals (animals, plants, insects, and so forth), were believed to have the ability to shift among several outward shapes. It was a common belief that animals and some plants had a human essence, evident when they were at home in house-like burrows or dens, but disguised by the appearance of their species when they ventured out. Immortals, too, had a human form, but an insubstantial one characterized by a shimmer or an iridescence caused by their powerfully charged condition. Throughout the Americas, these immortal spirits were the points of transfer for the energy that animated the cosmos. Spirits were thus the creators and custodians of the landscape, and occupied "holy homes" in caves, mountains, and other distinctive geographical features. Settled in the landscape, they were available to human petitioners and ever ready to intervene in daily life.

In addition to the capacity for thought, "people" also had emotions, expressed within close, caring, humanlike communities. Like humans, other "people" were also believed to organize themselves into groups which recognized the distinctions of ability, age, and gender.

All human communities had leaders, mature members of special families well versed in local lore, sacred history, and a concern for the greater good of everyone. Kindness and concern for all people were their hallmarks. Unlike other individuals, these leaders thought in terms of the larger whole, not just their own families and households. Yet their links with power sources, both religious and political, inspired suspicion in their neighbors. Jealousy, revenge, or selfishness might tempt a leader into dangerous behavior, even into witchcraft.

The intensity of life in each community was balanced against a suspicion and a fear of more remote peoples. Each community was its own world, operating in partial isolation from other groups in its regional network, save for various thresholds, charged spots at the edge of water, forest, sky, or earth. These sensitive gateways in the flow of goods and powers could only be transgressed with care. Kinship defined the common identity of a single community. The idiom of kinship related everything within a community or region to everything else, but the idiom did not necessarily apply to more distant peoples. Only kin, kith, and friends belonged to the same social and moral order of a known world. Other peoples were enemies, alien spirits, or monsters dwelling beyond the horizons. Contact between regions was left to leaders who benefited the larger community through their quests for knowledge, trade, or lucrative connections with outsiders. Trained in the proper use of etiquette, prayers, and gift offerings, leaders had the means to cross thresholds.

Many native languages of the Americas used the term "real people" to describe those who fully understood the close ties binding together spirit, land, and humans. Generation after generation, members of these special families taught their children how to keep the goodwill of the immortals of their territory, and mediate between all peoples. As outward signs of good faith, leading families had many healthy and productive members, were honorably wealthy, and, accordingly, were generous to everyone because of a strong sense of communal responsibility. "Real people" signaled their close bonds with the iridescent immortals by the use of shiny objects such as shells, feathers, crystals, or specialty goods like Panamanian carved blackwood bowls, Puebloan inlaid mosaics, or the gold and silver utensils of Aztec and Inca elites.

In most cases, leadership was a function of age. The older a leader, the greater was his or her access to power and possessions. A generous leader was honored, as long as he or she did not become senile, but a vengeful one was feared because his or her long life was judged to be a consequence of robbing life from others. Shamans were everywhere particularly watched because they worked closely with the immortals and, via the transfer of power, also had the ability to change their outward appearance and attack humans in disguise.

Even during a crisis, however, a suspect could never be charged directly. People should not be confrontational or directive. In general, indirectness constituted proper behavior. A leader never ordered anyone to do anything. Leadership was by example, not by command. If a leader believed that something was imperative, it was said to have been demanded by immortals, not by humans. Members of "real" families had the ability to invoke such command because their bond with local spirits affected the general welfare. Leaders shared all they possessed to build and keep a following, but followers were free to leave a community if they found better prospects elsewhere or felt affronted. Thus, subtle negotiation was required whenever a leader thought that an action needed to be undertaken. Through these negotiations—often extended councils to create consensus—the task would be accomplished, but not until everyone agreed or became resigned to the outcome. While based on consensus, the process was made easier by the obligations of kinship among all those involved in the decision.

On both continents, within a particular landscape, local communities were scattered along waterways, each one moving seasonally among available resources but returning to a home base on a stream to fish or farm or winter. Prior to 1492, communities were probably ranked according to their locations

Outside a stylized village and stockade, Huron men smoke and discuss community issues in council. Since consensus was the rule in American societies, people spent considerable time conferring so they could "know each other's hearts." This drawing is from a portion of a map of French Canada by Francisco Giuseppe Bressani, an Italian Jesuit who lived in the St. Lawrence Valley in the middle of the seventeenth century.

Concilium

PAGVS

along the waterway, with those downstream near the mouth being more populous, more elaborately organized, and more prestigious than those at the headwaters, who were less complex in organization and had fewer resources. Even so, both downstream and upstream communities were linked by the trading of local resources and by various marital or ritual interactions. Commonly, shellfish and crops from the river mouth were traded for meat and nuts from the hinterland, sometimes among in-laws or ceremonial lodge mates.

In addition to the factors of ability and age, every community was pervaded by a profound regard for gender, defined as a range of humanlike possibilities beyond the two polar opposites, male and female, accepted by Europeans. In the Americas, there were three basic types: men, women, and berdaches of a third, intermediate, or androgynous gender. In practice, moreover, these types often doubled into six: hyper-men, men, berdaches, amazons, women, and hyper-women. Within native languages, these genders were explicitly human, but male animals and plants were also called "men" and females of any kind were called "women."

To function, a society relied upon a range of genders productively organized as married couples and cooperating groups, which were led by someone of intermediate gender. Within leading families, the union of men and women was vital for the community web, but the androgynous gender was pivotal for all the "people" in a universe. For this reason, a Creator, High God, or founding ancestor, as befit a universal origin-point, was often believed to encompass all genders simultaneously.

To societies in the Americas, centerings at all levels, creating mutually reinforcing relationships, were more important than geographical or legal boundaries for defining a group. Arranged within the landscape—above, on, or under the earth of land and water—were various pivotal locales. The heart, for example, was the focus of a person, the hearth fire was the pivot of a household of men and women, the river was the crux for communities along its banks, the sun was the center of the earthly realm, and the Creator was the central source and summary for the universe. Each center, in varying degrees, was an intersection where time, space, and potent energy converged and then dispersed throughout the creative flow of life. Each pivot was a transfer station, simultaneously both source and summary, for the pulsating rhythms of the universe.

As an integrated whole, each society functioned like a slowly spinning top, its gyrations keeping time with ecological and social processes. Society thus had a distinctive sense of eternal rhythms that didn't fit with emerging European notions of chronological time, of an objective history set in a context of expected change.

A survey of several representative societies on both continents helps to convey a sense of their distinctive rhythms within the pre-Columbian moral order.

Each reflects the variations in gender categories that were so pervasive among Native American cultures. Between men and women, societies might emphasize one gender over the other, each one equally or each one separately.

WE BEGIN on the upper stretches of the Amazon River, among multilingual communities of Tucanoans, lowland South American societies that were male-based. They emphasized men above women in daily and public life, and relied on inheritance from fathers to sons, forming distinct patrilines.

Paddling their canoe up the Vaupés River and into one of its tributaries, a group of Tucanoan men, led by a Sunbird clansman, are returning to the site of a former maloca (a large rectangular communal house), which they had burned and abandoned five years before when their master shaman died. Now they are returning to exhume his remains from the center of the derelict house.

The maloca had been the home of the Fish clan, whose male members are related to the spirits who are believed to reside in a similar maloca of their own beneath the river rapids in front of the site. Other species have their own malocas under other landmarks along the river, while the master of the animals has his maloca inside a distant hill, where shamans meet with him to discuss limits on the size of animal, plant, and human populations in the region. Recognizing their common society, they envision a certain number of animal and human births and deaths in order to maintain the ecological balance of the region.

Along the river are also malocas of more than thirty clans, claiming descent from sky, earth, or water. Clan membership is passed down from fathers to sons. Each clan maloca is associated with a particular river bend or beach. Behind the house are fields tended by women who have married into the clan. Cleared by men for the women's use, the fields are one of the few places, apart from the public space of the malocas, where men and women can meet and have the privacy to conceive children. Every family possesses several plots of manioc and other tubers. Additional crops are gathered from the tropical forest, where the men hunt armadillos, rodents, birds, monkeys, deer, peccaries, and tapirs.

Ages of ingenuity go into the clearing and care of the fields. Generally, a gentle slope is selected and all of the trees are cut partially through so that a large tree at the top of the slope, cut at an angle to send it crashing down onto the other trees, can clear the forest with minimal effort. The trees are allowed to dry and are then burned before the start of the wet season, their ashes fertilizing the ground. Crops are planted on the same site for several years, although productivity declines with each successive crop.

The malocas have two doorways, one in the front, facing the river and used by men, and the other in the rear, facing the jungle and used by women. The

As depicted by Johann von Staden, among the Tupi, communal fishing required cooperation and hard work by both men and women. While men took fish with arrows and strung their catch through the gills, women on the shore would have been processing the fish for storage.

house fires and kitchen area are also toward the rear of the maloca, where women spend their time cleaning, cooking, and caring for their families. Men spend their time visiting with one another, either on the riverbank or, in some communities, in a separate men's house.

Clan malocas are ranked according to their location along the river, with the most important ones downstream at the mouth. According to the Tucanoan account of creation, humans had originally been deposited along the river by a giant anaconda serving as a canoe. Each load of settlers had been sent to their own territory by the Sun, guided by Hummingbird, a revered ancestor. The founders of the more important clans settled downriver, while the lesser-ranked ones built their malocas upriver.

The leadership of a maloca is shared by an elder, who manages ordinary activities, and a shaman, who cures the sick, safeguards fertility, and conducts communal rituals. The most adept shamans become the custodians of supreme knowledge, especially of the sacred texts which chart all ancestral traditions.

A Kinship of Spirit   **311**

The power of a shaman comes from the Sun, who also provides hallucinogens to heighten the curer's perceptions. A novice begins his training with an established shaman of a community other than his own. He learns formulae, mythology, and genealogy to enable him to understand the world of mortals and immortals, and to acquire the ability to change into the form of a jaguar or an anaconda. His primary responsibility involves the welfare and continuity of his clan. During ritual trance or seclusion, he confers with spirit leaders to exchange a certain number of human souls, preferably from enemy tribes, for those of animals, who will then allow themselves to be killed by hunters from his clan. Also, he advises couples to refrain from sexual relations at certain times; having numerous children is considered socially irresponsible and morally contemptible, since the existence of many human children imperils the biotic equilibrium with other species.

The master shaman, a member of the Sunbird clan and a direct representative of the Sun, devotes his life to the study of moral and ethical traditions, particularly those embodied in songs. To pursue his studies, he lives with his wives and children, apart from the maloca, in a separate dwelling. He is expected to devote himself to serene meditation, prayer, and continual good cheer. He joins with the maloca for public events and presides over feasts, but most of his time is taken up with spiritual matters.

Even after a Tucanoan shaman dies, his pivotal role continues to be emphasized. He is buried at the center of the maloca where he served, and the clan builds another house in the same area because they have a sacred bond with that portion of the river. While the grave of an elder or ordinary shaman is left undisturbed, that of a powerful shaman is opened after five years, sufficient time for the spot to have become impregnated with his power. His bones are carefully removed, and the larger ones, together with his ornaments and paraphernalia, are placed in a ceramic jar, which is buried in a secret location. The small bones of his fingers, hands, and feet are burned, ground into powder, and mixed with manioc beer, which the men drink to acquire some of his wisdom. Presumably, his knowledge has drained out of his heart, the central intersection of his body, through his extremities. Its last vestiges are therefore in his hands and feet. Drinking the concoction adds to the abilities the men have already acquired as members of their clan. While his wisdom was widely shared after death, the office of shaman passed from father to son.

The shaman manages all relations with the spiritual world, consecrating fresh food for immediate consumption and removing ritual restrictions on members of the community. He also supervises all major rituals, ranging from ceremonial visits by members of other clans—during which dancers, forming long lines evocative of the mythic anaconda that had delivered their ancestors along the drainages, enact incidents from the Origin Saga—to the Ancestor House rite, an initiation ritual that turns boys into men. In these rites, major aspects of the society are highlighted to revitalize them. During such events, the maloca represents simultaneously the human body, the river drainage, and the cosmos. In terms of the flow of energy, the centers of hearth, the heart, the rapids, and the Sun are interlinked to renew the Tucanoan world.

IN CONTRAST to a male-based community, let us now glimpse an example of the opposite—the female-based society of the Lenapes, later called the Delawares, who were organized in terms of matrilines of mothers and daughters located throughout the drainage of their namesake river and along the Atlantic coasts of modern-day New Jersey and adjoining states.

A Lenape girl comes back from a stream, carrying a fired clay pot filled with water. She is helping her mother make supper at the end of the day. They are camping in the hills, living in a bark wigwam. A few other families are camped with them, sharing in the fall bounty of berries, nuts, and fruits. Everyone helps out as they can, but most of the harvesting is done by adults. There are three generations working together.

Grandmother, the elder of the family, looks after the children while her daughters and daughters-in-law process foods for meals or storage. Grandfather advises on hunting activities, relying on his own long experience. Since he rarely hunts now, he devotes much of his time to making tools and utensils, mostly arrows and carved wooden bowls, which he trades for objects made by other old men who are equally proficient in their own crafts.

The younger men hunt in the area, ever watchful of wild animals that may endanger their families. Just last week a woman scolded some people on the other side of the berry patch for making too much noise among the bushes. When she went to confront them directly, she was startled to find that she had been chastising a bear. Immediately, she ran away and called for help. One of her sister's sons was hunting nearby and he drove the bear closer to the camp before killing it. Everyone in camp, particularly the children, took this encounter as a warning.

Only the oldest children help their parents with the hard work. Otherwise, siblings stay together, more mature ones looking after younger ones in the camp or in the playground that has been cleared for them nearby. The clearing is generally a safe area, except when a snake crawls there to bask in the sun. If it is harmless, the children leave it alone. If it is poisonous, then someone comes from camp and talks to the snake, asking it to leave for its own safety. Grandmother always teaches her family to respect life, because everything has a place. A snake will harm only those who hurt it, unless, of course, it has been compelled by a sorcerer, either for personal reasons or in return for payment, to avenge an actual or suspected insult.

Since theirs is a large and important family, the campers work hard to gather in many supplies. During the winter, other people will depend on them for food and comfort. Also, new grandchildren will soon be born, and their naming ceremonies will be occasions for feasting on stored supplies.

Soon the Lenape kin will pack up and return to their home, a compartment in a peaked longhouse in their town. Over its door is a carved and painted turtle, for the women are of the Turtle clan. Theirs is the largest clan in the town, proof that their ancient relationship with the Manitou of that place continues. Their senior man is also the town chief, and their head warrior is the town war leader. The Turtle clan chief manages the affairs of the town, except when a raid is planned or the town is besieged by enemies. Then the war chief takes control. Each clan has these two leaders, one civil and one military, concerned respectively with issues of life and of death. They gain their positions from the women of the clan by virtue of being brothers or sons, and hold them on the basis of continued ability. When they die or are deposed, the positions go to a younger brother or to the son of an older sister.

Within the longhouse, compartments are arranged on either side of a central hallway dotted by fireplaces. The families of two sisters on either side of the walkway share the same hearth, but domestic needs of the greater household are the concern of the oldest active woman of the matrilineage, the woman called Grandmother by all. While the chief and warrior speak on her behalf in public, in the private domain of the home she is in charge. At large gatherings hosted by the Turtles, she ladles out the food, giving a fair share to all. When the men deliberate in the great hall of the town, she brings food to the door, often favoring them with delicacies like beaver tail or elk lips.

Women are the foundation of society and work constantly to affirm that position. The town is near the farmlands where maize, beans, squash, sunflowers, and other crops are planted, tended, and harvested by the women. These towns are at the confluence of a tributary and the Delaware River. This Turtle town is larger than most of those nearby and, hence, is a regional center. Near the central plaza is the great hall, standing above the family longhouses. The chief's family lives there and cares for sacred objects handed down from the time when a Turtle Manitou befriended a woman ancestor of the clan. This great hall is where everyone in the area gathers for seasonal ceremonies which celebrate cycles of growth and harvest.

When the food-gathering families in the hills break camp and canoe down to the town, their kin meet them at the shore and help pack everything into the longhouse. There is not a lot of room, since the farm crops are already stored. Braided maize ears and woven strips of pumpkin hang from the rafters, and bark containers full of grain are stored under the side platforms that serve as both seats and beds. Other crops have been buried in storage pits both inside the longhouse, away from the walkway, and outside, behind the house. A few pits are outside the palisade of the town, for use in case of emergency or flight.

People concentrate on their tasks, and any distractions are discouraged as being rude. But after the goods are unloaded and secured, there is time for visiting. Grandmother learns that her youngest daughter has given birth to a girl. She is delighted with the news, because her daughters had previously borne only sons, and the lack of granddaughters did not bode well for her clan. She had even considered adopting the daughter of her brother, the chief, into the Turtles, but now this is unnecessary.

Grandmother is thankful, since the adoption negotiations would have been delicate. She would have had to approach the chief's wife, a matron of the Roundfoot clan, to which the girl also belongs. While the chief is responsible for everyone in the town, his wife is particularly concerned with coordinating female social activities and so functions as the senior woman of the town. Thus any settlement would have been tricky, particularly the matter of the size of the gift that the Turtles would have to make to the Roundfoot elders to com-

Women camped on scaffolds protect a corn harvest in modern-day Minnesota, as drawn by Captain Seth Eastman in the mid-nineteenth century. Using long-established patterns, communities spent the summer at favorite camps to take advantage of natural resources while their crops matured. As the harvest approached, families took precautions to prevent excessive loss to birds and other animals, who nevertheless shared some of the bounty.

A Kinship of Spirit

Lenape Thanksgiving Ceremony

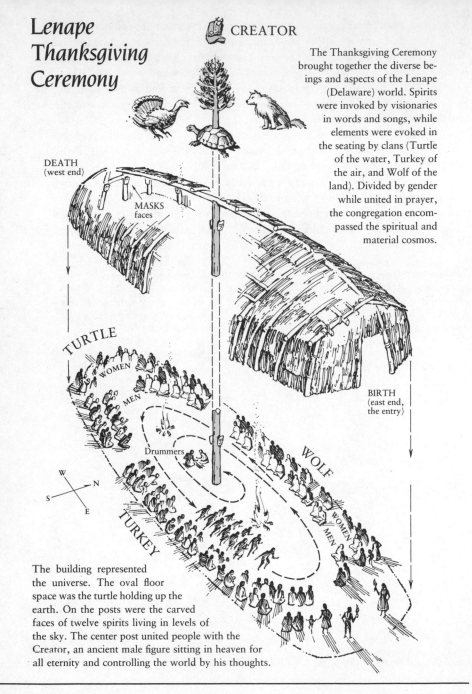

CREATOR

The Thanksgiving Ceremony brought together the diverse beings and aspects of the Lenape (Delaware) world. Spirits were invoked by visionaries in words and songs, while elements were evoked in the seating by clans (Turtle of the water, Turkey of the air, and Wolf of the land). Divided by gender while united in prayer, the congregation encompassed the spiritual and material cosmos.

DEATH
(west end)

MASKS
faces

TURTLE

WOMEN

MEN

Drummers

BIRTH
(east end,
the entry)

WOLF

W
N
S
E

WOMEN

MEN

TURKEY

The building represented the universe. The oval floor space was the turtle holding up the earth. On the posts were the carved faces of twelve spirits living in levels of the sky. The center post united people with the Creator, an ancient male figure sitting in heaven for all eternity and controlling the world by his thoughts.

pensate them for the loss of descendants. Still, all recognize the necessity of having daughters to perpetuate the clan. The only other clan in the town is the Turkey, represented by a few men who have married in, and their wives have borne only sons.

Grandmother goes to visit her daughter and new granddaughter. They have come out of seclusion and reentered the social life of the town. The baby wears tiny moccasins with holes in them so she can tell any of the dead who try to lure her away that she cannot travel because her shoes are so worn. Grandmother examines the baby carefully, looking for signs that she is a reincarnation. Sure enough, her ears have tiny dimples in the lobes, as though they had once worn earrings. Also, she is a quiet baby, almost as dignified as an old lady, and she keeps her hands open, not clenched like other babies. Grandmother suspects that she knows who this baby is, but, to be sure, she goes out and gathers up several other old women. They come back and look at the baby, agreeing with the signs already seen by Grandmother. They discuss the baby and decide that she is indeed Marsh Flower, Grandmother's great-aunt, returned.

The new arrival is cause for celebration. Grandmother begins to prepare for a feast the next day. She has left some of the harvest ready for just this event, but now, joyous at the birth of a girl, she adds more. Her daughters and granddaughters join in the preparations. She sends a child to tell her brother that the naming feast will take place on the morrow at his home, the great hall. Since they are the most important family of the town, generosity is expected. Later, at the fall harvest ceremony, when they thank Mother Earth for her bounty and the Creator for continued life, she will also feast guests and make the baby's name more generally known. And so, the next day, before they feast everyone with samples of all the food the Turtles had procured that summer and fall, cedar needles are smoked to purify the area, tobacco is burned to get the attention of the Manitou, and the baby girl is named. Through the medium of cedar and tobacco smoke, the girl's heart, the family's fire, and the Creator are aligned to intensify the flow of life-giving energy through all the realms of the community.

A few weeks later, another celebration, dedicated to general thanksgiving, is held in the great hall, with the Turtles hosting other clanspeople and neighbors who live in the region. Over the course of several days, leaders offer prayers to the Creator, and every man who has had a successful career conveys the manner in which he encountered an immortal, who took pity on him and provided a gift of supernatural power. These recitations alternate between speaking and chanting, accompanied by athletic movements evocative of the encounter. Only the Lenape have this ceremony, so its celebration serves to confirm their shared tribal identity. A fixed series of ceremonies bring them together seasonally, but this thanksgiving rite is the culmination of the year.

During the winter, families hold other ceremonies, feeding people and showing their generosity. In the spring, they move to rapids and waterfalls to process shad and other fish runs. Men do the heavy work of spearing and netting the fish, while the women gut, cut up, and smoke-dry the catch. At the towns, farm crops are planted, and many of the new green shoots of spring are harvested as fresh vegetables. People work according to their ability, by sex and age. The more successful, of course, also work to demonstrate their ongoing relationships with immortal benefactors. As the farmlands mature, a ceremony is held to safeguard the harvest and sample some of its early returns. Then the people scatter to upland camps to gather fall produce, before settling again into their towns for the winter.

FAR WESTWARD across North America, in present-day Washington State, the Skagits and other Salishan speakers exemplified still another society, one in which both genders were regarded as near equals, and relatives formed kindreds whose membership was traced through both father and mother.

Along the upper reaches of the Skagit River stands a longhouse made of split cedar planks. Its owner is a man named Shlaks, a title passed down through generations of his family. He is wealthy because of the power of his immortal, an inherited ally who also gave him the right to display in public two sacred carved poles. He is lavish with his gifts and food when these poles are activated during the dead of winter. As he leads the singing, the poles dance, propelling their holders around the house, then return quietly to their resting place. Other house owners have other wooden objects that come alive when their songs are sung, but those of Shlaks are renowned because their movements always correctly predict events to come.

Since Shlaks is wealthy, he has three wives and many children. Other residents of the house are his relatives, through both his father and his mother. He has relatives everywhere along the river, and even a few across the mountains among tribes of the sagebrush plateau or along the coast among the saltwater peoples. Some of these distant relatives have given their children hereditary names belonging to both sides of his family, but since these namesakes rarely encounter each other, it is not the cause for upset that it would be if neighbors used the same names without his permission.

Because he is wealthy, Shlaks also has a slave, an old woman who had been captured as a girl and traded upriver. She no longer has a name of her own, but is instead called Coast, since that is where she came from. She is treated kindly because Shlaks is a good man. Other slave owners can be cruel, beating and maiming their slaves. The upriver people are fairly isolated, but rich men near the river's mouth and the coast have several slaves, boys and girls captured in raids, or their descendants.

Except for Shlaks's own children, who belong to the nobility, the other residents of the house are ordinary people. They are near and distant relatives who decided to move into his home, use his resource areas, and help out at his feasts and celebrations. By doing so, they identify with his household. Along the river, people have many options open to them. They can live with any of their known relatives, who comprise all the kindreds linked to their great-grandparents. Specifically, these are the kinship networks of their father, mother, four grandparents, and eight great-grandparents. Frequent visiting and recitation of genealogy make people aware of who their relatives are. Among the families of leaders, knowing one's pedigree is a required part of the education of children. Since important names are hereditary, every time one of these names is assumed by a new person, its pedigree is recalled and celebrated. During a naming feast, other people will make speeches, mentioning that they also had a relative of that name in the past. In this way, relationships are forged anew in each generation.

The primary food of the people is salmon, caught each spring during the runs of several species and stored for winter food. Men take fish from traps, while women process the catch. Salmon are immortals who live in the west in plank houses, where they look just like humans. While paddling in canoes to come east, Salmon people go under the horizon and capsize, turning into salmon swimming in the water. After their flesh is removed, humans are careful to return salmon bones to the water, because then Salmon can return to their homes in the west. Such proper treatment is rewarded by a return of the salmon the next spring.

The first salmon caught is ritually welcomed to the community, just as any other leader is. Since it is the first fish to arrive, the community assumes that it is the leader of the run. It is carefully cooked and consumed at a communal meal, and its bones are tenderly returned to the river. Shlaks is in charge of this rite because he is the local peer of the salmon leader.

After the salmon have been processed and stored in baskets and wooden boxes, the household scatters to various camps near the headwaters of streams. Women collect wild plants, and men do some hunting. The most dangerous hunts, for bears and mountain goats, are a privilege of leading men since such meat and pelts are precious. These furs are traded for the dog-wool blankets made by downriver women of important families. The yarn is made from the woolly hair of large dogs that have been specially bred and tended for their fur.

During the fall, a great variety of berries are gathered and dried by women, and the men undertake hunting in earnest. These additional foods are stored for winter use, when people come to visit.

With the onset of winter, all of the immortals—whether appearing as mammals, birds, fish, or insects—revisit their human allies, making the man or woman sick. As this is expected, relatives quickly gather and begin to sing the patient's own song so that the patient's spirit will move easily through the throat when he or she joins the song. When Shlaks himself falls ill, everyone in the house sings for him, and, after he recovers, he feasts them well. Sometimes, the song gets stuck in the throat of a visionary or the person has other complications. Then a doctor has to be called to "straighten out" the song and cure the patient. As is usual in leading families, Shlaks and his brother both have curative powers and so can also help people recover. Their sister, too, has doctoring ability, but she is reluctant to practice in public. Once her family is grown and she is older, however, people expect that she too will begin to use her curative powers among the Skagits.

The Skagit Valley in 1492 constitutes a world of its own where kinship ties unite all of the inhabitants, mortal or immortal. Sacred places dot the land and water. In one place, a girl who married a water being resides beneath a waterfall, and, in another, a rocky hill with spiral striations marks the resting place of the rope that was used by a woman to escape from the sky world. Knowledge of these locations (and of their benefits) is held in families whose members have chosen to recognize their membership in that kindred as opposed to others to which they are entitled. By taking up residence in a particular household, they activate kinship ties with a place, a leader, and the privileges inherited from powers that are linked with the landmarks along a stretch of the river.

Membership in a family is expressed during a ceremony in which food is sent to the dead. A special fire is made, away from walkways, and the dead of a family are called in prayer. Only the native doctor can see them. When they arrive, favorite foods—such as salmon, berries, clams, and venison—are placed in the fire, a threshold between the worlds of the living and the dead. In the process, cosmic energy is concentrated at the intersection of fire, food, and shaman.

AN EXAMPLE of still another kinship system and society—one based on a separate regard for men and for women—existed in the present-day Southwest of the United States among the ancestors of some of the modern Pueblos, particularly the Keresans. Treating the genders as distinct encouraged the formation of dual social entities. When descent was traced from mother to children, the corporate groupings were known technically as matrilines, matrilineal clans, phratries, and moieties. Matrilines were composed of generations linked through women, while clans were matrilines which traced descent from a common spiritual ancestress. Phratries were clusterings of clans, and moieties were all-inclusive divisions, like Earth and Sky or Red and White, that organized a community into functional halves.

When transmission was traced through interlinked men—to boys from either fathers, mothers' brothers, or ceremonial godfathers—the result was patrilines of generations descended through men, patrilineal clans and phratries with a common spiritual ancestor, or male-based moieties. In particular instances, as below, inter-male links were expressed as priesthoods and other religious organizations, such as kiva (native church) groups.

The Keresan boy frolicking across the sand is part of a group returning from a visit to a neighboring pueblo. As he runs across the mesa, he thinks of home, a double row of connected, two-story rooms facing each other across a plaza. The boy is quiet, remembering the blessings that the kachina had brought to their hosts. It had rained a bit at the end of the dancing, a sure sign that all was well.

The boy dares not speak of the blessings of the kachinas because, as a recent initiate into the Kachina society, he is still extremely cautious about any mention of these immortals. He knows that beheading is the penalty for telling women or children that it is men who come in the guise of kachinas. Long ago the kachinas came in person, but humans insulted them. After a fight with great losses on both sides, the kachinas gave men the right to dress like themselves and gain their rain-bringing blessings by fervent effort. Soon the boy will take the role of a kachina at his own pueblo's celebration of the harvest.

As the pueblo comes into view across the arid landscape, he can see the fields of corn, beans, squash, and other crops. In the next day or two, everyone will be summoned to the fields by the town crier to begin the harvest. They will start with the field that the town had planted for their priest, the Tiamun-yi. He is like the mother of the town, devoted to fasting, prayer, and harmony. To protect him and the town, there is also a war priest, who visits the shrines along the perimeter of the pueblo's lands and leaves offerings in each one for its immortal patron.

Looking at the pueblo, the boy can see the Tiamunyi standing on the roof of the tower kiva, plotting the point where the sun is setting. Every day, he makes such solar and celestial observations so he will know when to schedule ritual events. Some of these are public, held in the kivas or plaza, but the important ones are celebrated by the various priesthoods in their chambers.

Nearing the town, the boy and his companions call out the proper kinship terms as greetings to the men working in the fields. At the plaza, families split up and go home. The boy goes to the notched log ladder leaning against the first story of his adobe-plastered home and climbs up to the roof. He walks through the door into the family room, where he sees his uncle, his mother's brother. Ever respectful, he gives his uncle a reserved greeting. He is hungry, since he has eaten only dried cornmeal on the way back, so he helps himself from a cooking pot full of cornmeal gruel flavored with animal grease. Then he goes into a back room to get his top and takes it outside to play.

A Kinship of Spirit   **321**

These woodcuts are based on original drawings by a nineteenth-century Eskimo artist known to Europeans only by his baptismal name, Aaron. Greenland Eskimo men engage in a rough-and-tumble ball game using a stuffed sealskin. Games played an important role in relieving social tensions. Teams were organized from disparate social groups who might be at odds with each other. Having fun contributed to the overall well-being of these remote communities.

The women of his family occupy a row of rooms running perpendicular to the long axis of the building. Most of the time, in good weather, they live outdoors on the plaza and on the roof. In the winter, they move into the front room, rolling up their sleeping mats and blankets during the day. The back rooms are for storage, stacked mostly with corn ears, beans, and dried pumpkin strips. Because rain is uncertain, the family has enough food stored to last them during a year of famine. They also have a reserve of planting seeds. The rooms on the first story, entered through a hatchway, are used for long-term storage, but one of them is set aside for the religious paraphernalia owned by the women of the family and used by its men.

Theirs is the mother house of the Sage clan, so the effigies of the clan children and the carved ancestral figures are stored in their home. In addition, the Sage clan sponsors the Beetles, one of the curing priesthoods, whose chief priest is the boy's maternal uncle. The slat altars and priestly emblems are kept in the chamber of the Beetle priesthood, but a few items of great antiquity are also stored in the boy's house. Under the paved floor of the lowest room is the grave of an earlier Beetle priest who died during a winter when the ash piles were frozen. He was too important a man to be accorded haphazard burial, so the paving stones were lifted up and the grave easily dug. Such a burial was unusual, because normally only infants are buried under house floors, to encourage their rebirth into mothers of the clan.

Other families, forming matrilines of mothers and daughters, occupy similar suites of rooms. The home of the family of the Tiamunyi has a slightly different arrangement. Because this priest has to avoid contact with his wife during periods of fasting and prayer, upper-level rooms are reserved for his use, particularly for his sun watching, and for the protection of the most sacred items in the community. His wife and family occupy a row of rooms that is larger than others because they are also used to store enough crops to care for the entire town during an attack or a famine.

Communal feeling is intense among townspeople. Everything done by a person must benefit everyone. Selfishness, an indication of sorcery, is avoided at all cost. Because of their greater knowledge of the workings of the universe, the priesthoods regulate all activities. In the arid environment, rainfall is crucial. As the custodians of age-old information, the priests are able to plan ahead for most possibilities. They divide their activities among the curing of internal and external diseases, the conduct of warfare, and the management of ceremonies. During the most vital of cures, they use "heart songs," which go to the very core of the patient and mobilize energies of earth, sky, and spirit to effect a recovery. Always, however, priests are concerned with the proper balance of moisture and heat needed by the crops and controlled by the Sun, who is prayed to as Father.

Greenland Eskimo men wrestle to test their stamina and skill inside a house. Clothing hangs on the walls and a continuous bench provides dry seats.

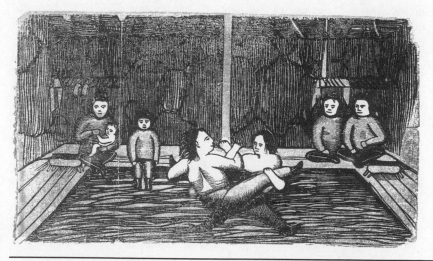

A Kinship of Spirit

An entire Eskimo community shares slabs of blubber and meat from a whale which has been killed by cooperative effort. Distributions like this one usually followed strict rules of kinship so that the maximum number of relatives could benefit from the success of hunters.

SUCH KIN TERMS were applied to all of the people in each world of the Americas. Some kin terms implied a notion of shared, usually inherited, substances, such as a common blood, bone, food, flesh, land, or spirit. Other terms implied that the relationship was acquired, usually as a result of the bonds of marriage. Linked together as kindreds, families were regarded in the broadest, most inclusive manner. These all-embracing relationships made native communities wonderful places to live, filled with close and caring residents who were nevertheless suspicious of outsiders. Community welfare depended on understanding that one's primary responsibility was to the group, not to the self. This ethic gave Native American societies a moral strength that enabled many of them to survive the consequences of 1492.

Thus, households were the building blocks for other social groupings. Among the elite, families often included several wives, together with their own and adopted children. While sisters married to the same husband shared the same home, among other wives each usually had her own hearth or home. Throughout the Americas, a family was regarded as quite expansive, embracing many generations, living or dead, and members who might not share the same substance (genes). In communities with small populations, kinship usually recognized both parents equally. In those contexts, families formed relational networks known technically as kindreds, tracing membership through various biological and social criteria along both the father's and the mother's side. In some cases, kindreds were the same as bands, political groups that shared the same customs, territory, and resources. In many instances, individual families and kindreds became associated with occupational specializations, either as the makers of particular craft items—pots, baskets, arrows, or mats—or as the holders of special positions—shaman, chanter, herbalist, or messenger.

Kin relationships were often complex, sometimes with different terms used for the same relative, depending upon whether someone was speaking directly to that relation or referring indirectly to him or her. No term was unique to any single person; rather, each term included a logical class or category. For example, the term used to speak directly to a "mother" might also be used for all the women whom a "mother" called "sister" and, in prayers, would also be used for the earth, certain plants such as maize, and particular features of the landscape representing petrified female beings, such as a girl who neglected puberty taboos and turned to stone.

Among some Pueblos of the American Southwest, men initiated to the status of priest-doctors were also called "mothers" because they played a nurturing or mothering role. While kinship terminologies relied heavily on biology for the basic categories, many of the finer distinctions involved cultural factors. Every term represented an intersection of several criteria.

Biological distinctions basic to all kinship terminologies were gender and age. All terminologies had separate words applying to kinsmen or kinswomen, but terms based on age were always complex, often referring both to generation and to relative birth order. Thus, generational terms distinguished grandparents, parents, children, and grandchildren. Within any generation, moreover, terms were used to indicate whether someone was older or younger in birth order (such as "firstborn," "older brother," "older sister," "youngest sibling"), whether a kinswoman belonged to a direct or side descent line (a "mother" in contrast to an "aunt"), and whether a relative was presently living or dead; when speaking of a dead relative, only circumlocutions could be used (such as "the woman who gave me birth" instead of "my mother").

Terminologies emphasizing generation, often associated with kindreds, used the same term for all same-gender siblings. Hence, the term for mother was also used for a mother's sisters, and that for father also included a father's brothers. All of their children were logically, therefore, brothers and sisters. When both generation and descent were involved, kinship lines were distinguished as direct or as collateral, separating parents from their own siblings (aunts or uncles), with their children being cousins. On the basis of gender, cousins were further divided in parallel and cross relations. The children of same-gender siblings (all brothers or all sisters) were distinguished as "parallel cousins," while the children of sisters for a brother or of brothers for a sister were "cross cousins." While parallel cousins were believed to share a common substance, cross cousins might be considered quasi-relatives or nonrelatives.

All societies had strict rules about who was and who was not eligible for marriage. Usually, shared-substance and same-clan relatives did not marry, although a few chiefdoms like that of the Calusa Indians of southwestern Florida encouraged brother-to-sister marriages among the ruling elite, as was done among the Incas and ancient Egyptians. In many cases, family pressures were applied to an individual to marry someone of a specific clan, name, or relationship, such as a cross cousin in communities with a sparse population. Over many generations, such marriages vitiated any genetic consequences for their heirs.

A distinctive feature of Native American kin systems was the emphasis given to grandparents, as elders of the family, leaders of community groups, and the primary agents of child care and instruction. Households included a wide range of ages. Since parents were often away gathering food and resources, grandparents and grandchildren were together most of the time, usually sleeping together when the children were toddlers. Grandparent terms ranged from systems with only a single term (applied to both "grandparent" and "grandchild") to a series including three different terms. Where gender was emphasized, two separate terms (for "grandfather" or "grandmother") were used. Triple terms distinguished same-genders (for "father's father" or "mother's mother"), together with another term meaning "grandparent of the opposite sex," used by grandsons for elders whom their fathers called mothers and by granddaughters for mothers' fathers.

These descent lines, relationships, obligations, and loyalties drew together in the definition of the "person" or "self," a notion of the individual very different from that of most Europeans in 1492. Basically, each self did not exist alone or separately, but rather was a facet of the larger, interconnected whole embodied by society. Communal identities were so strong and distinctive, moreover, that many have managed to survive into the present, even when other, more obvious features of pre-contact native society have not. Where Native American communities have remained viable entities, beliefs and values about the self, expressed best in the native languages, have been passed on to succeeding generations, encouraged by traditional patterns of child care.

In 1492 America, there were, indeed, as many notions of the person as there were separate communities. Yet, like kinship systems, they all seem to have been based on a range of logical principles from which each community selected alternatives. In general, cultures throughout the hemisphere viewed the self as an intersection of various inheritances, loyalties, and choices. In this sense, a person could not stand alone, apart from a network of people, but rather existed as a member of a community composed of several types of in-

A feast among the Acawai at the headwaters of the Orinoco River shows men dancing with rattles and women sharing fermented cassava. Usually, men and women organized their activities to keep genders separate. As with feasts among modern Amazon tribes, the food was served from a canoe.

stitutions concerned with the economy, the polity, kinship, and religion. Except for leaders, no one belonged to all of these institutions. Usually, a person had full status as an adult only after most of these identities had been acquired during a long life.

In the same way that the heart was the crux of the self, so the person was a pivotal link in society. Native American societies, however, generally emphasized selflessness because the predominant concern was the sustenance of others of like kind. Communities did not consist of individuals, but rather of "dividuals," persons who took their identity from membership in various groups and had little or no independent status apart from society. Hence, the self was not a unique entity, but rather was an intersection of family lines, social positions, and spiritual bonds, all intended to serve the whole community. While this was the norm, it was not always the practice, as beliefs in the effects of witchcraft and sorcery make clear. Such social ills were the result of selfishness, the use of special gifts for personal ends. Even so, witches were tolerated and, to a great extent, accepted by their community. Some groups, believing that witchcraft was inherited in family lines, could predict who would be suspected in each generation. Only during the greatest stress—during famine, drought, or cataclysm—were witches killed to reset the balance of the world. Otherwise, witches, either men or women, served to remind everyone of the unpleasant consequences of being selfish. Dread of being considered a sorcerer also helped to keep others on their best behavior. Besides, as most people hoped, witches always belonged to distant groups, never to friendly neighbors.

While each community had its own definition of the person, biological and life-cycle events provided a certain consistency to Native American concepts of selfhood, and it is to these shared features, seen in terms of a generalized lifetime, that we now turn.

A human life began with contributions from father, mother, and spirits. Usually, the father was understood to have contributed hard substances like bone, and the mother soft ones like flesh and blood. Elements from the tribal homeland, where ancestors were buried, also went into the creation of a baby. In the Pacific Northwest, the actual body for the baby was thought to come from a special place inhabited by unborn infants who lived much like other humans until they decided to find mortal parents and try life on earth. Among other groups, the actual animating force came from a Creator or God, or from a holy wind; life, particularly as breath and thought, was a gift from the supernatural.

The relative values of these contributions varied with the social structure of the community. Thus, among patrilineal native societies, a mother was regarded as akin to a tray holding the infant while it developed. Among matrilineal groups, in contrast, a father helped to start the process, but no more. It was the matrikin who saw to the development and well-being of both child and adult.

During gestation, parents were especially careful to avoid actions that might adversely mar the infant. Because of the interdependency of all life, the parents had to be careful in all that they did. If the mother blocked a doorway, she might obstruct her own delivery. If she stared at a rabbit, the baby might be born with a cleft palate (aptly called a harelip). If the father tied up a bundle, the umbilical cord might wrap around the infant's neck. Other members of the extended family, particularly the elders, were ever on the watch to prevent such linkages and to see that the mother ate proper foods in moderation. Nothing fresh or bloody was allowed, because that might lead to a miscarriage or to hemorrhaging. These restrictions were most severe for a first pregnancy.

When the time for delivery approached, the mother-to-be would move to a birthing hut or a partitioned-off section of the communal home. Men kept their distance at such times. Only in the event of difficulties was a male shaman or doctor called to ease the birth.

Generally, there was a period of seclusion for mother and baby during the first few days after the birth. Other women visited, but the men kept away, because birth was a female affair and separation of the genders was characteristic of the Americas. In much of South America, the father also went through a time of seclusion called couvade, a male version of lying-in. The couvade ranged from mild forms, involving his following the same dietary restrictions as his wife, to full ones, in which the father acted as though he had just given birth. This was a public way for the father to claim responsibility for his child and invoke universal life forces. Among "real" families, supernatural dimensions were frequently present when a new member was born. In most cases, the birth of important leaders was believed to be foretold by unusual weather conditions.

After the period of seclusion and/or couvade, the baby was presented to the community and named. In some cases, only nicknames were given until it seemed certain that the child would live. In others, particularly when clans were involved, the name or names conferred membership, since each one made reference to the clan emblem or history. Usually, names were marked for gender, either by subject (flowers for women, carnivores for men) or by special endings. Over the course of a lifetime, a person could earn or inherit a series of names. Among the more complex societies, such as chiefdoms, the important names were probably acquired in a fixed sequence, similar to the way in which the holder of the title of Prince of Wales eventually assumes the title of King of England.

Certain life changes were marked as they occurred. The more usual included the first step, first word, or first haircut, but some tribes also celebrated the first laugh or first whistle.

As they matured, children played at adult careers. Special attention was paid to the first time a child performed an appropriate economic role. Thus, the first berries or crops gathered by a girl were given to an elderly woman, with a request that she pray for a long life and many healthy children for the girl. When a boy made his first kill, however small, the game was given to an old man with a similar request for a prayer for bravery and longevity.

A successful career was validated, not by instruction or training, but rather by the intervention of a spiritual power. Only after the proper vision had been received and confirmed could adults teach a child the fine points of an activity. Over generations, families affiliated themselves with particular immortals, who provided certain careers to their members. Humans and spirits regarded each other as relatives and used appropriate kin terms. Families instructed their children about the location of the "holy home" of their immortal patron, and sent these youngsters out to quest with appropriate offerings and prayers familiar to that immortal. The "holy homes" were often distinctive features of the terrain, such as hills, buttes, pools, rapids, waterfalls, boulders, caves, or craters. Once entrance had been gained, the novice was instructed in the special songs, movements, and techniques for a successful career. In less formal encounters, the immortal simply appeared, in human form, to the visionary, gave the instructions, and left, after briefly assuming the guise of its species so the child would know with what aspect of nature he or she was now allied. For the rest of his or her life, the person could summon the ally by song, by offerings, and by thought. Throughout the Americas, religion impinged on everything, biology as well as society. A child's quest for an immortal ally was usually regarded as a prelude to puberty.

Female puberty was socially recognized in the Americas, although not always celebrated with elaborate ritual. The girl went into seclusion and learned to care for herself during subsequent menstruations. She was given tasks to occupy her time and prove her diligence. Intervals of singing and dancing with other women also marked the event. Her ability to bring forth a new generation was highlighted, usually with community feasting and expressions of goodwill. In rare instances, as among the Shipibo of the Peruvian Montaña, a girl's coming of age was also marked by the surgical removal of her clitoris, which was believed to remove a male aspect from her personality.

Male puberty was less universally celebrated by a ritual, although physiological changes were observed without ritual by the family. Cult initiations were often held during that period of life, frequently involving the use of masks and costumes to personify various immortals. Until then, boys were supposed to believe that the mask wearers were the spirits themselves. As an indication of their transition to adulthood, however, they shared in the "secret," supposedly unknown to women, that men took the roles in the rituals. At puberty, boys were reminded that fathering children was a primary responsibility to their community.

By puberty, a child accepted a fixed gender from as many as six types. The two primary ones were those of ordinary man and woman, defined socially by the careers appropriate to married adult members of the community. Other, less frequently recognized, genders included extreme, as well as overlapping, forms of the primary ones. The extremes, as mentioned previously, were hyper-men, renowned warriors or athletes, such as wrestlers in the Amazon, who kept apart from women most of the time, and hyper-women, who excelled at female crafts and domestic activities. The overlapping genders were the berdaches, males who assumed the female social role (with or without homosexual practices), and amazons, women who acted as men, preconditioned to do so by their greater size, strength, and bravado. While the "normal" genders of men and women were important, it was the intermediate (epicene) gender that provided the pivotal role. These individuals could mediate among different elements of society and tap into a full range of energies. Thus, members of the third gender often had prominent roles as leaders, shamans, and artists. In lieu of children of their own, berdaches adopted or had special naming or curing responsibilities with regard to the next generation.

Among elite families, babies and children were often betrothed to create or continue chiefly alliances. Other families left courtship more to chance, although elders were always careful to warn children away from involvement with forbidden relatives. Among clan societies, initial sex experiences were often between distant clan mates who, being quasi-kin, could never marry. With evidence of a successful spirit quest, and of increasing responsibility, marriages were arranged between families. For elites, these involved elaborate feasting and gift giving. The families themselves exchanged gifts, with the bride bringing tokens of her ability to prepare and cook foods associated with women and the groom contributing male foods, particularly meat.

All societies of the Americas recognized the marital bond as the basis for moral relations in the community. A married couple served as a social linkage, a responsible man and woman dedicated to the continuity of society.

In some regions, marriage choices were complicated by unusual factors. Along the upper Amazon in the Vaupés region, children belonged to the language community of their kinsmen and had to find spouses who did not speak their own father tongue. In this area of great linguistic diversity, communication was facilitated by a jargon (a common trade language) and a high incidence of polyglots. Similarly, along the Klamath River of northern California, elite families intermarried outside their speech communities, the better to inherit valued heirlooms important in several intertribal ceremonies.

Residence was usually congruent with social structure. Often, the groom joined the family of the bride until children were born. Then the couple would set up a separate household. As a general rule, houses belonged to the women. Where clans existed, the couple moved into the larger household of a clan segment. In a matrilineal home, the husband became an appendage to the matriline, and the mother's brother saw to the education of her children. In patrilineal societies, the wife joined her husband's patriline, subject to the authority of her mother-in-law, who herself had married into the family and community.

The birth of children confirmed marriages, providing parents with a means of public approval based on responsible actions. Full adult status and maturity came only with the birth of grandchildren, who were the special concern of grandparents. Political and social offices were open to good parents, contributing to their regard within the community. A good leader was also a good parent.

For ordinary people, marriages did not need to last. Because families were large, children were always welcome among relatives and, if need be, could be cared for by the extended family. Among the elite, however, marriages were alliances, so there were strong social sanctions against divorce. When such couples did separate, the social order might be shaken until new interfamily alliances were constituted.

With advancing age came a greater interest in religious matters. During the agile years, sexual activity was regulated by seasonal taboos and ritually imposed continence. In old age, sex might be forfeited in the interest of greater contact with immortal powers. Activities of the elderly focused on discipline and the perfection of knowledge, often evidenced by the production of superior artifacts. Such tokens of skill and dexterity were regarded as the result of close contact with spirit patrons.

At the moment of death, any bond with an immortal was severed and the spirit became something like a "lost puppy," actively seeking to renew the alliance with another family member. The elements that had formed the self became separated and dispersed. The spark or wind of life returned to its donor. Breath and clear fluids (saliva, lymph, tears) evaporated. The soul or souls wandered away or became a ghost, the flesh began to rot, and the bones and teeth began a gradual decomposition back into the ancestral soil.

These final processes were given different emphasis in various tribes. In the Pacific Northwest, the incorruptibility of shamans' bodies indicated their degree of power. In the same region, leaders were cremated so that their names could live on without evidence of corruption, which might have caused embarrassment to their kin by giving offense to others. In the North American Southeast, an elaborate cult was dedicated to the cleaning and reburial of human bones, the last residue of the life force of a person. The preserved bodies or defleshed remains of the most important leaders, preserved in fine baskets, were kept in temples atop earthen mounds.

In the rhythmic society before 1492, selves were linked to an ancestral homeland in perpetuity. During gestation, the earth and its bounty nourished them; in life, the environment supported them; and in death, they rejoined the land and the community of ancestors.

In life, every person relied upon various social institutions for the combination of loyalties making up an identity. The sources for these institutions were spiritual, inherited, and achieved, depending on the age, ability, and assumptions of a person. The characteristic expansiveness of native society can be seen clearly in the varieties of descent systems and corporate units, which were heavily influenced by factors such as population size and placement, ecological conditions, and regional interactions.

People lived together in households, but kinship extended beyond domestic walls to include all relations based on descent through kindreds, patrilines, or matrilines. Kindreds, bilateral networks related through both father and mother, were characteristic of much of the diffusely settled population of the Native Americas, but among more populous and complex societies, descent was traced in perpetuity and embodied in social units based on lineality, attributing different emphasis to the pedigree of one parent over the other. The most common pattern was patrilineality, tracing descent from father to son. Kinship systems associated with patrilines were distinguished by a special term that applied uniformly to those in the category of the mother's brother and all of his male descendants. This term recognized that the identity of the mother depended on her kinsmen, who transmitted their pedigree through sons born

Johann von Staden's illustration of a funeral in a Tupinamba village, from his account of his life among the South American tribe in the sixteenth century. Mourned by grieving relatives, the dead were buried within the palisade of the village, indicating the continuous role of the dead (as ancestors, ghosts, or reburied bones) in the life of the living.

of in-marrying wives. Less common was matrilineality, where kinship was traced through women. Kinship systems with matrilineal corporate units were characterized by a special term for the father's sisters, all of the female relatives of the father, since they carried on his matriline. In the most thoroughgoing systems, kinship terms, descent patterns, and residence coincided. These communities were both patrilineal and patrilocal, so the wife moved in with her husband's kin, or matrilineal and matrilocal, where the husband lived with the wife's kin.

Matrilineality should never be confused with matriarchy, which can only apply to the mythical realms of Amazons. Nor is matrilineality the mirror opposite of patrilineality, because in all known human societies males predominate in public settings. Male priority is both a characteristic of all higher primate species and an ingrained characteristic of humans. Thus, while members of the matriline traced descent through women, their leaders and public functionaries were men, who held office because they were related through mothers and sisters. Similarly, the children of these women were the responsibility of brothers because they shared the same corporate social identity. The fathers of these children belonged to other matrilines, where they were obligated to train their own sisters' children. This special relationship between mothers' brothers and sisters' sons was a hallmark of matrilineal systems. In some cases, these males and their families lived together in later life, enabling the heir to succeed his uncle ("mother's brother") with little disruption.

In a few instances, patterns of double descent occurred where father and mother each provided membership in corporate units having different functions. Thus among some of the Pueblos of the U.S. Southwest, membership in clan, household, and certain other kinship units was inherited through the mother and her kinswomen, while kiva and religious obligations were acquired through the father and his kinsmen.

Households and lineages belonged to clans, and these in turn often formed a clan cluttering called a phratry, held together by a common theme related to habitat, use, or mythic equation. Clans, while not universal in the Americas, nevertheless built upon the idea of kinship with the cosmos. In this way, members of the Turtle clan had an affinity with turtles, other amphibians, and shore areas. Other corporate divisions were moieties—two halves into which a community was divided, and which might or might not include clans and phratries—and sodalities—voluntary groups dedicated to specific tasks or interests, such as cures, crafts, festivals, or police functions.

A proper appreciation of the importance of clanship has been clouded among scholars by an overemphasis on the degree of a group's political integration, variously termed a band, tribe, confederacy, chiefdom, or state, in order of increasing complexity.

Tribe has been a term used to refer to a scale of society fairly typical of the Americas, although more as a localized congregation than as a political unit. A band was smaller than a tribe, composed of a few dozen relatives instead of several hundred. A confederacy was larger still, composed of allied tribes. A chiefdom was more strongly organized, with a dominant class of leading families at the apex of an intertribal system of trade, tribute, and religion. Not surprisingly, the intensity of the political organization and control was related to the degree and range of economic activities and prestigious offices. The more elaborate the social network, the more efficient and powerful the elite families.

Even so, in the Americas such control did not, for the most part, involve notions of total submission. There was still room for personal autonomy. A person usually could move away from an unpleasant situation. In general, leaders were followed because they were generous, not because they could command. Good leaders took care of the people and, in return, received respect and allegiance. Their wealth derived from good relations with important local immortals and far-flung trading arrangements that brought useful or exotic material into and out of the community, with a certain "trickling down" that kept everyone pleased. Through their skillful timing of events, whether

Théodore de Bry's engraving of a village, based on descriptions of Florida Indians supplied by the French explorer Jacques Lemoyne de Morgues. The concentric village plan was fairly typical of eastern North America. A town hall in the center is surrounded by houses arranged for convenience; gardens lie just inside the palisade. In lieu of gates, the palisade overlapped, although the guardhouses may well reflect European patterns.

rituals, harvests, or attacks, people led better lives. It is not surprising that archaeological evidence has repeatedly indicated that elite families ate better than others, often consuming more meat, because they led lives of more diverse experiences than others. Because "real people" kept things orderly, workers, in gratitude, donated some of their produce to them, knowing it would both feed the leaders and be shared with the needy. Rarely was a majority better and more diversely rewarded by the efforts of a few.

In the largest river systems, such as the Mississippi and Amazon, regional elites were involved in widespread exchanges among interlinked chiefdoms. Until the late thirteenth century, chiefdoms were the dominant political institution in the Americas. After that, with the ebbing of the Chacoan phenomenon in modern New Mexico and of Cahokia near present-day St. Louis, chiefdoms were on the wane. This was true even in the Southeast of North America, where the Mississippi and coastal trade gave them greater cohesion. They remained, however, the principal form of polity along the middle sections of both coasts of the Americas, impinged upon by the spreading empires of the Aztecs, Incas, and other expanding urban civilizations.

A hallmark of chiefdoms was a temple cult, an official intermeshing of temple, idol, and priesthood within an ancestral homeland. A famous example from the lower Mississippi River was the Natchez chiefdom, which limped into historical times until decimated by the French. In their central temple, a wooden box held a stone effigy, the petrified and diminished remains of the Sun's relative who came to earth to create the chiefly line. Since the stone was of the earth, the figure represented a complex linkage among the Sun deity, the human called the Sun who led the Natchez, the founding ancestor in the idol, the priestly elite, the royal temple, and the traditional territory. Intermediate between the kindred-based band and the lineally organized chiefdom was the tribe, a middle-range polity. In most cases, a tribe was synonymous with a waterway, particularly a major tributary. Tribes along a larger drainage might form a confederacy, sharing linguistic ties and ritual alliances.

Where clans existed, however, they were crucial for defining these regional networks. For example, in the Northeast, particularly in modern New York and New Jersey, three matriclans were characteristic of the people who would eventually become known as the Lenape (Delaware), Mahicans, Mohawks, and Oneidas. A clan was linked with amphibians, carnivores, or herbivores, variously represented as turtles, mammals, birds, or plants. Among the Delawares, the emblems were turtle, wolf, and turkey. Other tribal clans were turtle, wolf, and bear. What is significant about these kin units is that they cut across, if not ignored, features of politics and language that were otherwise considered important. Thus, the Delawares and Mahicans, though separate tribes, were both members of the Algonquian language family, associated, respectively, with the modern-day Delaware and lower Hudson rivers and with sacred fires that burned at central locations along these waterways. The Mohawks and Oneidas, who spoke related Iroquoian languages, became bitter enemies of the Algonquian tribes and, with the founding of the Iroquois League, recognized the priority of the sacred fire that burned among the Onondagas, the hub of the League near modern Syracuse, New York.

Similarly, along the Pacific Northwest coast, the confederated towns of people who became the Tlingit, Tsimshian, and Haida used different languages, but nevertheless shared the same moieties, localized along tributaries. In the Tsimshian country, these were branches of the Skeena River, while the Tlingit and Haida houses were along coastal rivers.

The moieties most developed among the Tsimshian were represented by the Orca (killer whale) and the Raven. As Raven was the culture hero who fixed the world in preparation for the arrival or birth of humans, it was not surprising that all three tribes shared the Raven moiety. The other half was variously known as Orca, Wolf, or Eagle, all carnivores emblematic of power and majesty. A town, in order to function and allow marriages, had to have members of both halves, one regarded as the owner, descended from the immortal ancestor or his human wife who founded the town, claimed its resources, and instituted its treasures, in contrast to the other unrelated half, which settled there later. Among the coastal Tsimshian, the Orca was the owner and the Raven was the other, while for the Haida, Raven was the founder. The elaborate equivalences among these three kinship systems suggest that these practices were ancient, probably a consequence of intermarriages among the royal families. With marriages went the inheritance of positions, resources, and treasures which were commonly understood among the elite in-laws because of shared cultural assumptions.

A characteristic of moiety societies was that they always included other crosscutting divisions. Among some communities like those of the Tewa Pueblos of New Mexico, priesthoods acted as mediators who stood between the moieties and coordinated community-wide activities. On special occasions, the towns divided into other dualities, such as teams of married versus unmarried members, which ignored the social moieties and forged another means for social cohesion.

In summary, society throughout the Americas relied on indigenous beliefs about ability, gender, self, immortals, and land, organized around a series of pivots such as the heart, hearth, waterway, and sun. In 1492, these beliefs reflected a uniquely unbroken aspect of the human record. American societies were each profoundly oriented to a landscape, reflecting a wealth of locally inspired ideas and customs which had slowly developed over millennia.

In 1492, society in the Americas was made up of households where men and women shared a hearth and belonged to groups that ranged from kindred-based bands, through tribes, confederacies, and chiefdoms, to the Aztec and Inca city-states. Regardless of their degree of sociopolitical complexity, all the societies tolerated a wide range of personal freedom and gender variations. In addition, these societies included many that were male-based, some that were female-based, and a few that treated genders equally or separately.

Above all else, these societies were rooted in the land, whose custodians were immortals, kinspeople living in "holy homes." Indeed, throughout the Americas, places were "people" in the sense that landmarks represented the petrified remains of individuals and acts depicted in mythology. Those who understood this constituted an elite of "real people" who partook of the flow of energy because they knew its transfer points were immortals, deeds, and rituals serving as pivotal crossroads in a cosmic network.

Knowledge of the land, along with respect for the centers rather than the boundaries of their communities, gave these Americans a belief in the sanctity of their land and in the moral superiority of their lifeways that has largely survived the destructive half a millennium that followed 1492.

FRANCIS JENNINGS

THE MULTIPLICITY and variety of pre-Columbian Amerindian societies are now generally recognized; no longer are the aboriginal Americans disregarded as an undifferentiated mass of "savages." As in Europe during the years of Rome's supremacy, so the Americas of 1492 included societies ranging from city-states to hunting-fishing-gathering subsistence bands. That their peoples had migrated originally from Asia is now generally recognized by scholars, sometimes with a vague reference to possible multiple waves of migration succeeding each other over long periods of time. There are implications in this fact that have not been much explored. Asia is a big place. Population movements from Asia into Europe are known and studied; the time seems overdue to try to see what happened in the Americas when varied Asians colonized this New World, settled down in some places, and became "Indians." ("Indian," of course, was Columbus's word. These diverse peoples knew themselves only by the names of their particular tribes or communities.)

The immigrants arrived from Asia at different times and traveled in different directions by land and sea, sometimes doubling back and always having to cope with each other when encounters took place. Encounters took varied forms: conflict, mutual toleration, or active cooperation. Plainly, commerce played a large role. Human curiosity guaranteed reciprocal visiting and investigating, and human material need and acquisitiveness resulted in the exchange of things valued. In short, when examining the political and economic rela-

A pochteca, or trader, member of a hereditary class of Aztec merchants which originated long before the founding of that empire. Pochtecas were multilingual and skilled in diplomacy. This image from the Codex Borgia shows a trader on the road with a woven backpack filled with merchandise (including a parrot). He carries a cane which identifies his status.

tionships between Native Americans in 1492, we can identify all the phenomena typically associated with international frontiers, despite difficulties inherent in the source materials.

In such respects, pre-Columbian American history shows much similarity to Europe's early eras, but there were also some distinguishing characteristics. For traditional historians, the most important of these distinctions was the absence in the Americas of a phonetic alphabet and the widespread literacy and accumulation of records made possible in Europe by the Greek and Latin alphabets. Lacking comparable archives in the Western Hemisphere, historians must piece together pre-Columbian accounts from the patient labors of archaeologists, ethnologists, and linguists, supplemented by native pictographs and glyphs, and by traditional lore recorded by interested Europeans.

All such means present special problems of interpretation. European observers embedded data in layers of dogma. Native peoples could be no less dogmatic; they frequently served interests of their own while reciting tradition. Dates and time scales are rarely specific. Archaeology necessarily leaves certain issues unresolved, such as whether some cultural traits traveled by migration of peoples or by diffusion of ideas or by parallel, but independent, innovation and change. A craft-worked seashell unearthed far inland is witness to trade, but it does not distinguish a long journey by one trader from a series of short-range exchanges by many. The operations of diplomacy are especially difficult to infer. Its results in war or peace may appear, but the negotiations leading to decision remain unknown.

Despite such handicaps, one may envision the Americas in 1492 as places in which two major city-states had arisen on foundations laid by much older urban civilizations. Beyond the imperial bounds lived other peoples, some of whom were influenced by the empires, some of whom descended from metropolitan colonies, but many of whom had originated independently, following lifeways as alien to Aztecs and Incas as Germanic or Hunnic tribes had been to ancient Rome.

The Americas were alive with activity during all those millennia before the Europeans came. Indians pioneered throughout the continents in making the land livable, sometimes by adaptation to their surroundings, sometimes by altering physical environments to suit human desires, always by using human intelligence to modify their cultures as needed.

This chapter attempts to show processes of interaction, especially at the farther reaches of urban influence. For comparison, some attention is given to dealings between tribes in the frontier regions beyond that influence. Finally, the chapter notes certain significant cultural traits that seem to have been common to city and tribe in the Americas, but sharply contrasts with what was developing among the Europeans who invaded later.

In what is now Mexico, a succession of city-states had culminated in the establishment of Aztec hegemony over many millions of people. Taking into account not only the Aztecs but their predecessors on whose cultural base Aztec civilization rested, the greatest intercultural frontier zone that the Americas have ever known—and the longest-lasting—was the vast periphery of Mesoamerican migration, colonization, and diffusion of culture to tribes at the frontiers.

Maize is an important clue to Mesoamerica's influence. Geneticists have established that maize cultivation had been innovated by at least 3500 B.C. in the Tehuacán Valley, about 150 miles southeast of today's Mexico City. Phenomenally productive, it supported a population explosion that led to imitations and variations of Mesoamerican cultures far to the north and south. Thus it came about, as will be shown, that the distant lands of the present-day eastern United States, washed by the Atlantic Ocean, imported maize horticulture long before much closer California, and that by means now unknown the peoples of the Andes Mountains learned maize culture thousands of miles south of its place of origin in central Mexico.

Maize was so essential to Mesoamerican culture that it is assumed here that the *influence* of Mesoamerica ended where no evidence of maize cultivation has surfaced. On the other hand, the presence of maize does not alone imply actual colonization by Mesoamericans, because maize became so marvelously productive that it would recommend itself to any people who learned about it and lived in an environment favorable to its cultivation.

A second benchmark of Mesoamerican influence is the surviving presence of great truncated pyramids or temple mounds. These are invariably found within regions of maize cultivation, though not in every region where maize was grown. By noting their presence or absence, it seems possible to infer a distinction between direct and indirect Mesoamerican influence, or, more explicitly, between colonization and diffusion.

It might seem likely that metal artifacts could also serve as "tracking" devices because they have survival value that endears them to archaeologists. Contrary to dogmas about Indians having Stone Age cultures in 1492, many crafted splendid works of art in gold, silver, copper, and bronze. Eastern Eskimos hammered meteoric iron into knives, but high-carbon steel had not yet been attained in the Americas. For present purposes, however, the distribution of items of metalcraft does not readily suggest vectors of either diffusion or migration. We must be content with the clues presented by maize and mounds (and, later, manioc).

At the center of their territory, the Aztecs depended utterly on facilitation and regulation of trade and tribute. The rulers of the twin cities of Tenochtitlan and Tlatelolco, on two linked islands that are now the heart of Mexico City, could not feed more than 5 percent of their population of more than 200,000. The remaining 190,000 or so persons depended on a daily stream of provisions and goods distributed in the cities' highly regulated markets, which were at the hub of a planned system of transportation by land and water. To facilitate trade, the Aztecs dredged canals through their horticultural islands (the chinampa) and across their surrounding Lake Texcoco to cities on the opposite shore. Thus, they created the prerequisite for the transportation of heavy freight by canoe through the shallow, reed-clogged waters. For carriage by land in a country without wheels, they adopted a system, already widespread in the Valley of Mexico, of portage by professional human carriers called tlamemes in relays from city to city. They supervised the construction of roads or trails for use by the tlameme porters, and they built causeways from their capital to the nearest opposite shores.

Further on, we shall consider Mesoamerican trade and colonization to the north. Here, however, let us travel southward. Possibly by way of traders, the cultivation of maize had diffused farther south. We can only speculate about its vectors of movement, but a reasonable hypothesis would take it from Mesoamerica through Ecuador, whence it continued farther south along the Andes, but also went eastward along the top of South America. An alternate hypothesis would carry maize by sea along the Pacific and Gulf coasts. We do know that it became one of the most important subsistence crops of the Inca empire of the Andes, supplementing the indigenous root crops of their highlands.

Here our concern is with the Inca rulers' outreach from their capital at Cuzco, which was probably in the opposite direction from the diffusion of civilization in the Andes. The Incas took good care to create myths that portrayed themselves as the fount of all wisdom, just as they tore down and rebuilt the architecture of their predecessors and liked to teach that they had conquered and civilized savages. The evidence of archaeology implies otherwise. Mesoamerica's urban culture was senior to that of the Incas, and maize certainly came from Mesoamerica, by however roundabout a route. The Incas taught that their culture came with them northward to Cuzco from Lake Titicaca on the Bolivian altiplano, but more than half a millennium before the Incas came to Cuzco, a people called the Moches built an enormous temple to the Sun in northern Peru. Even today it is the largest solid adobe structure in the Americas, though much reduced from its former size. Additional evidence of Moche cultural development has been unearthed in a spectacular tomb comparable in its treasures to Tutankhamen's tomb in Egypt.

Whatever the Incas may have inherited from Mesoamerica, they innovated a sharp contrast in their political economy. It is misleading to speak of their "trade," either internal or external. Goods were redistributed through kinship networks after tribute in labor left barely enough for subsistence. It was impossible for a peasant family to accumulate a surplus that might have been converted to capital. The functions that would be performed by a merchant class were carried out instead by agents of the bureaucracy. Probably there were pre-conquest traders in the seaport cities, plying along the coast, but from all appearances the Incas, after conquest, discouraged such traffic outside official control.

Like the Aztecs, the Incas preferred to use local nobles as agents of rule, but in direct contrast to them, they were not satisfied with "hegemonic" rule; they incorporated conquered peoples into their jurisdiction and converted local nobles into agents of their government. As to diplomatic relations with external governments, notices of such processes are rare. The Inca notion of diplomacy seems to have been an ultimatum to surrender, followed up by marching armies.

Incidentally, they were not always triumphant. Somewhere about 1473—Inca dates are conjectural—the great commander Topa Inca mounted a campaign over the Andes ridge to the eastern Montaña jungles with a plan to conquer Amazonia. His armies got bogged down among hostile peoples and rugged terrain, and he hurried back to Cuzco to suppress an uprising. (The Incas were constantly on the alert against uprisings, because they needed to be.) The Montaña peoples remained independent, and Inca territory remained limited to the western slopes of the Andes.

The Incas ruled, quite literally, from the heights and with the manpower of the sierra heights, partly because it was difficult for lowlanders to adjust to the thin air of the Andes. Even after conquest of the coastal peoples, the Incas did not draft them into their armies. What good would soldiers be who could not march more than half a mile without throwing themselves down panting for a rest? Loyalty was also a consideration, of course; the coastal peoples were far from trustworthy.

It is probable that Inca rule could not have survived for long even if no European had come near it. The restlessness of subject peoples and divisions within the ruling caste are some of the clues. More subtle, but wholly out of control, was the Incas' effort to manage the empire's economy by fiat. Suppressing the development of a merchant class, they rejected the concept of investment capital. They sank excess production into parasitic institutions that gobbled up goods and labor and could not be challenged or modified because of politico-religious dogmas. After the death of each emperor and his queen, their bodies were mummified and housed in elaborately equipped and richly ornamented palaces. Masses of retainers and concubines were sacrificed to serve the emperor in the hereafter. More deleterious to the economy, great estates and still more retainers were assigned to guard the palaces and serve the mummies in perpetuity. At the end of every reign, a huge new drain on the empire's resources was added to those already existing. It was literally a dead end for capital, and every new mummy made the situation worse. Productive labor lost to mummy service could be made up only by the conquest of more

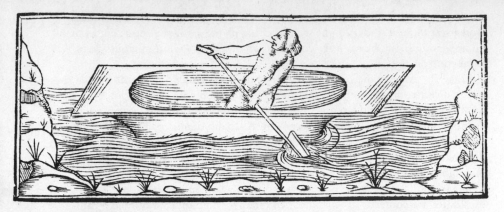

One of the first illustrations of a dugout canoe, from Gonzalo Fernández Oviedo y Valdés's report of 1547. Although his illustration fails to depict accurately the details of the dugout's construction, it shows how Caribbean natives managed this watercraft which was so vital to trade and transport.

people, which in turn implied still more loss of labor through casualties in battle.

Internalizing frontiers with diverse peoples implied acceptance of the disturbances endemic on frontiers. Despite the Incas' ingenious devices for suppressing varied cultures and traditions, their ultimate resource was state terrorism practiced horrifically on a large scale. Despite massacre, torture, and mass executions, simmering resentment among subject peoples broke out frequently into open rebellion. It appears that the Incas expanded their rule too fast and too far—too fast for cultural assimilation to take effect and too far for effective controls to be maintained from the capital at Cuzco.

Besides unrest among the subject peoples, dissension occurred within the ruling caste and the ruling family. As in all military despotisms, the generals vied for place and profit. Aided by the distance of Quito from Cuzco, the officers who had conquered Quito decided to keep it for themselves when Inca Huayna Capac died in 1527 and was succeeded by his son Huáscar Inca. The rebel captains set up Huáscar's younger brother, Atahualpa, as rival emperor. Thus, at the very moment when Francisco Pizarro's conquistadors appeared on the scene, the empire was being bloodily torn apart, and Pizarro was able to play the sides against each other. We know the consequence.

Cuzco, despite its grandeur, seems to have been a blip on the curve of culture, its ostensible importance magnified by the Incas' deliberate policy of destroying the evidence of their predecessors' accomplishments in order to vaunt their own praise. It is clear that, like the Aztecs, they built or rebuilt on foundations laid long before their time, especially in the essentials of agriculture, on which all else depended. In the long view, Ecuador outranks Peru as transmitter of cultural influence. Thousands of years before the Incas emerged to prominence, Ecuador was the crossroads through which maize cultivation and pottery styles passed. In the last and bloodiest of the Incas' great conquests, Ecuador's strong and independent people cost the Incas the finest of their troops and served as the base from which civil war was launched.

Easy, waterborne transportation was feasible from Ecuador to the vastness of South America east of the Andes. There was at least one system of Amazon tributaries that permitted navigation from the vicinity of Quito down to the mainstream. It was discovered and used by the expedition of Francisco de Orellana, which built boats and floated and fought in pursuit of El Dorado until its members reached the Atlantic. Their chronicler mentioned dense populations along the riverbanks which sent out large fleets of hostile dugout canoes. We need not be concerned about their adventures, except to note that communication along these waters was possible and probable long before the arrival of the Spaniards. It is well understood that a link exists between the Amazon and Orinoco tributaries.

A strong reason for believing in such communication is the cultivation and processing of bitter manioc. Some botanical scientists have put the probable origin of this tuber in eastern Ecuador, whence it traveled down the Amazon and Orinoco valleys and turned northward along the Antilles chain of islands stretching toward Florida. The odds are against so wide a distribution occurring by repeated independent innovation, because bitter manioc is poisonous when eaten raw and treatment is required to make it edible. Unlike most cultivated plants, which were edible in the wild state, manioc required someone to recognize its nutritious properties in the wild and to devise means to eliminate its toxic hydrocyanic acid, either by grating and pressing out the juices or by boiling them out. As remarked by an encyclopedist, "The wide area over which [manioc] has been distributed warrants the conclusion that the discovery of its value as a food and the means of separating its poisonous properties must have occurred at a very remote period." An alternative hypothesis originates manioc between 7000 and 5000 B.C. in the upper Amazon Valley.

Unfortunately, pre-Columbian Amazonia is still, to a large extent, a land of mystery. Whereas the cool and dry climate of the Andes preserved abandoned artifacts to leave evidence of their origins, the hot, soggy climate of Amazonia destroyed remnants of the past. From accounts of Spanish and Portuguese newcomers in the sixteenth century, we can glean some impressions—for instance, that large numbers of people were encountered by the Europeans. A modern estimate of Amazonia's population about 1492 puts it at five million persons, who lived in chiefdoms along the river valleys and fought fiercely with each other.

Besides these, the Tupinamba inhabitants of Brazil's coastal regions im-

Processing manioc. In the first illustration from the Antilles, a manioc plant grows next to a worker grinding manioc root into pulp. The second engraving demonstrates two techniques for squeezing the hydrocyanic acid from this pulp. With this toxin removed, the pulp is dried into flour.

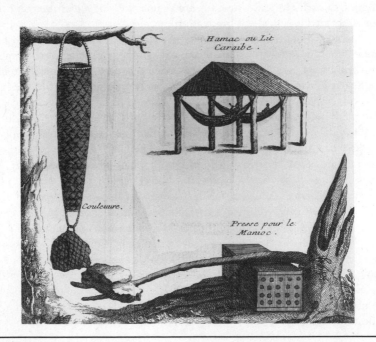

Hamac ou Lit
Caraibe.

Couleuure.

Presse pour le
Manioc.

pressed newly arriving Europeans. They were every bit as fiercely warlike against each other and neighboring tribes as the riverine peoples. We can only speculate as to how important trade became possible under such conditions of hostility, but so many people possessing dugout canoes in that network of waters could not have avoided each other.

In 1930, the respected archaeologist H. J. Spinden noticed evidence of a high culture at the mouth of the Amazon, and remarked that the "maize complex" was an "archeological bond between Central America, Venezuela and the lower Amazonas." Recently Anna Roosevelt and colleagues have found large platform mounds on the island of Marajó at the Amazon's mouth which testify to a long-lived city centered on 100,000 or more people. It had been abandoned by A.D. 1300. Nevertheless, dense populations along the entire length of the Amazon prevented Orellana's Spaniards from making a beachhead.

Pottery making and the cultivation of maize and manioc spread throughout Amazonia, whether by diffusion or by migration is not clear. The Arawak language—South America's most widely dispersed tongue— apparently originated in Amazonia and was carried into the Orinoco Valley, whence its speakers took to the sea and scattered along the Antilles Islands, stopping short of Florida, where they were rebuffed by hostile Timucua and Calusa Indians, who had come into the Florida peninsula from the opposite direction.

Attempts to trace the movements and communications of the peoples of northern South America and Mesoamerica must also take into account the surprising distribution of projectile weaponry, the pattern of which diverged greatly from the distribution of maize or manioc. The spear-throwing atlatl was favored by Incas, Aztecs, and Arawak-speaking Tainos of the Antilles, and the Tupinambas of coastal Brazil. Users of the bow and arrow surrounded these peoples and interpenetrated their territories; for example, in the backwoods of Brazil and among the Carib enemies of the Tainos.

Archaeologist Fred Olsen tried to trace manioc and the Taino speakers of Arawak to their assumed joint source, but he found no evidence farther up the Orinoco than Saladero, just above the river's delta in Venezuela. His earliest pottery find at Saladero is dated about 1000 B.C. He wondered whether the place may have been where migrants joined from several sources, including Colombia and Ecuador, to create the Arawak culture as now known to scholarship. This hypothesis could account for evidence in the Arawak culture of contact with the empires of Mesoamerica, but it does not explain the likelihood that Mayan merchants sent trading canoes along the northern coast of South America or that Arawak seamen journeyed to Mayan lands in Central America and the Yucatan.

Certainly much maritime trade was conducted in the Gulf of Mexico and the Caribbean Sea. According to the scholar Marshall B. McKusik: "Columbus and his companions saw large fleets of canoes in the Greater Antilles, and commerce and travel between the various large islands was well developed." McKusik, however, believed that not enough evidence exists to make a case for traffic between the islands and the mainland coast, and thought that "it is difficult to imagine what products other than cotton the islands could offer the mainland to stimulate an active and extensive trade." There is, nevertheless, very strong evidence of communication between Mesoamerica and the Greater Antilles, as well as with the southern coast of North America. And we know quite definitely of contact between Cuba and Florida, though that seems to have been irregular.

José M. Cruxent and Irving Rouse, archaeologists who have specialized in the West Indies, believe that the original settlers of the islands migrated to them between four and five thousand years ago from Central America. Others think that they came from the Florida peninsula or South America. Their descendants were displaced by invaders, perhaps more than once. Our concern here is with the principal peoples of the islands in 1492—the relatively recent invaders and colonizers, the Arawak-speaking Tainos and the Caribs. Both of these peoples practiced horticulture. The Tainos especially had created well-organized, socially stratified chiefdoms supported by the rich yield of three crops a year, and had prospered to the extent of pushing their predecessors, the Ciboneys, into remote corners of Cuba and Haiti. But the Tainos themselves were on the alert against raiding Caribs, whose expertise in war and canoe navigation made them formidable.

It is clear that the Tainos and their Carib enemies had come from South America to begin with. Their canoes (or pirogues) were capable of island hopping back to South America or north to Florida, or even across the Gulf of Mexico westward to the Yucatan, but the incoming Spaniards left no unambiguous report of islands-to-continent trade, and the archaeologists' inventories do not contain unambiguous artifacts testifying to it. It seems also that the Tainos and hostile Caribs, after sweeping through the chain of islands, failed to penetrate Florida in any significant way. William C. Sturtevant notes a Spanish report of a settlement of Cuban Indians in Florida about midway through the sixteenth century, but finds no long-term impact from it on the cultures of Florida's Indians.

The nature of maritime trade is to hide its tracks in the deep, so that it must be inferred from the presence of artifacts at the poles of the exchange. There are few enough of such artifacts on the islands, with one outstanding exception. This was the ball game so central to Mexican and Mayan cultures, which we know from the magnificent masonry courts later found by archaeologists. A thorough study by Ricardo E. Alegría concludes that "the similarities among the Mesoamerican, southwestern American, and West Indian ball courts indicate that the three areas shared a game which must have originated in one

A hollow clay figure of a Mayan ball player made as a whistle. Rubber ball games, which were played throughout Mesoamerica, were festive occasions. They brought fame to the participants, while attracting large groups of people, and stimulating visits, trading, and betting. Courtesy of the Milwaukee Public Museum.

of them." We are reminded of the elegant formality of a Mayan ball court at Copán, Honduras, but nothing so elaborate existed on the islands. Though more than 200 ball courts have been brought to light, those on the islands have none of the built-up structures found in Mesoamerica. Fred Olsen's wide travels disclosed "no example where any Arawak had deliberately placed one stone upon another." From this situation it would seem that the game had diffused from Mesoamerica out to the Antilles, but in a seeming contradiction the farthest of the Greater Antilles, Puerto Rico, had the most numerous and most elaborate courts, and is assumed to have been "the center of distribution of the ball-game complex in the Greater Antilles." How the game got there must be left to future experts. But unless the archaeologists reverse their findings dramatically, we must conclude that significant contact existed between the islands and the mainland, though not necessarily as systematic trade. We do know of likenesses between the island game and the Mesoamerican game through the reports of Spaniards who saw the island game played. Their accounts can be compared with the recorded descriptions of the Mexicans.

In this counterclockwise swing from Mesoamerica through northern South

A pitched battle among the Tupinambas of Brazil as depicted by the Huguenot missionary Jean de Léry. The warriors employ a trumpet, bows, arrows, shields, hardwood clubs, and their teeth. In the background are scenes catering to European expectations of cannibalism as well as other images of native life: hammocks, monkeys, parrots, and longhouses.

America and up along the West Indies, we have encountered a variety of contacts between peoples. Of these, the most important occurred where the highly organized city-states made contact with peoples beyond their jurisdictions. The influence of Mesoamericans seems to have spread beyond their borders chiefly through trade; certainly such essentials as maize cultivation ran far ahead of Mexican and Mayan armies.

But types of trade must be distinguished: there was the sort that took a trader off for long distances and the sort that moved goods within a region. Perishable commodities could not last a long journey, and bulky items with little value were not worth the effort. Such precious articles as obsidian, jadeite, and little copper bells were ideal for packing on the long haul. Sometimes, of course, goods could move along a series of short distances in a chain of regional trading stations. In either case, whether by one long jump or a series of hops, the influence of Mesoamerica gradually radiated outward, whether contact was direct or indirect.

In strong contrast, the influence of the Incas marched with their troops and seemed to have stopped where the troops stopped. To use an extreme figure of speech, the Inca power was a sort of "black hole" while the Mesoamerican city-states were exploding novas.

Mexican cultural influence also radiated in all directions. At its farthest, it extended along the northern coast of the Gulf of Mexico, up the Mississippi and Ohio valleys, and throughout the southeastern region of the present-day United States. Happily, for once, a narrative tradition has been preserved to supplement the evidence of archaeology. It was recited by the "keeper" of the Natchez temple in Louisiana to Antoine Simon Le Page du Pratz, one of Bienville's company who founded New Orleans. Le Page du Pratz had the recitation "confirmed to me by the Great Sun"—i.e., the current ruler of the Natchez people—and recorded it in 1758. The tradition fits what is known from other sources, and provides a rational, credible outline of a vast historical process:

> Before we came into this land we lived yonder under the sun (pointing with his finger nearly south-west, by which I understood that he meant Mexico); we lived in a fine country where the earth is always pleasant; there our Suns [Mexican rulers were called Suns] had their abode and our nation maintained itself for a long time against the ancients of the country, who conquered some of our villages in the plains, but never could force us from the mountains. Our nation extended itself along the great water [Gulf of Mexico] where this large river [the Mississippi] loses itself; but as our enemies were become very numerous and very wicked, our Suns sent some of their subjects who lived near this river, to examine whether we could return into the country through which it flowed. The country on the east side of the river being found extremely pleasant, the Great Sun, upon the return of those who had examined it, ordered all his subjects who lived in the plains, and who still defended themselves against the ancients of the country, to remove into this land, here to build a temple, and to preserve the eternal fire.
>
> A great part of our nation accordingly settled here, where they lived in peace and abundance for several generations. The Great Sun, and those who had remained with him, never thought of joining us, being tempted to continue where they were by the pleasantness of the country, which was very warm, and by the weakness of their enemies, who had fallen into civil dissensions, in consequence of the ambition of one of their chiefs, who wanted to raise himself from a state of equality with the other chiefs of the villages, and to treat all the people of his nation as slaves. During those discords among our enemies, some of them even entered into an alliance with the Great Sun, who still re-

mained in our old country that he might conveniently assist our other brethren who had settled on the banks of the Great Water to the east of the large river, and extended themselves so far on the coast and among the isles, that the Great Sun did not hear of them sometimes for five or six years together.

It was not till after many generations that the Great Suns came and joined us in this country, where, from the fine climate, and the peace we had enjoyed, we had multiplied like the leaves of the trees. Warriors of fire, who made the earth to tremble, had arrived in our old country, and having entered into an alliance with our brethren, conquered our ancient enemies; but attempting afterwards to make slaves of our Suns, they, rather than submit to them, left our brethren who refused to follow them, and came hither attended only with their slaves.

This unique source deserves respectful consideration for several reasons. It accords well with what we now know of Mexico's pre-Columbian history (and it could not have been hoaxed, because Le Page du Pratz did not know it except from his Natchez informant). We learn that the urbanites of some place in Mexico had been driven from some of their cities by the "ancients of the country"—who were called Chichimecs by the Aztecs—and that "after many generations" Mexico was conquered by "warriors of fire," who may easily be identified as Spaniards with firearms. Intriguingly, those Spaniards allied temporarily with the Great Suns of the Natchez tradition, which means that those Suns were *not* Aztecs. We may even hazard a guess that they were Tlascalans, because these were the people who first allied with Cortes, then rebelled against him. But such specific identification must await confirmation.

At the North American side of the Natchez tradition, Mexican influence is testified to immediately by the culture and customs of the Natchez themselves, beginning at the top with the mere existence of the omnipotent Great Sun (so different from the forms of government in most other North American polities) and ramifying down through a highly stratified social order.

The invading troops of Hernando de Soto, on their march from Florida to Arkansas or Texas (1539–43), encountered multitudes of Indians with identifiable Mesoamerican characteristics (as well as others who were "wild"). The anonymous Gentleman of Elvas, who recorded de Soto's campaign, repeatedly mentioned cacique lords carried in chairs or litters on the shoulders of their leading men. These caciques had such great authority that their men unhesitatingly obeyed orders taking them to certain death and often torture at Spanish hands. Many villages paid tribute and gave obedience to great overlords. Maize was grown everywhere; without the Indians' maize, de Soto's men "could not sustain themselves."

Marche du Calumet de Paix.

A procession of Natchez Indians, led by a calumet, or ceremonial pipe bearer, moves toward an arbor where Europeans await them. As a pledge of sincerity and an instrument of diplomacy, the calumet spread eastward from the Caddoan tribes in the lower Mississippi Valley in the decades before 1492.

West of the Mississippi they found cotton cloth and turquoise for the first time, and a town with the Toltec name of Tula. They even came across a variant of the Quetzalcoatl prophecy that the Indians "had learned from their ancestors that a white race would inevitably subdue them."

Archaeologists have traced the cultivation of maize up the Mississippi Valley and into Ontario and throughout the southern regions of the United States. Confirming the influence of Mesoamerica are many truncated pyramids with evidence that temples and administrative buildings had been built on top. But these "mounds" vary enough so that we must not assume they were all erected by the same people for the same purposes.

On the basis of present knowledge, we cannot be precise about the extent of Mexican immigration. Clear evidence exists of a mingling of peoples, some of whom had come *down* the Mississippi long before Mexicans started *up*. Perhaps the meeting peoples had remotely common ancestors whose paths had diverged millennia before they met again. Such a possibility is suggested by the massive earthworks at Poverty Point on the Mississippi at Floyd, Louisiana, which apparently were built about 1000 B.C. Architectural historian William N. Morgan attributed to the Poverty Point people a trade network "extending to Florida, the Appalachians, and the Great Lakes."

Until about A.D. 800, the earth structures in North America were dominated by circular or elliptical burial mounds, the excavated contents of which demonstate great skill in crafts and much trade extending from the Rocky Mountains to the Atlantic Ocean and south to the Gulf of Mexico. Naturally, the sort of artifacts found in these mounds included things thought to show honor to the dead. Morgan listed objects "of stone, obsidian, flint, fresh water pearls, bone, antler, bear teeth, mica, marine conch shells, textiles, and copper sometimes overlaid with iron, silver, or gold." The presence of textiles on that list is especially interesting because North American tribes beyond Mexican influence did not have true looms; directly or indirectly those textiles came either from Mexico or from peoples on the Mexican periphery. As a whole, the grave goods were luxury goods and as such they represented what has been called "primitive values" in order to distinguish such an inventory of goods from what might have been expected in European trade. Some of them indeed were crafted purposely as grave goods, but perhaps we should be careful about the condescension implicit in that word "primitive," as it is common enough in our own society nowadays to bury a corpse clothed in its finest garments in an expensively elaborate, silk-lined coffin, and often with a cherished piece of jewelry. What we can say positively about the artifacts unearthed from tombs is that these objects associated with mortuary ceremonialism cannot be taken as representative of those Indians' everyday life.

By "upstreaming" from practices observed after European arrival, we can infer that intertribal trade functioned for more exchanges than those of luxury and ceremonial goods, though perhaps not over such great distances. For instance, we know from recorded times of the arrangement by which Ontario's Huron and Nipissing Indians traded food with each other. The Hurons grew surplus maize at just about the northernmost possible latitude and exchanged it for the fish and game of the Nipissings, who lived beyond the climatic range of horticulture. And in especially severe winters, the Nipissings would be sheltered in Huron longhouses.

This sort of intertribal commerce and cooperation had two requirements: the tribes must be at formal peace with each other, and each must produce something needed or desired by the other. It seems reasonable to extrapolate cautiously this rule into the past to explain what made long-distance trade possible in the mound-building era, continuing to the time of European contact,

In his history of Canada published in 1664, François du Creux presents a Huron man smoking a pipe. Though the musculature is European, the hat, cape, moccasins, and tattoos reflect actual practice. The Hurons were middlemen in eastern Woodland trade.

when many practices changed. Caution requires notice that the Huron-Nipissing pattern of exchange occurred beyond the range of any possible Mexican colonization, so, as an example, it is removed in space as well as time.

Lacking written documents for the mound-building era, we can only guess whether regulated markets were maintained in Mexico's colonies in the elaborate style of what Cortés's men saw at Tenochtitlan, where state officials assigned spaces for particular kinds of goods and patrolled constantly to assure fair dealing. We do not know *how* trade was carried on by the mound builders—whether by entrepreneurs or by guilds of merchants as in Mexico—but we are fairly certain that it was done by barter, with all the implications of that sort of dealing, and we can trace some artifacts to origins far from their final resting place. Physical objects establish the existence of commerce, but equally limit the inferences to be drawn from them.

Similarly, a change in the mounds' architecture after about A.D. 800 demonstrates a probable northern extension of Mexican colonization or influence without revealing the process by which that came about, though we can be pretty sure that Mexican migration to Louisiana was responsible, directly or indirectly, for the introduction and spread of platform-topped pyramidal mounds in place of the older conical burial mounds. It appears also that the change in shape involved a change in function. Cahokia, the largest North American center of mound-building activity, located in Illinois across the Mississippi from present-day St. Louis, has been described as a city of more than 10,000 people, a "center of religion, trade, economics, government, and social activity for a tremendous area. Numerous and massive mounds were topped with temples and dwellings of the ruling class," wrote archaeologist William Iseminger. "Thousands of post and thatch dwellings of the city residents spread for miles throughout the surrounding bottomlands. Nearby were several satellite towns, much like suburbs, which contributed to the support of the main city."

That Cahokia required elaborate social, economic, and political structures to create and support its physical structures seems beyond question, but possibilities vary as to actual arrangements and operations. Cahokia was the supreme example of a culture type that the archaeologists call Mississippian, which has left remains extending as far north as the Aztalan site (Lake Mills, Wisconsin) and stretching along the Ohio and Tennessee tributaries of the Mississippi. The truncated pyramids associated with this culture have been found as far east as Florida's Atlantic coast and as far west as Spiro in present-day Oklahoma.

James Warren Porter has found cherts from Cahokia in Aztalan, and he concludes that Aztalan "had direct ties with Cahokia." Melvin L. Fowler writes plainly that "in a sense the entire American Bottom [of the Mississippi Valley] is one large Mississippian site."

Mississippian sites dominated by platform mounds suggest something more than simple administration of a homogeneous people. Major sites were surrounded by palisades, implying their location as colonialist centers in the midst of "native" tribal peoples. The farther out of these centers seem to have come to a fairly abrupt end about the thirteenth century A.D. James W. Porter suggests this "can be viewed in terms of the decay of the market system, and a return to the simpler and more individualistic redistribution system—a system never entirely lacking in the practices of the Woodland people." But this does not say *why* the market system ended.

In his magisterial study *The Southeastern Indians,* Charles Hudson observed that "the bearers of some elements of Mesoamerican culture may have been pochtecas, traveling Aztec traders, whose presence in North America may be supported by the fact that curious shell and copper masks of a 'long-nosed god' have been discovered at many Mississippian sites. It so happens that the god of the pochtecas was Yacatecuhtli who is often portrayed with a long nose." It seems likely that the pochtecas scouted before the migration reported in the Natchez tradition, and, considering the nature of the terrain, these movements probably took place by sea to the mouth of the Mississippi.

Images of the long-nosed god were associated with trade, probably with Mexico. Archaeologists have found objects like this one throughout the eastern United States. Another association between these artifacts and contact with Mexico is the fact that they were frequently associated with elaborate religious and political symbolism in Mississippian communities.

However, we must not assume that all the variants of Mississippian culture were dictated by diffusion from Mexico. Although the Natchez tradition establishes migration from Mexico in a time of troubles there, though the Mississippian platform mounds began to appear during one of Mexico's most turbulent periods, and though consensus exists that the introduction of Mexican maize was fundamental to Mississippian culture, it seems likely that the great dispersion of Mississippian culture was a phenomenon of a vast frontier region of mingling peoples. Strong evidence exists, even in the diverse forms and arrangements of the platform mounds, that local innovation and regional interaction modified the Mexican influence, however it was conveyed. The temple-mound peoples used bows and arrows like "barbarians" rather than the atlatl-using imperials. And we must not forget the tradition reciter's remark that "it was not till after many generations that the Great Suns came and joined us in this country, where . . . we had multiplied like the leaves of the trees." In human history, time and multiplication imply division. The farther that Mexicans got from home, the less their descendants felt and behaved like their ancestors.

Thus it came about that "Mississippian" culture manifested itself in variants identified by archaeologists as a core Middle Mississippian and, around its periphery (clockwise from "six o'clock" at the river's mouth), Plaquemine, Caddoan, Oneota, Fort Ancient, and South Appalachian. It appears that the Mississippians were aggressive at first, pushing outward from their core area, but withdrawing centuries later from their farthest expansion. These movements varied from region to region, and it is necessary to stress that what we

A cluster of mounds in what is now Georgia. These earthen remains of temple and house platforms were made by ancestors of the southeastern tribes encountered by Europeans in the sixteenth century. Such ceremonial centers thrived on various forms of exchange and tribute, and some were still being used in 1492.

know are vectors of culture, which may be independent of migrations of persons. Thus, when the Mississippian *culture* disappears from Wisconsin at about A.D. 1300, the reason may be that increasing aridity caused inhabitants to abandon planting for a hunting-fishing mode of subsistence that implied scattered small communities rather than cities, or there may have been physical withdrawal of populations to the south. At this stage, we can see only the signs of culture change.

In the Southeast, on the other hand, Mississippian cultures were still "full-blown" when Hernando de Soto used his troops to ravage the region between 1539 and 1543. It is not difficult to infer that his disastrous entrada was a powerful cause of culture change there.

Though much remains conjectural, it is certain that migration in North America was not a one-way street, nor was acculturation. Migrations from the North and Northwest were a constant over many generations, unavoidably encountering the northward-moving descendants of migrants from the South.

The migrants adapted to conditions as they traveled, and some of those conditions included the thrusting Middle Mississippians. What developed was a "local growth," in the phrase of archaeologist James B. Griffin—or rather a multitude of local growths—with "no single center."

We have yet to consider the more immediate frontiers north of Mexico's urban spread—i.e., the arid Sonoran territories of present-day Mexico and the southwestern region of the United States, which together form a single climatic region regardless of political boundaries. Perhaps the most important observation regarding this region is that the urban Mexicans were not much interested in it except for long-distance trade. This was the territory of Chichimec "barbarians." Opposite to the pattern of American colonization in the lush Mississippi Valley, Mexicans were on the defensive against Chichimec incursions from desert country. Legends bring the Aztecs themselves from somewhere in that harsh land into the opulence of the Valley of Mexico; and linguistics shows a relationship between them and the other members of the Uto-Aztecan family of languages, the Sonoran and Shoshonean or Northern Uto-Aztecan speakers, who stayed behind when the Aztecs migrated south.

Before the Aztecs, Mesoamerican trade reached out all the way to the turquoise mines in Chaco Canyon, in present-day northwestern New Mexico. Between the mines and the markets of Teotihuacán and Tula, the craftsmen of Alta Vista in Zacatecas and Casas Grandes in Chihuahua received the turquoise, worked it into jewelry, and sent it on to the major cities. As Richard A. Diehl describes them, these intermediaries had "colonialist" cultures in which the mass of common people were exploited and oppressed under an elite's harsh rule, but the rulers may have been local independents. "Although the north Mexican mining and trade centers maintained constant contact with the central Mexican cities, the degree of control exerted over them by the latter is not known. . . . In any case, the outposts could not have survived without the southern markets for their products," noted Diehl. The system broke up sometime in the thirteenth or fourteenth century (intriguingly close to the time when North America's Mississippian cultures showed traumatic decline).

One must distinguish between regional and long-distance trade, though certain centers probably dealt in both. The spectacular ruins of Chaco Canyon give evidence that its commercial activity was under some sort of political control, probably what anthropologists call a chiefdom. From A.D. 900 to 1130 or 1140, this canyon community built straight roads linking the settlements within the canyon to each other and radially to posts sixty miles, perhaps more, outside the canyon. Within this system, 125 planned towns have been identified. Such regional centers traded not only with each other and Mesoamerica but also eastward with Plains Indians and westward (for shells) to the Pacific coast. Some Southwestern cultural traits, such as the grooved ax, may have originated to the eastward.

Space is not available for detailed discussion of the rise and fall and rise again of the complex systems of commerce in the Sonora-Southwest region, and unfortunately much of such discussion would be based on speculation. It appears, however, that by A.D. 1500, trade had revived in northwestern Mexico, linking the outposts of Culiacán, Gusave, and Casas Grandes with central Mexico.

Southwestern archaeologists have disputed fiercely over how much of that region's general culture had been picked up by diffusion or colonization from Mesoamerica as compared with how much was the independent creation of indigenous peoples. Until more specific data are in hand, one must use common sense. Mexican influence is plain in ceremonial objects, in architecture, in irrigation systems, and in trade objects, and, as always, in the cultivation of maize. It is equally plain that Southwestern cultures were not mirror images of the Basin of Mexico; the resident peoples made their cultures out of what was at hand and what they had in their own heads instead of merely imitating patterns coming indistinctly from the distant metropole. If it is true that Mexico's influence extended vast distances, it is equally true, as Diehl remarked, that "civilizations cannot be understood without knowledge of happenings at their peripheries." In short, frontier regions have lives of their own that require study in their own contexts. In this respect, it is especially noteworthy that the bloodthirsty god of central Mexico did *not* travel to the Southwest, nor did the rituals of human sacrifice, although kinder gods in the form of kachinas went north and became an integral part of Pueblo ritual.

One of the oldest specifically identifiable cultures of the U.S. Southwest was the Hohokam of the southern Arizona desert, estimated to date from 300 B.C. and continuously discernible through artifact remains until about A.D. 1450. (The Pima and Tohono O'Odham, or Papago, Indians are believed to be Hohokam descendants.) There is reasonable agreement, we are told, that in pre-Aztec times "the Hohokam were a northern frontier Mesoamerican society." A more complex interpretation of the origin of Hohokam culture includes local evolution as well as trade and other forms of interaction with Mexicans and with other peoples of their own region. The Mexican influence, however exerted, spread across a large area of the Southwest, radiating beyond the Hohokams to the Mogollons, the Anasazi "old ones" of the "Four Corners" of Utah, Colorado, New Mexico, and Arizona, and a number of local and regional variant groups. Formerly hunting-gathering peoples of the Great Basin's age-old desert culture, they adopted agriculture and whatever else attracted them in Mexican importations and evolved a general Southwestern culture with regionally adapted subcultures. It was specific to that region, very likely for environmental reasons.

Again, something caused contraction at about the thirteenth century A.D., so that the Southwest today has a number of ghost towns like Mesa Verde from that general culture of the "old ones." Arriving Spaniards in the sixteenth century found the three major Pueblo centers still extant today: Zuni-Acoma, the communities of the northern Rio Grande Valley, and the mesa-country Hopis.

As invaders, the Spaniards were preceded by Apache-Navajo peoples who began reaching the Southwest about A.D. 1400, after migrating from the "great hive" of Athapaskan speakers in Canada's Mackenzie Basin. A pattern familiar elsewhere in the world repeated itself as the nomadic Athapaskan-speaking hunters harried the sedentary horticultural Pueblo. In due course, but not until Spaniards arrived from the south in "historical" times, the Athapaskan Apache-Navajos settled down after adopting pastoral ways from the Pueblos and horses from the Spaniards. The processes were turbulent and continued changing through the invasion of "Americans" in the nineteenth century. In all that time the most enduring and slowest-changing cultural tradition remained the one originally established in the frontier at the periphery of Mexico's city-states. Much is still visible today, even to the uninstructed eye, from Zuni craftsmanship in jewelry through Hopi ceremonialism to the adobe apartments of Taos.

Obviously the dry Southwest contrasts with the lush, well-watered Mississippi Valley, so that distinctions must be made when both are mentioned as frontier regions. Perhaps the physical connotations of *region* should be abandoned in order to compare these vast territories more abstractly as *zones*. What made them comparable was human activity rather than geography. Both were places in which outthrusting bearers of dynamic Mexican cultures encountered incoming bearers of quite different cultures, and where the peoples adapted by various means. Mutual acculturation plainly was one of the means. Just as plainly, wars were another.

It is hard to visualize all this vast area as a zone because it was tremendously larger than central Mexico, where the dominant impulse had been created, but the pattern is not unique in human history. Indeed, one can speculate that it was common. The tribes of Attica spread over enormous areas by trade and conquest and made the Hellenistic era, lasting for thousands of years, around the eastern Mediterranean Sea. Romans followed their example at the western end and in northern Europe. The general pattern is clear enough. What is needed for comprehension is acceptance of the basic assumption that the city-states of Mexico had the same expansive dynamism as Greece and Rome (and Persia and China). This underlying cultural power is hidden by Mexico's lack of political power; its rulers could not govern beyond their core population.

Let us return to that northern frontier zone and add one more segment to the area of Mexican influence. For this we must follow different patterns of migration. The great linguistic family of Algonquian speakers traveled primarily eastward from Alaska, instead of south, until some of them reached the Atlantic Ocean. The Ojibwas have a tradition that once they reached the Atlantic they reversed direction until they and their Ottawa kinfolk settled along the north shores of the Great Lakes. Northern Algonquian speakers, who lived where planting was impossible or chancy at best, continued a hunting-fishing-gathering way of life, but others spilled out, so to speak, from the general eastward surge and moved south, eventually making contact with Mississippians coming north.

The Algonquian Delawares traveled all the way to the Atlantic, and they recounted a tale of their most recent migration to Moravian missionary John Heckewelder late in the eighteenth century. He passed it on to the American Philosophical Society. According to this tradition, speakers of Algonquian and Iroquoian languages came to the Northeast from directions that may have been different; the Delawares came from the west and the Iroquois Five Nations "joined" them.

At some unspecified time (traditions are not strong on chronological particulars), the two peoples made war against an "Allegewi" people east of the Mississippi River who apparently were Mississippians. Heckewelder added that he had personally seen many of the Allegewi fortifications, one of which was "about 20 miles northeast of Detroit" with "large flat mounds" nearby. After the allies' triumph, the defeated Allegewi "abandoned the country to the conquerors, and fled down the Mississippi, from whence they never returned." This tradition's chronology is confused in ways too complex for analysis here, but it has enough confirmable data to suggest that the Allegewi had carried Mexico's influence as far as Ontario until forced into precipitate flight. Archaeologists have established that the Monongahela Valley—which may be presumed to have been Allegewi territory—was abandoned sometime after A.D. 1300.

From archaeological findings we learn that the eastern Algonquians and Iroquoians began to practice horticulture sometime around 1000 B.C., but maize became prominent in their planting only after A.D. 1300. Then, as Cadwallader Colden relates the Iroquois tradition, "The Five Nations made Planting of Corn their whole business" and exchanged it with northern, hunting Algonquians (of Canada, who lived beyond maize culture), "Corn for Venison," in a manner parallel to the historically reported trade between Hurons and Nipissings.

Iroquoianist scholars dispute the question of where those Iroquoians came from, but obviously they had come under Mexican-Mississippian influence at an early date. Linguistic study suggests that they may have come up from the South, "dropping" some of their people along the way. The Iroquoian Cherokees, whose language is closest to Proto-Iroquoian, settled in the mountains of North Carolina and Tennessee, and the "genealogy" of Iroquoian languages constructed by Professor Marianne Mithun strongly implies migration northward by other tribes until they spread around Lake Ontario and along the up-

A round dance. In this eighteenth-century illustration by Antoine Simon Le Page du Pratz, two rings of dancers circle a seated drummer. Women, some holding drums, form the inner circle, and men, using rattles, the outer one.

per St. Lawrence River. Professor Mithun does not suggest a migration source, and she cautions that thousands of years may have elapsed between migrations of separate branches of the Iroquoian family. Certainly it will be necessary to reconcile her findings with the chronologies of hypotheses about *in situ* development of material cultures, but no one is likely to deny that language is also part of culture.

However that turns out, the Mexican frontier zone in the Northeast came to an abrupt end at the line formed by the Canadian Shield escarpment. Horticulture was impossible beyond that line. As happened in the Southwest, a generalized culture evolved in the Northeast below the line. Intercommunication was constant and relatively easy. When European traders set up in business, they needed only to establish posts on the St. Lawrence, Connecticut, Hudson, and Delaware rivers and Chesapeake Bay to tap into the preexisting native network. Indian traders came to them over preestablished trails on land and by interlaced streams. Though much traffic and mingling characterized the Northeast, its peoples never homogenized. Iroquoians and Algonquians preserved distinctive styles of culture even as they borrowed from each other, and the Iroquois Five Nations became hostile to their surrounding neighbors. When Samuel de Champlain arrived on the St. Lawrence River in 1609, he joined war parties marching against the Iroquois Five Nations. Traditions of both the Delawares and the Iroquois stress their mutual hostility until the formation of the Covenant Chain bicultural confederation in 1677.

On the northwestern side of the Mississippian core, the Mexican influence was carried by Mandans, whose traditions told of migration from the upper Mississippi westward to the Missouri River. They had assimilated maize cultivation, directly or indirectly, while resident on the upper Mississippi, and they taught it to the Hidatsas when that people became their neighbors on the Missouri. Cheyennes, following a similar pattern, apparently engaged in horticulture while living in Minnesota on the highest reaches of the Mississippi, but were compelled by pressure from hostile tribes to migrate westward into North Dakota, where they again became horticulturalists.

Maize cultivation marks the farthest extent of indirect Mexican influence. Beyond the Mandans and Cheyennes there were peoples who planted tobacco for its symbolic significance in religious ritual, but they were hunters, and the significance of maize was primarily subsistence. Predictably, trading centers evolved among the maize growers on the Missouri, where exchange took place between peoples of complementary cultures. Ethnohistorian William R. Swagerty remarks, "A favorable geographical location as well as resource and craft specialization enabled these Middle Missouri tribes to assume the position of 'middlemen' in a cross-cultural and intertribal trade linking riverine horticulturalists with upland hunters."

When the expansion of Mexican influence appears in its entirety, one sees that topography and climate were not the only factors imposing limits. Everywhere around the periphery there was a perpetual surge inward of new migrants from the Northwest. Though these hunting peoples did not cultivate maize, they traded vigorously with one another. An annual "rendezvous," similar to European trade fairs, occurred at the Dalles near where the Columbia River cuts through the Cascade Mountains of Oregon and Washington. Salmon, instead of maize, played the central role where the fish swam upriver to spawn. Millions of pounds of salmon were taken and processed by drying or smoking every summer, and exchanged to Indian traders from all over the region.

Even the nomadic hunters of Alaska had a well-established pre-Columbian network of trade that included exchange of furs and wood carvings for Siberian metal utensils and reindeer skins. Annual summer trade fairs were held at

This complex Aztec mosaic depicts a ball game. It demonstrates the high value placed on lapidary work that used materials drawn from distant sources. The turquoise in this piece was probably imported from what is now the southwestern United States. Courtesy of the National Museum of the American Indian.

Kotzebue Sound, at Norton Sound, and on the Yukon Delta, where inland tribes brought jadeite, red ocher, and tailored skin clothing to exchange for sealskins and seal oil. Edward H. Hosley remarks that "before the intervention of Europeans in Alaska, all-native trading networks extended from northeast Asia into interior Alaska."

Obviously these trading systems were beyond even indirect influence from imperial Mexico. Just as plainly, the regular gatherings for trade served many functions besides exchange of goods. They were peaceful contacts between bands, during which socialization took place on a scale impossible out yonder in the wild. Such occasions promoted general unification: religious ceremonies were observed, intermarriages occurred, and alliances were formed. Besides trading goods, the participants exchanged ideas, knowledge, and skills. These were channels for the diffusion of culture over vast areas of territory. The hunting peoples who occupied the northern third of North America in 1492 varied in detail, but they shared an ancient general culture in which the summer assembly held prime importance everywhere. An astute French observer in eastern Canada, Father Joseph François Lafitau, remarked in 1724: "The Indian tribes have traded with each other from time immemorial. . . . The feasts and dances which they have when they go to deal with other tribes make their trade an agreeable diversion. . . . Their ways of engaging in trade is by an exchange of gifts."

Less information is available for the peoples of the Arctic Circle, but recent research discloses that even at the most northern latitudes "strong trade relationships existed side by side with fighting" between Eskimos and Indians. The Eskimos certainly moved about over great distances. About A.D. 1000, bearers of the Thule culture spread from western Alaska across northern Canada and Greenland.

When Columbus made his fateful landing in 1492, the Americas were home to two great city-states, the heirs to many generations of complex high cultures. In South America the Inca empire seems to have been implosively self-contained, but the older and more densely populated society of central Mexico had sent out colonies and spread vast networks of trade, probably into South America and confirmably into North America. If there is any validity to the idea of a "transit of civilization," Mexico must be credited as the source in the Americas. By whatever means it had come into being, we have traced this Mexican influence (predating the Aztecs) within a gigantic arc embracing the Southwestern United States, the entire Mississippi Valley, and the entire eastern region where maize cultivation is possible. Beyond that vast arc lived peoples who adhered to ancient lifeways of hunting, fishing, and gathering.

Especially noteworthy are the acculturative processes in frontier zones where peoples met and learned from each other while preserving individual identities. So to speak, these were historical laboratories of cultural pluralism, with lessons for modern times.

Some comparisons seem in order. In 1492, American Indians lived under forms of government almost as varied as Europe's. The popular myth that Indians were anarchists living in conditions of "wild license" is the product of ideological imagination. Despite technological lacks—of wheeled vehicles, draft animals, and large sailing vessels—the Indians everywhere maintained networks of trade and traffic, sometimes over thousands of miles.

But there were also substantial cultural differences less visible than the technological—not between savage Amerindians and civilized Europeans, but between particular institutions involved in their polities and commerce. One great European advantage was the simple, alphabet-based system of writing that made possible an impersonal, bureaucratic nation-state able to maintain and concentrate power for conquest and rule of subject peoples. Aztecs and Incas, though they conquered great territories, never managed to stabilize dominion; their armies were always busy putting down rebellions.

Europeans had another advantage in the possession of coined money—a universal commodity and means of keeping accounts. With money and literacy (and Indo-Arabic digits), Europeans had created by 1492 such benefits to commerce as credit, banks, insurance, bookkeeping, and—not least—classes and associations of merchants powerful enough to defend their individual properties and interests against the demands of nobles and priests. Essential to such merchant power was the cultural institution of private investment capital—something wholly alien to the conceptions of all Amerindians. Among Indians everywhere—in North and South America, among imperialists and tribalists—"wealth" (as defined by post-Renaissance Europeans) never developed beyond operating capital. Surpluses beyond immediate needs were redistributed in various ways. The merchants of Mexico bought sacrifices for the gods and gave expensive feasts to advance themselves in rank and prestige. In the Andes, the Incas seized surplus wealth and devoted it to their mummies' palaces. Among the tribes, men with wealth gave away much of it to gain leadership status, and sometimes destroyed it ostentatiously to gain prestige. (The Northwest Coast's Kwakiutls were the most famous practitioners of noble disdain, but something like the same attitude was displayed by Mohawk chiefs who flaunted their poverty.) It followed that the capital necessary to support sustained individual enterprise simply did not exist. Even the Hurons, who specialized in commerce, never became more than a tribe full of traders rather than merchants.

Thus, when the first fury of armed European conquest was succeeded by *intersocietal* trade, the Europeans held great advantage not only in quantity and quality of material goods (excepting certain craft specialties) but in the methods by which trade was conducted. Intersocietal exchange assured that conquest would be continued quietly, though no swords were drawn, through odds stacked in favor of the more mercenary Europeans.

For a long time, scholars lost sight of the vast pre-Columbian *intertribal* trading networks because such commerce was seriously disrupted when the differently conducted and more immediately visible intersocietal trade began. Now, however, we can understand that the tribes were drawn out of their own pre-Columbian systems into the world market dominated by Europeans. What happened then may well be studied by statesmen today, as computers and conglomerates draw commerce into a new sort of world market that functions according to its own rules and controls nations more than it is controlled by them.

W.H. HOLMES

CLARA SUE KIDWELL

ON A CLEAR, COLD predawn morning in Arizona, a Hopi man leaves his home and walks some distance to a rise of land near his village. He settles himself at the top of the rise to watch in the growing light for the sun to make its first appearance above the eastern horizon. The Hopi sun watcher on this morning is carrying out a duty that his ancestors were carrying out in 1492 when Columbus first sighted land from the deck of the *Santa María,* and when Francisco Coronado first arrived in the country of the Pueblo peoples in 1540. Throughout the months before the winter solstice, the sun watcher sights the progress of the sun along the horizon, observing its points of rising by natural markers such as hilltops and valleys, and, in the present, by the point of rising over the roof of the Hopi Cultural Center on Second Mesa.

The sun watcher's observations of the sun's movements allow him to tell the leaders of his village when the sun will reach a certain point in its travels across the sky. There, the sun has reached the extent of its southernmost journey and will rest before it resumes its travels back across the sky toward its northern house. The observation of the winter solstice is a key to the timing of the Soyal Ceremony, which celebrates the first appearance of the kachina spirits in the villages. The kachinas, the spirits who bring rain and fertile crops, are an essential part of Hopi life. The solstice is also the predictor of the change of the seasons that is crucially important to people who depend on agriculture for their subsistence. It is essential to know the time of the last killing frost so that planting may begin.

In Pueblo towns the chief priest had among his duties the responsibility for tracking the movements of heavenly bodies, particularly the sun. This idealized picture of a cliff dwelling by a nineteenth-century American anthropologist includes a tower kiva from which such observations were made. Courtesy of the National Museum of the American Indian.

A tool for straightening the wooden shafts of arrows. While straighteners were present in all parts of the Americas, this one (made of ivory) was found by archaeologists in western Alaska. Courtesy of the Field Museum of Natural History.

The sun watcher's observations allow him to predict the future actions of the environment—that is, that cold weather and frost will cease and that plants will be able to grow. The sun watcher can tell not only when the sun reaches the extreme points of its path across the sky; he can also tell where the moon stands in relation to the sun during the year. He can tell when the moon will appear each month, and what time of night it will rise. By observing not only the points of solstice but the relationship of the moon to the sun throughout the yearly cycle of the seasons, the Hopis demonstrate, as they have for centuries, a sophisticated understanding of celestial relationships that have been integral to their own subsistence patterns, because they predict planting and harvesting seasons.

Prediction in 1492 was also an essential aspect of science as it was understood by the Europeans who first arrived in the New World. The same kind of sophisticated celestial observations that governed Hopi agriculture allowed Columbus to find his way across the uncharted waters of the Atlantic. He simply did not know about the landmass that stood in the way of his passage to India. But his skill at navigation was based on a tradition of systematic observation of nature that characterized both the Hopi Indians and the European explorers in 1492. The science that brought Columbus to the New World stemmed from an intellectual heritage of inquiry about how the natural world worked. In that respect, Columbus and the Hopi sun watcher shared a common belief—that there were patterns in nature that were important. Those patterns allowed people to predict what future events would happen in their worlds.

Although there were similarities in the traditions of observation of natural phenomena that allowed the Hopi sun watcher to know about the turning of the sun and Columbus to reach America, there were significant differences in the ways that each explained the reasons for the sun's motion. To the Hopis, the sun was a being who acted of his own will, albeit in predictable ways. To Columbus and the intellectual tradition predominant in Europe in 1492, the sun was a physical object moving according to predictable patterns that never varied. But to both Columbus and the Hopis, the sun revolved around the earth. And the idea that physical bodies could have will was very much a part of European science. The intellectuals of the time explained falling bodies in terms of natural place, an Aristotelian belief that objects fell because they had an inherent desire to reach their natural place (the center of the world). And natural place explained gravity.

The terms "science" and "technology" in the modern world carry the learning of the last five centuries of knowledge and experience. They mean many different things now than they did in 1492, and the practices of the Native Americans of that period cannot be judged by present-day understandings of those terms. The science and technology of the New World in 1492 must be understood in the context of what Europeans understood about the world then. It was full of intangible forces that acted on things. Philosopher's stones could transmute base metals into gold. Invisible fluids could move between objects to influence their behavior. To the common and uneducated people of Europe, the world was alive with spirits who lived in the woods, and witches and others had powers to manipulate the forces of the world to cause illness or bad luck.

The real divergence of Native American and European beliefs about the nature of the world came after 1492. In Europe, the rational traditions of the Greeks came increasingly to mean natural laws. They melded with Christian beliefs in an omniscient, omnipotent, and omnipresent God, and nature ceased to be spiritual and became increasingly material and governed by the will of that God.

In 1492, although their ways of understanding the natural environment may have differed, both Europeans and Native Americans had similar ends in view—to be able to control the outcome of events in the world around them. Knowledge of the environment came from systematic observation of a body of physical phenomena that existed apart from human beings (a statement of belief in itself), and that knowledge allowed humans to exercise a measure of control over the forces of nature and to predict the outcomes of situations and their own actions.

One way of controlling the environment is to utilize human energy more efficiently through the use of machines, what one generally calls technology. Native people of 1492 used the same kind of simple machines that Europeans did, although they did not theorize about why they worked. Many machines in Europe were more complex, but they were based on the five simple machines of classical Greek mechanics: the wedge, the inclined plane, the level, the pulley, and the screw. The point of a machine is that it increases the force exerted on it. On the Northwest Coast of North America, there were examples of mechanical devices. Gigantic cedar trees were sometimes felled by chipping cavities into their sides with an adze (an application of the wedge) and setting a slow fire therein. The trunk burned through until the tree toppled. Cedar is straight-grained and splits easily. To split cedar logs into planks, Indian men would open a small split in the side of a log and then drive in a series of wooden wedges to widen the split until a plank could be peeled off. A simple pulley was used in a Plains Indian medical technique. To reset a dislocated joint, a man would tie a rawhide rope around the affected limb, throw the rope over a tree branch, and pull on it—a generally effective method of exerting sufficient force to pop the joint back into place.

Some of the techniques for making things were simply and sheerly ingenious. To build canoes, Haida craftsmen smoothed the outside of a giant log to the appropriate shape, burned into it with slow fires, and chipped away the charred wood to form the canoe. At the crucial stage of hollowing the shell to a uniform thickness, very small pegs of the desired length were driven through the outside, and as the carver smoothed the inside, he could tell that he had reached the desired thickness when the tops of the pegs appeared.

Beyond this use of technology, Europeans and Indians of 1492 shared the practice of systematic observation of natural phenomena. They predicted the outcome of events on the basis of those phenomena. But while European intellectuals of the fifteenth century looked for ultimate causes whose results could always be predicted, the native peoples exercised control over the forces of nature by establishing personal relationships with spirit beings through ceremonial actions or visionary experiences or dreams. These personal relationships allowed people to call on the spirits for assistance in obtaining desired results. To Europeans, the natural world was ruled by laws; to native people, it exercised will. To both, it was the object of careful observation which led to ability to predict the outcome of events. Native American science in 1492, then, constituted the activities of the native peoples of the New World in observing physical phenomena and attempting to explain and control them.

The major point at which European and native science diverged was in the matter of experimentation. It would not have occurred to the Hopis to cease their ceremonies to see if the sun would indeed continue north rather than turning in its path. However, by the late seventeenth century, European scientists believed that they could test the outcomes of events by controlling the circumstances and observing the results. Modern science is concerned with proof of scientific hypotheses—that is, their power to predict the outcome of a set of circumstances controlled by the experimenter. Native people believed

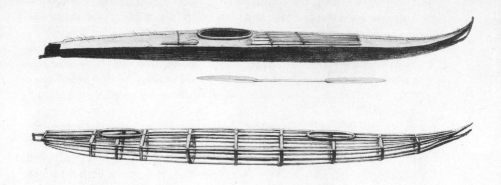

Louis Choris, a French artist who accompanied a Russian expedition to the Pacific coast in the late eighteenth century, was fascinated by the variety of watercraft encountered on the trip. Here he presents the inner and outer forms of kayaks from the Aleutians and of boats from St. Lawrence Island in the Bering Strait.

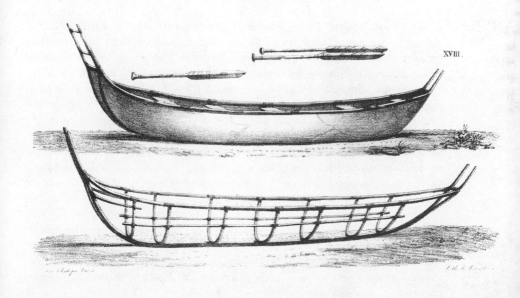

XVIII.

that their personal relationships or the formal relationships of their groups with spiritual forces would bring about results. Thus, the ceremony performed by the Hopis at the instance of the sun watcher's observations of the solstice actually caused the sun to turn in its journey and return across the sky.

Another principle of twentieth-century science is the importance of uniformity in nature. European science by the eighteenth century was concerned with similarities of things and events that would indicate natural order. However, to native people, importance was attached to the unusual, the mutable or changeable.

A. Irving Hallowell, an anthropologist working in Canada in the 1930s, asked a Saulteaux (Ojibwa) Indian man, "Are all the stones we see around us alive?" and after the man had thought about the question a while, he replied, "No, but some are." To Hallowell as a scientist, it is the "all" that was important. He was looking for a generalizable principle. To the Saulteaux man, it was the "some" that were significant—those rocks that exhibited some unusual behavior, that were observed to move of their own volition, or to speak to people. These attributes were signs of special spiritual power. These actions reinforced the idea of the reality of spiritual beings acting in nature.

This is not to say that Native Americans were not interested in the similarities of things, or that they did not put things into categories. It is simply to say that things that were unusual were of greater interest than things that were similar.

The ways in which people classify things indicate what qualities or characteristics are most important to them. Aristotelian categories of earth, air, fire, and water reduced the diversity of phenomena to a few elemental forms and qualities. The modern system of scientific plant classification, the Linnaean system (devised by Carl von Linné in 1735), is generally accepted as a significant achievement in Western science. It divides plants into categories based on sexual characteristics and other morphological features.

Indians were also interested in similarities of form and function, and one can find many examples of New World naming systems that classified things or indicated similarities. The categories that native people devised were based on systematic observation, as were European systems. The difference was in the elements that were considered similar.

Plants were closely observed and widely used, and there were many examples of classificatory names. The Navajos characterized plants as male and female, depending on characteristics such as size and hardness or softness of stems and foliage. The system was based on analogy to personality traits distinguishing men and women, rather than on the idea of the physical sexual characteristics of plants.

The Aztecs used three major categories of plants: trees (quauhtli), bushes (quaquauhzin), and herbs (xihuitl). Plant names generally included a word or suffix that indicated whether they were food (quilitl), ornamental (yochitl), medicinal (patli), or economic, or plants used for building, clothing, or material objects, for which a number of suffixes were used. The Thompson Indians of British Columbia named some plants according to their use, as ilie'litu'nəl, "cough medicine," or cuxcuxuza, "grizzly bear berry," one eaten by grizzly bears. They also recognized categories in the fact that certain plants generally grew together, and they could predict the presence of them together. Thus, they named the wood betony "companion of willow weed," because they found it with the willow.

Indian classifications were not always based on physical properties. The Navajos put bats in the same category as insects because of an origin tradition in which insects and bats had lived together in a previous world. The badger was classified with the wolf, mountain lion, bobcat, and lynx (which were grouped as predatory animals) because he was their friend.

Classification systems were important to native people, and they revealed the results of careful observation and thinking about the nature of the world. The categories in those systems were more likely to be based on their usefulness to humans or associations with other beings in the physical world than to simple physical form. Contemporary science judges the validity of Native American classification systems by how well the Indian names distinguished among animals and plants of different genera and species—that is, how closely native people recognized the same features that scientists do. The Tzeltal Mayas in Chiapas, Mexico, for example, distinguished relatively few of the modernly designated botanical categories of plants in their environment. They did, however, distinguish a number of different kinds of beans within a single currently known species. They also lumped numbers of species together in single names. In other words, they found many differences in plants that were important to them, and very few in those that were not.

The observation of plants directed the Native Americans' attention to their immediate surroundings and the cycles of life and death of living things. They noted the conjunction of those cycles with events in the sky above them, and they regulated their own lives by the movements of the sun, moon, and stars. The systematic observation of the movement of celestial bodies constituted one of the most dramatic facets of Native American scientific activity.

In 1492, astronomy in Europe was primarily the basis for astrology—that is, the prediction of human events. The earth was the center of the universe. The Copernican doctrine of the sun-centered universe had yet to be proposed. The movements of the earth and the planets were observed against the background of the fixed stars with their distinctive patterns that constituted the zodiac. Observations were oriented toward events occurring overhead, and those events were thought to have a significant impact on the lives of humans on the earth.

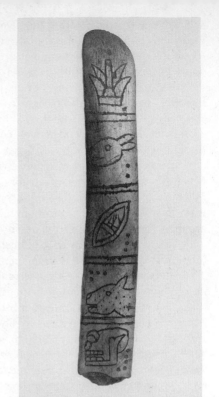

A bone handle from Mexico covered with marks of day signs designating particular dates, probably birthdays or other important family events. In 1492, calendars were important regulators of daily life throughout Mesoamerica. Courtesy of the Milwaukee Public Museum.

In the Americas, at the same time, the horizon was the main reference point for observation of celestial events. Although some observations of zenith events—those directly overhead—took place, the horizon was still the most important marker. We can infer this fact from the numerous orientations of physical structures or their parts to events occurring on the horizon, and it distinguished Native American from European astronomy.

The horizon-based system of observation led to practices such as those of the Hopi sun watcher. Throughout North and South America, people built structures that aligned with certain points on the horizon where important celestial events took place. These structures allowed for observation of regularly recurring phenomena. In the ruins of pueblos dating back to at least A.D. 1100 in the present-day U.S. Southwest, there is evidence of Indian knowledge that the sun moved in relation to the earth in regular cycles. Casa Rinconada, a large circular kiva in the Chaco Canyon region of northwestern New Mexico, has twenty-eight niches spaced equally around the interior of its stone wall. It also has six somewhat larger and irregularly spaced niches below those. At the time of the summer solstice, for four or five days around that date, light from a window placed high on the northeastern side of the kiva shines on one of the six niches.

Some of the curiously placed corner windows of the ruins of Pueblo Bonito in Chaco Canyon have also been examined as possible observation sites for solstices or other celestial phenomena. Although the condition of the ruins makes it hard to determine exact alignments, the unusual placement of the windows draws attention to them. It seems that they were there for a specific purpose, and when the light of the rising sun at the summer solstice shines directly through a window into the room beyond it, the purpose becomes clear. The window was placed to alert the occupants of the dwelling that a crucial point in the year had arrived.

On Fajada Butte, near the large pueblo ruins in the canyon, is another apparent pre-Columbian observation site. There, three large rock slabs rest on a small outcropping and lean against the side of the butte. In 1989, one of the slabs shifted slightly, but prior to that time, on the day of the summer solstice, a thin dagger of sunlight passed through the exact center of a spiral design carved into the butte's side behind the rocks. At the winter solstice, two daggers of light just grazed the sides of the spiral. Whether the placement of the stone slabs was deliberate or accidental, the spiral in the rock is definitely of human origin, and the conjunction of light and shadow with the spiral made the sun dagger a solstice marker.

On a bluff among the Big Horn Mountains in Wyoming there is another site, also obviously the product of human activity. Known as the Medicine Wheel, it consists of a ring of piled stones or cairns, some twelve feet in diameter, from which twenty-eight stone spokes radiate to an outer stone circle abutting six other piled-stone cairns. The point of the rising of the summer solstice sun can be observed along a line sighting from one of the outer cairns across the center cairn. Other lines along the spokes of the wheel serve to sight the rising of the bright stars Rigel and Aldebaran, which precede the solstice by a matter of weeks.

Constructions such as the Medicine Wheel are evidence that systematic observation of the stars and knowledge of celestial occurrences allowed people to predict important events. If the Indians of North America did not have written languages, they recorded their observations in other ways. The Medicine Wheel both predicted and marked the summer solstice.

There are remains of many medicine wheels in North America. Two sites in the territory of the Blackfeet in modern Saskatchewan show evidence of the placement of stones similar to that of the Medicine Wheel in Wyoming. The orientation of lines of boulders and stone cairns on Moose Mountain points to the summer solstice. Other alignments toward the rising of Sirius and Aldebaran can also be observed. The Blackfeet traditionally had calendar men who used bundles of sticks to mark the time for certain ceremonies, and although contemporary Blackfeet elders deny knowledge of a connection between the stones and the solstice, these boulders might have been placed to help the calendar men correlate their stick counts with the solar year. The coincidence between the orientations and the knowledge of calendar men that allowed the timing of the ceremonies may indicate the observational powers of the Blackfeet.

The sun is the largest and most observable of celestial bodies, and the solstices are crucial events in the lives of agricultural people because they mark the changing of seasons. But other celestial bodies were used as markers as well. The Pleiades were an important point of reference for astronomical observation. The Pleiades appear in the sky in the fall, and they remain in the night sky in the Northern Hemisphere until the spring, when they disappear below the horizon. The dates of their first and last appearance depend upon the lat-

This chart drawn on buckskin, from a Skidi Pawnee medicine bundle, depicts constellations and stars of varying magnitudes. Keenly aware of the sky, tribes of the Great Plains had a wealth of astronomical lore, elaborated in mythologies, for finding their way through the sea of grass that was their home. Courtesy of the Field Museum of Natural History.

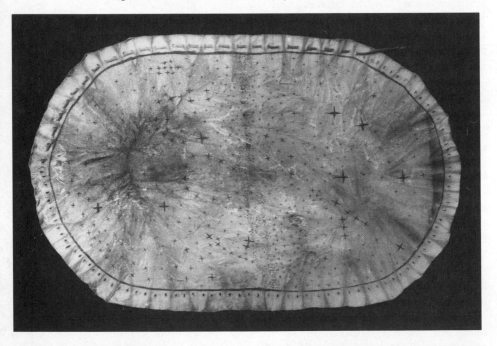

itude of the observer. However, their presence corresponds generally with the planting seasons of agriculturalists. They appear at about the time of the first killing frost, and they remain in the sky until about the time of the last frost. They are thus a distinctive marker of the seasons.

At approximately 42 degrees north latitude, the Seneca communities in present-day New York State observed the first rising of the Pleiades by the middle of October. They timed the beginning of their traditional Midwinter Ceremony by the passage of the Pleiades directly above the central longhouses of their villages. This event happened in early February, and it predicted the beginning of their planting season. The Pleiades disappeared from the night sky in about mid-May. The type of corn grown by the Senecas required approximately 120 days of frost-free weather to appear and mature. The zenith passage of the Pleiades in mid-February marked the midpoint of the frost season. The disappearance of the Pleiades from the sky about May 5–19 and their reappearance around October 10–15 encompassed a period of 153 to 163 days, a comfortable margin for the growth of corn.

The Pleiades were observed by agricultural people throughout North America, and various explanations were given for their origin. A charming story related by Sauk and Fox Indians in the heart of the continent told of six brothers, and the youngest brother's little dog, who were hunting one day. They began to chase a particularly large and strong buffalo. As they pursued the beast, they suddenly realized that they had left the earth and were running up to the sky. But it was too late to stop, and so they had to continue the chase forever. The six bright stars of the Pleiades are the six brothers, and the faint seventh star is the youngest hunter's little dog. The story is myth rather than scientific explanation. It is important because it reveals how Native Americans related to the phenomena of their world on a personal basis. It embodies, however, an understanding of the importance of the appearance of the Pleiades as a significant, predictable event in nature.

The Aztecs observed the Pleiades for a different, but equally important, reason. Their zenith passage marked the end of one of the significant cycles of the Aztecs' calendar system. When the Pleiades passed directly overhead at midnight in the final year of the 52-year cycle called the Calendar Round, a ceremony named toxiuhmolpilia, or "Binding of the Years," occurred. The event was marked by a period of sweeping and cleaning and disposing of rubbish, the putting out of old fires, a ceremonial procession to a temple in the city of Tenochtitlan, and a human sacrifice; the victim's chest was cut open and in the cavity a new fire was kindled. New fires were then lit throughout the empire, and the Aztecs were assured that their world would continue. The 52-year cycle marked by this ceremony was a conjunction of two different Aztec calendrical systems—one of which had no connection with the seasons—that were profoundly important in Aztec life.

A Zuni cornfield draped with ropes festooned with rags to ward off birds. Scarecrows made to resemble kachinas dot the field. On the far slope, two shelters will house families who move to the fields as the crops mature. Courtesy of the National Museum of the American Indian.

Although explanations of the origins of heavenly bodies varied significantly among the different peoples of the Americas, the physical reality of the phenomena of the sky existed for all of them. Recognizable cycles in the sky corresponded to cycles in the peoples' lives, and, as stated, were particularly crucial to agriculturalists. But among some societies, the passage of time itself became important, and observations of complex cycles of celestial events were recorded.

Chichen Itzá is a Mayan site in Yucatan dating to about A.D. 800. There, a curiously shaped and partially ruined tower, the Caracol, resembles closely a modern astronomical observatory. It is a circular tower rising two stories above a flat-topped base. Sir Eric Thompson, the eminent Mayanist, described it as "a 2-decker wedding cake on the square carton in which it came." It has four outer doors oriented toward the cardinal directions, and inside is a circular corridor, from which four doors open into yet another round corridor. That inner one surrounds a central core within which is a spiral staircase leading to the top of the tower. Near the top, three shafts (originally six) pierce the thick walls. These shafts serve as observing sites. They align with the vernal and autumnal equinoxes, when the sun rises in the midpoint of one or the other of two shafts. The appearance of the Pleiades in the fall and their disappearance on the date of the vernal equinox can be observed from the tower. In addition, the alignments, corresponding to the most northern and southern risings of Venus on the western horizon, allowed prediction of the heliacal rising—or the first appearance of the star in the sky just before sunrise—on the eastern horizon. The importance of these observations reflected the significance of the planet in the lives of the Mayas.

The appearance of Venus as the morning star at sunrise or the evening star at sunset is impressive. After the sun and the moon, it is the brightest object in the sky. Its movements are closely related to those of the sun, but it is elusive in that it disappears for periods of time. The Mayas called Venus noh ek (great star) and chac ek (red star), and they followed its movements through the sky closely. They knew that Venus completed its apparent orbit around the sun in 584 days, although the concept of physical bodies spinning in endless space was foreign to them. Venus was a deity, not only to be observed but prayed to and propitiated with sacrifices. They knew that Venus was present in the sky as the morning star for 236 days, invisible then for a period of 90 days, that it reappeared as the evening star for 250 days, and was invisible again for a period of 8 days. That the Mayas knew these things about Venus we know from examination of one of the few surviving records written in the Mayan pictographic language, a codex now housed in Dresden.

From a handful of such codices, scholars have tried to reconstruct the calendar system devised by the Mayas and later appropriated by the Aztecs. That system constituted a significant intellectual and scientific achievement. It also comprised a system of thought much different from that of the Europeans who arrived in the New World in 1492, who subsequently destroyed most of the codices that preserved Mayan knowledge.

The fragments of their knowledge that still exist lay out numerical systems that present-day scientists can recognize because they resemble those of twentieth-century science. They tell virtually nothing, however, about the premises from which the makers of the calendars proceeded. Similarly, a ceremony like the Binding of the Years explains something of the importance of cycles to the Aztecs, but the processes of deduction from observed events cannot be reconstructed. From the numerically recorded results of these systems, we must work backward to try to reconstruct the systems on which they were based. Whereas modern mathematics works from premise to result, we must work from result to premise.

Mayan Calendars

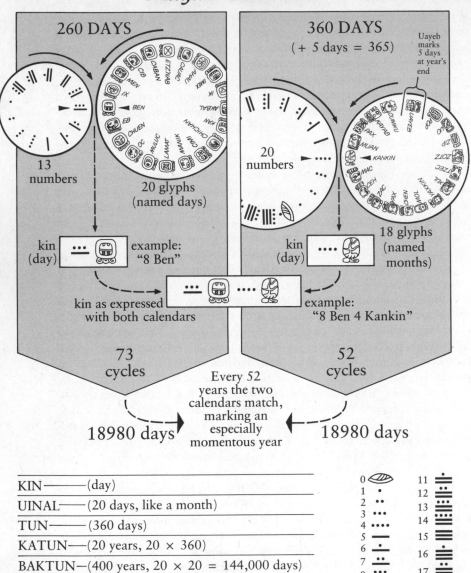

KIN ——— (day)

UINAL ——— (20 days, like a month)

TUN ——— (360 days)

KATUN ——— (20 years, 20 × 360)

BAKTUN — (400 years, 20 × 20 = 144,000 days)

"GREAT CYCLE"
5200 years—100 52-year cycles. We are still
in the first Great Cycle of the Mayan calendar,
which began on 13 August 3114 B.C. (Gregorian).

0
1
2
3
4
5
6
7
8
9
10

11
12
13
14
15
16
17
18
19

20

The Mayan calendar system counted time by two systems. One was a sacred calendar of 260 days (the tzolkin) formed by the interlocking of a series of 20 named days (as we name the days of the week) and a series of 13 numbers (as we count 29, 30, or 31 days in a month). Since the 20 named days had to go around 13 times to get back to the beginning of their cycle, there were 260 days in this sacred year.

The origin of the 260-day year, unique among calendar systems, is obscure. One theory is that it is based on the major interval between two zenith passages of the sun—260 days. Observation of this 260-day interval can be made near the Mayan city of Copán in present-day Honduras, which is at approximately 15 degrees north latitude. Here the sun passes directly overhead at intervals of 260 and 105 days. It is important to keep in mind that the 365-day year is an arbitrary convention, since the earth actually completes its path around the sun in somewhat over $365^1/4$ days. The insertion of a leap day every four years is necessary to keep the calendar aligned with actual seasons, and even so, periodic adjustments of several days have been made throughout history. The Mayan calendar had no such arbitrary adjustment, and over time, the calendar months drifted through the seasons. That is, by a modern calendar system, the month of May would at some point occur in midwinter. For the Mayas near Copán, the passage of the sun overhead at intervals of 260 and 105 days was an absolutely predictable event. They were also aware, however, of the number of days that their calendar was ahead of or behind the seasons, and they knew that it took 1,508 of their calendar years for it to realign with the seasons.

The two zenith passings divide the solar year into periods of 260 and approximately 105 days, and the latter period was the typical planting season. For this reason, the tzolkin may indeed have had some correlation to the environment, although its purpose in the lives of the Mayas was, and remains,

---

The Mayas tracked the passage of time with two major calendars that operated simultaneously. In their everyday activities, they followed the 260-day calendar on the left. Each day sign was the conjunction of a number, from 1 to 13, with a day glyph, one of 20 such. (In this example, "8 ben" is followed by "9 ix.") In the lower left are indicated the names for groups of days (kin, uinal, tun, etc.). On the right is a 360-day calendar, used apparently for ceremonial or political purposes, in which the day signs were each composed of one of 18 numbers and one of 20 glyphs. Here, too, both parts of the day sign changed every day. For this second calendar, a 5-day interlude called an uayeb occurs at the end of each 360-day cycle.

Each day sign functioned like a horoscope for the Mayas. In addition, points at which the two calendars converged were regarded as cosmic junctures which required ritual renewal. The most important of these occurred at the end of 52 years, when the two calendars coincided. There was also the "great cycle," made up of 100 52-year cycles. The Mayas' first Great Cycle is still in progress.

A pottery jar in the shape of a squash, probably Mochican. One of the earliest New World domesticated plants, squash came in many varieties and had many functions, from food to containers and ornaments. Courtesy of the Field Museum of Natural History.

more important for prediction of events in a person's life—that is, for its astrological significance. Other theories relate the 260-day year to the cycle of the planet Venus, to the 260-day gestation period of the human female, and to the base 20 numerical system of the Mayas. Whatever its origin, it was profoundly important to the Mayan calendar system.

The Mayas also had a year that corresponded roughly to a solar year—the 365¼ days that it takes the earth to return to its same position relative to the sun in its revolution. That year was marked by 18 named months, each consisting of 20 numbered days. At the end of the cycle, a period of five days was added. These days had religious significance since they were an addition to the regular cycle, and they marked a period of uncertainty before the next cycle of months and days began. But, again, it must be remembered that the Mayas did not attempt to keep this calendar in line with the seasons by inserting a leap day every four years. Indeed, the calendar gained time on the seasons without any correction. Generally translated as the Vague Year, its purpose was not to keep time for seasonal planting activities. Rather, this Mayan calendar followed progressions of days through cycles. The Vague Year's purpose was more likely to mark certain ceremonial or political events. Since it was not concerned with strict correlation with the seasons, it indicated concerns beyond those of pure subsistence.

Another major cycle was made up of the respective revolutions of the sacred and calendar years. Like two interlocking gears, the 260-day tzolkin and the 365-day solar year began at a certain point and revolved against each other until that same point was reached again. It took 18,980 days (or 52 years) to complete this cycle, which was known as the Calendar Round. The Round gave a unique identity to each day in the cycle, and it made it possible to record unique historical events.

Finally, the Mayas had a day count, by which they reckoned the absolute number of days in their history. As Europeans reckoned their era from the birth of Christ, so the Mayas reckoned theirs from an event far back in time. The uncertainties of interpretation of the Mayan hieroglyphic system have made it difficult to know precisely what that first event was or to correlate it with certainty with the Europeans' calendar. However, using best estimates from interpolations of the Mayan calendar, their day count went back to approximately the fourth millennium B.C. A specific date that has been proposed for the beginning of the Long Count is August 11, 3114 B.C. It is far earlier than the accepted beginning date of precursors of the Mayas among whom the intellectual tradition of the calendar system started. But the number of days in the Long Count is certain from pure mathematical manipulation. What we may well have is a native record of what can be described as mythic time—that is, a count back to a point before anything literally within human memory or written record.

One of the most intriguing aspects of the Mayan astronomical system was the importance of Venus. Its synodic period of 584 days was observable from the earth as two cycles. The orbit of Venus is closer to the sun than that of the earth, and so when the three bodies begin from a common point, Venus is visible from the earth for a period of time, then disappears behind the sun as it seems to speed ahead of the earth, and reappears for a time before it, the earth, and the sun reach the same point in the sky once again. The Venus table in the Mayas' Dresden Codex recorded time periods that corresponded to the number of days that Venus was visible from the earth as the very bright morning star. Although the numerical values in the table were consistent in recording the 584-day cycle of Venus, they did not correspond closely with the actual intervals of the planet's disappearance in the sky. Several conventions were designed to bring the numbers and the actual dates of sightings into alignment. But it is clear that the Venus table corresponded with some reality other than purely physical observations. It appears likely, too, that the Venus table served as a marker for ceremonial or political events.

The Mayas also observed the cycles of the moon. These cycles comprised one of the most obvious celestial phenomena, but it was also obvious that they did not correlate with the cycle of the sun that constituted a solar and seasonal year. The Hopi sun watcher recognized that fact. Various calendar systems use moon cycles to record important events. The Christian celebration of Easter, for instance, is timed to the first Sunday after the first full moon that follows the vernal equinox. The Mayas not only observed the cycles of the moon but recorded one of their most dramatic features, the periodic eclipses.

Observations of the moon in modern scientific terms are complicated because it has phases and it appears in different parts of the sky in its different phases. Eclipses are likely to occur at certain points in the conjunction of the moon's orbit around the earth and the earth's orbit around the sun. The plane of the moon's orbit around the earth is inclined about 5 degrees from the plane of the orbit of the earth around the sun. If one could envision a juggler spinning rings around a central point, with the sun and moon as points on the rings, these intersecting orbital planes become clear. The conjunction of these planes at certain points, called nodes, produces the condition where the shadow of the earth blocks the sun's rays that illuminate the moon, creating a lunar eclipse.

The Dresden Codex contains a table in which two numbers, 6,585 and 177, predominate, and an occasional 148 appears. The first number corresponds to the number of days in the saros cycle—similar patterns of eclipses that repeat, beginning every 6,585 days. A period of 177 days is equivalent to six cycles of the moon, at the end of which it is possible for the orbits of the earth and moon to cross each other in a way that causes an eclipse. A person observing the night sky on a regular basis would see a full or partial eclipse of the moon after some sequence of periods of 177 days, or within a period of days that could be broken down into sequences of 177 and 148 days.

Although their own reasons for observing celestial phenomena were religious and political, rather than scientific, the Mayas demonstrated their keen interest in and sophisticated observation of those phenomena. In that they moved beyond a concern with the purely physical phenomena of seasons, they became scientists in the European sense. Their interests and knowledge became more abstract but never divorced from religious beliefs. Their records, particularly the Long Count, show their concern with lengthy periods of time. And it is only over very long periods that observation of the skies allows men (and we will have to assume, given what we know of Mayan culture, that the observers were men) to record the extended cycles of the sun, moon, and planets. How many repetitions of a pattern did it take to lead to the conclusion that, indeed, a pattern existed? In tables of numbers that correspond to average intervals of celestial conjunctions, the Mayan codices indicate that their writers were well aware of patterns in the conjunction of celestial events. They recorded them, and they regulated their lives by certain of them. And if their reasons were not scientific, the records they left are.

The astronomical records of the Mayas were kept in numerical form. Our knowledge of their mathematical system derives from their calendar system. The written records of the Mayas, hieroglyphic inscriptions on stone stelae or in codices, show the use of mathematics only in calendar systems. There are no records of other forms of mathematical records. The mathematics of the system were lodged in a base-20 system of counting. Numbers proceeded as units up to 20, and by powers of twenty thereafter, as we count by 10s, 100s, 1,000s, etc. Except that because the numbers explain the calendar system, the third number stood for 18 units rather than 20—the number of months in the calendar year, rather than the number of days in the month.

Rather than using digits from 1 through 9, the Mayas employed dots and bars to indicate numbers. One dot stood for 1 and five dots made a bar. For numbers from 2 through 19, dots or dots and bars were combined. Numbers above 19 were indicated by the placement of sets of dots and bars, higher-order numbers being indicated by groups of dots and bars written one above the other. Numerals written in this system were used for counting and addition.

Some scholars have asserted that the Mayas understood the concept of the zero—that there was a position in a sequence of numbers that was empty. The expression 101, for example, means that there is no multiple of 10 to count. Although it is true that the Mayas used a symbol to show that one sequence of 20 was complete and another was beginning, scholars do not agree that it constituted a true mathematical zero. The zero is mathematically important in the manipulation of numbers such as in multiplication and division. The Mayas were concerned primarily with counting in long sequences, although they certainly understood the multiplicative power of 20. There is no evidence that they used their numbers for mathematical manipulation such as multiplication or division of different numbers, or that they used them in record keeping other than calendric.

Much of the Mayan calendar system and its mathematics, derived largely from the Olmecs and other earlier Mesoamerican peoples, became, in turn, part of the intellectual legacy of the Aztec peoples of 1492. The Aztecs may have put their inherited numerical system to uses other than calendar counts. Evidence from Aztec codices indicates the recording of amounts of tribute received from subject nations and the notation of areas of land. Again, the evidence is only for counting, although it is possible to infer algorithms for computing land areas.

To Native Americans in 1492, abstract numbers were not as important as the passage of time, the gathering of tribute, or the recording of land. In the Inca empire, mathematical knowledge was recorded in quipus, a system of information storage relying on a number of strings tied in patterns (see page 236). Generally, a series of strings hung from a main cord, and some of them might, in turn, have dependent strings. The strings were often of different colors, which recurred in sequences. On each was a series of knots, again tied in distinct groups. If one views the quipu as an elaborate coding device, perhaps analogous to a Chinese abacus, it is obvious that the variables of color sequences, number of knots, number of dependent strings, and patterns of knots could convey an immense amount of information. But, even if one assumes the quipu to be a highly sophisticated code, the problem is that no one has

CŌTADOR·MAÍOR·ÍTE3ORERO
TAVANTIN·SVIO·QVÍPOC
CVRACA·COИ ☙ DOR·CHAVA

con tator ytgoure   con tator

The chief auditor and treasurer of the Incas holding a quipu. This drawing is by Felipe Guaman Poma de Ayala, the native Peruvian chronicler of Incan life. Quipus, which consisted of a train of knotted strings of varying colors, were used for accounting and calculation and were essential to the administration of this Andean empire.

yet broken it. There is no Rosetta Stone to provide a translation of the meaning of quipus into a language recognizable to European-based science.

The quipu as a series of knotted strings may have had a larger analogy in Inca culture in a system of geographic locations encoding observations of celestial phenomena. Early Spanish chroniclers of the Inca empire, writing primarily to record its overthrow, reported the existence of a unique calendar system. Around the city of Cuzco, there were 328 huacas, or shrines, which were aligned in 41 directions along ceques, or lines radiating out from the Temple of the Sun and reaching to the horizon. Although the numbers varied somewhat, there were approximately eight shrines along each ceque. This system might have functioned like a giant quipu laid over the city. One could imagine the ceques as strings radiating from a central knot, and the huacas as knots on each string. This imaginary quipu divided time into units, because the sun traverses the arc of distance on the horizon between any two lines in a set time. The system may have worked as a calendar, and also probably organized the space around the city into political units from which certain groups of individuals came to a central plaza to blow horns and announce the arrival of a "month" when they had special responsibilities.

The system of ceques and huacas, with its values of 41 and 328, obviously did not correspond to the 365¹/₄-day solar year of modern astronomy. The numbers did correspond, however, to certain aspects of the lunar year, raising the important point that for many cultures the moon was as important a marker of time as the sun because of its waxing and waning. The aspect and movements of the sun in Cuzco, a tropical city, varied less dramatically from day to day than they did in more extreme latitudes. The sun passed high overhead during the greater part of the year. The moon was the more variable of celestial bodies and, thus, the lunar cycle may have been much more important for marking units of time.

Evidence for the importance of certain numbers in the Inca system of ceques and huacas has been inferred from two pieces of fabric, one woven in a very complex design of circles and squares, and the other in rectangles. The intricacy and symmetry of the pattern in the weaving has attracted the attention of contemporary scholars familiar with the mathematical and astronomical systems described in historic accounts of the Inca empire.

The first piece of fabric is actually two pieces separately woven and sewn together. Each piece has ten rows of 36 circles, and the diagonal rows of circles across the pieces are of different colors. The diagonal arrangement of elements in the fabric divides the circles into groups that add up to 365, the approximate number of days in the solar year. The second fabric has rectangles in patterns that can be added together to make the number 28, which is close to the average number of days (29.5) in a lunar month. The calendar system that one can infer from the ceques and the huacas appears to have been based on sidereal lunar months—the period of time at the beginning and end of which the moon appeared in the same position with respect to the stars. The phase of the moon might be different, but its position was the same, relative to the stars. The system seems also to have contained references to synodic periods— when the moon returned to its same position relative to the sun after it had completed a phase.

At the same time, the ceques as imaginary lines stretched to a very real horizon. The observation of the passage of the sun along that horizon may have marked certain crucial events such as solstices. The reconstruction of this system of astronomical observation can never be certain because many of the huacas have been destroyed over time, but the possibilities for its interpretation are intriguing.

Native American systems of knowledge are often encompassed in sources that do not conform to Western ideas of written language. Hence, they have seemed undecipherable to Europeans. Astronomical knowledge, for instance, may be read from the physical remains of buildings such as Chichén Itzá's Caracol tower. The technology of building thus becomes an expression of Indian knowledge preserved in stone.

At Uxmal, another Mayan center in Yucatan, there are buildings whose walls do not form right angles and whose doorways make odd patterns in walls. The art of construction is impressive, with corbeled arches, sculptured friezes, and carefully fitted stonework. The building identified as the Nunnery at Uxmal is quadrangular in shape, but all its sides differ in length and meet at different angles. If some scholars preoccupied with the perfection of Euclidian geometry have ascribed the strange angles of the building to sloppy workmanship, others with a different perspective have attributed them to alignments with the rising and setting of celestial bodies. The Mayas who built the complex at Uxmal were capable of laying out parallel walls with an accuracy comparable to that of modern buildings. But in the Nunnery, doors and walls align not to right angles but to sight lines that appear to indicate risings and settings of the planet Venus.

Uxmal is evidence of the ability of Mayan builders to lay out structures along their own survey lines and accommodate different angles in their construction techniques. The buildings indicate a highly developed Indian architectural technology as well. Corbeled vaults cover buildings. These served the same purpose as the curved arch with keystone, a characteristic European building technique. The monumental structures at Uxmal, as at many other sites in Mesoamerica, include elaborate detail in carved façades, pillars, and fascias.

In North America above the Rio Grande, building technology was not as sophisticated, but it certainly allowed for the development of large-scale complexes, including the Mississippian temple-mound centers and the Pueblo towns, both in what is now the United States. The most impressive dwellings in North America north of the Rio Grande were those at Chaco Canyon, in New Mexico. Pueblo Bonito was an apartment complex of some 800 rooms, parts of which rose to a height of four and five stories. The building technique was straightforward. Slabs of rock were laid in courses to form walls, which were often braced with logs, either set within the walls or as supporting rafters between them. The corner windows of some rooms may have served to indicate the rising of the solstice sun. If the building's construction was not particularly innovative, it served its numerous inhabitants well while they lived there, and it far outlasted their occupancy.

High on a ridge of a great mountain chain in Peru was another city, Machu Picchu, built by a civilization that probably predated and was ancestral to the Inca empire. Perched at an elevation of some 10,000 feet between two peaks in the Andes about fifty miles from Cuzco, it was a remarkable feat of Indian design and engineering. The city was a walled citadel, surrounded by terraced plots of cultivated land and watered by mountain springs that were channeled through a stone conduit supported in part by an aqueduct that passed above a moat and dipped under a wall into a series of fountains and basins through-

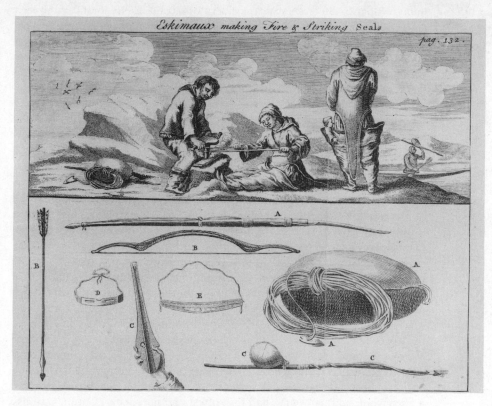

A depiction of Eskimo technology published in 1748 shows two men making fire by using a leather thong to rotate a rod being held in place by a wooden plate. Next to them, a woman carries a baby in her hip boot, and beyond, a kayaker harpoons a seal. Eskimo tools and ornaments are displayed below: a whale harpoon (A), a bow and arrow (B), a seal harpoon and thrower (C), snow goggles (D), and a bone pendant (E).

out the city. The mountains were granite, and in a sense Machu Picchu was carved out of living stone, since its buildings were constructed of granite blocks. The tools of its builders were stone hammers and bronze crowbars. Most of the houses were built of roughly finished stone laid in courses with clay mortar. But its finest structures were of carefully smoothed granite blocks, some weighing several tons, and walls faced with ashlars (smooth granite slabs). Retaining walls stabilized almost vertical mountainsides. One structure that may have been a temple was built upon a foundation of natural rock that sloped upward at an angle of about 40 degrees. The rock walls that rose from the base were constructed without mortar. The great achievement of the in-

Systems of Knowledge   **391**

habitants of Machu Picchu was their development of a system of carving their granite building blocks and slabs with interlocking ridges and projections that fitted them together. They often followed the terrain and laid walls in irregular but carefully joined sections rather than in regular courses. Such walls, almost like jigsaw puzzles, became single units. In a mountainous area where earthquakes were fairly frequent, although not as severe as they were at lower elevations, the walls were very stable.

The mountain fortress of Machu Picchu is evidence of a highly organized society, where time and materials were available in abundance. That society was a precursor to the great Inca empire that ruled the central Andes in 1492, an empire that tied together its parts with an elaborate system of paved roads and religious shrines stretching out in linear patterns to its horizons.

Quipus, huacas, and ceques give glimpses of a highly sophisticated system of preserving information. Woven strings and woven textiles can also serve as a system of writing. The sophistication of textiles in Mesoamerica may represent as complex a system of knowledge as metallurgy in Europe. Knotted string encoded information. Cloth was required as tribute, a sign of its value in an exchange system. Cotton armor and cotton slings were instruments of war. The technology of cloth was as important to the Incas as the technology of metals was to Europeans.

The art of weaving cloth reached a high point in the Incan empire prior to the European conquest. The Incas had domesticated llamas and alpacas both as beasts of burden and as sources of wool. They hunted the vicuña for its coat. The domesticated llama served as a source of coarse wool to be woven into utilitarian garments and bags as containers for storage. The alpaca provided a finer wool, and the vicuña had the softest and finest coat. Cotton was also raised or traded with neighboring groups. To the Incas, fabric was probably more important than ceramics for storing things. It became readily associated with the status of rulers, who wore the finest garments. Given the number of yards of finely woven thread necessary for the finest garments (the average diameter was $1/125$ of an inch), one can appreciate the amount of time devoted by workers in Inca society to preparing the materials and spinning the thread. Some 125 separate shades and tints have been identified in Incan textiles, evidence of the sophistication of dyeing techniques and knowledge of the mordants used to set the dyes. All of the major weaving techniques known in Europe in 1492 were known to the Incas—tapestry, brocade, gauze, and double cloth. Peruvian weavers also had a distinctive technique, interlocking warp.

The use of spindles, looms, wool fibers, and dyes appeared by about 500 B.C. in cultures on the coast of South America that were antecedent to the Incas'. The technology of cloth had undergone a long period of development by 1492.

One of the hallmarks of technological development in Europe was the use

Indians panning for gold as depicted by Gonzalo Fernández de Oviedo y Valdés in 1547. This aboriginal practice obviously attracted wide attention and inflamed European greed. The man on the right hoes up gravel, while the figure in the middle carries a basin of gravel to the stream. On the left, a man pans for the heavier particles of gold, which settle in the bottom of his basin.

of metals. The course of Western civilization had changed because northern Hittite invaders used iron weapons to overcome the bronze-armed Mesopotamians. Although the historical formulation is too simple, it dramatizes the importance of metalworking in human history. Knowledge of metalworking existed in the New World, but the ends to which it was put differed greatly from those in Europe (which, in 1492, included significant weaponry). In North America, raw copper ore was beaten into ornaments by native people around the Great Lakes, where the ore could be found on the ground. But this use was very primitive compared with the technologies of metalworking in South America.

If the Incas were sophisticated weavers, they were also superb goldsmiths, as were their predecessors, the Mochicas, and various other peoples who dwelled farther north in such places as present-day Colombia and Panama. The main technique for creating artifacts with golden surfaces involved smelting an alloy of gold, silver, and copper called tumbaga. The ingot was then beaten and annealed. The process produced copper oxide, which was removed with an acid solution. By progressively removing the copper, the process brought the gold to the surface of the increasingly thinned sheet metal. The silver was then removed with a paste of iron sulfate and salt. The gold remained in a granular state at the surface of the metal sheet, and it was heated and burnished to produce the shiny golden surface characteristic of Andean metalwork.

The technique described destroyed much of the copper and silver substrate in the original alloy. Obviously, such a technique was not thrifty with mate-

In this eighteenth-century illustration, Antonio de Herrara depicts Central American hunters armed with lances driving wild javelinas (a variety of wild boar) into a net.

rials, and it was not as efficient as simply plating with gold foil. But the end was not beauty for beauty's sake, but the investment of the object with a meaning beyond simple form. The objects were representative of the religious and social power of those who held them.

If gold is an emblem of material wealth in the world of today, it was a metaphor for spiritual and political power in pre-Columbian South American societies. Quechua religious texts of the sixteenth and seventeenth centuries in the Andes make important use of the term "camay," the act of infusing life spirit into an inanimate object. It was not the act of fabricating an object that was important, but the act of somehow infusing the object through its whole form with gold as an essential quality. Gold was not important for the shape of the object, but for its substance and meaning. Metallurgy to the craftsmen of the Andes was not simply technology, the ability to use energy to melt and re-form metals. It was the power to transform the very essence of material and imbue it with religious significance, giving it an inner form that was more important than the outer one.

This concern with the inner forces that gave meaning and life to outer forms was the essence of Native American science. The development of agriculture in both Europe and the New World in 1492 was scientific, because it was based on the power to predict events—the growth of crops—and technological, because it allowed people to control forms of energy.

The main sources of energy available to native people in the New World in 1492 were the sun and their own physical effort. If the sun was the main motive power for human activity, then part of that activity was using human energy to produce the greatest return from the environment in the form of food. There were many techniques which Indians employed to achieve this control. One of the most prevalent was the use of fire to promote new growth and provide increased browsing areas for wild animals that were a source of food. In California, for example, Indians systematically burned off areas of chaparral (the low-growing piñon/juniper/scrub oak shrubbery) that was the characteristic cover of the Sierra foothills. Through these deliberately set fires, and also through natural fires caused by lightning, the brushy undergrowth was kept thin so that the fires were not very intense. They served to burn back the older growth without killing the shrubs themselves, and this hastened the production of fresh and tender new growth that was especially attractive to deer. Contemporary animal biologists have shown that deer feeding in fired areas produce more and healthier offspring than those in other areas.

On the North American plains, fire drives were used for buffalo hunting, and they also caused the growth of new grass in the burned-over areas. This periodic burning not only replenished the browse for the buffalo but held back the perimeters of forests and maintained the extent of grasslands.

On the Atlantic coast of the present-day United States, early European travelers and explorers described the parklike aspect of the forests. Stands of trees shaded grassy areas that the Indians maintained by periodic burning. The brushy understory, characteristic of the New England forests today, was burned off frequently enough to prevent its providing accumulated tinder for very hot fires. Consequently, burns took place without damaging the large trees, and new grasses grew back to provide forage for the deer that were hunted there. The parklike environment made it easy for hunters to move through the forests and use their bows without hindrance.

Control of animal feeding areas by fire was important for hunters, since game animals were essential to their diets. The domestication of plants and animals, however, was another matter. Domestication means bringing some living thing under the control of human beings. In the Native American understanding of the world, all living things had their own lives and wills, and they acted independently of men. This understanding probably accounted for the relative lack of domesticated animals in the New World. The Andean peoples of South America domesticated the llama and the guinea pig, but these were not primary food sources. In North America, the dog was domesticated and used as a burden bearer, and occasionally dogs were eaten as part of ceremonial meals, but, again, dogs were not a primary food source.

The domestication of plants and animals implies certain scientific principles. In all cultures where domestication has taken place, it has been based on observation of the actions of plants and animals, human ability to predict those actions, and human intervention to control them. In Europe, the domestication of plants and animals meant that they were deprived of spirits and means of independent action. In the New World, domestication of animals was minimal, and domestication of plants was achieved through an interaction of humans with the spirits of the plants.

The term "camay" for the inner essence of Incan goldwork has a parallel in the Navajo concept of inner forms. Every outer form or active physical phenomenon had its inner form that motivated it. All living and moving things, thus, had a spiritual sanction. In the European sense of science, agriculture is the most concentrated use of human energy to control the environment to produce food. It falls within our contemporary definition of science because it entails systematic observation of plants, prediction of their future action, and deliberate intervention in the processes of nature to select and promote certain things. It depends upon an understanding of the outcome of events—such as that seeds will reproduce their own kind. People observed that new plants grew more readily where they had dug or pulled roots and disturbed the soil. They knew that the clearing of areas by gathering or by controlled burning promoted new growth. They brought water to wild plants or dug them up and replanted them someplace else. When they gathered plants, they selected them for specific characteristics. By selecting certain plants and controlling their environments with fire and water, they altered them and made them dependent upon human action for reproduction. That Native Americans domesticated such plants as sunflowers and chenopodium is shown by the differences in the size of the seeds of the wild species and domesticated species.

In 1492, Indians in many parts of the Americas had domesticated and were cultivating an immense number of plants. The list of their crops unknown to Europeans at the time contained numerous products that have since become familiar throughout the world: maize or Indian corn, white and sweet potatoes, manioc, squashes, beans (kidney, navy, and lima), cacao, pumpkins, peanuts, avocados, tomatoes, pineapples, tobacco, and chili peppers. In the Andes, some 3,000 different types of domesticated potatoes were being grown. Other New World crops included chenopodium, quinoa, amaranth, jicama, pacay, yacón, cranberries, and guayaba, lucuma, pepino, cherimoya, pitaya,

Girolamo Benzoni illustrates the making and use of bread in the West Indies. At the left, a woman grinds cornmeal on a metate; in the center, another woman shapes and cooks tortillas; and at the right, a woman serves them with a bowl of stew.

canistel, sapote, and papaya fruits. Both fossilized seeds and some that are still viable have been found in archaeological sites. Ceramic reproductions of many cultivated foods, from manioc and maize to beans and peppers, have been discovered in pre-Columbian tombs along the Peruvian coast.

Plants domesticated in the northeastern part of North America included sunflowers, sumpweed, goosefoot, maygrass, and giant ragweed. All were grown as foods, though today they are considered weeds because of their intrusive nature in cultivated fields and their ability to withstand a wide range of environmental conditions. Another North American domesticate is the Jerusalem "artichoke." Squashes, tepary beans, gourds, and devil's-claw were domesticated in the Southwest of the present-day United States. The gourds were used as containers, and the fibers of the devil's-claw were employed in making baskets.

Maize, or Indian corn, had become the major food source for numerous peoples throughout the Americas long before 1492. Maize was descended from teosinte, a wild grass that at least 7,000 years ago began to be modified in

A corn popper from the Mochica culture of the northern coast of Peru. The Mochicas emerged during the first millennium and were later supplanted by the Chimu people around A.D. 600. Courtesy of the Field Museum of Natural History.

Mesoamerica by human selection. The primary source of food energy in plants is the seed. Wild plants reproduce by being able to scatter their seeds freely. However, humans collecting seeds want them to stay in one place, and thus a feature in the domestication of plants for food involves selection for seeds that stay attached to the plant for easy harvesting. But because humans must then remove the seeds from the plants, the plants become dependent on humans to disperse the seeds so they can reproduce. This is what happened with the teosinte, whose seed cases modified into rigid containers characteristic of the kernels of maize. Although the process of human selection was not systematic in the beginning, it became deliberate, and it served to alter the structure of the corn plant.

Corn became dependent on human intervention, and humans became dependent on corn. The domestication of corn was a form of scientific activity. It was the result of systematic observation of plants and the deliberate selection of some of them over others. Humans became responsible for deciding which varieties would reproduce. The Hopis produced a corn plant whose seed was adapted to the arid growing conditions of their mesas. The taproot was very long, enabling it to reach down to the deep, underlying subsurface moisture. The seedling itself adapted to grow a long way also, to break the soil before putting out its first leaves. The colors of Hopi corn—red, white, blue, and yellow—were the result of selection and the careful preservation of seeds.

The relationship between humans and corn was a symbiotic one, a fact that became evident in the religious significance of corn in ceremonial activities in the American Southwest. Pueblo peoples used corn mothers (perfect ears of corn) in ceremonies, and gave perfect ears, representing corn mothers, to children at birth. The life cycle of the corn mirrored the human life cycle. The continuation of life for the Hopis depended as much on their appropriate relationship with the spirits of corn as on their ability to domesticate and select varieties that would survive in their harsh environment. Just as planting with a digging stick allowed each seed to be placed deep into the soil in order for the long taproot to reach moisture, so the Hopi snake dance was essential to the growing of the crops because the snakes handled by the dancers were released to carry the respect and wishes of the people to the spirits deep in the earth.

Although the Hopi agriculturalists dealt with the need for moisture by modifying the corn, many other Pueblo people devised irrigation techniques to control water. In the Chaco Canyon region, where several communities began to flourish about A.D. 920, dramatic expansion of the culture was made possible by sophisticated water control systems. The Chaco River, actually a seasonally flowing stream, had formed the canyon, and people had probably lived there for hundreds of years, but the region now became a major center of population. Prior to 900, the Chaco River had flooded seasonally, and crops had been planted on the floodplain. Water had also collected in natural basins along the rim of the canyon, and in heavy rains had run over the rim and down the sides of the canyon. By about 900, however, the river had cut its way so deeply into the canyon bottom and become so entrenched that it would not flood. If the inhabitants of the canyon were to grow crops, they had to devise irrigation techniques. These included earthen dams to contain the stream's waters, diversion walls and canals to bring the water to the fields, and sluice gates to control the flow. Additional diversion walls were built along the slopes of the main and side canyons to channel the runoff water into canals. Bordered and gravel-mulched gardens preserved the soil moisture.

Today, the remains of nine major Pueblo towns are located along a nine-mile stretch of lower Chaco Wash. In the surrounding area were four other pueblos, ranging from 30 to 100 rooms each, and at least fifty small villages of 10 to 20 rooms. At its peak, the population may have been close to 10,000 people. During the great building phase in Chaco Canyon, from about A.D. 1020 to 1120, perhaps 100,000 pine trees were cut down for construction uses and firewood. After 1120, however, virtually no new building took place, and by about 1220, the population of the canyon had drifted away, and the towns and villages were virtually abandoned. The most likely explanation for the exodus was a great drought in the San Juan River basin that lasted from 1130 to

Girolamo Benzoni's depiction of the way the Caribbean Indians navigated their dugout canoes. While four paddlers position themselves along the sides, the man at the stern uses his paddle as a rudder to keep the vessel on course.

1190. Although the water control systems in Chaco Canyon were sophisticated, they could not deal with a severe and extended dry period. Technology had its limits, and the response of the population to its failure was to seek other locations.

In parts of Mesoamerica, the problem for agriculturalists was not too little water, but too much. Water control techniques in low-lying, swampy areas included the use of raised platforms of soil and various methods of drainage. Land was also artificially terraced to create raised growing areas.

Around Lake Texcoco and in the lake itself, Aztec farmers created chinampas, artificial islands. Rafts were built out of timbers or intertwined reeds, and the rich bottom mud of the lake and nearby swamps was brought up and piled on top of the rafts. The pressure of neighboring hostile people on the mainland prevented the Aztecs from utilizing extensive farmlands, and the chinampas were an ingenious solution to the problem. They were also remarkably productive because of the richness of the soil and the ease with which it could be replenished.

The Indians in the New World were able to control their environments through the technology of fire, agriculture, and irrigation. But they also had a sophisticated understanding of the wild plants that grew around them. They depended on plants not only for food, shelter, and material for baskets and clothing but also for curing sickness. Since plants were considered living beings that shared with humans the ability to grow and change and reproduce, to live and die, they could affect human beings, and through use and systematic observation, native people were well aware of the effects of plants on the human body.

Animal behavior probably provided them with clues to the effects of plants. Scientists in Africa observed chimpanzees swallowing the leaves of *Aspilia* plants whole. They presumed that this constituted a medicinal use, since the chimpanzees chewed other plants that they used for food. Analysis of those particular leaves showed that they contained a chemical, "thiarubrine A," which is an antibiotic. Similar active components have been found in South American species of *Aspilia,* leading to the possibility that New World monkeys might have been observed making similar use of their leaves.

Born in Milan, Girolamo Benzoni traveled through Spain's American colonies in the sixteenth century and published a report in 1565 which was sharply critical of the Crown's treatment of both Indians and African slaves. Here, Benzoni presents a sympathetic portrait of a native healer tending to a patient who is lying in a hammock.

Based on a painting by Jacques Lemoyne de Morgues, this engraving by the Flemish publisher Théodore de Bry, which appeared in 1591, depicts various Timucuan healing practices. The man resting on his back is having blood drawn from his forehead, while the man on his stomach is inhaling the fumes of burning seeds. The man in the center rear is using tobacco smoke to cure an infection.

The greatest similarity between modern practices and those of the native people of the New World in 1492 is in the field of medicine. Despite sophisticated technology and understanding of the processes of the human body, physicians in contemporary society still work partly in the sphere of science and partly in that of belief. Powerful drugs have potent effects on the human body. Native American healers knew from observation that plants caused significant changes in the body. And, indeed, much of the medical practice of fifteenth-century Europe was based on the use of medicinal simples, or plant medicines.

Plant medicines from the New World have proved effective by modern medical standards. A hormone extracted from stoneseed, a plant used by Paiute Indian women as a contraceptive, suppresses gonadotropins in the ovaries of laboratory mice and thus interferes with the ovulation cycle. The tlepatli prescribed in Aztec medicine as a diuretic and as a treatment for gangrene contains plumbagin, which is an antibacterial agent, particularly useful against staphylococcus.

The point, however, is not to judge herbal medicines by the standards of modern medicine, or the efficacy of chemical properties, but to recognize that native people experienced and assessed the powers of plants in consistent ways. Certain plants always produced certain results. To the Indian, the cause was not chemical, but the inherent spiritual power of the plant as a living being.

Medicine is a combination of science and belief. Science is also a matter of belief. In 1492, European scientists believed that objects sought their natural place, and that the philosopher's stone would transmute base elements into gold, and that plants had the power to cure illness. Native American scientists believed that plants could cure, and that golden objects could be imbued with power, and that all things had their proper places in the great scheme of the world.

The essence of science is an understanding of the world, but the premises of modern science have changed significantly from 1492 to the present. From natural place to black holes, from humors to superstrings, the enterprise of science has sought an always elusive truth. To Native Americans in 1492, the world was alive with forces that could be understood in certain ways. They observed the world around them, and they knew its patterns and its effects on their own lives. Systematic observation of the environment and prediction of the effects of forces in the environment allowed native people in the New World to adapt to a wide range of conditions and evolve their relationships with the natural world.

On the eve of Columbus's landing in the New World in 1492, the native people of the Americas maintained a delicate balance with the resources of their world. That balance between control and faith was soon to be disrupted. Confronted by invaders from the Old World, it would be overcome by the onslaught of European diseases, plants, and animals introduced into the New World environment and by beliefs that dismissed as pagan superstition the systems of knowledge that constituted the science of the Indians.

CHRISTIAN F. FEEST

IT MAY HAVE BEEN in the year 13-Flint, the sixth year of King Ahuit-zotl's reign, that the stoneworkers of the palace took their tools to Chapulte-pec. Their lord had requested that his image be carved into the rock of Grasshopper Hill next to the portraits of his predecessors, his father, Mocte-zuma I, and his brother, Axayacatl. It would help later generations to remem-ber those who had made the Mexicas the masters of all the riches of the universe, and to be inspired by their deeds as conquerors, as builders of the temples, and as wise rulers.

Ahuitzotl presented himself at the rock, attired in his regalia and badges of office, so the artists could observe all the details as they sketched his frontal, full-length portrait on the smoothed surface. It would be a perfect likeness, surpassing in every respect those of his antecedents. The stoneworkers, the best in the country, those who otherwise were employed in making the images of the gods in the temples of Tenochtitlán, had progressed marvelously in their craft in recent years. They would be rewarded richly for their labor with food, clothing, salt, cocoa, and slaves from the hot country.

About the same time, a hunter sat in front of his lean-to shelter in the wind-swept and barren plains of Tierra del Fuego, peeling off the bark from care-fully selected branches that had been drying in his hut for some days. While he turned the sticks slowly in his hand, he made them swell toward the center by scraping the wood with a piece of mussel shell that he occasionally whetted against a block of sandstone. After warming them over the embers of his campfire, he drew one stick after the other through his mouth, using the mois-ture of his saliva and the force of his teeth to straighten them out. This was

Ceramic bowl crafted in the late fifteenth century and later excavated at Awatovi, on An-telope Mesa in Arizona. Courtesy of the Museum für Völkerkunde, Berlin.

important, because the sticks were to be used as shafts for his arrows, whose stable flight would depend on their having a perfect shape.

Smoothing the shafts came next. The hunter grasped them with a piece of guanaco skin and moved them back and forth over a grooved piece of sandstone, catching the abraded dust in a fox-fur rag. The rag and its dust were used finally for polishing the sticks. The hunter was satisfied. Once they had completely dried out, the sticks would make good arrows, fletched, notched, and armed with a triangular slate point. His friends would envy him for having arrows as fine as these, and he would bring home plenty of meat.

In another part of the hemisphere, in what is today the Southwest of the United States, another creator was at work. Gathering the fine gray clay from a pit just off the trail that led from the village on the top of Antelope Mesa down to the fields, an Awatovi potter had sprinkled sacred cornmeal over the site, as one would exchange gifts with a friend. She was grateful for the dense quality of the clay that shrank so little when fired that nothing had to be added to keep her pots from cracking. The surface would be smooth and good for painting.

After modeling the base of the vessel in an old bowl, she built up its body by adding coils of clay to the top edge and pinching them in place. Then she shaped its gentle outline evenly by patting the outside with a flat stone while pressing her left hand against the inside of the thin wall. After the pot had dried sufficiently, she polished the surface with another stone, applied a thin layer of liquid clay to seal it, and polished it again. Now it was ready for painting, and few other women were more skilled than she in rendering complex designs of birds, feathers, and intricate geometric patterns with a yucca-leaf brush. In a few days, she and her daughters who lived with her would have made enough pots for firing. They stacked them, bottoms up, in a huge pile, placed slabs of coal around them, and covered them with wood. It would take a whole day for the smoldering fire to turn the gray clay into a nice buff sherd and make the pots ready for use.

Meanwhile, on the coast of Brazil, a Tupinamba woman readied herself for the sacrifice of a captive brought in by the men from a raid on a distant village. Using urucú and genipa, she began by painting herself half red and half black and then gluing feathers all over her body, which was covered only by the oily paint. When the woman was ready, she reached for a club, six feet long, carved from brown palm wood by one of the men. Shining like her own body, it was a long staff with a flat, disk-shaped head. First covering it with a resinous glue, she proceeded to sprinkle crushed gray and green shells all over it.

Now she scratched lines into the sticky cover: checkers, spirals, and waves, like those she usually scratched into the soft clay of the unfired cooking vessels. Surrounded by the other women, who were singing songs of mockery and revenge, and discussing who would be entitled to which cut of the captive's meat, she would soon turn to the prisoner to paint his body black and to decorate his face in much the same manner as the club, which would then crush his head. How they would feast!

On the island of Haiti, at the same time, a Taino shaman was putting the final polish on a grayish-green stone whose conical body protruded from an oval base. The front end clearly depicted the head of a woodpecker, the creature which in mythical time had used its beak to make women out of sexless beings. Another man had recently been up in the hills, and from the corner of his eyes he had seen that stone moving and beckoning to him. Only a shaman could tell which being was hiding in the stone, and so the shaman had sniffed a powerful drug in order to communicate with it and to discover its true nature.

The woodpecker had ordered the shaman to carve the stone in its shape, to make it a zemi, in which it could dwell and bring fertility to the fields of the man who had seen the stone move. Everyone asked the shaman for help when encountering the powers in nature, or when the spirits came in dreams, and the shaman would always have to discover the spirits' intentions and make their idols of stone, shell, wood, or cotton. People had many such zemis, and they cherished them for the power of their supernatural inmates, who ate the food that was offered them, and would sometimes even speak when asked to foretell the future. The world was full of spirits, and often it was hard to recognize them in their disguises. Recently, the islanders had seen some of them out on the sea, as if they were huge dugout canoes under a white cloud.

No matter how many stops we make for glimpses of life in the Americas in 1492, the infinite variety of forms, functions, and meanings of the arts that were thriving could not be adequately described. The universe of shapes, colors, sounds, and movements produced by men and women between the Bering Strait and Tierra del Fuego defies generalizations. But it mirrored faithfully the individuality of native cultures, their relative needs, and their common desire to express themselves.

It would be unfair to compare the monumental stone sculpture of the professional Aztec artisan at the royal court in Tenochtitlán with a roughly hewn idol in a rural temple carved by the local stonecutter, or even with an arrowhead made by a hunter in the Canadian Subarctic forests. Yet all three works may represent the highest achievements in shaping stone in their respective cultural worlds.

Social, economic, and religious complexity controlled the demand for art, but the availability of resources and technologies limited its forms of expression. The treeless desert of the Arctic tundra offered little opportunity for the development of wooden sculpture, just as the lack of metallurgical knowledge prevented native peoples inhabiting gold-rich regions in what is now California from becoming goldsmiths. Nomadic hunters and gatherers had second thoughts before creating objects like heavy and breakable pots that would encumber them in their movements. These limitations weighed heavily on the visual arts, but literature and music were not without their own specific constraints. Musical versatility depended to some extent on the ability to fashion adequate instruments. And while all languages lent themselves to the creation of verbal arts, their grammatical structures and even their sound systems influenced appreciably the results of such efforts.

Forms of expression must also be seen to be a result of complex historical developments. By 1492, native peoples had perhaps inhabited the American continents for tens of thousands of years. After so many millennia, the common heritage they had carried with them out of Asia had become modified beyond recognition by changes that had been far from uniform. The ancestors of people like the Fuegians of the southern tip of South America had slowly traversed the whole of both continents, adapting and readapting their lifeways and arts to the changing environments they had encountered as they had moved south. Even those whose journeys were much shorter had experienced dramatic changes in climates and plant and animal life. Straddling the Bering Strait, the Eskimos had maintained contact between the Old World and the New, but had only selectively accepted and transmitted innovations that had reached northeastern Asia.

All of the migrating peoples had encountered numerous others with different traditions, often causing them to adopt new techniques, new songs, and new ideas, which they had reshaped according to their own needs and desires. Some had been forced to live under foreign rule, as had happened to many Andean peoples during the time of the expansion of the Incan empire. Others had never even heard rumors of dramatic developments occurring outside their own world. And sometimes native peoples found themselves facing the visible remnants of their predecessors, such as the burial mounds in the Ohio Valley or the ruins of the classical civilizations in Mesoamerica.

All of the cultures and all of their arts had changed, each at their own pace, sometimes imperceptibly, sometimes in great leaps. None of the arts of any of these peoples was the same in 1492 as it had been five hundred years before. Those that survived were vastly different, yet still distinctive after five centuries. The inter-American network of encounters and exchanges before Columbus provided for some regional commonalities in the arts, but it never led to any unity in expressive terms. The only universal feature was the presence of the arts themselves.

But the "arts" were not "art" as we know it today. Although we may not entirely agree on what art really is, we all think that it exists as a separable part of our experience. To say that none of the indigenous languages of America had a word for art (or religion, for that matter) simply means that their speakers did not consider aesthetics as separable from the rest of their activities. "If you expect them to value or admire any art," a later observer explained, addressing "the great and almost general indifference" of the Indians of northeastern North America toward works of art in the narrow European sense, "it must have a reference to hunting, fishing, or fighting."

Thus, there was no art for art's sake. Every object, every sentence, every melody, and every dance served a clearly defined purpose, but they also enjoyed the "luxury of form" within and beyond the necessities of usefulness. The Fuegian was pleased with his arrow because it was perfectly useful, and it was useful because it was perfectly well shaped. Certain forms of Aztec sculpture were lavishly decorated on their underside, which was never seen, because the symbolic meaning thus expressed far outweighed the purely visual aspect. Just as a concern for nonhuman powers in the world permeated the people's lives, the concern for form was unlimited, differing in intensity, as it might, from occasion to occasion and from culture to culture.

This greater wholeness of experience was one of the reasons why it may be misleading to speak about the indigenous arts in the Americas in 1492 in terms of "beauty." The appreciation of created forms was not based on aesthetic considerations alone, but also on their usefulness and their meaning. While standards by which forms were judged existed in every native culture, they were hardly ever identical. The well-formed sentence carried its message, the well-shaped pot held the water, and the well-carved image was recognized as the god it had been made to represent. Yet in a different culture, the same message sounded different, another pot held the water just as well, and even the same god was rendered in a different local style. While style was only the medium through which messages were transmitted, it shaped the message and became part of it.

Another aspect of this encompassing outlook on the world affects the question of what constituted the "arts" in pre-Columbian America. Our neat categories of "painting," "sculpture," "literature," "music," "dance," and "drama" are once again based on the categorical ideas of separation, as well as on the importance attached to professional specialization. Neither of these premises was shared by the majority of indigenous American cultures.

Purely instrumental music was quite rare all over the continent, because melodies were usually combined with words into song, and rhythms with movement into dance, as when the dancer wore rattles or bells which translated his steps into sounds. Masks were not carved to be displayed in the isolation of a showcase, but to be worn in dramatic reenactments of mythic events, stories come alive to the movement of music.

If the "arts" are to be seen as comprehending all the sensuous experiences of human expression rather than just the productions of people regarded as "artists," smell and taste become equally part of the artistic universe. The Aztecs, it was said, found "gladness and joy in spending the entire day smelling a little flower or a bouquet made of different kinds." The effect of the Aztec florists' art was thus based as much on fragrance as on color and shape. The metaphoric term for poetry was "the flower, the song," and the composition was likened to cutting "flowers of delightful scents."

Elsewhere, the smell of incense, whether it was copal, tobacco, or sweet grass, was an integral part of performances of ceremonial drama; and few feasts of song and dancing were complete without the taste of food prepared according to specific recipes. Small effigy breads in the shape of gods, flowers, or birds were prepared and eaten at the feast of Xochiquetzal, the divine patroness of Aztec painters, weavers, silversmiths, and sculptors, and the skill of the makers of decorated bread was regarded as equal to that of other artists. Foods and fumes carried as much symbolic meaning in aboriginal America as other forms of expression and were an important part of the experience of the world shaped by human beings.

The arts existing in America in 1492 can therefore be truly understood and evaluated only if we know how they were embedded in the fabric of their respective culture. The shock and aftermath of 1492 closed the door to a full comprehension of these arts forever. Every approach, however careful, can take us only part of the way.

Not all artists were created equal. Skills varied to a considerable extent between individuals. Poor hand-eye coordination affected the execution of the best image that ever came to mind; an insufficient sense of rhythm spoiled the efforts of the clearest voice and the nimblest foot. Probably all native peoples in America recognized these differences in artistic performance, but they did not attach the same importance to them.

The hunters of Tierra del Fuego knew the individual talents of every person in their band, and they admired mastery of a craft. Yet everyone was expected to produce the same kinds of objects for his or her own use whenever the necessity arose. Never were objects made for stock, because of the inconvenience of carrying them from camp to camp. Occasional trades had to be made with items already in use, and these would have to be replaced instantly.

Eskimo singers would try to excel in the regular song festivals held during the dark season of the year. This was especially true of dispute-settlement songs, in which no mercy was shown in exposing the opponent to public ridicule and silencing him—although not for good. Victory in the contest simply made up for past wrongs and put an end to further enmity. The song festivals were not reserved for the best singers; everyone, including children, talented or not, would step into the circle formed by the participants.

The Aztecs likewise knew the difference between good and bad stonecutters. The good stonemason, said the ancient text of the Mexicas, was "of skilled hands, able hands . . . He quarries, breaks the rocks; pecks, smooths them

. . . splits them with a wedge, marks them with black; forms curved stone, cuts it . . . sculptures in stone, forms work of artifice, of skill . . ." The bad carver, on the other hand, was "of lame, feeble arm; a crooked cutter, a crooked builder; a mocker—as if he were a builder of curved, leaning walls. He mocks people, builds crooked, builds with mud." But unlike the less articulate Eskimo singer, the negligent Aztec stonecutter was a professional craftsman who worked for others and, his reputation being what it was, he could hardly expect to receive prestigious and rewarding orders.

Only a few of the native societies of America knew professionalism in the field of arts and crafts. Most practiced the much simpler division of labor by sex, which made the family ideally the self-sufficient unit of economic and artistic production. Wives and daughters supplied the family's need of hide clothing, baskets, textiles, and pots (wherever they were made); husbands and sons carved in wood or stone, and worked metals. The line between male and female arts was not always drawn in exactly the same fashion, and some arts like face painting were commonly done by both sexes. In the verbal arts, in music, and in dance, there were similar distinctions based on sex. The use of wind instruments, for example, appears to have been limited to men, whose dominance over drums, on the other hand, was probably a result of ritual specialization, rather than of sexual division. But everyone was able and expected to create the needed forms, and excellence was praised, although not necessarily in a way that set the individual apart from or above others. Even the most gifted Eskimo poet and performer did not think of himself as special, because poetry was not an individual achievement, but a gift which everyone possessed to some extent.

In these common art traditions, where everyone was a creator of forms and the wholeness of the experience was still maintained, the distinction between artist and audience retreated into the background. Arts were not judged by passive viewers, but by a community of fellow creators according to shared standards of competence. The sexual division of creation was not only complementary; it also led to distinctive male and female styles. Some of these differences were based on technique (basketry exerted different constraints on form than carving); others followed from the segregated transmission of male and female arts from father to son or mother to daughter.

Access to local resources often promoted trade both of raw materials and of manufactured goods. Carved maple bowls were "of highe price" among the tribes of coastal New England in the 1620s and perhaps also in 1492, "and these are dispersed by bartering one with the other, and are but in certaine parts of the Country made, where the severall trades are appropriated to the inhabitants of those parts onely." Such local specialization was even more characteristic of Mexico, where the exchange of products between villages took place in regular markets. Producing stock for trade obviously led to higher average standards of quality, but again not necessarily to individual excellence.

Sometimes specialization in the arts was a result of the control over non-human powers. Many forms of art had religious aspects, meanings, or functions, and the most clearly defined form of religious art was that made by religious specialists. Healing formulae, incantations, and other sacred words could be based on esoteric knowledge in the minds of a few shamans or priests, who were best suited to deal with such powerful and potentially dangerous material. Ritual objects, such as charms and sacred images, were similarly the works of religious specialists, who generally were not chosen to perform their tasks because of their aesthetic inclinations.

Frequently the manufacture and control over such religious art was appropriated by secret societies. Only the initiated men among the Fuegians or among the Pueblo people knew the secrets of their masks, and only they could make them and wear them in their impersonations of the gods and spirits. Only the members of the Northwest Coast dancing societies knew the secrets of the stage that baffled their unsuspecting audiences during the winter ceremonials. These societies, though not professional, acted in fact as theatrical groups. Specialization of this kind caused inequality. Based, as it was, on the control over esoteric meaning no longer shared by the community and on the special powers of a select few to deal with the sacred, it ultimately led to a control over form.

True professionalism in the visual arts occurred in stratified societies, in which elites patronized the services of the makers of goods fashioned to meet their specific needs. This was the case in the civilizations of Mesoamerica and in the Andean highlands, in the chiefdoms of the area intermediate between the two centers, and probably in southeastern North America. At the time of European contact in the eighteenth century, the wealthy clan chiefs of the Northwest Coast of North America also supported the work of professional artists. The presence of a group of spectacular and highly formalized carvings among much less exquisite products in archaeological sites of the area suggests that this specialization had begun to take place by 1492.

Mass production for the market enhanced the technical excellence of the products, but works made to order for the elites by professional artists brought about greater refinement. The result was an ever-widening separation between maker and user, between high and folk arts, as well as between the centers and the periphery. The major survival of the former wholeness of the creative process was the continuing unity of form and function.

Under such circumstances, some artists also enjoyed higher prestige associated with their special status. In the Inca empire, the silversmiths, the tapestry weavers, the makers of the finely lacquered wooden beakers, and other such specialists not only were hereditary servants of the government but were also exempt from taxes. Their products belonged to the Inca himself, who distributed the surplus among the nobility. The taxpayers, on the other hand, had to supply their own needs and were furnished by the authorities only with raw materials, such as wool. Commoners were allowed to wear only plain clothes with simple patterns, while the fine tapestry-woven textiles with complex designs in many colors were reserved for the upper class.

Professional artists were not necessarily selected on the basis of their established competence, although individual excellence certainly made all the difference within their ranks. The Aztecs, who strongly believed in the importance of day signs, thought that persons born under the sign of xochitl, "Flower," were destined to become artisans, musicians, or entertainers. Upon birth they received symbols of their prognosticated calling, such as a brush for a painter or an adze for a carpenter. Thus, in a way, some Aztecs were born artists.

Specialization also existed in some of the verbal arts and in music. Many of the greatest poets and singers in Aztec Mexico were members of the nobility, like the famous poet-king Nezahualcoyotl of Texcoco. Others lived in the palace or temple compounds and were paid to compose divine songs or to glorify the deeds of the kings and their ancestors in epic verse. Through training in the temple schools, they acquired the historical and religious knowledge necessary for their creative work. There were other schools, "the houses of song," attached to the temple of every Aztec city, in which twelve- to fourteen-year-old boys and girls were taught the performing arts of song, dance, and instrumental music in order to be able to participate in public rituals.

The creation of expressive forms by artists was closely linked to human ideas about the creation of themselves and the world around them. The peoples of America possessed different explanations of how the world had come into being, but many of their accounts spoke of the destruction of previous worlds before the creation of the present one, or of the transformation of pre-existing shapes into their current forms. Rather than proposing a unique and perfect creation by a single creator-god, these beliefs viewed creation as often imperfect and subject to improvement and renewal.

In Eskimo belief, the first human beings of the present age were two men who had emerged from two hummocks of earth. By means of a magical song, one of them was transformed into a woman and bore the first child. At the same time, Eskimos believed that all songs came to man from the souls of the land of the dead, and that the power of the sacred word was sufficient to heal or kill a person. Not only was creation perceived as something generic rather than individual, it was a process in which the distinction between mythic time and the present was voided. The power to create or transform lived on in the shaping of forms.

In the Inca empire with its professional craftspeople, creation was not looked upon as an anonymous event. Wiraqoca, "the Lord," had first carved men of giant shape from stone. It was thought that the pre-Inca monumental

Bone panpipes held in a copper sheath. Pipes like these existed in many places; these were discovered by archaeologists in present-day Ohio. Courtesy of the Field Museum of Natural History.

stone sculptures were the remnants of this first creation, which Wiraqoca—dissatisfied with his own work—had turned into stone again in order to form a new generation of beings from clay and in his own size. Clothing them by painting their dress on the clay bodies and bringing them to life, the creator also gave his creatures their customs, food, language, and song.

Just as the creation of the world was caused by supernatural beings, human creativity was often seen as resulting from an encounter with nonhuman powers. Protective designs painted by warriors on shields or clothing, or facial decorations worn by shamans, were frequently derived from a person's vision or dream in which the soul had left the body. Although the designs were conventionalized within certain patterns specific to the given culture, they derived their legitimacy and efficiency from their nonhuman origin. Conversely, in many indigenous American cultures the acquisition of power was identified with the visionary acquisition of a song. The Fuegian shaman knew he had received his calling when his guardian spirit taught him his song in a dream.

These powers also came into play because all the materials used in the visual arts were drawn from a world animated by spirits. As an act involving the manipulation of these powers, artistic creation was often surrounded by taboos, prayers, and self-mortification. Eskimo women were careful not to use caribou sinew to sew sealskin garments, owing to a general belief in the impropriety of mixing the products (and spirits) of the land and the sea. Aztec embroiderers, just like other professional craftspeople of their culture, were expected to do penance and to fast for several weeks, so "that their embroidery or design might be a work of art well fabricated and well painted."

The preparation of ritual objects involved even greater ceremonial attention. The Mayan wood carvers of Yucatan showed much reluctance when it came to "making gods" from cedarwood. They knew of the dangers involved in careless transgressions of taboos, and made all sorts of excuses before accepting the commission and the payment in food, cacao beans, and stone or shell beads from the sponsors of the images. The best time for the work (usually the Mayan month of Mol) was determined by the priests. While specially selected ceremonial attendants began to fast, and the sculptors refrained from sexual intercourse, the sponsors gathered the cedarwood and brought it to a straw shelter built for the occasion. No one was allowed to come near the workshop, except the priests, attendants, and carvers, all of whom drew blood from their ears by means of the spine of a stingray and applied it to the nascent sculpture. It is not surprising that the wooden idols were highly prized by their owners, but they were held in esteem not because they were thought to be divine, but because they had been ceremonially made.

Musical instruments were not only the means to produce a form of art but,

Papago flutes. While sometimes employed in ceremonies, flutes like these were frequently used by young men during courting. Courtesy of the Field Museum of Natural History.

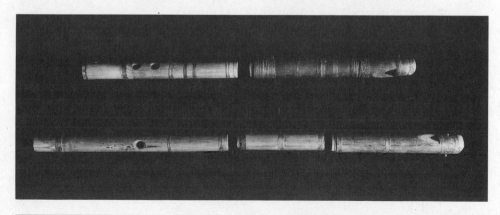

given their own voice, were themselves often regarded as being animated or even sacred. Their makers among the Mayas prayed while producing them and gave them alcoholic drinks to keep them happy and well tuned. The Tupinamba offered food to their rattles, and among many tribes of the South American lowlands sacred trumpets, flutes, and bull-roarers were taboo to the women, who sometimes were even supposed to be killed by the instruments upon sight.

The high regard accorded some of the arts by Native American societies was well illustrated in later encounters with European goods and art. The Potawatomi of Wisconsin looked upon a French trader who supplied them with iron implements in the seventeenth century "as one of the chief spirits, since thou usest iron," and proceeded to incense his knives and hatchets with tobacco smoke. Painters like George Catlin, Rudolf Friedrich Kurz, and Paul Kane were viewed by nineteenth-century Plains Indians as having the power of medicine men—a power that was both bewildering and potentially dangerous. The creation of a likeness gave the creator some control over the model, whether it was a spirit depicted in the Taino zemi or a carved wooden doll used to bewitch the enemy represented in it.

But not all human creations were as obviously inspired by supernatural powers or modeled after divine acts; nor was creativity always a highly prized goal. In many basketry traditions there appears to have been little desire for innovation, especially when satisfactory solutions for the problem of spacing designs on the body of the basket had been found. Knowledge of inherited patterns and the excellence of their execution were of overriding importance.

Given the wide variety of indigenous American notions of creativity, it is hardly to be expected that at a time when even European cultures had a less individualistic view of art, our contemporary Western idea of art as an individual expression should have been shared by Native Americans. Instead, we find a wide range of variation in this respect, although in general the product was considered more important than the maker.

Aztec stone carving, for example, was done collectively by members of a guild, not unlike the situation in a medieval workshop. The same may have been true of other professional art traditions that were flourishing in 1492, such as Northwest Coast wood carving. Collective endeavors were even more typical for the performing arts, in which a reliance on organized group effort was necessarily much greater.

Later evidence for the presence of craftswomen's societies among the village farmers of the North American Plains suggests that such guilds existed even where work was done individually, and that one of their major purposes was the preservation and cultivation of specialized technical and spiritual knowledge. The right to use the "sacred knowledge" to make baskets, pots, or tipis had to be purchased from a member of the guild, whereas other crafts, such as mat weaving, were regarded as "free." Even though some of the latter were in fact quite laborious, they were viewed as less prestigious and valuable than the restricted arts.

Cooperation occurred also outside of organized groups, especially in a family when men painted on hides tanned and prepared by their wives or when mothers and daughters shared the work of pottery making and painting. Given the constraints imposed by tradition on form and function, the individuality of the maker was generally less important, even when—as in the majority of cases—work was done individually.

In Western art the signature is the individual artist's claim to responsibility for his achievement. Such signatures seem to be missing in pre-Columbian American art, even where systems of writing were present. Especially in the common art traditions, however, there was no need for a signature, since individual work was characterized and recognized by subtle differences. But both for the artists producing primarily for their households and for those who produced luxury goods for a narrowly circumscribed elite, individuality was of little consequence.

Even where professional artists were at work, as in Aztec Mexico, individual achievements in the arts were hardly ever remembered. The major exception may have been in the highly developed field of poetry, where the works of members of the nobility, such as Nezahualcoyotl, were remembered long after their death. It is likely, however, that this fame rested as much on a poet's social prominence as on his ability.

In most native American societies there was no individual right to specific forms. The Californian basket maker would laugh at the suggestion that somebody might actually claim copyright to a certain design, although not all the weavers were able to produce all known patterns. Only a few experienced "pattern makers" could memorize the necessary counts of weaving elements for all the designs and were asked for help as the occasion arose.

A not uncommon exception to this rule was heraldic designs. But even here the form was owned by a kinship group rather than by the artist. In the late eighteenth century, and probably also by 1492, many of the motifs of Northwest Coast art were the property of clans or lineages, because they related to that group's history and mythical origin. Abstract designs on men's tunics and women's shawls in the Inca empire similarly appear to have been of a heraldic nature, and so were many of the face and body decorations used all over the American continents. Kinship groups or ritualistic societies could also own the rights to certain songs or dramatic performances.

It is important to recognize that the ownership of a theme or motif did not imply its fossilization. Indeed, such themes were continually modified. A certain war song performed in the year 13-Reed for the Aztec King Axayacatl, for example, was the property of the people of Chalca; the version rendered at that time was one that had been invented originally by a noble composer but had been improved upon later on by others.

The individual nature of every artistic creation makes it an extension of the maker's personality and a symbol of his or her identity. Californian women knew their own baskets, and Pueblo women their own pots, when it came to separating the various containers at the end of a communal feast to which everyone had contributed. The heraldic devices served to mark the identity of corporate kinship groups, just as the shared traditions and styles of towns, tribes, and nations were used to signal their shared identity. The latter was, of course, especially important in encounters with other groups, such as in markets, where the local style of dress immediately identified the origin of a person.

Art styles did in fact often reflect the character of the culture of their origin. The technical excellence that characterized Inca art of Peru, including the repetition of a limited number of simple forms, a tendency toward geometric and abstract designs, and a love for simple, but functional surfaces, speaks of a highly organized, technocratic, no-nonsense society. A look at Aztec art reveals that all builders of late empires need not be identical. While it shared a predilection for clarity and strict organization of form, and also lacked a marked concern for individual expression, it encouraged virtuosity and a realism rich in metaphor.

Western civilization is a rare exception among the cultures of the world in that it consciously and sometimes artificially preserves its works of art (and lately also those of other cultures). Visual art is stored and displayed in museums or conserved as monuments. Language arts and music are written down, printed, and recorded, and kept in archives and libraries. Even the performing arts are being documented on film or video. This preservation has important consequences for the arts themselves, as it creates a strong consciousness for their historicity and development, and makes them subject to reevaluation, reinterpretation, and even revitalization. It is therefore of substantial interest to look at the arts of indigenous America in terms of their life span and preservation.

The fleeting movement of dance was clearly the most difficult art to freeze in time. Although it was the purest art of the moment, the steps of the dancers were not only firmly prescribed but often keenly watched, and sometimes even enforced. As with all ritual behavior, the close observance of the required activity was held to be important for the achievement of the intended purpose of the ceremony. Especially in areas with well-organized structures of authority, such as the Northwest Coast or southeastern North America, dancers who deviated from the rules were punished on the spot for their mistakes. The enforcement of dance rules was intended to maintain ritual propriety and continuity and must have added to the notion of the perpetuity

BUFFALO BULL DANCER. One of the central features of the four-day Okeepa ceremony of the Missouri River Mandans was the buffalo bull dance. In this dance, eight men were painted with black, red, and white paint and covered with the skin of a buffalo. Each dancer carried a rattle and a staff and had a bundle of willow boughs tied to his back. Courtesy of the Newberry Library.

A SILVER GOBLET of Chimu manufacture, probably from the fifteenth century. Chimu craftsmen made this goblet by hammering a sheet of silver over a carved wooden form. Following the incorporation of the Chimus into the Inca empire, many of their renowned metalworkers were taken to Cuzco to make objects of this kind for their new leaders. Courtesy of the Milwaukee Public Museum.

EMBOSSED GOLD MUMMY MASK from the Chimu region of the Peruvian coast. A three-dimensional nose was attached to this hammered sheet of gold to create a mask which was sewn over the face of a mummy bundle. The object reflects the extent to which dead leaders were honored throughout this region. Courtesy of the Milwaukee Public Museum.

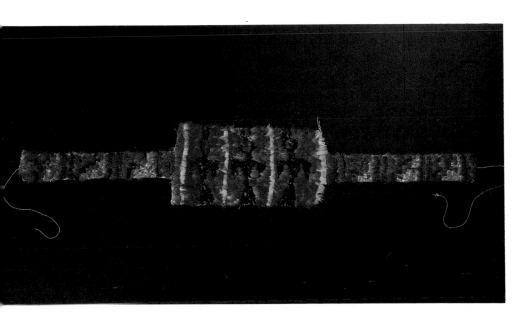

FEATHER BELT. Made by Inca feather workers in the late fifteenth century, this sash testi-
fies to the level of artistic specialization in
America in 1492. The feathers were imported,
probably from the Amazon Basin, indicating
the extent of Inca trading networks. Courtesy
of the Milwaukee Public Museum.

BIRDS ON NATIVE COTTON. One of the very
earliest known examples (ca. 2,500 years old)
of Peruvian painted fabric. Courtesy of the
Lowie Museum of Anthropology.

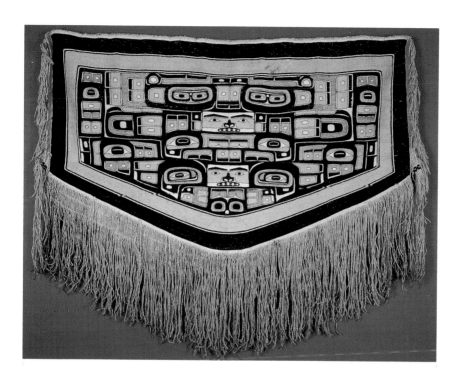

CHILKAT BLANKET. Woven from mountain
goat hair and cedar root, these blankets were
adorned with abstract representations and
were elaborately fringed to be worn while
dancing. Photo by Eduardo Calderon, courtesy of the Thomas Burke Memorial State
Museum.

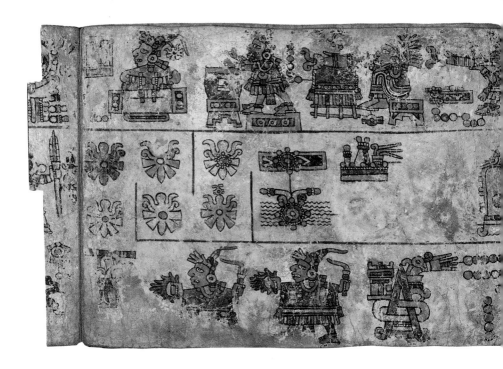

AZTEC MUSICIANS. These figures playing a rattle, a horn, and drums were painted on skins. The image is a detail from the Codex Becker. Courtesy of the Museum für Völkerkunde, Vienna.

KWAKIUTL MASKS. Used in tribal ceremonies, these "transformation masks" enabled the wearer to assume several identities simultaneously. Courtesy of the American Museum of Natural History.

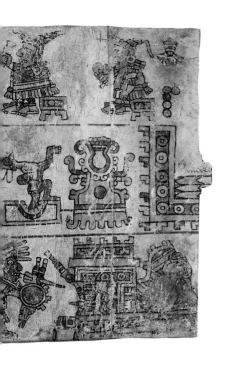

ZEMI. These objects, believed to hold different levels of religious power, were used in a variety of ceremonial settings. Zemis were usually made in response to a vision. This zemi is from the Caribbean. Photo by R. Delpiano, courtesy of the Museo di Etnografia et Antropologica di Torina.

of this art, rather than invited speculations about past and future changes.

The situation was similar in the case of music. But music was generally more closely tied to words (even if purely instrumental, it tended to refer to song), so that musical features could be rather easily transposed into language. (That the reverse is also true can be seen in the occurrence of drum or whistle languages and other acoustical signaling methods, which were used in several regions of pre-Columbian America.) Whenever writing systems were developed for a language, there was always the chance that musical notation might also occur. The rhythms of Aztec songs were expressed through nonlexical or meaningless syllables. These were notated in early Spanish colonial times, but it is doubtful that this was already the case in 1492.

Human memory was also the primary repository for the preservation of the verbal arts. As with all memory culture, oral tradition suggested the illusion of timeless continuity and persistence. Ironically, it was only the advent of writing, with its intention to create a permanent record of the spoken word, that exposed the otherwise unrecognized changes. True writing systems, in which the words as written could be read without additional knowledge of the contents, were limited to Mayan hieroglyphic writing. Even this system was in decline in 1492, and it remains doubtful how much of the inscriptions of the classical period of the first millennium could be read at that time. Their presence and the recognition of the changes, however, must have been the occasion for reflections about the past on the part of the literate Mayan elite.

Aztec and Mixtec writing contained some phonetic features, but was largely pictographic and ideographic. Aztec scribes were therefore trained not only in the technical aspects of writing but more importantly in memorizing the oral commentaries that went with the manuscripts. The codices, whose contents were partly ritualistic and partly mytho-historical, helped to systematize at least part of the vast amount of traditional verbal genres. Given the small number of literate Aztecs, however, the oral delivery remained the major form of expression. The same was true of other pictographic and nonpictographic memory aids, such as the quipus of the Incas or the calendric pictographs of eastern North America. Rather than being records of the word, they were repositories of data and ideas.

Of all the forms of human expression, the visual arts had the longest potential life, as most of them could be preserved directly rather than only by means of memory or writing. Yet in actual fact, some of the works were extremely short-lived while others appeared to last forever.

Face or body painting was an art that by its function and technique was designed to last for only a few hours. Some of the more elaborate designs took longer to produce than the time they would be displayed. The other major group of works designed for extremely short periods of appreciation was intended for religious ceremonial use. Like all culinary art, the monumental divine images made of amaranth-seed dough, for instance, were eaten in Aztec Mexico at the end of the ritual for which they had been made. Other examples are documented or can be inferred for the Pueblo culture of the North American Southwest: the dry paintings of colored sands, pollen, and/or cornmeal that formed part of altar arrangements were destroyed immediately after the ceremony; the painted leather masks worn by the impersonators of the kachinas were not preserved, but were redesigned for each appearance; and even the polychrome mural paintings of complex design on the walls of ceremonial rooms, which probably served as backdrops for the altars, were whitewashed and repainted for every new ceremony. Apart from the inherently impermanent nature of the dry paintings, fear of potential misuse of the powerful art may be held responsible for the destruction of the works, despite the great amount of labor that was expended in their production. In all these cases, no other purely mental models were available to the artists setting out to do their tasks.

Things made for common use, such as decorated clothing and items of personal ornamentation, pottery, baskets, weapons, tools—the vast majority of all visual arts—were employed according to their function until they were worn out. Depending on the material and the intensity of use, this could mean anywhere from a few days to many years. Little beyond an occasional repair was done to prolong their life expectancy. When no longer useful, they were discarded or, more often, recycled.

Most of these arts probably did not survive their makers (this is obviously true of tattooed body art), and some were indeed buried with them as grave goods. But there were always enough intact examples of recent manufacture around to be looked at, copied, and possibly improved upon.

The destruction of ceremonial items was far from universal in aboriginal America. No Taino would have destroyed his zemi, the abode of his spirit helper, which could even be stolen without losing its power. Among the Yucatecan Mayas, the cherished wooden images of gods were passed down from generation to generation. And most religious images made of stone were carved to last as well.

In most of these cases there may not have been a conscious effort to produce works that would last forever. But among the Aztecs, a people with a keen awareness of history, we find examples of art purposely made for those who would come afterward. As they themselves looked back on the monuments of ancient cities, such as Teotihuacán, they must have realized that some works were to remain and be marveled at by posterity. The series of relief portraits at Chapultepec commissioned by the Aztec kings were a prime example of this sense of historicity. Moctezuma I, who initiated the practice in the 1460s, hoping "to be glorified and adored like Quetzalcoatl," mused that the permanent record would "be a reward for our endeavors, and our sons and grandsons will see our images there, remember us and our great deeds, and will struggle to imitate us."

The Aztecs were also one of the few pre-Columbian peoples who consciously collected both foreign and ancient art. In offering caches at the great temple of Tenochtitlán, objects were deposited that had been brought to the city from areas recently incorporated into the empire, but also works from the Olmec and Teotihuacán periods. The former were obviously symbols of their hegemony; the latter imply an attempt to place themselves in a tradition of dominant cultures. This was a serious matter for a people who had only lately come to share the glory of Mesoamerican civilization, and who despite their sense of superiority knew of their shortcomings as far as refinement was concerned. It is significant that their honorary term for artist-craftsman was toltecatl, "like a Toltec," because they thought highly of the achievements of their immediate predecessors: "The remains of what they made and left behind, all of their work were good, all were exact, all well made and admirable." Aztec copies of pre-Aztec sculptures and pottery prove that their collecting also served the practical purpose of providing models of the arts of older traditions to imitate.

The inhabitants of the old Ica chiefdom of Peru had a different reason for collecting and imitating antiques. After being conquered by the Incas, members of the lower strata of Ica society began to glorify a past free of foreign rule. Items from this period of independence became a symbol of an unbroken identity, and copies of old forms were made as the custom began to spread.

The collecting of antiques placed a value on their association with the past, but also on their rarity. A similar intensity by rarefaction for the viewer was achieved by other means as well. One was the production of exquisite goods for the elites in stratified societies, which were often used only once before being discarded. In the verbal arts this was paralleled by the use of class-specific language, in terms of both accent and vocabulary or figures of speech. Even more common was rarefaction in religious contexts where, apart from the destruction of ceremonial works, art was kept from view in shrines or temples, to be seen only rarely, if at all, by commoners. The effect on the female viewers of the simple but strikingly painted bark masks worn by the men of Tierra del Fuego was heightened by the short duration of their public presentation during this emergence from the ceremonial shelter. The words spoken by the Subarctic shaman in an esoteric language, when communicating with his spirit helpers, increased the awareness of the importance of his action.

Displays of the rare and unusual were always a demonstration of religious or political power. Public art serving the same purpose had to compensate by monumentality for the lack of restrictions on exposure. The height of the carved wooden stools used by the Ica nobility varied according to their rank. Temples were frequently elevated on artificial mounds or pyramids. And on the Northwest Coast, ambitious chiefs glorified their ancestry and privileges by commissioning monumental carvings for public display.

All arts were extensions of the human mind into the reality of sensuous experience. As this transformation was achieved through activities of the body, often aided by tools, it was the tools that to no small extent shaped the expressions. Some of the characteristics of the American arts in 1492 may therefore be explained by the presence or absence of certain means of production.

Language being the technology of the word, the verbal arts were heavily indebted to linguistic structures for the organizing principle they suggested to thought as well as to form of expression. Polysynthesis, a common though far from universal feature of American languages, allowed an infinite variety of constructions, expressing the finest shades of meaning by the accretion of affixes. The number of conjugations of a simple verb like "to go" could run into the hundreds of thousands, whereas abstract nouns denoting categories might never occur without specific qualifications. Later European observers often understood such expressions as metaphors, or—lacking analogous possibilities in their own language—at least tried to translate them as such. But metaphors and other ways of intensification of meaning occurred besides, and in addition to, the hues allowed by literal expression. Given the almost complete absence of the written word (as distinguished from the representation of data) in 1492, it is hard to evaluate the specific achievements of American verbal arts at that time. The enormous variety and richness of the languages spoken on the two continents, however, were definitely responsible for the complexity prevailing in respect to verbal aesthetics.

The voices of Native America produced not only sentences but also melodies (some of the languages were indeed tone languages, in which the rising and falling contours of vowels affected the meaning of words). While song was universal, other forms of music were not. Some people, like the Fuegians, totally lacked musical instruments; others, like the Eskimos, had only drums. Stringed instruments were extremely rare and perhaps even generally absent.

As elsewhere in the world, the greatest variety was found among idiophones, in which sounds were produced by causing a rigid piece of material to vibrate. The range extended from two wooden sticks struck against one another, plank "drums" or baskets beaten with mallets, slit gongs made of hollowed logs, and notched rasps, to rattles made of wood, gourds, eggshells, dewclaws, cocoons, metal bells, turtle shells, and a host of other materials. Like the true drums made of hide stretched taut over a frame, most of these idiophones served to mark the rhythms of song and dance, but some, like the Aztecs' teponaztli, could produce sounds of different pitch.

With the rare exception of a few simple reed instruments, such as were used on the Northwest Coast, the majority of wind instruments were flutes and trumpets. None of the trumpets had finger holes, so only a series of overtones could be produced by overblowing. Among the flutes, on the other hand, were ocarinas and other instruments capable of playing complex melodies, either by finger holes or by a serial arrangement of several instruments (panpipes). By 1492, the latter were confined to the area from the Andean highlands to Panama, but had been present earlier in eastern North America and Mexico, where they had led to the development of multiple flutes with finger holes, by which an individual player was able to produce polyphonic melodies.

In the vast arena of the visual arts, Native American craftspeople were apparently disadvantaged by the absence of several technological developments that had taken place in the Old World. In particular, all applications of the principle of technical turning motion were unknown in America: potter's wheels, turning lathes, spinning wheels, and of course wheeled vehicles, which would have helped in hauling raw materials from their source to workshops. With minor exceptions, iron tools were equally absent. The exceptions included small amounts of meteoric iron, mostly used for ornamental purposes, and some tools traded from Asia as far south as the Northwest Coast.

Indigenous metallurgy had originated in the Andes and spread as far north as Mexico (with trade items reaching the North American Southwest). But it was limited to copper, silver, gold, and alloys made of these metals. A much older copper-working tradition had been present in eastern North America, but had never developed from cold hammering and annealing into a full-fledged metallurgy. The same low capacity of heat control that limited the smelting of ores also affected the firing of pottery. As kilns were unknown and open firing techniques were the rule, true glazes were not achieved.

Given these disadvantages, the results surpassed the expectations. Just as the lack of writing was made up for by improved memory skills in purely oral traditions, the lack of certain technological aids was compensated for by exceptional manual control in the visual arts.

In view of the diversity of the American arts in 1492, any attempt to summarize the universe of forms in a few paragraphs is bound to fail. The following survey can only highlight some of the achievements and suggest the range of differences.

Visually, indigenous American arts ran the whole gamut from abstract through ornamental to representational, from rectilinear to curvilinear, and from symbolic to realistic, without regard to social complexity or technological advancement, and sometimes existing side by side in the same culture. By and large, basketry and weaving lent themselves more readily to abstract decoration (with exceptions to be noted below), whereas the major portion of sculptural artwork was representational. Floral motifs were relatively rare, as compared to the use of anthropomorphic and zoomorphic designs. In the use of color, polychromy—especially traditions of red and black on a white or neutral background—was steadily gaining ground over the purely graphic arts.

Perhaps the most widely distributed genre of painting was rock art, both as pecked and engraved petroglyphs and as rock painting. Although it was apparently of great antiquity and was often practiced into the period after 1492, problems of dating it form a major obstacle to any synchronic overview. Some of the works may have related to shamanistic practices, others to hunting ritual, or individual records of achievement. In the urban centers of Mesoamerica, rock art was mostly replaced by architectural relief sculpture or murals, with the portraits of the Aztec rulers on the living rock of Chapultepec perhaps a reminder of the recent humble origins of the Aztecs.

We are on somewhat safer ground with regard to mural painting, whose distribution was concentrated in Mesoamerica and the North American Southwest, where plastered walls formed an ideal base for the application of fresco techniques. (By contrast, the stonemasonry walls in the Inca empire were decorated with products of the weaving arts.)

Body painting and tattooing must have had as wide a distribution as rock art, although the evidence for it is mostly indirect. The quality of some of it may be gleaned from sixteenth-century European reports, like that of a French observer in Florida who found the blue, red, and black tattoos of the Timucua "painted so well and properly, that the best painters of Europe could not improve upon it."

Judging from early historic evidence, painting on animal skins was well established in North and South America outside the centers of textile traditions, where the practice was transferred to bark cloth or woven fabrics (and eventually replaced by appliqué, embroidery, or woven designs). Apart from painted skins used as clothing, the genre notably included painted shields and drumheads.

The best attestations of painting, engraving, and relief carving on wood come from Mexico, Florida, and the Northwest Coast, while the majority of the lavishly lacquered wooden cups and pipes from Peru are now believed to date from early colonial times, and definitely after 1492. However, a much wider distribution, including the painting and engraving of bark, must be assumed. The incrustation of wood, shell, or stone with mosaic was highly developed in Mexico and Peru, but was practiced also in the Zuni pueblo of Hawikuh and, in a simpler variety of inlays, elsewhere.

Thanks to the less perishable nature of potsherds, the information on the distribution of pottery decoration is more complete. As in rock art, two basic techniques—pigmentation and mechanical surface treatment like scratching or stamping—were used, and painting was steadily gaining ground. In terms of sophistication and complexity, however, the trends were less uniform. While Pueblo pottery was reaching its highest development around 1492, the contemporaneous wares of the Andes had become relatively simpler than those of the earlier classical period.

In the textile arts, it appears that basketry had a nearly universal distribution, embracing the range from undecorated utilitarian to elaborately designed works. The technically most sophisticated products may have originated among sedentary but non-pottery-making groups, such as the peoples of California or the Northwest Coast (for whom direct evidence is rare). In some of the finest American basketry, the inherent tendency to produce rectilinear, abstract designs was overcome. Bold curvilinear patterns are known from the early historic period in southeastern North America; representational motifs show up in the Northeast and on the central Northwest Coast. In better-documented regions, such as the Pueblo area, the development of pottery had certainly led to a decline in the importance and virtuosity of basket weaving.

Loom weaving was restricted to the urban civilizations and their sphere of influence. While direct evidence is poor for Mesoamerica, archaeological finds in Peru have yielded overwhelming proof of the high quality of Inca textiles that was to be expected in an area with professional textile artists and a refined weaving tradition of some two thousand years. Life-forms had long been part of the design repertoire of Andean warriors. Although the Incas employed the services of textile specialists from among the conquered peoples of their empire, a certain decline in overall quality (similar to that in pottery) was noticeable. Native South America also saw the highest achievements in various techniques of interlacing, while fine twined textiles were produced in North America outside the weaving area of the Southwest.

Among the many decorative techniques related to the textile arts, special consideration must be given to feather work, if only because of its later stereotypical association with indigenous America. The splendid variety of birds and their strikingly colored feathers, especially in the tropical lowlands, had given rise to their use for decorative purposes. This, combined with the achievements of the textile arts in the urban civilizations, led ultimately to the manufacture of spectacular feather capes and mantles in Mexico and Peru, of whose splendor the few surviving examples can convey only a faint idea. Of early Brazilian feather work, a few sixteenth-century Tupinamba pieces may represent the standard of 1492, while of the turkey-feather mantles, which greatly impressed early European visitors in eastern North America, the reputation is all that remains.

With the exception of wood carving, the sculptural arts of pre-Columbian America are far better known than any of the other branches of creative activity. Works of shaped stone ranged from the simple, flaked implements of hunting peoples to the realistic images produced by the Aztec artists. Apart from a predilection for monumentality, Mesoamerican stonecutters accepted the challenge of working glasslike obsidian and the extremely hard jadeite, which was consequently valued more highly than precious metals. Monumental stone sculpture (although on a smaller scale and of a simpler style) flourished also in

Central America and in the Andes; small stone sculpture, especially of easy-to-carve stones, had a wide distribution all over the Americas.

Ceramic sculpture not only included molded or hand-formed images, generally of a religious nature, but also continued an old American tradition of effigy vessels, containers in the shape of gods, humans, or animals. Ivory carving was prevalent in Alaska, although the most accomplished examples dated from periods earlier than 1492. Exquisite wooden sculpture survives in rare examples from the Mesoamerican and Andean centers, as well as from the Northwest Coast and from a single site attributable to the ancestors of the historic Calusa Indians on the Gulf Coast of Florida.

The unchallenged center of metalworking was the region of the northern Andes and lower Central America. There gold and a gold-copper alloy were fashioned into ornaments, utensils, ceremonial items, and small sculptures in a wide range of local styles and techniques, including lost-wax casting and filigree. In Peru, where silver also played a major role in metallurgy, the Incas were the first to make large-scale use of bronze for utilitarian and ritual purposes.

Of the American building arts of 1492, only a very few examples survive to this day, and most of them are in a rather fragmentary condition. The monumental stonemasonry walls of the Inca period are a faint reminder of the engineering skills of their imperial architects; a look at the remains of Tenochtitlan tortures the imagination anxious to catch a glimpse of the glorious city in its original state; and only the Pueblo ruins of southwestern North America can be reconstructed more reliably by analogy with their living descendants. Most of the other building traditions, from the domed house built of snow bricks in the central Arctic to the gigantic longhouse of tropical Brazil, each important in its own way, can only be inferred on the basis of more recent evidence.

Our vision of the verbal arts, music, dance, and drama is even more blurred. The Aztecs classified their own genres of formal expression into metrical verse and prose. The former included the works of the "songmakers," such as hymnic divine songs, epic war songs, meditative songs of joy and privation, and erotic songs of pleasure. Narrative sacred word of mythology, historical word of the ancient times, and imaginative tales comprise part of the prose legacy. Comparatively little is known about Inca verbal arts, since almost nothing was recorded at the time of the conquest. We can only speculate that genres vaguely similar to those of the Aztecs existed here and elsewhere, and that the formal structure and theory of the forms of verbal expression were perhaps somewhat less sophisticated.

The existence of schools, where not only singing but also instrumental music was taught, reflected the degree of formalization present in Aztec music. Yet even without such schools, musical cultures existed throughout the hemisphere. Sometimes purely social, more often of religious significance, man-made sounds provided important accents and symbols to life. Kokopelli, the humpbacked and sexually aroused flute-playing kachina of the Hopis, who may be recognized in pre-Columbian Pueblo depictions, suggests the frequent association between flute music and sexuality and fertility. The sounds of instruments were often regarded as the voices of supernatural beings themselves, and sometimes, as the Eskimo word for drum implies, "that by means of which the spirits are called up."

Many of the ritual dramas of aboriginal America, including that of Aztec human sacrifice or the seasonal appearance of the Pueblo kachinas, not only reenacted myths but made them part of the experienced reality. The human participants were not detached actors but genuine impersonators of the non-human dramatis personae. Other performances, however, were of a purely secular nature, such as the Aztec plays that ridiculed the Huastecs as well as other foreigners and "savages," or the simplest of all mummeries, the animal disguises used by hunters stealthily approaching their prey.

What do we really know about the American arts of 1492, and how much will we ever know? Virtually all of the material evidence we have comes from archaeological research, which continues to increase the data base. But archaeology can supply only tangible remains, and that with some limitations. The verbal arts of nonliterate cultures are beyond the reach of the spade and the trowel. Music shows up in the record only as far as nonperishable musical instruments, such as clay flutes, are concerned. Glimpses of dance and drama can at best be gleaned from depictions on murals and pottery bowls or other graphic representations. Even the visual arts are far from being fully known. Dry climates have helped to conserve organic material in the coastal regions of Peru and in the American Southwest. Similar insights can be gained from sites covered by mud slides (as on the Northwest Coast) or from frozen remains in the Arctic. But elsewhere we may never know about feather work, basketry, or wood carving.

The artifacts that have been preserved are often not the best products fresh from the artist's workshop, but rejects or worn-out examples of the various crafts. Most important, none of them provides direct evidence of the cultural context in which they were once made and appreciated. This context could only be observed in the thriving cultures of 1492. By the time the first reasonable descriptions of the various native ways of life were written, years, decades, and centuries had passed. The changes that had occurred in the meantime, both before and after European contact, were more pronounced in the urban centers than in some of the outlying areas. The feather work collected in Mexico in the years immediately following the Spanish conquest was technically and stylistically much more sophisticated than anything that had been produced in 1492. The Aztec literature that was recorded in the native language in the sixteenth century was at least partly affected by the colonial experience—perhaps to a greater extent than the arts of the central Eskimos of Canada in the early twentieth century.

Approached cautiously, the surviving traditions of present-day Native Americans are a valuable source, allowing at least some inferences about the cultural principles and backgrounds of the arts of their forebears. But they are the descendants of only a fraction of the traditions existing in 1492. As far as the civilizations are concerned, the exquisite achievements of the elites were doomed by the process of conquest, and a similar fate was in store for many of the tribal cultures. For the folk cultures of Mesoamerica and the Andean highlands, as well as for the peoples elsewhere, survival depended on their ability to adjust to outside changes. Only dead cultures are impervious to modification. So ultimately, the vitality of the living traditions compensates for the gloom of 1492.

Afterword

VINE DELORIA, JR.

THE PRECEDING CHAPTERS have presented, as best as can be described, the peoples and their lives as they existed in the Western Hemisphere at the time of Columbus's "discovery." But our knowledge is changing constantly, and a generation from now, if the same topics are discussed, one might well find that many truisms of today are no longer considered valid, that additional research has thrown new light on some of the puzzling subjects about which today we merely hypothesize. Nevertheless, this present synthesis will, one believes, withstand critical scrutiny for many years to come.

Everyone would like to believe that the story of the Western Hemisphere after the Europeans' discovery of the New World is a straightforward chronology of events leading to the present, and indeed we write history with that goal in mind. History, the wise men say, is written by the winners, and after they have recast events to show themselves in a favorable light, it resembles nothing so much as an apology for their shortcomings. It is not difficult to arrange a chronology of subsequent events and describe the invasion and conquest of this part of the planet by peoples of European descent. Great disagreement exists, however, in the choice of interpretive themes by which we try to understand this most unique migration of peoples and the social, political, and economic experiments which characterize their time on these two continents.

Increasingly, American Indians are understanding the European invasion as a failure. That is to say, in spite of severe oppression, almost complete displacement, and substantial loss of religion and culture, Indians have not been completely defeated. Indeed, the hallmark of today's Indian psyche is the realization that the worst has now passed and that it is the white man with his careless attitude toward life and the environment who is actually in danger of extinction. The old Indian prophecies say that the white man's stay on these western continents will be the shortest of any who have come here. From an

Indian point of view, the general theme by which to understand the history of the hemisphere would be the degree to which the whites have responded to the rhythms of the land—the degree to which they have become indigenous. From that perspective, the judgment of Europeans is severe.

American history is usually cast in the light of progress—how a wilderness was tamed and brought to production by a hardy people who created a society in which the benefits of the earth were distributed to the largest percentage of people. From a short-term perspective, there is much to be said for this interpretation. Luxuries virtually inundate the United States, and even the poorest person in this society is in a much more comfortable position than the majority of people in most other human societies. This evaluation cannot be true for all nations of the Americas, of course, but for the peoples influenced by the English tradition it is most certainly a fact. The people of the United States prefer to credit their success to an intense commitment to progress, although at odd moments the Deity does get a bit of a compliment, and progress is almost always defined as an increase in material wealth. But in recent years, as the United States has begun to resemble a Third World nation saddled with insurmountable debts, the argument about the superiority of the United States is wearing a little thin. We are now living on future wealth, not on what we are able to produce ourselves. Today we have mortgaged the future.

It is fitting that we understand the conditions which once existed in this hemisphere, because this generation is facing a particularly difficult time grasping the meaning of the American experience. History, it appears to some people, is drawing to a close—at least the view of history that has nourished, inspired, and oriented us for most of our lives. The titanic struggle known as the Cold War is over and it is no longer clear in which direction world history is moving, if indeed there is movement at all.

In a rare and almost eerie prophetic analysis of the potential contained in the world situation in 1830, Alexis de Tocqueville observed:

> The American fights against natural obstacles; the Russian is at grips with men. The former combats the wilderness and barbarism; the latter, civilization with all its arms. America's conquests are made with the plowshare, Russia's with the sword.
>
> To attain their aims, the former relies on personal interest and gives free scope to the unguided strength and common sense of individuals.
>
> The latter in a sense concentrates the whole power of society in one man.
>
> One has freedom as the principal means of action; the other has servitude.
>
> Their point of departure is different and their paths diverse;

nevertheless, each seems called by some secret design of Providence one day to hold in its hands the destinies of half the world.

To what degree has this prediction been fulfilled? Russia no longer fights men and apparently has abandoned one-man rule, but has the United States transcended its struggle with nature so that it is, in a sense, the leader of the beginning of a new global history shared by everyone?

If we have understood the rage for democracy that has recently swept the earth, toppling long-established dictatorships and gnawing at the foundations of the monolith of Chinese communism, we must come to see that even American democracy, the oldest and most prosperous on earth, faces a gigantic task of redefinition. It may well be that the United States has worn out the democratic forms which were once so comfortable and reassuring. The United States must either make a gargantuan leap forward to a new global society of peace and justice or become a relic of vested privilege that will be swept aside with the old political structures of the Old World.

Russian communism and the American experiment with democracy represented two paths which the European emergence from feudalism could have taken. That these possibilities were realized on lands away from Europe is significant because the Old World could not have survived the stresses which the escape from feudalism required. Indeed, Nazism can be regarded as the true response of Europe to its declining role in the world: the *Lebensraum* of the National Socialists was simply Russian and American imperialism written in the small space of Central Europe. If the struggle for living space has ended, and it was always a quest for a secure national identity, then our present and future task is to create, once and for all, an adequate history of the human race, a history in which even the smallest and least significant people are understood in the light of their own experiences. For Americans that means coming to grips with the real meaning of the past five centuries and understanding what actually happened between the original inhabitants of this hemisphere and those who tried to erase and replace them.

A good way to begin an evaluation of the American experience is to look honestly at the experiences of the Americans, red and white, and to determine from their collective and shared experiences some themes and attitudes that have remained reasonably constant during these five centuries of contact. Discovery, whether it occurred on October 12, 1492, on a remote Caribbean island or in the wilds of California in 1911 when Ishi surrendered to civilization, brought with it profound cultural and historical shock. This trauma still remains a potent context for understanding Indian-white relations, and to the degree that the strangeness of the other being has not been overcome or assimilated, it remains a filter through which all other relations are passed.

At the time of discovery, Indians could not fathom the degree of danger which the new people represented. With Europeans appearing as individuals or in small groups no larger than the average native village, it was not possible for Indians to see in these few strangers the magnitude of the population they actually represented. Enormous populations and large settlements were completely unimaginable to most Indians. Even in the closing decades of the Indian wars of the American West in the 1870s and 1880s, the Indian chiefs had to be brought to the eastern cities on a grand tour before they could understand the magnitude of forces facing them. Even today it is impossible to get most Indians to understand that their problems and their solutions are not merely local affairs, that they live in an incredibly large and complex society.

After discovery, Europeans strove desperately to understand the meaning of the New World. Their knowledge of the world was derived primarily from their theological perspective, which accepted the literal creation of our species in a remote garden somewhere in the Middle East and saw no possibility that human societies could exist outside the historical framework given by the Holy Bible. It was not very difficult to assimilate the fact of two massive continents previously unknown to European minds. Ancient maps and legends suggested the existence of fantasy lands, and the discovery of the Western Hemisphere simply gave credence to some aspects of old mythologies, thereby inspiring expeditions in search of the Northwest Passage and the Fountain of Youth when the explorers did come ashore. And it was exceedingly difficult to understand who the people were who inhabited these continents.

Identification of the peoples of the New World revolved about two major strands of thought, both highly detrimental to the eventual treatment of the natives. One line of thought sought to identify the Indians with missing peoples of the Old Testament, and at various times the Indians were described as remnants of the survivors of the Great Noachian Flood, as the Ten Lost Tribes of Hebrews who had vanished during the Babylonian Captivity, or perhaps as fugitives from one of the periodic purges of heretics which swept Christendom in the centuries after Christianity became the dominant European religion. The Book of Mormon represents one of these traditional ways of understanding Indian origins. But Mormonism's tolerance for Indians was no greater than that shown by the zealous Spanish missionaries at the beginning of the conquest, and its doctrine that the dark skins of Indians and later of African blacks were a sign of divine displeasure has inhibited racial harmony and cooperation in the decades since its founding. There was no way that Indians could be identified with people of the Old Testament in a manner that would have given them status and respect.

The technological achievements of the Indians whom the first Europeans met did not suggest that these people were able to sail across the vast oceans that separated the two worlds. Consequently the idea grew up that at one time the continents of the planet were connected by land bridges and that most probably the lands underlying the Bering Strait had once been above water, providing a vast plain across which the ancient Indians migrated. The evidence for such a land bridge is exceedingly sparse and depends more upon the academic training that scholars receive than on physical evidence. Anthropologists do not agree on the dates during which this land bridge existed. In order to have a land bridge at all they must invoke an Ice Age which absorbed a sufficient amount of water from the world's oceans to lay bare the land under the Bering Strait. They then must create a mythical corridor between massive glacial sheets in order to get the Indians over to North America, through the ice, and into the interior, particularly to the southern parts, where they could survive.

The Bering Strait theory is tenaciously held by white scholars against the varied migration traditions of the natives and is an example of the triumph of doctrine over facts. Excavating ancient fireplaces and campsites may be exciting, but there are no well-worn paths which clearly show migratory patterns from Asia to North America, and if there were such paths, there would be no indication anywhere which way the footprints were heading. We can be certain of only one thing: the Bering Strait theory is *preferred* by the whites and consequently becomes accepted as scientific fact. If the universities were controlled by the Indians, we would have an entirely different explanation of the peopling of the New World and it would be just as respectable for the scholarly establishment to support it. The theory does illustrate a constant theme to which we shall return later on: a good many scientific and/or scholarly beliefs about Indians originated as religious doctrines. As religion lost its influence as an opinion maker, the idea was picked up by secular scholars, transformed into scientific theory, and published as orthodox science.

The scholarly Bering Strait fiction has a bizarre corollary which today has produced some dangerous elaborations. Facing evidence of massive contemporary ecological breakdown in North America, conservative scholars argue that our planet has survived many previous human trashings of the environment, thereby presumably nullifying the effects of our own errors, or at least minimizing the moral question of what modern Americans have done. Paul Martin, a paleobiologist, not only has ancient Indian hunters trekking across the Bering Strait but, upon reaching the New World, embarking on a program of extermination which eliminated all the big game animals of the Pleistocene era. Not all scholars endorse this idea, at least partially because it is ludicrous, but the popular mind, particularly that of the avid sportsmen, now cites the theory during discussions of Indian hunting and fishing rights as a means of proving that the blame for declining game resources should be placed on the Indians and not on themselves.

Like the Bering Strait theory, the Pleistocene overkill by ancient Indians has very little hard evidence to commend it. There are, to be sure, some sites which indicate that a group of Indians once drove a herd of buffalo over a cliff in what appears to have been an extravagant hunting episode. But since we have no idea how many guests were at dinner that day, even this evidence cannot be called wasteful without further data. The overkill theory, like the shifting ice corridors that move back and forth across the northern parts of the continent in accordance with scholars' requirements, falls apart of its own inadequacies as soon as it is examined. We are asked to believe that Indian hunters waded through massive herds of buffalo, deer, elk, antelope, and other tasty game animals in order to exterminate dire wolves, saber-toothed tigers, giant sloths, giant armadillos, and other creatures of similar size. If this slaughter was for food, we must credit the Indians with being the world's foremost chefs to make such fare edible. If the killings were for fun, then the Indians played very dangerous games and should be given credit for unusual courage, since these animals could easily have destroyed the hunters.

The other strand of European thought in identifying the origin of the natives of this hemisphere was that they might not be humans after all. Closely following the reporting of the discovery of the New World, intense political struggles commenced behind the scenes in Europe. The Papacy, ever responsive to the desires of the kings of Spain, made a gift of the lands of the New World to the Spanish Crown with the understanding that the Spaniards would bring the natives to embrace the True Faith. Thus armed with a totally bogus title issued by God's representative on earth, the Spaniards then began a brutal conquest in the Americas which virtually obliterated the native populations in the Caribbean within a generation. Such deeds did not go unnoticed among the more humane Spanish clerics, and reaction against the cruelty began to discomfit the King.

To justify conquest of the natives, the conquistadores added a theological twist. Approaching an Indian village, they would read a document known as the "Requirement," which recited the history of the world as they knew it, from the Garden of Eden to the recent discovery, and demanded that the natives accept this fable as true and submit themselves to the Spanish Crown and the Catholic Church. If the natives refused, it was argued, they had rejected the revealed truth of God and could be dealt with summarily. That the natives did not understand either Spanish or Latin or that they might have had their own version of world history was inconsequential. They were attacked, subjugated, and baptized in that order. Even this practice and the subsequent enslavement of natives on encomiendas repelled liberal Church leaders and added to the King's uncertainty.

In 1550–51, King Charles of Spain convened the leading Spanish theologians and philosophers at Valladolid to debate the criteria by which a just war could be waged against the natives of the New World. The debate revolved around the question of whether Indians were true human beings, possessing law, culture, religion, and a sense of family, or whether they were not really brutes according to the definitions of Aristotle and therefore could justly be reduced to the status of servants of the civilized peoples. The Indian cause was represented by Bartolomé de Las Casas, who had considerable experience in the New World and believed that Christianity should be spread by kindness and example and not by the sword. His opponent, Juan Ginés de Sepúlveda, who had no experience whatsoever with the New World, adopted the Aristotelian doctrine with great zeal.

After extensive debate, fifteen of the leading scholars were asked to write their opinions. No winner was ever pronounced. A massive document, the *Apology,* prepared by Las Casas and giving a detailed defense of the humanity of the natives, was suppressed by the Spanish authorities and modified versions of Sepúlveda's arguments were quickly circulated in the New World, where they were used as popular justifications for enslaving the natives. But there were tangible benefits for the Indians also: When native villages were put to the sword, and it came time to disembowel pregnant Indian women, a priest was always present in case the premature infant lived for a moment after it had been ripped from its mother's womb. During its few seconds of life, the baby was baptized before being unceremoniously dashed against a rock or wall. Thus religion maintained a place in the conquest of the Americas.

With some modifications for time and occasion, the arguments used by Sepúlveda have been cited with approval whenever it has been necessary to suppress the nonwhite races in America: nonwhites are not quite human and can be exploited by whites. Black slavery was once charitably described as a benign internship during which the Africans could be taught the rudiments of Christianity and civilization while toiling in the fields for their natural masters. Chinese workers were given the most hazardous work on the railroads on the premise that they were something less than human and could endure physical hardships far better than civilized whites. And as late as the 1920s, Mexicans were described by some social scientists as having been intended by nature to do stoop migratory labor because they were built close to the ground. Predictably, when the Great Depression deepened in the United States and jobs were needed for the influx of "Arkies" and "Okies" in the fields of southern California, the scientific classifications were no longer regarded as important. In summary, then, the pattern of dehumanization first voiced at Valladolid and applied to American Indians became the justification for the racism that has been a key characteristic of the American experience.

In the American perspective, science has adopted the beliefs of theology, transformed them into respectable secular theories, and then held them tenaciously in spite of all evidence to the contrary. Beginning most impressively with Thomas Jefferson and continuing until the present, American scientists and men of leisure have made it a practice to investigate the origins of American Indians by excavating Indian graves and burial sites, usually retaining the personal burial goods they fancy. By the end of the nineteenth century, during the formative years of formal anthropology and archaeology as sciences, the demand for Indian skeletal remains had risen with a frenzy. Indian dead on western battlegrounds were shipped East for inspection and examination by scientists. Considerable correspondence exists to show that grave-robbing was a common activity among the federal employees charged with taking care of Indians. Most distasteful was the practice of decapitating Indian skeletal remains during a brief period when some anthropologists believed that brain size, as determined by skull measurements, had something to do with intelligence and cultural behavior. It is impossible to estimate the number of Indian skeletal remains residing in American museums, primarily because most museums are afraid that if Indians know of their existence, they will want the return of their ancestors' bones for reburial.

Museums, state historical societies, and the United States National Park Service today insist on calling these remains "specimens," "resources," or other scientifically impressive names to cloak the fact that they are indeed human remains. They loudly argue that the Indian remains are needed by science to study a variety of important questions and that if the remains are returned, science will suffer irreparable damage. In order to insist that Indian bodies are within the domain of science, it is necessary to argue that Indians have no sentiment for their relatives, living or dead, and that consequently there is no need to acknowledge the religious claims of the people. We know of very few societies that did not have reverence for their dead. Even graves of very ancient times display clear evidence that a well-developed understanding of life—and death—was present.

The laws in this situation are complex and askew. When the tribes have sought legislative protection from scientific intrusions on religious grounds, they have been told that no protection can be granted because to do so would "establish" the tribal religions above others. Deliberately omitted in this analysis is the fact that it is decidedly not commonplace behavior among Americans to dig up the graves of the deceased and that only in the case of American Indians, because of their supposed subhumanity, can grave-robbing be done with impunity.

The belief that Indians are subhuman was an integral part of federal land policy from the very beginning. The Great Plains was originally called the Great American Desert because it was believed that civilized people could not live there and that the area was fit only for herds of grazing animals and Indians. Treaties frequently dispossessed Indians of the most fertile lands and located them on wastelands far from sources of game and water. During the Depression in the 1930s, the Department of Agriculture had a program whereby it could purchase the lands of bankrupt farmers who had ruined their lands by destructive farming practices. Once the lands were held by federal agencies, and classified as "submarginal," which is to say that they could not be used to produce an adequate living, they were loaned to the Bureau of Indian Affairs for use in relocating Indian families on them. Presumably Indians, being something less than human, could make these exhausted lands produce sufficient vegetation to stay alive.

The basic question of Valladolid remains unanswered. It is only with great difficulty that we can begin to conceive of the conditions under which it could be answered. If humanity as a whole has made significant progress in understanding itself during these past five centuries, the people of the Western Hemisphere have not changed their perception of the basic elements of humanity or they have deliberately rejected the possibility that these characteristics also are found among American Indians.

The perception of the people who inhabited these continents and the perception of the land itself seem to be intimately related in the minds of the immigrants and their descendants. If the people were classified as savages, the land took on the aspect of a wilderness, treacherous and without mercy. So frightening was the prospect of living in a strange land that early immigrants went to extravagant lengths to ensure their own physical and psychic stability. The first Swedish colony on the Delaware River, afraid of the land and not certain how to make it produce, imported their own food for almost a generation before they felt comfortable enough to farm the land.

In the closing reflections of Nick Carraway at the end of *The Great Gatsby,* F. Scott Fitzgerald portrays what must have been the unforgettable emotions of the first experience with the New World: "For a transitory moment man must have held his breath in the presence of this continent, compelled into an aesthetic contemplation he neither understood nor desired, face to face for the last time in history with something commensurate with his capacity for wonder." Whenever Western men walked in this hemisphere the same sentiments were expressed—the wonder of a land virtually uncorrupted. It was, unfortunately, too late in human history for the newcomers to adapt to the land and embrace the symbiosis with nature which it demanded. After the initial moment of wonder, Europeans saw the land as raw material for reproducing the European way of life on their own terms. Paradise had been discovered, but in the discovery was paradise lost.

European settlements on both continents reflected the effort to transfer European culture and build in America what people felt had been denied them in Europe. Thus, we had initial colonial settlements named New Spain, New England, New Haven, New Bedford, and later, with the establishment of white hegemony, Syracuse, Troy, Athens, Sparta, and Cairo in the eastern United States. Lands coming under the control of Spain and Portugal mirrored the intense ecclesiastical concerns of the Crown: Santa Fe, Los Angeles, Las Cruces,

Trinidad, Santiago, and so forth. It was not until relatively late in these centuries of colonization and settlement that cities and towns began to reflect the names of prominent politicians such as Washington, Jefferson, Jackson, Monroe, Lincoln, Juárez, and Bolívar.

Names tell us that the half millennium of occupation has been primarily a task of establishing new settlements in a land that has stubbornly kept its own identity. Other than the Hudson and Columbia, most rivers, mountains, and lakes have kept their original Indian names, and there remains a great deal that is still wholly Indian in our landscape. Indeed, the basic sacred geography of the Indian remains virtually untouched after five centuries of conflict. American history has really been a hard-fought compromise between efforts to reproduce the European way of life on these shores and the incessant demands of the land itself to remain free with its own identity.

The intense sense of wonder of which Fitzgerald writes must have been a shock of the first magnitude. It certainly gave the people who settled in the Americas a distorted sense of their own importance. From the beginning, European immigrants believed they were the "first" to do something. Balboa is regarded as the first person to see the Pacific Ocean, the Indians and Orientals apparently having lived on its shores for millennia without ever glancing at it. The list is dazzling, and it was not too long ago that schoolbooks pretended that no one had ever done the marvelous things which the first explorers had accomplished in charting the wilderness. Even though today these outrageous claims of primacy have been tempered to read "first white man," people in the United States today continue to believe that their way of life is unique, admired, and precedent-setting for all of humanity, that they are "first" in everything. Thus national sporting events are called "World" Series and "World" Championships even though the rest of the world is not allowed to compete in them. Our politicians continually worry that they will set a bad precedent in some field of endeavor. Thus Richard Nixon doggedly remained in Vietnam because he did not want to be the first American President to "lose" a war. We will know that the shock of discovery has worn off when Americans accept the fact that they are just a passing episode in the larger human story of life on the planet.

Another persistent attitude stemming from the discovery of the two western continents was the belief that their natural resources were inexhaustible. Europeans had grown up on a continent that had been systematically exploited for millennia. Other than a few forests set aside for the King, there were no unsettled lands in Europe, and imperial and dynastic wars beginning with the early Roman intrusions had pretty well changed the face of Europe and exterminated its indigenous birds, plants, and animals. The incredible variety of flora and fauna in the New World must have stunned the immigrants and convinced them that its resources could never be consumed. Thomas Jefferson was said to have remarked that with the riches of the New World available to them, each man should live like a king in America after three generations of settlement.

Most important in relation to the natural resources of the continents was the fact that there were no rigid rules determining how people were to use these riches. European governments encouraged the rapid exploitation of lands and animals because it brought immediate wealth into the mother country. The freedom from political oppression which had been experienced in Europe was quickly transformed into the freedom to exploit the natural resources of the hemisphere. Indeed, economic and political rights became closely related and have been partners ever since. Whites did their best to change the lands. Hardwood forests were cut and burned to get lands to farm; mountains were stripped away to make it easier to extract the coal underneath; swamps and wetlands were drained or filled in to provide space for settlements and later shopping centers and luxury hotels. The story of the past five centuries might well be told as the destruction of localities and the radical change of natural environments.

Every place that the immigrant put his foot, he ravaged the land, killed the plants and animals, and substituted an artificial setting for himself. With placer mining and irrigated agriculture, most river systems became merely channels for moving water to places where it could be used. Settlements wholly dependent on technology, and incapable of supporting themselves naturally, now characterize the American landscape. It now appears that we may have reached the outer limits of possible exploitation. Large portions of North America are incapable of supporting life, and as the environment continues to deteriorate, we face the prospect that the whole edifice of settlement will come tumbling down around our ears. Paradise may soon reveal itself as a threatening hell.

North America is not alone in this respect. Recent studies have shown that the South American rain forest is being destroyed at the rate of a football field a minute. A large smoke pall now exists as a permanent feature of the South American atmosphere. But the smoke from burning forests appears to be trapped in a depression where it can never be blown clear by winds or dissipate by its own response to rains or to changes in temperature. With the final destruction of the rain forest will go mankind's last best chance to avoid a greenhouse effect that will severely change living conditions on the planet.

Strangely, even though the mood of white Americans encouraged the rapid exploitation of natural resources, it was in the United States that the concept of national parks originated. In 1872, four years before the Custer fight, Yellowstone National Park was set aside as a national heritage, and in the decades since that first step, an incredible number of parks, forests, and monuments have been dedicated to present use and to future enjoyment by Americans. We have even tried to establish a wild rivers system and wilderness areas where the footprints of man will be minimal. Private groups today are beginning to have an impact on national decision making with respect to the use and exploitation of lands. And the knowledge of what must happen to preserve and even restore lands is becoming commonplace. The United States appears to be moving toward radical change in the way that it looks at its landed heritage.

Shifting attitudes toward land use mark the beginning of a transition from the European tradition to the indigenous American matter of living on the land. Theologically it means accepting that we are part of nature and not an entity standing above it. From the Indian perspective, however, proper land use means a sharing of the land with other forms of life. Indeed a major purpose of Indian ceremonials was to ensure a proper relationship to plants, birds, and animals who provided food, clothing, and shelter for human beings. It is therefore both comforting and puzzling to see the emergence of the Animal Rights Movement. Although not yet related to ecological and land conservation concerns, the appearance of regard for animals suggests that the major elements of the traditional Indian understanding of the universe are coming together in new ways.

There are now a number of effective national organizations raising the question of how we treat animals. The subject is rather a novelty for most Americans accustomed to heavy diets of beef and pork, and the first response to this concern, as might be expected, attempts to satirize the issue. In view of the many human problems which we are as yet unable or unwilling to solve, it seems strange that people would wholeheartedly devote themselves to ensuring that certain species of animals are not extinguished and that our use of animals has a recognized ethical content. While many scientists are supportive of land conservation efforts, the majority of the scientific community balks at granting some protective legal rights to animals, claiming that animals are needed for laboratory experiments which benefit humans. But their argument is based primarily upon a mechanistic and materialistic science which in many instances is no longer feasible or intellectually coherent. And in truth many useless experiments are performed on animals for purely cosmetic purposes, some scientists performing experiments primarily to keep their federal grants income as a continuing source of financial aid for their institutions.

Assuming that the Animal Rights Movement continues to flourish, we may be facing a future in which the basic tenets of the Indian view of life become the central themes of our society. In such a case, the five hundred years of exploitation and development would seem to have been a tragic mistake of unsuspected proportions. We would then have to do reappraisals of American history that would be completely different from what we have presented in this volume. The presence and persistence of American Indians, their way of life, practices, and beliefs, would form the central theme of historical interpretation and the ideas of civilization, progress, and economic Darwinism would fade out, as former superstitions once held by our species have always done.

Reviewing the five centuries since the European discovery of the Western Hemisphere, and choosing these themes to emphasize, one finds that the major issues separating Indians and non-Indians are not resolved, but that in some critical areas the non-Indians are beginning to adopt the perspective of the Indians. Carl Jung was struck by the fact that his American patients were always possessed of an incredible fascination for, and almost a haunting by, the Indians. He also commented on the fact that American sports were the same rough-and-tumble activities favored by the Indians and that the American earth seemed to change the body configurations of the immigrant stock, so that they began to appear as if they had some Indian blood.

These speculations are interesting because we do not yet know the whole story of the American earth. Outside the academic setting where orthodoxy reigns supreme, there is an incredible amount of study being done on miscellaneous rock paintings and inscriptions with the intent of providing proof that there were a multitude of ancient expeditions to this hemisphere by Celts, Phoenicians, Hebrews, Greeks, Romans, and fugitive groups of early Christians. Most of these studies concentrate on specific sites and discoveries that appear to be anomalies which orthodox anthropologists and archaeologists either ignore or misinterpret.

The famous Bat Creek stone in Tennessee has an inscription long thought to be in early-nineteenth-century Cherokee writing but recently deciphered as Hebrew. In Las Lunas, New Mexico, in a remote gully, has been found an inscription of the Ten Commandments and above them on a mesa what appear to be the ruins of an ancient fort. These inscriptions were long attacked as a hoax because certain letters in them appeared to vary significantly from any known forms of Hebrew letters. Recent discoveries in the Old World, however, show some of the same letter forms, thus adding a measure of authenticity that is difficult to explain. And for generations farmers in the Midwest and the eastern United States have been digging up old coins from the Old World when they do their spring planting. The orthodox response to the presence of these coins has been to hypothesize an early American coin collector who carelessly dropped parts of his treasure in the abandoned cornfields of Illinois, Indiana, and Tennessee. If any of these discoveries were to prove authentic, the way we look at the history of this hemisphere—and world history—would have to be changed.

If these unsettling developments were not enough, there is a further mystery to be solved in the American lands. In October 1924, the Doheny Scientific Expedition left Los Angeles for the Grand Canyon specifically to explore the junction of the Supai and Lee canyons. There, etched in the red sandstone under considerable "desert varnish"—a black scale that forms on the surface of the sandstone because of the weathering of the iron in it—they found a set of pictographs that drastically challenge our view of world history. There is a dinosaur, identified as most likely a diplodocus, standing upright with its tail extending in a discernible curve. There is also an elephant striking a human being on the top of his head with his trunk, and a herd of ibex being hunted by men. Up on the plateau that embraces the Grand Canyon, the expedition found an ancient fortress with walls made of gigantic blocks of stone that appeared to have been hoisted in some manner to the top of the little mesa known as "The Thumb." This scientific report was published by the expedition's director, Samuel Hubbard, and copies reside in the Peabody Museum, but it is never mentioned by anthropologists and archaeologists.

We seem to know a great deal about the conditions existing in the Western Hemisphere at the time of discovery. But we certainly do not know very much about the actual history of these continents. If there were ancient expeditions, they either perished or were so radically changed by the American lands that it is impossible to find more than a puzzling trace of them. And if the pictographs found by the Doheny Expedition have any relevance, we have a great deal more thinking to do about ourselves before we know with any certainty who we are and where we are going—or where we have been. So the Americas stood poised that October day when Columbus came ashore, containing mysteries that we have not even begun to fathom.

We now stand at a similar threshold in human history. We do not know how the pieces will fit together yet, but we do know that the world is now irretrievably one. And the Americas stand as the crucial elements in the new order. The future writing of American history must seek to integrate the American experience into the much larger context of human strivings. It cannot be regarded as the final product of an evolutionary march toward greatness or as a unique experiment in how people should organize themselves as a society. America and Canada, Australia and New Zealand, remain the primary lands where the native and immigrant histories have not yet been reconciled. These lands yet contain mysteries about the human past which we cannot fathom. We must solve them so that they can become part of the complete human heritage.

Scott Momaday suggests at the beginning of this book that Columbus made a voyage in time as well as space, that he moved the world from the Middle Ages to the Renaissance. Since that time, we have moved beyond the Renaissance, through the Reformation and the Industrial Revolution, suffered a series of world wars, and now envision a period of relative global peace. The native peoples of the American continents suffered total inundation, lost a substantial portion of their population, and in coming into the modern world surrendered much of the natural life which had given them comfort and dignity. But they have managed to survive. Now, at a time when the virtues they represented, and continue to represent, are badly needed by the biosphere struggling to remain alive, they must be given the participatory role which they might have had in the world if the past five centuries had been different. The attitudes and beliefs that have kept the natives of the Western Hemisphere hidden and neglected must be changed so that world history becomes the story of mankind on this planet and not the selected history of a few people and their apology for what has happened to our species.

There are old Indian prophecies that forecast the coming of the white man, and some of them predict the disappearance of tribes because of the actions of these invaders. Other prophecies declare that the white man will be the shortest-lived of all those who have sought to live on these lands. We have yet to write the final chapter of the human story, and we must now attempt to live out the final chapter of the American story. How closely it will resemble the contents of this book in another five centuries is for this and future generations to determine.

APPENDIX

Genetic Classification of the Languages of the Americas

JOEL SHERZER

This classification represents genetic relationships among Native American languages both as they were in 1492 and as they are today. Since languages are always changing, the divergences between and among them have become even greater than they were five hundred years ago, even though those that were genetically related in 1492 are still considered to be so.

What follows is an amalgamation of various proposed classifications, and represents a variety of degrees of relatedness of languages. For the most part, the classification falls within a relatively narrow time frame of the last three to five thousand years. Areas where speculation and controversy exist are so indicated. These latter tend to involve the grouping of language families into relationships—known as phyla—that have a greater time depth. The helpful commentary of Lyle Campbell, Terrence Kaufman, Brian Stross, and Greg Urban provided consensus on many units.

The classification is divided into three broad geographic areas of the Americas: North America, Mesoamerica, and South America. The fact that these three areas are all relatively self-contained linguistically is a reflection of their relative independence, culturally and historically. At the same time, there are spills and overlaps linguistically among them, some at greater time depths and therefore in realms of greater speculation, but also of interest for cultural and historical interpretations.

In the presentation of genetic relationships, not all of the languages of each family are listed, but, rather, a representative sampling of the best-known languages. Languages which have no close genetic relations, often called isolates in the literature, are listed separately, and without the "-an" ending which indicates the name of a family.

Following are the many different linguistic families and some of the genetically related languages within them:

ESKIMO-ALEUT: Eskimo, Aleut

ATHAPASKAN: Dogrib, Chipewyan, Kutchin, Tanana, Beaver, Carrier, Tanaina, Chasta Costa, Hupa, Kato, Mattole, Navajo, Western Apache, Chiricahua Apache, Jicarilla Apache

EYAK

TLINGIT

It is generally agreed that Athapaskan, Eyak, and Tlingit are related to one another within a phylum called Na-Dene.

HAIDA

ALGONQUIAN: Cree, Ojibwa, Menominee, Fox, Shawnee, Potawatomi, Delaware, Penobscot, Malecite, Micmac, Blackfoot, Cheyenne, Arapaho

YUROK

WIYOT

It is generally agreed that Algonquian, Yurok, and Wiyot are related to one another within a phylum sometimes called Algic.

MUSKOGEAN: Choctaw, Alabama, Mikasuki, Creek, Seminole

NATCHEZ

ATAKAPA

CHITIMACHA

TUNICA

TONKAWA

SIOUAN: Crow, Hidatsa, Winnebago, Omaha, Dakota, Tutelo, Catawba

IROQUOIAN: Seneca, Mohawk, Oneida, Huron, Tuscarora, Cherokee

CADDOAN: Caddo, Wichita, Pawnee, Arikara

YUCHI

It has been proposed that Siouan, Iroquoian, Caddoan, and Yuchi are related to one another within a phylum called Macro-Siouan.

YUMAN: Walapai, Havasupai, Yavapai, Mohave, Yuma, Cocopa, Diegueño

SERI

POMOAN: Northern Pomo, Northeast Pomo, Central Pomo, Southwest Pomo, Southeast Pomo, Southern Pomo

PALAIHNIHAN: Achomawi, Atsugewi

SHASTAN

YANAN

CHIMARIKO

WASHO

SALINAN

KAROK

CHUMASHAN

COMECRUDAN

COAHUILTECAN

ESSELEN

It has been proposed that Yuman, Seri, Pomo, Palaihnihan, Shastan, Yanan, Chimariko, Washo, Salinan, Karok, Chumashan, Comecrudan, and Coahuiltecan are related to one another, within a phylum called Hokan. It has also been suggested that Hokan, Siouan, Yuchi, Iroquoian, Caddoan, Coahuiltecan, Tonkawa, Muskogean, Natchez, Tunica, Atakapa, and Chitimacha are related to one another within a phylum called Hokan-Siouan.

YOKUTSAN

MAIDUAN

WINTUN

MIWOK-COSTANOAN

KLAMATH-MODOC

SAHAPTIAN: Sahaptin, Nez Perce

CAYUSE

MOLALA

COOS

YAKONAN: Alsea, Siuslaw

TAKELMA

KALAPUYA

CHINOOKAN

TSIMSHIAN

ZUNI

. It has been proposed that Yokutsan, Maiduan, Wintun, Miwok-Costanoan, Klamath-Modoc, Sahaptian, Cayuse, Molala, Coos, Yakonan, Takelma, Kalapuya, Chinookan, Tsimshian, and perhaps Zuni are related to one another within a phylum called Penutian. Within this proposed phylum, there is mostly general agreement that California Penutian (Yokutsan, Maiduan, Wintun, and Miwok-Costanoan) constitutes a valid genetic grouping.

KIOWA

TANOAN: Tiwa, Tewa, Towa

It is generally agreed that Kiowa and Tanoan

are related to each other within a larger grouping called Kiowa-Tanoan.

UTO-AZTECAN: Mono, Northern Paiute, Shoshone, Comanche, Southern Paiute, Hopi, Tubatulabal, Luiseño, Cahuilla, Cupeño, Serrano, Pima-Papago

There are also Uto-Aztecan languages in Mesoamerica, notably in Mexico. It is generally agreed that Kiowa-Tanoan and Uto-Aztecan are related to each other within a phylum called Aztec-Tanoan.

KERESAN: Keres, Laguna, Acoma, Cochiti

YUKIAN: Yuki, Wappo

It has been suggested that Keresan and Yukian are related to Hokan within the Hokan-Siouan phylum.

BEOTHUK

Many scholars suspect a genetic connection between Beothuk and Algonquian, though the extant data on Beothuk are too meager to prove it.

KUTENAI

KARANKAWA

CHIMAKUAN: Quileute, Chemakum

SALISHAN: Lillooet, Shuswap, Thompson, Okanagon, Pend d'Oreille, Coeur d'Alene, Tillamook, Twana, Upper Chehalis, Southern Puget Sound Salish, Halkomelem, Squamish, Comox, Bella Coola

WAKASHAN: Nootka, Nitinat, Makah, Kwakiutl, Bella Bella, Kitamat

It has been proposed that Kutenai, Salish, and Wakashan are related to one another within a single phylum.

TIMUCUA

Mesoamerica

UTO-AZTECAN: Tepehaun, Tarahumara, Yaqui, Mayo, Cora, Huichol, Nahuatl, Pipil

As noted above, there are also Uto-Aztecan languages in North America. This language family thus cuts across two of the major areas of the Americas and is thus one of the most extensive of American Indian language families.

CUITLATEC

SERI

TEQUISTLATECAN (CHONTAL of OAXACA): Huamelultec, Tequistlatec

JICAQUEAN: Eastern Jicaque, Western Jicaque

It has been suggested that Seri, Tequistlatecan, and Jicaquean belong within, or are distantly related to, the Hokan phylum of North America.

TLAPANECAN: Tlapanec, Subtiaba

OTOPAMEAN: Chichimec, Pame, Matlatzinca, Otomi, Mazahua

POPOLOCAN: Ixcatec, Popoloca, Chocho, Mazatec

MIXTECAN: Amuzgo, Mixtec, Trique

ZAPOTECAN: Zapotec, Papabuco, Chatino

CHINANTECAN: Chinantec

MANGUEAN: Chiapanec, Mangue

It is generally agreed that Tlapanecan, Otopamean, Popolocan, Mixtecan, Zapotecan, Chinantecan, and Manguean are related to one another within a larger family that has been called Otomanguean.

HUAVE

MAYAN: Huastec, Yucatec, Lacandón, Itzá, Mopán, Chontal, Chol, Chortí, Tzotzil, Tzeltal, Tojolobal, Chuj, Kanjobal, Acatec, Jacaltec, Motocintlec, Teco, Mam, Aguacatec, Ixil, Uspantec, Quiche, Sacapultec, Sipacapa, Cakchiquel, Tzutujil, Pocomam, Pocomchí, Kekchí

MIXE-ZOQUEAN: Mixe, Tapachultec, Sayula Popoluca, Sierra Popoluca, Zoque

TOTONACAN: Totonac, Tepehua

It has been proposed that Mixe-Zoquean and Totonacan are related to Mayan within a phylum called Macro-Mayan.

TARASCAN

XINCAN: Guazacapan, Chiquimulilla, Jumaytepec, Yupiltepeque

LENCAN: Lenca, Chilanga

CHIBCHAN: Paya

MISUMALPAN: Misquito, Matagalpa-Cacaopera, Sumo

It has been proposed that Misumalpan is genetically related to Chibchan, a language family that includes Paya as well as languages within South America, thus constituting a linguistic bridge between Mesoamerica and South America.

CHIBCHAN: Talamancan (Bribi, Teṛraba), Rama, Guaymí, Kuna, Paez, Chibcha, Kogi, Kamsá

While there is general agreement that Chibchan languages are genetically related, the languages listed here constitute a very broad grouping (which includes smaller families within it), with a much greater differentiation and at a greater time depth than most of the language families listed heretofore.

CHOCOAN: Waunana, Emberá

YANOMAMAN

ANDAKI

PAEZ

BARBACOAN: Cayapa, Colorado, Cuaiquer

It is generally agreed that Andaki, Paez, and Barbacoan are genetically related.

WARAO

MURA-MATANAWI

YUNCA

ATACAMEÑO

ITONAMA

It has been suggested that the languages listed above, from Chocoan through Itonama, are genetically related to Chibchan within a phylum called Macro-Chibchan.

ALACALUFAN

ARAUCANIAN (MAPUCHE)

CHON: Ona, Tehuelche

QUECHUAN: Quechua languages and dialects

AYMARAN: Aymara, Jaqaru

Quechua and Aymara share many linguistic features owing to a long period of mutual contact. If, in addition, as has often been suggested and debated, they are also genetically related, this genetic relationship is an ancient one with a very great time depth.

ZAPAROAN

OMURANO

SABELA

LECO

SEC

CULLE

CHOLONAN

CATACAO

JIVAROAN: Aguaruna, Jivaro (Shuar)

ESMERALDA

YARUṚO

There is good evidence that Esmeralda and Yaruro are genetically related.

COFÁN

TUCANOAN: Siona, Bara, Desana, Cubeo, Tucano, Tuyuca

CATUKINA

TIKUNA

MUNICHE

MACÚ

CANICHANA

MOVIMA

PUINAVEAN

It has been suggested that all of the languages listed above, from Tucanoan through Puinavean, are genetically related within a phylum that has been called Macro-Tucanoan.

ARAWAKAN: Amuesha, Apolista, Arauá, Chamicuro, Maipurean, Goajiro, Island Carib, Campa, Taino

TUPIAN: Tupi-Guaraní, Guaraní, Cocama, Guayakí, Siriono, Mundurucú

TIMOTE

ZAMUCOAN: Ayoreo, Chamakoko

GUAHIBOAN

SÁLIVAN

OTOMACO

TUYONEIRI

YURACARE

TRUMAI

CAYUVAVA

BOROROAN: Bororo

BOTOCUDOAN

FULNIO

GE: Shavante, Apinayé-Cayapo, Eastern Timbira, Suyá, Kaingang, Shokleng

KARAJÁ

PURÍ

CHIQUITO

GUATÓ

It has been proposed that all of the languages listed above, from Botocudoan through Guató, belong to a single phylum, which has been called Macro-Ge. Some scholars would include Bororoan in this hypothesis.

PANOAN: Amahuaca, Cashinawa, Conibo-Shipibo, Pano, Culino, Arazaire, Caripuna

TACANAN: Arasa, Chama, Maropa, Tacana

It is generally agreed that Panoan and Tacanan are genetically related to one another and constitute a phylum which has been called Pano-Tacanan.

MATACO/MATAGUAYO: Choroti, Mataco

LULEAN: Lule, Vilela

MASCOI

GUAYCURUAN: Toba, Mocoví, Pilagá, Abipon, Mbaya-Guaycurú

NAMBICUARA

HUARPE

CARIBAN: Akawaio, Apalai, Carare, Motilon, Panare, Waiwai, Trio, Wayana, Xingu Basin Carib

It has been suggested that Tupian, the proposed Macro-Ge, and the Cariban languages are all genetically related.

PEBA-YAGUAN: Yagua, Peba, Yameo

BORAN

WITOTOAN

It has been proposed that Boran and Witotoan are genetically related.

CUCURA

TARUMA

FOR FURTHER READING

2. Northern Hunters

Good overviews of the Arctic and Subarctic region are *Athapaskan Adaptations: Hunters and Fishermen of the Subarctic Forests* by James Van Stone (AHM Publishing, 1974), *The Netsilik Eskimo* by Asen Balikci (Natural History Press, 1970), and the classic *Naskapi: The Savage Hunters of the Labrador Peninsula* by Frank G. Speck (University of Oklahoma Press, 1975).

Readable early studies of the Inuit-Eskimos include Franz Boas's *The Central Eskimo* (Bureau of American Ethnology, 6th Annual Report, 1888), *The Life of the Copper Eskimos* (Canadian Arctic Expedition, 1922) by Diamond Jenness, *Across Arctic America: Narrative of the Fifth Tule Expedition* by Knud Rasmussen (Putnam's, 1927), and Vilhjalmur Stefansson's classics of the Canadian Arctic: *My Life with the Eskimo* (Macmillan, 1913), *The Friendly Arctic: The Story of Five Years in Polar Regions* (Macmillan, 1921), and *Hunters of the Great North* (Harcourt, Brace, 1922).

The history of the area is well treated in *Part of the Land, Part of the Water: A History of the Yukon Indians* by Catherine McClellan (Douglas and McIntyre, 1987), *Athapaskan Women: Lives and Legends* (Canadian National Museum of Man, 1979), and *Life Lived Like a Story* (University of Nebraska Press, 1991) by Julie Cruikshank, and *Mom, We've Been Discovered* by Decho (Yellowknife Dene Cultural Center, 1989).

Important recent studies are *Living the Arctic: Hunters of the Canadian North* (Douglas and McIntyre, 1987) and *Maps and Dreams* (Douglas and McIntyre, 1981), both by Hugh Brody; *Make Prayers to Raven: A Koyukan View of the Northern Forest* (University of Chicago Press, 1983) and other works by Richard K. Nelson, and paired books by Robin Ridington, *Trail to Heaven: Knowledge and Narrative in a Dunne-Za Community* (University of Iowa Press, 1988) and *Little Bit Know Something: Stories in a Language of Anthropology* (University of Iowa Press, 1990).

Standard reference works are the Smithsonian's *Handbook of North American Indians: Arctic* (Vol. 5, 1984) and *Subarctic* (Vol. 6, 1981). Lavishly illustrated, *The Way of the Animal Powers* by Joseph Campbell (Times Books, 1983) and *Crossroads of Continents: Cultures of Siberia and Alaska* (Smithsonian Institution Press, 1988) by William W. Fitzhugh and Aron Crowell are also recommended.

3. People of the Salmon

A general overview of the early prehistory of the Pacific Northwest is to be found in Luther S. Cressman's *Prehistory of the Far West: Homes of Vanished Peoples* (1977). Jesse D. Jennings's *Prehistory of North America* (Mayfield Publishing, 1979) also represents an overview, but it deals more thoroughly with later prehistoric cultures. *Exploring Washington State Archaeology* by Richard D. Daugherty and Ruth Kirk (University of Washington Press, 1978) presents the findings of that state for a general reader, with numerous black-and-white and color plates. These same authors discuss the archaeology of the Ozette site for young readers in *Hunters of the Whale* (Morrow, 1974).

For the cultures of the Northwest Coast, Philip Drucker's *Cultures of the North Pacific Coast* (Chandler & Sharp, 1965) is general and comprehensive. *Indians of the North Pacific Coast* (University of Washington Press, 1966) edited by Tom McFeat, includes a number of classic papers on the region written by authorities in the field. In *Coast Salish Essays* (University of Washington Press, 1987) Wayne Suttles collects articles from a lifetime of research.

A well-illustrated introduction to the sophisticated art of the area is *Looking at Indian Art of the Northwest Coast* by Hilary Stewart (University of Washington Press, 1979).

The acknowledged synthesis of the lifeways of the Plateau region is Verne Rays's *Cultural Relations in the Plateau of Northwestern North America* (Los Angeles: The Southwest Museum, 1939) and his classic ethnography *Sanpoil and Nespelem: Salishan People of Northwestern Washington* (University of Washington Press, 1932). Other detailed studies include James A. Teit's *The Salishan Tribes of the Western Plateau* (Bureau of American Ethnology, 1930) and Leslie Spier's *Klamath Ethnography* (University of California Press, 1930).

4. Taking Care of the Earth and Sky

Handbook of North American Indians, published by the Smithsonian Institution, includes volumes with definitive analyses of various Indian communities in the American West. These include *California* (Vol. 8, 1978), *Southwest* (Vols. II 9 and 10, 1979 and 1983), and *Great Basin* (Volume II, 1986).

Of the general surveys now available, *The Native Americans* by Robert F. Spencer, Jesse D. Jennings, and others is particularly good. For the Southwest, the later portions of Linda S. Cordell, *Prehistory of the Southwest* (Academic Press, 1984) present a thorough picture. W. Raymond Wood and Margot Liberty, *Anthropology on the Great Plains* (University of Nebraska Press, 1980) includes many fine chapters. For California, important work was done by Robert Heizer, as in *The Natural World of the California Indians* (University of California Press 1980), co-authored with Albert B. Elsasser, which nicely introduces different environments inhabited by native societies.

R. Douglas Hurt, *Indian Agriculture in America: Prehistory to the Present* (University of Kansas Press, 1987) focuses in part on pre-Columbian agriculture. Gilbert Livingstone Wilson, *Agriculture of the Hidastsa Indians: An Indian Interpretation* (University of Minnesota Press, 1917) is an insightful and pioneering work.

For religious beliefs and worldviews, many studies exist, though they are usually concerned with more recent eras. Gene Weltfish's *The Lost Universe: The Way of Life of the Pawnee* (Basic Books, 1965) is an especially vivid portrait. John C. Ewers has edited and written an introduction for the classic description etched by George Catlin, *O-kee-pa: A Religious Ceremony and Other Customs of the Mandans* (Yale University Press, 1967).

Students of life in the arid West have employed fiction to bring us a sense of real lives in days gone by. The Swiss ethnologist Adolf Bandelier wrote *The Delight Makers* (Harcourt Brace Jovanovich, 1971; original 1890) about the world of the New Mexico Pueblo Indians. D'Arcy McNickle, an Indian scholar and novelist, wrote *Runner in the Sun* (University of New Mexico Press, 1987) to illustrate rivalry, heroism, and community survival over a vast area of the Southwest prior to the arrival of Europeans.

5. Farmers of the Woodlands

The cornerstones for this region are the Smithsonian's *Handbook of North American Indians: Northeast* (Vol., 1978) and *The Atlas of Great Lakes Indian History,* edited by Helen Hornbeck Tanner (University of Oklahoma Press, 1987).

For Iroquoians, books range from the classic study by Lewis Henry Morgan, *League of the Ho-de-no-sau-nee or Iroquois* (Sage or Brother , 1851), to the works of William N. Fenton, particularly his *The False Faces of the Iroquois* (University of Oklahoma Press, 1987), and Bruce Trigger, *The Children of Aataensic: A History of the Huron People to 1660* (McGill-Queen's Printer, 1976). The best general treatment is Anthony F. C. Wallace, *The Death and Rebirth of the Seneca* (Random House, 1969). For a neighboring tribe, a useful study is Clinton A. Weslager, *The Delaware Indians: A History* (Rutgers University Press, 1972).

Readable works about representative Great Lakes communities include *Ojibwe Religion and the Midewiwin* and *The Prairie Potawatomi,* both by Ruth Landes (University of Wisconsin Press, 1968 and 1970), and *The Winnebago Tribe* by Paul Radin (University of Nebraska Press, 1970).

For the Plains, before the horse and the Hollywood image, Gene Weltfish gives a vivid re-creation of Pawnee life in *The Lost Universe* (Basic Books, 1965).

Helen Roundtree, *The Powhatan Indians of Virginia: Their Traditional Culture* (University of Oklahoma Press, 1989) provides a good portrait for the Southeast, while the classic overview remains John R. Swanton, *The Indians of the Southeastern United States* (Smithsonian Institution Press, 1979).

For New England, important works are William S. Simmons, *Spirit of New England Tribes: Indian History and Folklore,* 1620–1984 (University Press of New England, 1986), and, though dated, Frank Speck, *Penobscot Man: The Life History of a Forest Tribe of Maine* (Octagon Books, 1970).

For the past of this region, Dean Snow's *The Archaeology of North America* (New York, 1976) and *Atlas of Ancient America* (Facts on File, 1986) by Michael Coe, Dean Snow, and Elizabeth P. Benson present syntheses.

6. Men of Maize

The archaeological background of Mesoamerica is explored in Michael D. Coe, *America's First Civilization* (American Heritage, 1968); Ignacio Bernal, *The Olmec World* (University of California Press, 1969); Sven Loven, *Origins of Tainan Culture, West Indies* (Elanders, 1935).

Sources for the details of the Columbus voyages include *The Four Voyages of Columbus,* trans. J. M. Cohen (Penguin, 1969); *The Life of the Admiral Christopher Columbus by His Son Ferdinand,* trans. Benjamin Keen (Rutgers University Press, 1959); Carl Sauer, *The Early Spanish Main* (University of California Press, 1966); and Friar Ramón Pané, *Relación acerca de las Antigüedades de los Indios,* Mexican edition by Juan José Arrom (Siglo Veintiuno, 1987).

Classic sources for the encounter and conflicts are Bartolomé de Las Casas, *Apologetica Historia Sumaria,* 2 vols. (Mexican National University Press, 1967); Peter Martyr d'Anghera, *De Orbe Novo: The Eight Decades of . . . ,* trans. Francis Augustus MacNutt (G. P. Putnam's Sons, 1912); Hernán Cortés, *Letters from Mexico,* trans. A. R. Padgen (Grossman Publ. ; 1971); Bernal Díaz del Castillo, *The Discovery and Conquest of Mexico* (Farrar, Straus and Cudahy, 1956); and Miguel León-Portilla, *The Broken Spears: Aztec Account of the Conquest of Mexico* (University of Oklahoma Press, 1963). An overview is Fredi Chiapelli, *First Images of America,* 2 vols. (University of California Press, 1976).

Indigenous epics include the *Popol Vuh,* the Book of Counsel of the Quiche Mayas of Guatemala, trans. Munro S. Edmonson (Tulane, 1971) and *Book of Chilam of Chumayel,* trans. from Yucatec Mayan by Ralph Roys (University of Oklahoma Press, 1967). Other sources are *Codex Florentinus,* 12 vols. (School of American Research, 1950–69), trans. J. Arthur Anderson and Charles E. Dibble; *Mesoamerican Writing Systems,* ed. Elizabeth Benson (Dumbarton Oaks, 1973); and Friar Diego Durán, *Book of the Gods and Rites and the Ancient Calendar,* trans. Doris Heyden and Fernando Hurcasitas (University of Oklahoma Press, 1971); Miguel León-Portilla, *Pre-Columbian Literatures of Mexico* (University of Oklahoma Press, 1968, revised 1987) and *Native Mesoamerican Spirituality: Ancient Myths, Discourses, Stories, Doctrines, Hymns, Poems from the Aztec, Yucatec, Quiche Maya, and Other Sacred Traditions* (Paulist Press, 1980).

Other important references are Nigel Davies, *The Aztecs* (University of Oklahoma Press, 1980); Miguel León-Portilla, *Aztec Thought and Culture: A Study of the Ancient Nahuatl Mind* (University of Oklahoma Press, 1963); J. Eric Thompson, *Maya History and Religion* (University of Oklahoma Press, 1970).

For the Caribbean and environs, useful works include Gonzalo Fernández de Oviedo y Valdéz, *Natural History of the West Indes,* a translation of *Sumario de la Natural Historia de las Indias* by Sterling A. Stoudemire (University of North Carolina Press, 1959) and Mary W. Helms, *Ancient Panama: Chiefs in Search of Power* (University of Texas Press, 1979).

7. A Continent on the Move

The classic, comprehensive overview of South American peoples in pre-European times is the seven-volume *Handbook of South American Indians* (Smithsonian Institution Press, 1946–59). Its editor, Julian H. Steward, organized articles from more than ninety international contributors into chapters ranging from archaeology and ethnography through linguistics and physical anthropology. In Vol. 5, Steward wrote a long Interpretative Summary of the varieties of South American cultural achievements. Some years later, Steward and Faron wrote *Native Peoples of South America* (McGraw-Hill, 1959), which provided a much more wieldy but ethnographically detailed summary of the *Handbook* and which brought into sharper focus the ecological bases of the multitude of social developments among aboriginal peoples. Both of these studies are widely available in libraries.

The anthropological literature of South America has, since the 1960s, mushroomed into thousands of journal articles and a great many monographs. Very few of these, however, discuss the historical period covered in this chapter and are not cited, with the exception of the minimal listing that follows.

Napoleon Chagnon, in his *Yanomamo: The Fierce People* (Holt Rinehart & Winston, 1968), writes about Indians in the Venezuelan and bordering Brazilian tropical lowlands who until recently lived a harsh existence quite apart from contact with Western society and maintaining historical continuity back to pre-Columbian times. Michael Harner's *The Jivaro: People of the Sacred Waterfalls* (Natural History Book, 1973) deals partly with age-old traditions in the high jungles of Ecuador. Other books which attempt some historical reconstruction of traditional culture back to the contact period include Jules Henry, *Jungle People: A Kaingang Tribe of the Highlands of Brazil* (J. J. Augustin, 1964); Allan Holmberg, *Nomads of the Long Bow: The Siriono of Eastern Bolivia* (Natural History Books, N.Y., 1969); Betty Meggers, *Amazonia: Man and Culture in a Counterfeit Paradise* (Aldine, 1971); Johannes Wilbert, *Survivors of El Dorado: Four Indian Cultures of South America* (Praeger, 1972).

There are a number of interesting explorations of more specialized topics. See, for example, Janet Siskind, *To Hunt in the Morning* (1975); Yolanda and Robert Murphy, *Women of the Forest* (1974); and Louis C. Faron, *The Mapuche Indians of Chile* (1986). Finally, in the English translation of *Tristes Tropiques* (1964), Claude Lévi-Strauss presents an intriguing appraisal of the timeless aspects of several South American Indian cultures.

8. In the Realm of the Four Quarters

For a regional summary of general Andean prehistory, see *Ancient South Americans*, ed. J. D. Jennings. (W. H. Freeman, 1983); also for Andean archaeology and the social impact of environmental diversity on the region, see *Andean Ecology and Civilization*, eds. S. Masuda, I. Shimada, and C. Morris (University of Tokyo Press, 1985).

A classic general account of Inca social and political organization, technology, and ritual life can be found in John Rowe's "Inca Culture at the Time of the Spanish Conquest," in *Handbook of South American Indians*, Vol. 2, ed. Julian Steward (Smithsonian Institution Press, 1946). John Murra's *The Economic Organization of the Inca State* (JAI Press 1980) provides a penetrating, comprehensive analysis of Inca state economic policies, institutions, and patterns of economic production. Burr Cartwright Brundage's *Empire of the Inca* (1963) and *Lords of Cuzco* (1967), both from the University of Oklahoma Press, offer accessible and engaging descriptions of life in the court of the Incas, and of the processes and events that led to the expansion of the Inca empire.

The complex relationships between local cultures and the Inca state in the far north of the empire are explored in depth in Frank Salomon's *Native Lords of Quito in the Age of the Incas* (Cambridge University Press, 1986). Craig Morris and Donald Thompson provide the best single archaeological treatment of an Inca provincial capital and its surrounding regions in *Huanuco Pampa: An Inca City and Its Hinterland,* (Thames & Hudson, 1985 while Graciano Gasparini and Luise Margolies have compiled a handsomely illustrated, detailed description of the Incas' remarkable achievements in domestic and ceremonial architecture in *Inca Architecture* (Indiana University Press, 1980). Another specialized study of great interest to readers fascinated with the Incas' ingenious solution to problems of logistics and transport within their vast empire can be found in John Hyslop's *The Inca Road System* (Academic Press, 1984).

Readers interested in early eyewitness accounts of the Incas as recorded by the Spaniards will find two excellent English-language versions of chronicles in *The Incas of Pedro Cieza de León,* ed. Victor Von Hagen, trans. Harriet de Onís (University of Oklahoma Press, 1959), and Bernabé Cobo, *History of the Inca Empire,* trans. Roland Hamilton (University of Texas Press, 1979).

9. A Richness of Voices

General surveys of the native languages of the Americas, focusing especially on their genetic classification, are provided by William Bright, "North American Indian Languages" *(Encyclopaedia Britannica,* 15th ed., 1974); Terrence Kaufman, "Meso-American Indian Languages" *(Encyclopaedia Britannica,* 15th ed., 1974); and Jorge A. Suarez, "South American Indian Languages" *(Encyclopaedia Britannica,* 15th ed., 1974).

Joseph H. Greenberg's *Language in the Americas* (Stanford, 1987), though controversial, offers broad schemes for classifying all of the native languages of the Americas. Two collections of articles deal with issues in the classification and history of American Indian languages for North America and Mesoamerica: Lyle Campbell and Marianne Mithun, eds., *The Languages of Native America: Historical and Comparative Assessment* (Austin, 1979), and for South America, Harriet E. Manelis Klein and Louisa R. Stark, eds., *South American Indian Languages: Retrospect and Prospect* (University of Texas Press, 1985).

Joel Sherzer, *An Areal-Typological Study of American Indian Languages North of Mexico,* North-Holland Linguistic Series 20 (North Holland Publ., 1976), deals with North American Indian languages from an areal and typological point of view. Jorge A. Suarez, *The Mesoamerican Indian Languages* (Cambridge University Press, 1983), provides information about Mesoamerican Indian languages from descriptive, typological, and historical perspectives. Harold E. Driver, *Indians of North America* (University of Chicago, 1961), has a chapter on language which provides descriptive, typological, and historical information about the languages of Native North America. Edward Sapir's *Language* (Harcourt, Brace & Co., , 1921), a classic general introduction to linguistics, draws on North American Indian languages for many of its examples. Harry Hoijer, ed., *Linguistic Structures of Native America,* Viking Fund Publications in Anthropology, No. 6 (1946), is a collection of short descriptive studies of selected American Indian languages.

The question of the relationship between language and culture and language and thought is dealt with in a number of papers by Benjamin Lee Whorf, *Language, Thought, and Reality: Selected Writings of Benjamin Lee Whorf,* ed. John B. Carroll (Beacon Press, 1956), which draws mainly on the Hopi language for illustrative examples. Harry Hoijer, "Cultural Implications of Some Navajo Linguistic Categories," in Dell Hymes, ed., *Language in Culture and Society: A Reader in Linguistics and Anthropology* (Harper & Row, 1964); Clyde Kluckholn and Dorothea Leighton, *The Navaho* (Natural History Press, N.Y., 1962), and Gary Witherspoon, *Language and Art in the Navajo Universe* (University of Michigan Press, 1977), examine the Navajo language in relation to patterns of Navajo culture.

The way languages enter into ritual and ceremony, including politics and religion, is the subject of Joel Sherzer, *Kuna Ways of Speaking: An Ethnographic Perspective* (University of Texas, 1983). Gary H. Gossen, *Chamulas in the World of the Sun: Time and*

Space in a Maya Oral Tradition (1974) describes the full gamut of speech forms in Chamula, one of the modern descendants of the ancient Mayas. Diego Duran, *The Aztecs: The History of the Indies of New Spain* (1964) describes language use among the Aztecs. Garcilaso de la Vega, *Royal Commentaries of the Incas,* trans. Harold V. Livermore (University of Texas Press, 1966) does the same for the Incas. Bernardino de Sahagún, *Florentine Codex: General History of the Things of New Spain,* eds. Arthur J. O. Anderson and Charles E. Dibble (School of American Research, 1950–79), is full of fascinating descriptions of how language was used among the Aztecs.

Joel Sherzer and Greg Urban, eds., *Native South American Discourse* (1986) and Joel Sherzer and Anthony C. Woodbury, eds., *Native American Discourse: Poetics and Rhetoric* (Cambridge University Press, 1987) are collections of papers dealing with Native American oral literature. Munro S. Edmonson, trans., *The Book of Counsel: The Popol Vuh of the Quiche Maya of Guatemala,* Middle American Research Institute Publication 35 (1971), and Dennis Tedlock, trans., *Popol Vuh: The Mayan Book of the Dawn of Life and the Glories of Gods and Kings* (Random House, 1985), are two different translations of a classic work, the Mayan *Popol Vuh.* Angel Maria Garibay K., *Historia de la Literatura Nahuatl* (1953) deals with Nahuatl literature. Miguel León-Portilla has written a series of books on Aztec and Mayan thought, culture, and literature: *Aztec Thought and Culture: A Study of the Ancient Nahuatl Mind* (University of Oklahoma Press, 1963), *Literatures of Mexico* (University of Oklahoma Press, 1969), and *Time and Reality in the Thought of the Maya* (Boston, 1973).

10. Religious Forms and Themes

The literature on the religions of Native Americans is enormous. General works that set their scopes at the hemisphere include Åke Hultkrantz, *The Religions of the American Indians* (University of California Perss, 1967), and Walter Krickeberg, Hermann Trimborn, Werner Muller, and Otto Zerries, *Pre-Columbian American Religions* (Weidenfeld and Nicholson, 1968). Other general studies have a continental scope. Lawrence Sullivan's *Icanchu's Drum* (Macmillan, 1988) provides general patterns that help introduce the almost overwhelming complexity of the religions of South American peoples. Many native perspectives from North American tribes as well as a wealth of classic accounts may be found in Peggy V. Beck and A. L. Walters, *The Sacred: Ways of Knowledge, Sources of Life* (Navajo College 1977). A stimulating selection of essays on North American religions is Walter Capps, ed., *Seeing with a Native Eye* (1976). An introduction to understanding and appreciating Native American religions and an accompanying selection of sources and texts, concentrating on North American peoples, are Sam Gill, *Native American Religions: An Introduction* (Wadsworth Publ., 1982) and *Native American Traditions: Sources and Interpretations* (Wadsworth Publ., 1983).

The record of stories and mythology, so important to Native American religions, fills scores of volumes. Some collections help to introduce these rich traditions: Harold Osborne, *South American Mythology* (Peter Bedrick Books, 1986); Stith Thompson, *Tales of North American Indians* (University of Indiana Press, 1929); and Alfonso Ortiz and Richard Erdoes, *American Indian Myths and Legends* (Pantheon Books, 1984). Also helpful is Susan A. Niles, *South American Indian Narrative: Theoretical and Analytical Approaches: An Annotated Bibliography* (Garland Publ., 1981).

Finally, Åke Hultkrantz's survey, *The Study of American Indian Religions* (Crossroads

Publ., 1983), is an excellent bibliographic source and provides insight into the interests and biases that have shaped what information has been collected and the interpretations that have been made of it.

11. A Kinship of Spirit

While there have been many detailed treatments of the societies of particular tribes, there have been few synthetic studies of the Americas. A standard book summarizing distributional details of Native North America is Harold Driver, *Indians of North America* (University of Chicago Press, 1961). For features of political organization, from an older perspective, an important article is Robert Lowie, "Some Aspects of Political Organization among the American Aborigines," in Lowie's *Selected Papers in Anthropology,* ed. Cora Du Bois (University of California Press, 1960). Much of early Americanist research all but ignored history, casting descriptions in a vague "ethnographic present." A notable exception is *North American Indians in Historical Perspective,* eds. Eleanor Burke Leacock and Nancy Oestreich Lurie, and recently reprinted (Waveland Press, 1988).

South America, as described by the subtitle of the collection of essays by Patricia Lyon, *Native South Americans: Ethnology of the Least Known Continent* (Little, Brown, 1974), has been receiving superb scholarly attention during the past few decades. The classic overview remains Julian Steward and Louis Faron, *Native Peoples of South America* (McGraw-Hill, 1959).

While modern studies are technical, they are clearly written to convey the natives' sense of their own societies and meaningful categories. For central Brazil, some of the most significant books are David Maybury-Lewis, *Akwe-Shavante Society* (Oxford University Press, 1974) and the edited volume by Maybury-Lewis, *Dialectical Societies.* The Bororo of central Brazil are the subject of Jon Christopher Crocker, *Vital Souls: Bororo Cosmology, Natural Symbolism, and Shamanism* (University of Arizona Press, 1985).

An important study of native personal life, otherwise missing from the record, is Thomas Gregor, *Anxious Pleasures: The Sexual Lives of an Amazonian People* (University of Chicago Press, 1985). As he details, actual practices make clear that romantic notions of "free love" belong only to European fantasy, not to existing societies.

The fascinating complexities of the Vaupés region on the Colombia-Brazil border have been the subject of several contemplative books. A primary work is Irving Goldman, *The Cubeo Indians of the Northwest Amazon* (Illinois Studies in Anthropology 2, 1963). A work of great insight into elite knowledge is Geraldo Reichel-Dolmatoff, *Amazonian Cosmos: The Sexual and Religious Symbolism of the Tukano Indians* (University of Chicago Press, 1971). An overview of the region is provided by Jean Jackson, *Fish People: Linguistic Exogamy and Tukanoan Identity in Northwest Amazonia* (Cambridge University Press, 1983).

For particular regions, useful works include John Swanton, *Indian Tribes of the Lower Mississippi Valley and Adjacent Coast of the Gulf of Mexico* (Bureau of American Ethnology, Bulletin 1911); Vi Hilbert, *HABOO: Native American Stories from Puget Sound* (University of Washington Press, 1985).

For a regional perspective on the integration of tribes and nations, great insight is provided by John Dunn, "International Moieties: The Northern Maritime Province of the North Pacific Coast," in *The Tsimshian: Images of the Past: Views for the Future,* ed. Margaret Seguin (University of British Columbia Press, 1984), with additional discussion in Jay Miller and Carol Eastman, *The Tsimshian and Their Neighbors of the North Pacific Coast* (University of Washington Press, 1984).

Other ramifications of beliefs with respect to society can be found in Jay Miller, *Shamanic Odyssey: A Comparative Study of the Lushootseed (Puget Salish) Ritualized Journey to the Land of the Dead in Terms of Death, Potency, and Cooperating Shamans in North America* (Ballena Press Anthropological Papers, 32, 1988). A fascinating perspective on the elite's quest for knowledge beyond the horizons of their own communities is provided by Mary Helms, *Ulysses' Sail: An Ethnographic Odyssey of Power, Knowledge, and Geographical Distance* (Princeton University Press, 1988).

12. American Frontiers

A fine overview of pre-Columbian societies in North and South America which illuminates cross-continental contacts is Michael Coe, Dean Snow, and Elizabeth P. Benson, *Atlas of Ancient America,* ed. Graham Speake (Facts on File Publications, 1986). See also *Archaeological Frontiers and External Connections,* eds. Gordon F. Ekholm and Gordon R. Willey, *Handbook of Middle American Indians,* Vol. 4 (University of Texas Press, 1966). Worthwhile for text as well as illustrations is David S. Brose, James A. Brown, and David W. Penney, *Ancient Art of the American Woodland Indians* (Harry N. Abrams, 1985). Variety of mound construction is clearly depicted in William N. Morgan, *Prehistoric Architecture in the Eastern United States* (MIT Press, 1980). The Natchez tradition of migration from Mexico is recorded in Antoine Simon Le Page du Pratz, *The History of Louisiana* (1774), ed. Joseph G. Tregle, Jr., reprinted facsimile (Louisiana State University Press, 1975). Because its subject is too rarely discussed: *The Sea in the Pre-Columbian World,* ed. Elizabeth P. Benson (Dumbarton Oaks Research Library and Collections, 1977).

13. Systems of Knowledge

Archaeoastronomy is one of the most complex yet most interesting areas of native knowledge. In *Skywatchers of Ancient Mexico* (University of Texas Press, 1980), Anthony Aveni explains the terminology of modern astronomy to make archaeoastronomy accessible and to introduce complex phenomena like the Venus cycle and eclipse cycles as they were explained by the Mayas and Aztecs. Ray Williamson, in *Living the Sky* (1984), surveys sites and practices in both North and South America that give evidence of archaeoastronomical activity. The essays collected in *Archaeoastronomy in Precolumbian America* (University of Texas Press, 1975) and *Archaeoastronomy in the New World* (Cambridge, 1982), both edited by Anthony Aveni, give ample proof of the importance of systematic observation of celestial phenomena in the New World.

Alignments of buildings indicate both sophisticated observation and importance of architectural technology. The most impressive structures are in South America and Mesoamerica, and Doris Heyden and Paul Gendrop introduce *Pre-Columbian Architecture of Mesoamerica* (H.N. Abrams, 1975). In North America, the Chaco Canyon region of New Mexico includes the largest concentration of prehistoric Pueblo architecture. Stephen Lekson has edited *The Architecture and Dendrochronology of Chetro Ketl, Chaco Canyon, New Mexico* (Natural Park Service, 1983). Although somewhat technical, it provides a thorough and interesting discussion of one of the large pueblos in the canyon. A more general overview, with lavish illustrations, is found in *Native American Architecture*, by Peter Nabokov and Robert Easton (Oxford University Press, 1989).

The mathematical systems of a number of Indian tribes in North and South America are described in essays in *Native American Mathematics*, ed. Michael P. Closs (University of Texas Press, 1986). Of particular interest is the inference of Mayan and Aztec mathematics from their calendar systems. Even more inferential, but equally fascinating, is *Code of the Quipu: A Study in Media, Mathematics and Culture*, by Marcia and Robert Ascher (University of Michigan Press, 1980). Although their reconstruction of a mathematical system is very complex, their discussion of Inca culture and the quipu as an expression of it is excellent.

The exquisite metalwork of the Incas and other South American people is the subject of essays in *Pre-Columbia Metallurgy of South America*, ed. Elizabeth P. Benson (Punbanton Oaks., 1979), and Heather Lechtman and Robert S. Merrill discuss native technologies in *Material Culture: Style, Organization, and Dynamics of Technology* (St. Paul, c. 1977).

The development of agriculture in the New World can be traced in the essays included in *Prehistoric Food Production in North America*, ed. Richard Ford (University of Michigan Press, 1985). Corn is the great triumph of indigenous agriculture, and Paul Manglesdorf's classic study, *Corn: Its Origin, Evolution and Improvement* (Harvard University Press, 1974), is elegantly written and argued, albeit as an example of genetic science rather than human intervention. The mention of Indians as domesticators is disappointingly brief. Gary Nabhun presents the human dimensions of native agriculture and the use of wild plants in a contemporary Indian community in *The Desert Smells Like Rain: A Naturalist in Papago Indian Country* (North Point Press, 1982). One can see the persistence of values that probably existed among the ancestors of the Tohono O'Odham (Papago) in 1492.

An important use of plants was for curing illness. The most extensive survey of Indian medical practices is Virgil Vogel's *American Indian Medicine* (University of Oklahoma Press, 1970), an encyclopedic volume whose extensive bibliography is a useful guide to further study. The discussion of the cultural context of native healing practices is superficial, but the wealth of factual information makes the book valuable as an introduction to the subject.

14. The Pervasive World of Arts

Writings on the arts of the Americas have been presented in terms of materials, techniques, and regions. Useful overviews are provided by Edwin L. Wade, *The Arts of the North American Indian: Native Traditions in Evolution* (Philbrook Art Center, 1986); Frederick Dockstader, *Indian Art in America* (New York Graphic Society, 1961); Ralph T. Coe, *Sacred Circles: Two Thousand Years of North American Indian Art* (Arts Council of Great Britain, 1976); George Kubler, *Art and Architecture of Ancient America* (Penguin Books, 1962), William N. Morgan, *Prehistoric Architecture in the Eastern United States* (MIT Press, 1980); Christian Feest, *Native Arts of North America* (Thames & Hudson, 1980); and Samuel Marti, *Music before Columbus* (Ediciones Euroamericanas, 1978).

Major regional surveys have been presented by Raoul d'Harcourt, *Textiles of Ancient Peru and Their Techniques* (University of Washington Press, 1962); Kate Peck Kent, *Textiles of the Prehistoric Southwest* (University of New Mexico Press, 1983); Doris Hayden and Paul Gendrop, *Pre-Columbian Architecture of Mesoamerica* (Harry N. Abrams, 1975);

John Hemming, *Monuments of the Incas* (Little, Brown, 1982); Frank C. Hibben, *Kiva Art of the Anasazi at Pottery Mound* (KC Publishers, 1975); Ruth Bunzel, *The Pueblo Potter* (Dover, 1972); S. Abel-Vidor, *Between Continents—Between Seas: Precolumbian Art in Costa Rica* (Harry N. Abrams, 1981); and George Warton James, *Indian Basketry* (Dover, 1972).

Important works on Aztec arts include Miguel León-Portilla, *Aztec Thought and Culture* (University of Oklahoma Press, 1963) and *Pre-Columbian Literatures of Mexico* (University of Oklahoma Press, 1968, revised 1987); Esther Pasztory, *Aztec Art* (Harry N. Abrams, 1983); Samuel Marti, *Dances of Anahuac: The Choreography and Music of Precortesian Dances* (Viking Fund Publications in Anthropology, No. 38, 1964); and H. B. Nicholson with Eloise Quiones Keber, *Art of Aztec Mexico: Treasures of Tenochtitlan* (National Gallery of Art, 1983).

Page numbers in italics denote illustrations

The Contributors

RICHARD D. DAUGHERTY is professor emeritus of anthropology, Washington State University. He has served as chairman for both the Northwest Anthropological Conference and the Great Basin Archaeological Conference and as the director of the Washington State Archaeological Society. In 1968 he was appointed to the President's Advisory Council on Historic Preservation. Among Professor Daugherty's publications are *The Yakima People* and *Exploring Washington Archaeology* (with Ruth Kirk).

VINE DELORIA, JR., is professor at the Center for Studies of Ethnicity and Race in America (CSERA) at the University of Colorado at Boulder. A Standing Rock Sioux, he is best known for his many books and articles on the history of Indian–white relations, including *Custer Died for Your Sins; Behind the Trail of Broken Treaties; God Is Red;* and *We Talk, You Listen.* He is also editor of *American Indian Policy in the Twentieth Century* and co-author (with Clifford Lytle) of *The Nations Within: The Past and Future of American Indian Sovereignty.*

LOUIS C. FARON, professor emeritus of anthropology, the State University of New York at Stony Brook, is a veteran of many years of ethnographic research in Central and South America. His numerous publications include *Native Peoples of South America* (with Julian Steward); *History of Agriculture in the Chancay Valley, Peru;* and *From Conquest to Agrarian Reform; Ethnicity, Ecology, and Economy in the Chancay Valley, Peru: 1533 to 1965.*

CHRISTIAN F. FEEST is curator of the North and Middle American Indian collection of the Museum für Völkerkunde, Vienna, and teaches anthropology at the University of Vienna. His publications include *Native Arts of North America* and *Indians and Europe.* He is editor of *The European Review of Native American Studies.*

SAM D. GILL is professor of religion at the University of Colorado, Boulder. Among his books are *Songs of Life: An Introduction to Navajo Religious Culture; Sacred Words: A Study of Navajo Religion and Prayer;* and *Native American Religious Action.*

FREDERICK E. HOXIE is director of the D'Arcy McNickle Center for the History of the American Indian at the Newberry Library in Chicago. He is the author of several books, including *A Final Promise: The Campaign to Assimilate the Indians, 1880–1920,* and editor of *Indians in American History: An Introduction.* He is a former associate professor of history at Antioch College.

PETER IVERSON is professor of history at Arizona State University. He is the author of *The Navajo Nation; Carlos Montezuma and the Changing World of American Indians;* and *The Navajos;* and editor of *The Plains Indians of the Twentieth Century.* He has received the Chief Manuelito Appreciation Award from the Navajo Nation for his contributions to Navajo education and fellowships from the Newberry Library, the National Endowment for the Humanities, and the W. K. Kellogg Foundation.

FRANCIS JENNINGS is director emeritus of the D'Arcy McNickle Center for the History of the American Indian and a past president of the American Society for Ethnohistory. He has also served on the executive boards of the Organization of American Historians and the Pennsylvania Historical Society. Dr. Jennings is the author of the *Invasion of America* and the *Covenant Chain Trilogy,* of which the most recent volume is *Empire of Fortune: Crowns, Colonies, and Tribes in the Seven Years War in America.*

ALVIN M. JOSEPHY, JR., historian and author of prize-winning books and articles on American Indians, is a former editor in chief of *American Heritage* magazine and vice chairman of the Indian Arts and Crafts Board. The recipient of a Guggenheim Fellowship, he is currently chairman of the board of trustees of the National Museum of the American Indian and a member of the executive committee of the Society of American Historians and the Institute of the North American West. Among his books are *The Patriot Chiefs; The Nez Perce Indians and the Opening of the Northwest; The Indian Heritage of America; Red Power;* and *Now That the Buffalo's Gone.*

CLARA SUE KIDWELL, a member of the Choctaw and Chippewa tribes, is associate professor of Native American studies at the University of California, Berkeley. Having concentrated her teaching and research on American Indians since 1970, she is presently completing a book on the Choctaw Indians in Mississippi.

ALAN KOLATA is associate professor in the Department of Anthropology, the University of Chicago. His major academic research interests are pre-industrial urbanism, pre-Hispanic architecture, and the history of agricultural technology in Mesoamerica and South America. The author of many articles and essays, Dr. Kolata is author of a forthcoming book, *An Architectural and Social History of Chan Chan, Peru.*

MIGUEL LEÓN-PORTILLA has served as professor of anthropology and history at the National University of Mexico and as Mexico's Ambassador to UNESCO and has held visiting professorships at universities in the United States, Japan, Israel, and Europe. Among his numerous publications, dealing mostly with the literary creations of the ancient and contemporary Nahuas (Aztecs) and Mayas, are *The Broken Spears* and *The Pre-Columbian Literature of Mexico.*

JAY MILLER is editor and assistant director of the D'Arcy McNickle Center for the History of the American Indian. His specialty is the cultures of Native North America. He has done fieldwork among the Pueblo, Delaware, Tsimshian, Salish, Numic, Creek, and Caddo Indians. His most recent volume is *Shamanic Odyssey: The Lushootseed Salish Journey to the Land of the Dead.*

N. SCOTT MOMADAY, Pulitzer Prize-winning Kiowa author, is Regents Professor in the Department of English, the University of Arizona. He has held the appointment of visiting professor at many domestic and foreign universities, including the University of Regensburg, West Germany, and the State University of Moscow, U.S.S.R. Novelist, poet, historian, and artist, Dr. Momaday's best-known writings include *The House Made of Dawn; The Way to Rainy Mountain; Angle of Geese and Other Poems;* and *The Names.*

PETER NABOKOV is Assistant Professor of Anthropology at the University of Wisconsin, Madison. His many essays on Native American history, art, and culture have appeared in scholarly as well as popular journals, including *The Nation* and *The New York Times Magazine.* His books include *Native American Architecture* (with Robert Easton); *Indian Running; Two Leggings: The Making of a Crow Warrior;* and *Native American Testimony: An Anthology of Indian and White Relations,* Vols. I and II.

ROBIN RIDINGTON is associate professor of anthropology at the University of British Columbia in Vancouver. His recent articles concern the worldview and technology of Subarctic Indians and the ceremonial traditions of the Omaha tribe. He is the author of *Trail to Heaven: Knowledge and Narrative in a Northern Native Community* and *Little Bit Know Something: Stories in a Language of Anthropology.*

JOEL SHERZER is professor of anthropology and linguistics at the University of Texas, Austin. His research deals with the languages and cultures of native peoples of North, Central, and South America. He is the author of *An Areal-Typological Study of American Indian Languages North of Mexico* and *Kuna Ways of Speaking: An Ethnographic Perspective.* He is also co-editor of *Native American Discourse: Poetics and Rhetoric* and *Native South American Discourse.*

DEAN SNOW is professor of anthropology at the State University of New York, Albany. He is the author of *The American Indian: Their Archaeology and Prehistory* and *Native American Prehistory: A Critical Bibliography* and co-editor of *The Atlas of Ancient America.*